THROUGH FEMINIST EYES

ESSAYS ON CANADIAN WOMEN'S HISTORY

Joan Sangster

THROUGH FEMINIST EYES

AU PRESS

Published by AU Press, Athabasca University
1200, 10011 – 109 Street
Edmonton, AB T5J 3S8

ISBN 978-1-926836-18-8 (print)
ISBN 978-1-926836-19-5 (PDF)
ISBN 978-1-926836-40-9 (epub)

Cover and book design by Natalie Olsen, Kisscut Design.
Cover image by Fototeca Storica Nazionale / Photodisc / Getty Images,
"Feminist Reunion of the Socialist League."
Author photo by Lesli Onusko.
Printed and bound in Canada by Marquis Book Printing.

We acknowledge the financial support of the Government of Canada through
the Canada Book Fund (CBF) for our publishing activities.

Library and Archives Canada Cataloguing in Publication

Sangster, Joan, 1952 –
Through feminist eyes : essays on Canadian women's history /
Joan Sangster.

Issued also in electronic format.
ISBN 978-1-926836-18-8

1. Women — Canada — History.
I. Title.

HQ1453.S26 2011   305.40971   C2011-900870-X

CONTENTS

ACKNOWLEDGEMENTS

This book would not have been possible without the support I received from everyone at Athabasca University Press. Alvin Finkel especially has been an exemplary editor; his smart and perceptive comments flew back almost immediately when I sent him emails, and he was always on the mark with his suggestions. Betsy Jameson also offered important encouragement and feedback, and all the staff at AU Press, including the director, Walter Hildebrandt, have been wonderful. I also want to thank the anonymous reviewers of the manuscript for their comments and input. At Trent, Meghan Buckham and Kirk Niergarth provided me with much-needed technical aid, organizing the manuscript and magically turning old articles on paper into modern computer files. As always, Bryan Palmer provided unconditional love and support; indeed, when I was reluctant to proceed with a retrospective collection of my own work, he encouraged me to do so.

My thinking about women's history has been shaped by many factors over the past thirty years: I've been inspired by the writing of scholars whom I have never met and by friends and colleagues with whom I've shared new ideas over glasses of wine. I've also benefited tremendously from my interactions with undergraduate and graduate students, whose engagement with historical writing can be energizing, enlightening, and inspiring. Because of them, my job is far more than 'work'; it is also a pleasure and a joy. This book is dedicated to them.

All royalties from this book will be donated to the Barbara Roberts Memorial Fund, which provides support for projects relating to workplace issues, unions, and radical social movements, to the pursuit of peace, social justice, and human rights, and to women's studies education, all examined from a feminist perspective.

INTRODUCTION REFLECTIONS ON
THIRTY YEARS OF WOMEN'S HISTORY

I did not grow up wanting to be a historian. As a well-socialized child of the 1950s, my early fantasies centred more on the frilliest wedding dress possible. Luckily for me, I abandoned the 'say yes to the dress' dream for a life in history. After an undergraduate career in which I managed to avoid Canadian history almost completely and focused instead on African subjects, I worked, travelled to Africa, and came back thinking about the radical possibilities of history on the home front. From the time I returned to school, first part-time at Glendon College, then to do graduate work at McMaster University, I had a dual devotion to labour and women's history, though there were inevitably tensions and challenges in that pairing. Yet as I was a relatively new feminist at that time, women's history often felt like 'home,' and I have never lost the sense of discovery, excitement, involvement, and pleasure that reading women's history entails. Trying to pass a fraction of that excitement along to students has taken up almost thirty years of my life, and I have thoroughly enjoyed the 'wow' factor in students' responses to previously unimagined views of the past, whether it was Sylvia Van Kirk's wonderful reinterpretation of women in the fur trade, Constance Backhouse's disturbing account of the Ku Klux Klan and intermarriage, or Rusty Bitterman's tale of Isabella MacDonald, a stick-wielding rural woman defending her family and property against Prince Edward Island landlords.[1]

This collection grew out of a desire to reflect critically on the evolution of women's history over the past thirty-some years. My original intent was to pen a historiographic text, but other research passions always intervened. Another feminist historian suggested using my own writing as a basis around which to discuss women's history in Canada, and Athabasca

1

University Press responded to her suggestion with enthusiasm. This is not, however, an autobiographical text detailing my personal experiences as a historian. Nor do I claim that the essays gathered here are a perfect reflection of the evolution of Canadian women's history, since the interpretive paths of gender historians have sometimes approximated each other but have at other times diverged. I chose a number of pieces that explore some of the changing concerns and debates in women's history, though ultimately they illustrate how I wrestled with concepts, theories, and the peculiarities of Canadian gender history. One advantage of taking a retrospective view of writing about women's history is that it helps to contextualize our own writing, reminding us how significantly women's and gender histories were shaped by the social milieu, political background, and theoretical debates of the time. I do not pretend to hide my own research interests (how could I?), which have centred on themes such as class, work, legal regulation, and colonialism, or my theoretical predilections for a feminist historical materialism, if influenced also by some of the 'post' writing. While my ideas have shifted over time, productively challenged especially by critical race theory and anticolonial writing, I also believe that not everything new is automatically better. Some 'old' ideas and positions may be, and should be, defended.

It is not my aim to offer a detailed 'from then to now' description of the writing of women's history in this introduction, though a few very general observations do come to mind. First, Canadian women's history has always existed at the crossroads of, and in dialogue with, international writing, particularly that emanating from the United States, Britain, and France (the last more so in Quebec). As colonialism has taken on greater significance in women's history, scholarship on empire, and comparative research on British white settler societies have also become more important. Second, writing on women and gender has been intimately connected to, and stimulated by, movements for social change, most notably, (but not only) the women's movement. Whether it was challenges to the gendered division of labour, patriarchal legal structures, or the regulation of women's bodies, feminist critiques of existing power structures have had an inestimable impact on women's history. In turn, feminist efforts to construct our own 'herstory' offered insights into, and also lent weight to, specific political struggles. As racism increasingly became a political issue for the women's movement, for instance, new questions about 'race' and whiteness emerged in women's history, though political concerns always take some time to register in published scholarship.

Third, it also goes without saying that our project has been intertwined with that of women's studies and with feminist theorizing. Women's studies has both sustained and been sustained by women's history and has created a vibrant space for interdisciplinary dialogue. Feminist theory may appear less important in historical writing than in other disciplines in which theory is the sole topic of conversation, but this is in part because historians often interweave theory with their historical narrative. We might even argue that historical knowledge is vital to the development of feminist theory, though this imperative would not be universally embraced.

Fourth, the subject area of women's history, while marginalized in its infancy, increasingly gained acceptance and moved closer to the centre of the historical profession: this was registered in many ways, including the awarding of prizes, articles in journals, the hiring of professors, and our participation in professional organizations. Gender has been integrated into some general history texts and courses, and far more departments now have at least one gender specialist. The danger, of course, may be a perception that one is just enough. Finally, Canadian women's history does have its own peculiarities, shaped by distinct patterns of economic and social development, by Canada's own version of colonialism, and by in- and out-migration, not to mention historians' past preoccupation with the nation-state and nationalisms. The receptiveness of Canadian women's history to international scholarship and theoretical currents has been by and large very positive and productive. One problem, however, is that Anglo-American historiography is so dominant, even hegemonic, and almost always so unaware of Canadian scholarship that we have to be careful to question the conclusions and historiographical certainties enshrined in this writing, as there may well be Canadian exceptions to these 'rules.' Raising these would-be distinctions in international audiences can make one sound like an irritating Canadian nationalist demanding attention, but there is no way around this problem of scholarly marginalization.[2]

In the following discussion, I have assumed, as Judith Bennett has suggested, that we can use the term 'women's history' with the understanding that it encompasses gender history, for the longer 'women's and gender history,' or WGH, is a larger mouthful (or an awkward acronym). Some historians have seen these projects as distinct, and where that is the case, I try to note their standpoint on this issue. A few still see a pecking order of sophistication, with women's history superseded by gender history.[3] My own view is that hierarchies in this regard are not particularly useful. More historians would probably now concede, I hope, an overlap and interplay between these two approaches, in which other distinctions — theory, theme, method, evidence — are at least as important as the woman/gender distinction. Perhaps of greater value than setting up this hierarchy of methodological sophistication is a different, more general question: does our writing effectively uncover and understand power relations in the past, and, if so, how and why does it do this? In this regard, both gender and women's history can be considered 'feminist' history (or not), depending on their commitment to feminist politics and perspectives. This might mean approaching a past without sexist or racist preconceptions, understanding the 'why' of women's agency, analyzing women's inequality where it existed, or probing the multiple power relations that have created and sustained social inequalities.

Historians like Cecilia Morgan and Beverly Boutilier have explored the history of Canadian women's history, offering intriguing examples of women — often amateurs shut out of the corridors of academe — who valued, rescued, and recounted Canadian women's history, long before our time. Many were animated by their own political and cultural beliefs, including feminism for some, or more often a particular vision of progress, 'Canadianness,' nationalism, or imperialism. Taking a different view, Aboriginal historians like Ethel Brant Monture were keenly aware of the ways in which the dominant Canadian histories had discounted and marginalized Indigenous peoples, and folklorists like Edith Fowke attempted to rescue the disappearing history of the 'common people' by preserving their stories and songs.[4]

While recognizing the importance of these pre-1960s historians, we usually associate the rise of women's history with the late 1960s and the 1970s, and the explosion of curiosity, creativeness, and political energy that shaped the emergence of this new women's history is undeniable. Inspired by the ferment of the 'long sixties' political movements of feminism, the New Left, and civil rights organizing, and shaped by new currents in social history that validated a focus on ordinary people rather than high politics, women's history burst onto the academic scene with considerable optimism and political vitality. In Canada, it announced its presence with books like *Women at Work: Ontario, 1880–1930*, with new journals like *Atlantis*, and with the founding of the Canadian Committee on Women's History (CCWH) in 1975.[5] The foundation story of the CCWH, already told effectively by Veronica Strong-Boag,[6] was intricately tied up with overt challenges to the barriers women faced in a profession that was not only male-dominated but also shaped by class and ethnocentric biases. However, we were not entirely alone: our attempts to question what was of scholarly significance, as well as existing professional power structures, were shared by other insurgent groups, including labour historians. Both challenged a hierarchy in which workers and women appeared to be nonentities on the historical stage, and both redirected attention to groups, themes, and power relations previously ignored in historical writing: the patriarchal relations of family life, the class relations of the workplace, or the intermingling of the two.[7] As our historical gaze shifted to the streets, the home, and the workplace, older nationalist versions of history, so closely tied to the narrative of nation-state building, came under critical scrutiny, though Quebec social and women's history moved in parallel *and* different directions, shaped by a distinct cultural history and a concern with Quebec's own national subordination.

This "moment of discovery" was very much a project of the women's movement, for feminists recognized that women needed an understanding of the past in order to reshape our present and imagine a better future. Popular women's publications were hungry for any tidbit of women's history. In *Kinesis*, a feminist newspaper produced in Vancouver, for example, a feature article on women's history in 1976 insisted that revising our understanding of history was essential to the feminist project. History books reflected the ideas of those in power, thus "excluding women, the non-white and the poor." A history of "working women, Native peoples, and the poor," the author argued, would reveal a completely different story, including their struggles for "equality and justice." This popular article relied on the limited research to date, including material on the vote, social reform, and British Columbia women elected to office from all political parties, but it was also deeply critical of the conservative agenda of early suffragists, detailed actions of working-class women, and was critical of "racism" against Aboriginal peoples. Its politics, in other words, were more radical than the historical writing it was able to cite, an interesting comment on this time period.[8] Some of the earliest popular texts that inspired us were far-reaching, venturesome overviews that spoke to an unbounded sense of political discovery and commitment: Sheila Rowbotham's examination of "300 years of women's oppression and the fight against it" is but one example.[9] I taught my first women's history course in the summer session at UPEI in 1979, using material on women in the United States, Europe, and Canada, galloping over centuries and topics — a rather audacious reach that I would not attempt so blithely now.

There is no doubt that some of the earliest attempts to delve into women's history 'added' women into the existing historical concerns, whether it was the story of white settlement, industrialization, or movements for social reform and equal citizenship. Fewer applied their feminist insights directly to a retelling of the 'old' dominant stories of the Canadian nation, though an exception might be Barbara Roberts's refreshing re-examination of national hero Sir John A. Macdonald through the prism of his historically maligned wives in "They Drove Him to Drink."[10] And yes, some pieces written in the 1970s and 1980s looked at the suffrage and feminist movements, in part because they represented one early, significant campaign for equal rights — admittedly, campaigns that involved only some women and excluded others. I never wrote about suffrage, but I have tried to imagine the context that encouraged these studies, since they are sometimes cited as evidence of the limitations and narrowness of early women's history. In contemporary politics, this was a period when campaigns for some basic rights for women, from maternity leave to marital property rights, were ongoing and in the courts.[11] Feminists, newly aware of forms of contemporary oppression that had never before been 'named,' were understandably interested in explanations for oppression, but, as Andrée Lévesque argues for the case of Quebec, there were also attempts to understand how, where, and why women made their own history (even within the cloistered sphere of the male-dominated church). She adds that feminist historians were caught in a difficult situation: they might be accused of creating a history of "victimologie," yet if one stressed women's agency, they were 'idealizing' their subjects![12]

Even historians who likely would not have called themselves liberal feminists sometimes started with the stories of more visible political women who had led public lives, left accessible archives, or whose struggles seemed, on the surface at least, to resemble more contemporary feminist concerns, such as campaigns for legal reform or reproductive control. Still, not everyone wrote about suffragists: to claim, as late as 1996, that Canadian historians "have given lavish attention to the winning of female suffrage between 1916 and 1919 as the critical watershed in the construction of modern feminism" oversimplifies, and thus fails to do justice to, the range of historical writing that did emerge in women's history.[13] While the early efforts to insert women back into history by looking at their contributions to society were part of the overall impetus for women's history, feminist writing, argues Andrée Lévesque, was more complicated than this. In Quebec, she notes, one of the first key statements on women's history, by Micheline Dumont, moved decisively away from traditional French-Canadian biographical celebrations of women settlers and saints, focusing on the economic and social conditions of women.[14] Moreover, women's 'contribution' to history, Lévesque suggests, was not necessarily interpreted in the vein of public, political history but took in previously neglected areas such as the history of motherhood, contraception, and so on.[15] I am not sure that proportionally more biographical (or 'great woman') monographs were actually written in the very initial stage of women's history than more recently. When I first began writing, I saw biography as a more elitist and traditional genre, as I'm sure others did too. An interest in biography, however, has been resurrected by some authors as a very effective method of probing prominent, influential women's ideas about power, 'race,' and colonialism. Biographies of the prominent can provide insights into the imposition of, and challenges to, dominant ideas about race and class. However, they do inevitably leave us more focused on these notable figures rather than on the female subjects they were categorizing and describing, who appear to us only from a distance.[16]

To label early writing on women's history as 'adding women and stirring' (a rather negative domestic analogy) thus captures only part of the project of discovery and diminishes how important (and thus radical) even adding women and stirring was in the eyes of many establishment historians. In the 1970s, women's history was typecast in some graduate studies programs as marginal at best, trendy at worst, and there were almost no women professors teaching in this area. Those of us who survived in unsympathetic environs often found sympathetic male supervisors (as I did), but a refrain I heard from faculty and students was that women's history was too political, biased, and partial, "an excuse for our prejudices" as someone put it. How could we *not* study men's gender roles as well, we were asked, and those who asked were not usually early advocates of gender history; rather, they often assumed the 'minimal' importance of women's history! Women were a smaller proportion of the graduate cohort than now, and though we treasured those few, beleaguered, kind women faculty who offered us support, we could also see that they were the targets of masculine marginalization: those who stuck their necks out on issues like sexual harassment might be mocked or sidelined.

Adding and stirring also misses the sense of unbounded and exciting potential at a time when almost no women's history was written; moreover, the intent to add women to history, in its most basic form, persisted well into the 1990s and beyond, producing invaluable accounts of women within certain time periods, as well as in the professions, politics, unions, and so on.[17] Nor was the intent of early writing to reconstruct a world of women, severed from society and the larger social formation. One of the initial Canadian statements on the subject urged that women's history be integrated into social history to create an entirely new history of society.[18] Influential writers like Joan Kelly (whose work inspired me) declared that we needed a more holistic history that took in a "double vision" of productive and reproductive relations, while Gerda Lerner called for a "new vantage point" and new questions for traditional history, rather than simply 'filling in the blanks.' We need a new "history of humanity," she too declared, a slogan similar to one popular in the women's movement at the time: "Women's liberation is human liberation."[19] This dual commitment did not seem at all contradictory: as I began to explore women's history, I was won over by feminist writers like Linda Gordon and Sheila Rowbotham, who produced impassioned and pointed feminist indictments of male domination, while simultaneously conveying a critique of class and capitalist relations, and I found that political journals committed to social justice politics, like *Radical America* and *Socialist Review*, provided the medium for these messages as much as academic journals.

It is hard to say exactly when a moment of discovery became a moment of expansion and complication. Perhaps they proceeded together. Rather than always tracing our steps in linear terms of improvement, I think it is useful to draw on Susan Friedman's description of the "dialogic" tension continually operating within women's history between efforts, on the one hand, to "reclaim" and restore women's history and, on the other, an ensuing "anxiety" about the "possibility that our feminist reproductions of history may risk repeating patterns of thought that distorted or excluded women from the master narratives to begin with."[20] As a result, our enthusiasms about recovery have to be continually checked by critical self-reflection. Women's history does make "compensational and oppositional truth claims"[21] (and decidedly political ones) that counter existing hegemonic views of history, but feminist critiques of the production of androcentric (hardly 'value-free') knowledge have also made us wary of speaking for others and of generalized truth claims. This ongoing tension between "positivism and subjectivism," between truth-telling and critique, Friedman suggests, is a productive one, although she concludes that the current inordinate influence of poststructuralism risks pushing the balance too far towards "relativism, a fetishization of indeterminacy," political paralysis, and a stereotyping of the "naïve" project of recovery.[22] Perhaps we are always walking a tightrope between recovery and reflection, negotiating a "continuum between objectivity and relativism."[23]

Women's historians could claim that we were simply retrieving a new narrative, a new version of history from a feminist point of view, but it was clear that there was not *one* feminist history, just as there were many methodological and thematic pathways into women's history. Certainly, historians increasingly pursued many divergent areas of research, from Wendy Mitchinson's pioneering work on operations on insane women to Bettina Bradbury's quantitative analyses of Montreal censuses and her discoveries of "pigs, cows and boarders" in working-class households.[24] Some areas of study, such as lesbian history, were initially more fully developed outside of Canada but, over a period of twenty years, moved from virtual obscurity to greater prominence within Canada. Employing something of a whig perspective of progress, Gail Brandt suggested in a historiographic piece that, by 1990, the earlier "monolithic and static interpretations" of women were superseded by an increasing "variety and richness" in our writing, not only because the range of topics proliferated (that seems undeniable) but because ideas like the social construction of skill were developed more fully, traditional periodization was questioned, and concepts like 'separate spheres' interrogated.[25] Still, complication, in the form of analyzing differences between women, had been a theme running through feminist writing from the 1970s on, whether it was with respect to the imperialist bourgeois project of importing female domestic servants into Canada to help propagate the Anglo-Saxon race, working-class women resisting their 'improvement' by middle-class reformers, divisions within the suffrage movement between labour and bourgeois women, or the distinctive experience of groups of European immigrant women.[26] There were, of course, lacuna in our exploration of difference, particularly with reference to race and sexual orientation. While US writing focused more on race and class, with some feminist historians exploring the separate, unequal, but interconnected worlds of white and African-American women, Canadian writing focused more on class to the exclusion of race — again reflecting the women's movement well into the 1980s.[27]

Inevitably, we were influenced by ideas defined as new and significant in Anglo-American writing at the time. An interest in the notion of distinct women's cultures — so evident in the United States in the late 1970s and 1980s in work by Carol Smith-Rosenberg and others — was indicated also in Canadian writing that employed a life-cycle analysis or that focused on women's diaries, recollections, and social networks, and this writing was frequently linked to the specificities of region, place, or women's rural work.[28] Nonetheless, writing on 'women's culture,' often shaped by both cultural and liberal feminism, was arguably less prominent in Canada, though we too wrestled critically with the concept of 'separate spheres.'[29] Regional differences in our writing were probably inevitable. More pieces on industrialization emerged in central Canada; women writing about the prairies were concerned with the division of labour in farm families; and women studying Newfoundland probed the changing nature of the family economy of fishing. Quebec was a culture unto itself and developed particular strengths related to its own social history, including explorations of both religious and lay women professionals nurtured in a Catholic milieu and among discussions of French-Canadian nationalism and the woman question. Although women's history in its early incarnations "was an important aspect of the awakening of regional history," it is not clear, as Suzanne Morton says of Atlantic Canada, to what extent women's history really "transformed" how regional themes are examined — even if it has added immeasurably to that history.[30] Western-based feminist collections, often transborder ones, are still very common, perhaps indicating a stronger sense that prairie and coastal history has been altered in the wake of feminist critiques, as well as a regional feeling that women's history is still defined too much by central Canadian themes and examples.[31]

One could argue that an increasingly self-critical moment emerged by the mid-1980s and into the 1990s (a rather long span of time, I admit) as feminist historians interrogated their own early assumptions, almost immediately asking what was missing, even from the newly emerging story of women's history. An answer came from historians exploring themes such as immigration, sexuality and the law, criminalized women, or those in marginal political parties, to name only a few areas.[32] Influenced in part by the demographic and political changes in Canada ushered in by the end of an ostensibly 'white-only' immigration policy in the late 1960s, and especially pushed by critiques penned by women of colour, women's history did increasingly attempt to confront issues of ethnicity, race, and racism, as well as the colonial project of dispossession and subordination that defined our nation-state and shaped the lives of Indigenous women so profoundly. The latter, of course, had not been completely absent: we should not discount the pioneering work done by scholars like Sylvia Van Kirk and Jennifer Brown in fur trade studies.[33]

New political priorities did mean that the way we posed our questions had to be rethought: rather than examining women factory workers, we had to look more closely at domestic work and the informal economy; rather than looking for women's political activism in feminist groups and political parties, we had to explore women's organizing on the basis of their ethnic, racial, linguistic, and cultural identities; rather than associating 'race' solely with women of colour, we had to address white identity as well. Although poststructuralist writing on difference and identities may have shaped this new concern with ethnic and racial differences, it was also a profoundly political response to critiques circulating within the women's movement at the time. Feminist historians — and I include myself — may have imperfectly integrated a race analysis into our writing of women's history, but there has been a shift over time in our sensibilities in this regard. I think it inaccurate to suggest that there is an immoveable group of feminist historians who see a 'race' analysis as "abandoning gender."[34] Rather, many historians are struggling to understand the specificity of women's lives within the categories of analysis that are most salient to their research context, with race being one of those. In the early twentieth century, for instance, Newfoundland outport women's lives were profoundly shaped not only by gender but by merchant and industrial capitalism, regional poverty, and religious and cultural identity.[35]

We can also make some very broad generalizations about feminist and critical theory: earlier works in the 1970s and into the 1980s were influenced by varieties of 'modernist' feminist theories, including those trying to understand 'patriarchy' or, like the pioneering *Women at Work: Ontario, 1880–1930*, by Marxism and Marxist-feminist writing.[36] Some historians put more emphasis on gender oppression, seeing this as a means of "changing the past and the present,"[37] while others drew on E.P. Thompson's 'Marxist-humanist' vision of history and feminist-socialist debates about the relationships between capitalism and patriarchy. My socialization was shaped particularly by the latter two currents: Thompson's emphasis on class formation as both a material and cultural phenomenon, on experience as a dialectical process, and on the importance of human agency seemed to offer a vision of the past that opened up rather than closed down the possibilities of a feminist and socialist analysis.[38] Still, there was never an entirely either/or distinction between class and gender: even those stressing gender as a 'primary category' in their writing, for instance, were not completely inattentive to class, at least in Canada.

Interdisciplinary exchange also played a role in shaping emerging theoretical approaches. Feminist political economists, many of whom were sympathetic to structural and materialist approaches, produced historical studies on women, work, and the welfare state, and their work was not insignificant to the emerging feminist oeuvre. I suspect that women's history was less influenced by literary theory here than it was in the United States — though certainly there was some interchange between the two fields.[39] Poststructuralist theory — the 'linguistic turn' — and a parallel thematic interest in culture, representation, and identity were clearly increasingly influential by the 1990s onwards,[40] though other theoretical proclivities, including feminist materialism, did not completely wither away. The influence of queer theory, postcolonialism, and some poststructuralist writing on language was also evident by the mid-1990s. On the international scene, some historians went so far as to suggest that gender history had literally been brought into being by poststructuralist theory. While this claim did not dominate Canadian writing, it was a distortion of the historiography that understandably irritated socialist feminists.[41]

There was perhaps less debate about the theoretical benefits of 'post' theorizing in Canadian women's history than there was in Anglo-American social history more generally. This can hardly be chalked up to younger historians' "timid" fears of one Marxist historian, a rather facile claim (and an insulting one to the historians who were using theory) put forward by Mariana Valverde.[42] It is more likely that the insights of 'post' theory were simply taken for granted as Canadian historians followed an international trajectory in which materialism and Marxism were on the decline. They looked outside our borders for the key texts shaping this debate, and, following some Anglo-American social historians, some suggested that a more a pluralist 'accommodation' between materialism and poststructuralism was the answer.[43] The latter accommodationist or integrationist enterprise (summed up most recently by Geoff Eley and Keith Nield's claim that "we do not have to choose") persists in some writing.[44] However, I am not alone in seeing some of these attempts to find a 'third way' as problematic, not only because they can become a new form of liberal pluralism,[45] but also because many authors ultimately do choose which theory to validate and which to undermine or reject, even if subtly so, and it was more likely to be historical materialism that was portrayed as lacking or 'myopic.'[46]

In her 1991 historiographic piece, "A Postmodern Patchwork," Gail Brandt suggests that women's historians in Canada were drawn to poststructuralist notions of "diversity and mutability," as well as its dislike of "generalization and discrete categories of analysis."[47] Yet generalization and categories of analysis were not banished from historical writing in the wake of poststructuralism, and few Canadian feminist historians truly embraced forms of radical deconstructionism advocated by writers like Hayden White. Poststructuralism certainly had an influence, perhaps a discreet, subterranean one that persists today, and many women's historians paid an almost ritual homage to Joan Scott's writing on language and gender. However, this does not mean they embraced poststructuralism in a thoroughgoing manner, and this was perhaps especially true in Quebec.[48]

Still, for those of us who are sympathetic to historical materialism, class seemed increasingly to become a silent partner in women's history, and, symbolically, labour historians' texts were judged by their attention to gender, while feminist histories were not held to account for class in the same way.[49] In international circles of Anglo-American writing, the theoretical shift away from a social history shaped by Marxism was well documented, though the same trends were not necessarily found in non-Western 'third world' contexts. Not only was social history not supplanted by cultural history in Latin America, argues Barbara Weinstein, but Anglo-American assertions that the integration of gender into social history signals the highest pinnacle of scholarly "theoretical sophistication" creates a hierarchy in which Latin Americanists appear to be "lagging" behind, surely an insulting equation. Her warning connects to the arguments of some Indigenous women in North America who lay claim to different historical priorities than non-Aboriginal women; for them, categories of imperialism or race, rather than gender, may yield more significant master narratives.[50]

In feminist theory more generally in North America, class did not disappear; indeed, it was often invoked as a marker of difference, but it was described more in terms of identity than with reference, as it had been earlier, to the productive and reproductive relations undergirding capitalism. In the wake of a "new individualism" evident in politics and theory by the 1990s, argues Beverly Skeggs, class was seen as redundant or as a "relic from modernism which had no applicability to the ability to travel through differences, unencumbered by structure and inequality." "Class," publishers informed her dismissively, no longer "sells."[51] A

movement away from class was even the case for those using intersec-
tionalist theory (as I did too), perhaps suggesting that I/we should have
been more cognizant of some of the problems with intersectionality. We
looked to intersectionality as a means of avoiding an 'add-on' analysis
of compounding inequalities, focusing instead on the interconnected,
seemingly indivisible aspects of social life. It also promised an analysis
still interested in listening to multiply marginalized "outsider" voices.[52]
However, at one end of the spectrum of intersectionality writing, all
categories of analysis were simply deconstructed,[53] and attention was
focused on the multiplicity of differences within individual identity.
Some of the intersectionality writing paid relatively little attention to
class,[54] and indeed, key ontological differences between *kinds* of inequality — race, class, gender, and so on — were occluded. The "methodological murkiness" of intersectionality, a failure to address the "structural
level" of oppression, and the tendency to "skirt questions of origins" thus
remain problems with intersectionality writing.[55] The different ways
in which intersectionality has been used by feminists are increasingly
under critique and reconsideration,[56] offering the possibility that insights
about the interconnectedness of social life may be retained without neglecting the importance of structural inequalities. Interestingly, in the
last two years, some prominent US-based feminists have suggested a reconsideration of class analysis and Marxism, in light of their recognition
that global capitalism was able to accommodate and reconfigure key demands of 'second wave' feminism. One might argue that the 'fit' between
feminism and capitalism was encouraged far more by postmodern and
liberal feminism than socialist feminism since the latter group did not
completely abandon the much-maligned metanarratives of Marxism or
their critique of structural inequalities. Nonetheless, even if this insight
about accommodation is not entirely new, a renewed look at it may take
feminist theory in productive new pathways.[57]

The National Question and Feminist History

One example of how Canadian women's history both intersected with international scholarship and followed its own distinct path is to be found
in debates concerning the 'nation.' Although Anglo-American and French

feminist historians have certainly written about the ways in which gendered power relations and discourses have shaped definitions of the nation,[58] Canadian women's historians have arguably wrestled with a more fragmented notion of the nation. Within our nation-state, there has long been more than one group constructed as a nation, and this has inevitably complicated gender history. Early on, both French- and English-speaking feminists defined themselves as part of a specific nation, and there are other groups of women who would still define themselves as located within a cultural nation shaped by ethnicity and history. There are also feminists within Canada who see their own liberation not simply in gendered terms but in national and anticolonial terms as well. For those writing women's history, in other words, the 'nation' had not only been problematic because it was originally equated with a masculine story of political evolution, thereby marginalizing aspects of women's history deemed less central to this 'public' realm, but also because the notion of a homogeneous nation has been so contentious for many groups. This is particularly true for Québécois and Aboriginals but also for those on the economically regional outskirts of the nation. It is for this reason that one commentator has suggested that an understanding of fragmentation and critiques of essentialism were already known to Canadian feminists before postmodern critics popularized them.[59]

It may seem peculiar to explore the concept of the nation when the current emphasis is on creating transnational histories that escape or 'rise above' the limited categories of past analyses: too often, claims a group of new scholars who are somewhat dismissive of their predecessors, we continue to "fall back on the comfortable fiction of the nation."[60] While this historiographical assertion needs some interrogation, the value of thinking transnationally about women's history, as many historians have already rehearsed, is obvious: it allows us to research and write comparatively; trace the movement of populations, cultures, and ideas across national boundaries; analyze the common and distinct social forces that shaped women's lives and gender relations; and highlight divergent patterns of colonialism, class, and 'race' politics shaping feminist thought and practice, to name a few areas.[61] Historians of empire have made particularly good use of transnational work, though some of this is essentially comparative history with a new name.[62] Still, the legal regimes, environmental resources, and political cultures of the nation-state were important influences on women's lives, as were their loyalty to, and critiques of, national identity. So we must ask why and how these influences affected their histories and history writing. Moreover, even though Canadian historians have offered critiques of national and/or nationalist metanarratives, they have often circled back, interpretively, to the nation as their focus or as a means of framing the parameters of their study.[63] I see no reason to privilege transnational history as far superior to those histories bounded by the nation, since good transnational histories must ultimately be built on accounts of the relationships, entanglements, and conflicts between the local, regional, national, and global. One could even argue that Canadian history is itself transnational given the multiple nations within its boundaries (an idea some American colleagues looked on rather askance when I tried it out on them).

From the early 1970s and into the 1980s, feminist historians often had an ambiguous if not contradictory relationship to the concept of a Canadian nation and to nationalism. Feminists wanted women included in the nation's history in order to fill gaps and silences and, ultimately, to transform that history itself. Like feminist historians in many countries, they opposed a traditional nationalist history of wars and high politics, often promoted by leading malestream historians as *the* pre-eminent and most significant metanarrative to be studied. Standing at the core of both teaching and research in the post-World War II period, this national history had often focused on the nation as either a progressive, optimistic story of Canada's liberal political evolution or as a more pessimistic, conservative story in which Canada went from British colony to nation to American colony. In Quebec, the nation was highly contested, but in different ways, with English Canada rather than the United States the focus of anticolonial critique. National identity was also theorized as a product of our distinct relation to the environment, the North, and the emergence of a 'peaceable kingdom.' However, this comforting image of the 'peaceable kingdom' ignored public and private histories of violence and dissention, occluded gender, and as one critic has suggested, implicitly valorized the superiority of the white Euro-Canadian founding nations.[64]

When feminist historians first argued that we needed to redefine the meaning of the political and interrogate a national history that excluded workers, women, and Aboriginals, we were not, however, completely questioning the very basis of nation itself as a category of historical analysis.[65] One reason was probably that English-Canadian feminists like myself, who came of political age in the 1970s, had lived through intense political discussions, across ideological and party lines, about our colonial relationship with the United States; remnants of this concern with the cultural and economic domination of the Canadian nation likely lingered on. Second, nationalism was a key organizing principle of activist and academic politics for Quebec feminists who were deeply involved in their own nation-building project in the years after the Quiet Revolution of the 1960s. The impressive synthesis of women's history first published by Le Collectif Clio in 1982 was an attempt to bring to light the distinct history of the Québécois. Rather than rejecting a nation-based identity, the authors sought to recast Quebec's history, questioning its traditional categories and periodization, by integrating women and a feminist perspective into the narrative.[66] At the same time, the ongoing political concern with recognizing Quebec as a nation likely left Quebec feminists in a difficult situation: their case for historical redress could be seen as less important than the overall need for national redress from a confining federalism. Feminist historians were not necessarily hostile to nationalism, but they could be critical of it, as Micheline Dumont was in her analysis of the sexist language and assumptions in some nationalist literature.[67]

These two national solitudes of feminism have been an ongoing element of Canadian women's history.[68] Quebec feminist historians have rightly questioned why relations with their English-speaking colleagues are so often 'one way,' with the English language dominating, while Quebec women's history written in French remains largely unexamined by anglophones. Although English and French-Canadian women's history have shared many concerns, differences — in how we periodize history (especially with respect to feminist activity), in the dominant methodologies used, and in the themes explored — still exist. A form of 'implicit separatism' has come to operate, as Denyse Baillargeon has suggested.[69] This may be in part because of an increasing focus on transnational rather than national histories, but it is also because Quebec no longer commands the same political attention in English Canada that it once did. Opportunities for comparative work or, better, examinations of our "entangled" histories, as Magda Farhni argues, have not been developed.[70] When the CCWH was first founded, it was cognizant of the need to address the two solitudes, and we found some commonality in co-operative professional efforts. The problem remains, however, and is not helped by the fact that many of us imagine that, intellectually and culturally, Quebec has already gone its own separate way.[71] Even if the solution, as one Quebec feminist colleague tells me, is to sustain our 'internationalist' ties with each other, we cannot do so in linguistic solitudes.

Another shift in the view of nation emerged from those writing Aboriginal history, whose work challenged that long-established cornerstone of Canadian history, the idea of two founding nations. Instead, Aboriginal historians spoke of the First Nations and the white settler newcomers. Feminists influenced by postcolonialism also began to critically dissect the nation as an imaginary that was synonymous with gendered, racist, and ethnocentric discourses and practices.[72] In this historical work, women were not added to the nation as much as the nation itself was held up for scrutiny, including its racialized and gendered dimensions (though class, notably, is not so visible). If in the 1970s feminist historians sought to make women historical subjects and actors within the nation, by the turn of the century scholarship increasingly examined the symbolic meanings of the nation, using a gender and race critique. Race was deeply woven into the nation-building project, it was argued, including in terms of exclusion/inclusion, as immigration policy de facto kept Canada an overwhelmingly white country until the later twentieth century. This question was extended to the constructions of nation within a global context: Sherene Razack has asked how the Canadian state created an image of a protective, gentler peacekeeping military nation while remaining violently complicit in racism and imperialism.[73] Research on ethnicity has also indicated the complicated creation of women's national loyalties. The Ukrainian communist women of the 1920s that I wrote about (who were left out of the dominant definitions of an Anglo, 'white' Canadian 'nation' at the time) related to multiple nations: their cultural nation of origin, their current national home, and the nation of their political ideals, the Soviet Union.[74]

Despite the impact of feminist and other criticisms of traditional national history, it has proven hard to escape the nation. This holds true even if our aim is to critique it, and even if it is important that we continue to question and "trouble" the nation, particularly the ways in which it is defined by inclusions and exclusions.[75] And given that the local state is often first in our line of political sight when we fight for rights and resources for women, our interest in understanding the mechanics of the nation-state is not entirely misplaced. Moreover, contra postmodern calls to 'deconstruct the nation,' metanarratives that focus primarily on the nation remain a central part of Canadian history making, even if they are presented under the rubric of new theoretical or political forms such as 'the liberal order' or 'cultural communications.'[76] It may be preferable, then, to recognize their influence, engaging with them critically and productively.

Daiva Stasiulis offers one feminist suggestion as to how we might reinterpret the 'nation' without focusing solely on identity and sacrificing all systemic analyses, including structural investigations of race and class. Examining the stark reality of competing feminist nationalisms in Canada — English, French, First Nations — she argues that we should put aside an accommodationist liberal pluralism and instead analyze the relational "positionality" of these nationalisms, with attention to the relative economic and social positions of these groups. [77]

Interrogating Historiographical Certainties

As historians, we may look, rather instinctually, for a chronological narrative of historiography, for change over time, assuming that insight builds on insight, leading us to a 'better' history. As Chris Dummitt noted, certain origin stories and narratives of onward-and-upward progress often take hold in our writing.[78] This moves us precariously close to a whig interpretation of women's history, something we need to continually question. I too have invoked a 'progressive narrative' when I described labour history moving from a narrow focus on male artisans to a more expansive focus that also took in women, family, and community. Perhaps, however, we can make some distinctions between recognizing certain advances in our writing (as well as possible setbacks) and claiming an ever onward-and-upward improvement over what came before, a problematic whig view that critics have located even within some poststructuralist writing seemingly dedicated to decentring existing narratives of progress.[79]

Another problem with a historiographical narrative of progress is that contention and different points of view may be suppressed. As I reviewed many books for this introduction, I was struck by the number of exceptions to some of the widely accepted narratives of feminist historiography in Canada. And contra my colleague Chris Dummitt, I do not see Canadian women's history as a homogenous feminist project of attempts to advance political "inclusiveness," with few lines of distinction between authors.[80] Indeed, this very claim, along with the sentiment repeatedly articulated in the same book that debates of the older generation were simply "polarizing and polemical," whereas the arguments advanced by the book's 'new scholar' contributors are expansive and innovative, should also be held up for scrutiny as a problematic whig claim.[81] It may be true that one of the code words for inclusiveness, 'difference,' has become fetishized, overused, and quite compatible with liberal pluralism. We should perhaps also heed the warning of political theorists like Himani Bannerji who argue that liberal pluralism can slide into an acceptance of neoliberalism because, in its avoidance of master narratives, it "precludes the use of larger concepts of social organization, such as class, capitalism, imperialism, even patriarchy."[82] That statement in itself suggests differences between those feminist scholars who still see the need for such metanarratives and for structural explanations and those who are far more suspicious of such approaches.

If feminist historians are to locate and analyze those differences, we may need to continually rethink the narratives and historiographical certainties that become reified and are thus taken for granted in the profession.[83] Understandably, when feminists think they have opened a new door of interpretation that had previously been hidden or shut, they may embrace that newfound insight, or sense of mission, rather enthusiastically. Casting an ongoing critical glance on our claims making is thus essential. For example, by the late 1990s, after 'race' had become a more central preoccupation for Canadian feminists, one scholar warned that by trying to overcome too singular a focus on gender (what she calls "gender essentialism"), feminist writing slipped into "race essentialism." In so doing, writing assumed an automatic hierarchy of racial oppression, warned against any and all appropriation, homogenized women of colour (as well as white women), and dealt in guilt at the expense of analysis, thus obscuring a more complex analysis of power.[84] Similarly, a feminist theorist has suggested that our fears of making generalizations across differences and of being labelled an 'essentialist' (a designation no self-respecting feminist wants) have resulted in our methodologies becoming far less diverse, more "essentialist," and more limited.[85] Another social scientist has questioned the "airbrushing of history"[86] involved in the whig notion that, over the past thirty years, feminist theory went from being simply white to diverse.

Although these questions have not emerged in the same way in Canadian history as they have in the field of feminist studies, they usefully challenge taken-for-granted narratives of feminist theoretical progress. Questions like these would help us interrogate our definitions, methods of categorization, and a priori assumptions. It may be worth asking, in this vein, if historians are using categories like colonialism and race with an eye to historical context and specificity, rather than imposing current definitions on the past. Is it not acceptable, for instance, to use the word 'colonial' when referring to Quebec-Canada relations in the past, even though we now associate the word primarily with white-Native relations? I have been criticized for doing so, including by students, yet words and categories that seem dissonant now may characterize past relations quite well — and vice versa.

One example of a productive rethinking of historiographical issues is Janice Fiamengo's nuanced discussion of early suffragists' understanding of 'race,' in which the author avoids a dichotomous reading of her subjects' ideas that either indicts their racism or sidesteps the question of race.[87] However, another piece by the same author indicates precisely the problem with historiographical certainties that become entrenched and are widely reproduced. In this article on Nellie McClung — reprinted in *Rethinking Canada: The Promise of Women's History*, a very influential collection read by scores of students — Fiamengo positions her research within an accepted version of historiography that sees Canadian women's history evolving progressively into a more complex analysis of gender history. To support this narrative, Fiamengo cites a much-quoted introduction to *Gender Conflicts: New Essays in Women's History*.[88] This *Gender Conflicts* introduction was itself particularly important, I would argue, since it seemed to represent a new group of historians different from those who had put out the very first feminist collections like *The Neglected Majority* or *A Not Unreasonable Claim*, and also exploring some exciting new thematic areas of social history.[89] It may have appeared that women's history was moving in new directions, symbolized by the title's emphasis on gender, not women, and indeed this was the claim of the book's authors, often made by counterpoising the 'new' gender history, with all its complexity, to older, "unfruitful models" and writing associated with women's history.

According to Fiamengo, women's history was first exemplified by a "celebratory" phase.[90] Veronica Strong-Boag's early writing, for instance, "championed" Nellie McClung's contribution to feminism. This one-dimensional approach was challenged to some extent in the later 1980s by Carol Bacchi's critical take on the suffragists' class, ethnic, and eugenic biases. But the key interpretive shift, it is implied, comes in 1992 with *Gender Conflicts*, since this book represents an embrace of complexity and difference, a challenge to the previous celebratory approach, and a more thoroughgoing call for attention to race. "Gone is the assumption of commonality in women's experiences," repeats Fiamengo; gone is the singular emphasis on the "contributions of women" in past writing. Fiamengo admits her interpretation is "schematic," but there is nonetheless an assumption of a movement from a more naive, celebratory form of women's history to a more complex one.[91] Concentrating on one or two key texts, as Fiamengo does, can be a useful method of interrogating historiography, but it has dangers: how do we decide what constitutes a key text? Should we not explore a broader range of historical writing? Does this method literally make these texts iconic?

On the basis of that same introduction, other pieces on women's and gender history make similar assumptions about a positive shift in the historiography: these claims are picked up on as 'fact' in an international publication as well.[92] What is interesting is that this introduction, co-authored by all the contributors to the book, actually opens with a more generous interpretation of previous writing. Although it claims that the field of Canadian women's history has been characterized by a liberal "preoccupation with white middle-class women," there is some acknowledgement that other topics have been examined, including the lives of working-class women. Yet it is the ensuing whig-like assertions that seem to captivate readers, and that have been repeated so often.

The authors contrast their book to earlier scholarship that was limited, among other things, by its concentration on "articulate, white middle-class women" (categories seemingly always elided) and by its tendency to create "romanticized heroines," whether they were "middle-class reformers" or "working-class victims."[93] Earlier social history writing was also restricted by its reliance on generalizations about the "tired" dichotomy of "top-down domination and bottom-up resistance,"[94] whereas their collection showed that some women with little power could "exercise a measure of control over their own and others' lives."[95] In contrast to previous scholars, these authors claimed to avoid "creating heroines of any type," particularly those women who were "morally pure."[96] But were not some earlier authors also trying to understand this dance of power, control, and human agency involved in women's history?

Leaving aside the question of whether the contributors' individual essays reflect their collective self-description, we need to ask if their portrait of past writing is accurate. After all, who exactly wrote about these one-dimensional and morally pure heroines? There were almost no citations offered for all these bold historiographical claims.[97] Yet earlier scholarship suggests a more complicated picture, particularly with regard to class. Wayne Roberts's work on working-class women contradicts the *Gender Conflicts* characterization, and his writing was not merely an anomaly. Nor were women merely "described," rather than "analyzed," by previous historians (the former more simplistic, the latter denoting a more complex stance).[98] Articles dealing with upper-class women's efforts to create an imperialist Canada through British working-class women's immigration, class-based efforts to reform working-class women, political efforts to mobilize working-class women against bourgeois women, or white settlers who marginalized Native and Métis women: all suggest that conflict was not totally ignored. Our interpretations of historiography, like history, will always differ, but there are some cautionary principles we might agree on: the need to understand the political, social, and intellectual currents shaping historians' scholarship, to look at a broad range of writing, to actually cite texts to support our argument, and to be wary of too easily impugning historians with accusations of one-dimensional ideas or political motivations. The latter three are of particular concern in this case.

Fiamengo's critical comments on the limits of so-called contribution history, aligned with this particular historiographical narrative, also raise questions about how we define 'contribution' history and where the line is drawn between celebratory or uncritical histories and sympathetic or empathetic ones. Does taking a sympathetic view of working-class women who are on strike, or who are struggling to keep the family economy intact, amount to celebratory history?[99] How does this differ from the sensitive and empathetic portrayals Karen Dubinsky offers of female victims of violence who protested their treatment in court? Should we always disguise our sympathy for women who found a myriad of ways, formal and informal, to avoid, protest, or dispute their oppression?

One can thus cite enough exceptions to the historiographical narrative extracted from the *Gender Conflicts* introduction to suggest that a straw feminist historian is being set up and a whig narrative sustained. Because few published pieces took direct issue with this interpretation it could become 'common sense' in the field.[100] Indeed, there are other examples of similar claims making. In one article, a group of feminists posited that gender history offered a superior perspective to women's history since it went "beyond descriptions of 'women's experience'" and looked at the "whole social formation," not "just women": as a result, the "unitary category" of woman was productively questioned, not simply assumed.[101] In a similar vein, Mariana Valverde suggested that women's history represented a "first stage" in feminist writing that was characterized by the naive, "positivist" assumption that one could simply "collect quantities of facts about 'women's experiences.'" In contrast, poststructuralist writing by authors like Denise Riley offered a more sophisticated, open, "tension filled methodological approach" far from the proven "dogmatism" that characterized both "grand theory and empiricism."[102] Yet one could argue that historical materialism, a maligned 'grand theory,' also examined tensions and contradictions and, at its best, encouraged an "open" reflective assessment of truth claims.[103]

One can dispute the historiographical assertions made by some authors but still commend the thematics and subject matter they are addressing. Situated as it was in the early 1990s, the *Gender Conflicts* introduction also represented two broad shifts in the field: a growing concern with questions of 'race,' and an increasing interest in poststructuralism.

The latter trend was visible in other monographs as well, though their use of theory was not of one piece. Carolyn Strange's positioning of her study of the 'girl problem' in Toronto as a project less concerned with locating women's 'experience' than with the discourses shaping their 'regulation' drew consciously on Foucault, while Cecilia Morgan's study of Upper Canada used discourse theory to dissect the meanings of masculinity and femininity in the colonial period.[104]

This shift towards poststructuralism was also visible in a second key historiographical statement also often taken as definitive, that of Joy Parr's "Gender History and Historical Practice," which won the Hilda Neatby prize for the best article in women's history. This piece (published in 1995) is also a good reflection of debates and ideas circulating by the mid-1990s: first, it argues for gender as an improvement on women's history; second, it indicates the increasing interest in masculinity; and, third, it offers a poststructuralist critique of previous notions of experience in women's history. Gender history, Parr suggests, emerged very much because of theoretical innovations of poststructuralism. Moreover, the latter's emphasis on contingency, "temporariness, impermanence" is in fact the "greatest contribution" gender history has made, as well as the source of opposition to it.[105] It is gender history's emphasis on impermanence and 'not knowing,' Parr argues, that threatens an older "generation" of historians, who were "cleaved" to the humanist "roots of history," including nineteenth-century notions of truth.[106] "The writing of history has moved on," she declares, asserting an implicitly whig view of progress.

"Highlighting the partialness of our understanding of the past," Parr claims, is seen as "dangerous" by these older critics, though she cites only two Canadian pieces reflecting this stick-in-the-mud generation: Michael Bliss's much-criticized and discussed piece on fragmentation and an unpublished paper by Jim Miller. Without Miller's unpublished piece that was cited, it is difficult to assess this claim, but I do not think the published version falls under the category of being "ferocious and hostile" to gender history.[107] On the contrary, he praises many of the innovations and advances of women's history. However, he does argue there are certain dangers inherent in new methods and theories of the 1990s, not only because of poststructuralist rejections of the idea of truth but also because historians may, he fears, sacrifice what they see as the truth to political considerations or invest too much in a feminist emphasis on the personal and experiential. I do not agree with all of Miller's points: using the usually antifeminist term 'political correctness' was a mistake, and assuming that women's history was deeply invested in the experiential was actually a misreading of the times, since that is precisely what Joan Scott was critiquing. But some of the questions Miller raises about an abandonment of all notions of truth and about the perceived problems of researching across Native and newcomer cultures are thoughtful and timely. Indeed, given his research on residential schools, it is not surprising that Miller might be concerned with the undermining of truth claims, which are often the path to redress. A defender of traditional humanism he may be, but he is hardly a reactionary 'von Rankean,' opposed to historiographical innovations, including gender history.[108]

Those critical of a poststructuralist emphasis on impermanence, fluidity, and 'not knowing' are not all in one older, passé generation, nor do they necessarily reject the need for diversity or the insight that society and history, not biology, lie behind the construction of gender and race, as Parr suggests in her article. To be critical of poststructuralism is not the same as being critical of gender history or feminism. Poststructuralists see positions as "multidimensional and specific" rather than "universal and totalizing," Parr claims, again making those she criticizes appear to be inflexible absolutists.[109] Others have argued that an emphasis on seeing history as 'unfinished,' on questioning "interpretive assumptions" and the "strategies used in constructing texts," are not specific to poststructuralism and have long been tenets of historical practice.[110] Even though Parr concedes this might be so, she adds that poststructuralism is a needed antidote "after three decades of the social sciences" leading historians to seek out "immobilized structures" and ignore "local colour."[111] This is not a characterization that to my mind reflects Canadian social history in the mid-1990s, which had long welcomed local studies and which was increasingly sceptical of mechanical 'structural' interpretations.

Parr's influential article also undoubtedly reinforced the view that a focus on women was limited because, as she put it, the very questions asked about 'woman' "presupposed" the answers given, "isolating woman from the social relationships that created her."[112] In her discussion of masculinity, however, Parr discusses similar problems of assuming a 'unitary' masculinity. One could argue that extracting any one group from its social context or presupposing answers based on the questions asked are potential perils for histories of men or women, masculinity or femininity, depending on how the history is done. They are not intrinsic to a more "limited" women's history.

Parr also rightly points out that writing in the 1970s and 1980s often aimed to reclaim women's experience, and, in accordance with Joan Scott's 1991 influential article, Parr sees this earlier approach as flawed by a lack of understanding that experience itself is not foundational: rather, "experiences were claims, not irrefutable foundations," for "meaning precedes experience."[113] Earlier feminists did often claim to be recovering women's experiences, and some of these works undoubtedly assumed women's words could be read as an 'authentic' rendering of their lives. However, not all feminist historians naively relayed women's words as simple 'truth,' or failed to ask the question Parr sees as crucial: "What made some parts of experience notable and others unmarked?"[114]

To swim against what is persistently presented as the tide of historiographic *progress* and innovation can be daunting: to argue against the apparently definitive insights of poststructuralism could put one in the camp of the absolutists, the naive humanists, and maybe even the economistic, determinist Marxists (perhaps the worst label of all). To admit to really liking or agreeing with books like *Against Postmodernism, The Retreat from Class,* or *Descent into Discourse* (as I did) might classify you in the latter unfashionable category.[115] Whatever the beneficial insights of feminist poststructuralist writing (and there were significant ones), there were significant disadvantages as well, including for those women who had been marginalized even within women's history, as their 'authentic' voices of experience could be undermined — a point Karen Flynn makes very well in the context of African-Canadian women's history.[116] There may indeed be some areas where the insights of modernist and postmodernist thought have been mutually beneficial and productive, even — or perhaps especially — when they existed in tension, as, for example in feminist writing on sexuality and regulation that drew selectively on Foucault but also engaged with him critically. The same might be true for writing on gender and colonialism that drew in part on postcolonial theories. However, in the latter case, even third world scholars sympathetic to postcolonial scholarship are critical of the depoliticizing tendencies evident in some highly culturalist postcolonial theory that has strayed completely from the earliest (anti-imperialist) meaning of the term.[117] I believe we need to heed their words.[118]

The theoretical sentiment in Joy Parr's article clearly struck a chord at the time, and it is a cogent reminder that, by the mid-1990s, the concept of experience had become problematic for many feminist historians, associated as it was with erroneous, even dangerously 'essentializing' foundational concepts.[119] And this critique did have a tangible effect, shifting historians' approaches to their subjects, creating a wariness of depicting women's experiences with any certainty, of being able to get inside their minds and feelings — especially when one was crossing barriers of race. It is precisely for this reason that representation became more central to feminist history writing. For feminist historians like myself whose socialization had been in Thompsonian social history, the poststructuralist critique could not but unsettle a core concept of 'lived experience' that encompassed both social relations and human interpretations of those relations. Debates about experience were hardly new; indeed, earlier structuralist critiques of Thompson had also argued (not unlike some poststructuralists) that he endowed the notion of human experience with too much 'authenticity.'[120] Despite the confident assertions of some social historians that Thompson's rendition of experience had been "disposed of" by Joan Scott and others,[121] it has not been without its defenders. By the late 1990s, feminists and materialists of various stripes were publishing critiques of Scott reaffirming the importance of "retrieving experience,"[122] although many such works came from feminist and cultural studies theorists rather than historians. For precisely this reason, I revisited these debates in one of the final articles in this book.

Even accounting for some reticence vis-à-vis this debate, American women's historians seemed more ready to discuss interpretive and ideological differences than their Canadian counterparts. As Andrée Lévesque noted with regret, "one cannot help but notice the paucity of theoretical debates by historians, including Canadians, which so enliven the practice and development of women's history."[123] Why is this?

Debatophobia

When I began working on this book, Alvin Finkel commented that some critical discussion of feminist historiography would be a welcome addition to Canadian scholarship: after all, he quipped, Canadian women's history seems to suffer from 'debatophobia.' His comment forced to me to reflect critically on whether this was really true, and if so, why? And were the consequences of agreement really that bad? After all, many feminists have seen building consensus as a positive and community-enhancing enterprise.

As 1970s' feminists discovered, however, consensus can simply paper over or even suppress differences in ideas, feeling, and power. Debate, in contrast, is more open, and while it may not lead to resolution, it does clarify what our differences are and why we feel one interpretation is better that the other — and is interpretation not at the core of how and why we do history? Think of the debates within feminist studies over the years. The Nancy Fraser–Judith Butler debate about the politics of recognition and redistribution was sometimes sharp, and certainly critical, but it was also enlightening and stimulating.[124] If nothing was resolved, positions were developed, ideas expanded, and feminist theory was certainly enriched — whichever side you oscillated towards. The exchanges between Linda Gordon and Theda Skocpal about social policy, or between Linda Gordon and Joan Scott about violence and women's experience, similarly highlighted different approaches to history, politics, and feminism[125] — and one can cite many other examples of incisive feminist critiques and theoretical differences.

Such drama is not the stuff of Canadian women's history, and it is not simply that we are a more polite nation, prone to be accommodating even when someone steps on our toes. Is it possible that we actually all agree? I think there may be a measure of truth to this characterization. The early CCWH was built on attempts to draw together feminists from a variety of occupations, politics, and regional areas. Since many of those who initially became interested in women's history were already sympathetic to some brand of feminism we were drawn together by a common sense of political purpose. No matter what our age or background, many of us have dealt with instances of sexism, marginalization, fear, or derision relating to our gender at some point in our lives. A feeling of being 'embattled' was probably especially prevalent in the early ten to fifteen years of the CCWH, when women's history was more decidedly on the margins, when women were struggling to get courses on women accepted, and when there were fewer women in history departments, let alone universities. This feeling of being in the same boat — and a lifeboat at that — likely engendered a sense we should stick together, and there certainly were instances of women supporting other women in the profession. Unlike our counterparts in the United States, where there are hundreds of feminist historians working in universities, we are also a much smaller group, with more personal connections.

Perhaps we also had some political role models: Canada's national women's organization, the National Action Committee on the Status of Women (NAC), worked for many years as an uneasy political coalition of women drawn from different political stripes, constituting a form of feminist politics that Jill Vickers and others define as particularly Canadian.[126] There seem to be far fewer high-profile right-wing commentators and antifeminists in Canada à la Camille Paglia or Katie Roiphe, peddling their wares in our country (which is not to deny that some organizations like REAL [Realistic, Equal, Active, for Life] Women of Canada are pernicious promoters of antifeminism), and an enduring social democratic tradition has often become the home of many feminists attracted to its gentle critique of capitalism, its long-standing voice on women's issues, and its investment in democratic processes of change. Still, not everyone stumps for the NDP, and the assumption that we are all 'progressive' feminists of this variety, or even that this tradition is the one and only way forward, leaves out some feminists and assumes an ideological consensus that may well paper over differences. Social democracy, as history suggests, can be quite sectarian in its sense of moral superiority.

This problem of a seemingly agreeable progressive left-centre perspective being taken as the superior norm is not confined to women's history; this pluralistic vision, lauding attention to race, gender, ethnicity, colonialism, sexual orientation, and disability has also been celebrated as the primary achievement of social history.[127] But pluralism can also be a form of liberalism or can become a confining creed of consensus whose dominance is assumed, not questioned.[128] The solution to a cozy sameness, one commentator has lightly suggested, is to have more "conservatives" writing Canadian history, since leftists supposedly split hairs rather than debate real differences.[129] I think not.

A more generalized example of this aversion to debate was symbolized by the decision of the Canadian Historical Association (CHA) years ago not to have commentators at sessions as they might be too "critical" (precisely the word used). Yet commentators can tie papers together, raise questions we had not thought of, and yes, create a critical, engaged, intellectual community. I have not heard a harsh critical commentary since 1985 at the CHA, and I don't think the turn towards consensus has made the conference academically superior. Moreover, shutting down open debate simply takes it into a more closed, private realm. If we refrain from making a critical comment during a session or in a book review but then go and complain about someone's paper (and perhaps them, too) behind their back, this is not creating a scholarly community. It is recreating the atmosphere of 'junior high school' (as one historian put it to me), an experience some of us would rather forget. To be sure, at one time we had to guard against antifeminist and pejorative comments about women's history, but they are far less commonplace now, and feminists must be ready to face the same questions about how we use evidence, argument, and theory that define all of us as historians. We also need to distinguish between antifeminism and critique. To disparage women's history and feminism in general is one thing, but to criticize a particular text for not using evidence carefully, or taking a quote out of context, or drawing the wrong conclusions is a valid and useful academic exercise.[130]

It is true that disciplines differentially and differently foster debate as part of their ethos. Canadian political economy would seem at first glance to engage in more debate, whether one is addressing race and essentialism, the national question, or the need to discuss gender.[131] Within the historical profession, writing in British social history has never escaped sharp debate, and the much larger, more diverse and variegated American profession, including women's and labour history, also seems less reluctant to disagree. Consensus is thus not endemic to Canadian research or history more generally; indeed, other areas of the discipline have witnessed more disagreement. When women's history burst upon the scene in the 1970s, its sometime ally was labour history, which was characterized by more ideologically charged debates, in part because an established cohort with social democratic loyalties opposed an upstart group of Marxists whose politics, priorities, and international perspectives challenged theirs.[132]

Our views are likely shaped also by our own academic and political socialization. I suspect that being exposed to the 'far left' political milieu of the late 1970s encouraged me to see political agendas as worth fighting over. I may not have always liked the way these debates unfolded, including in gendered terms, but I did not see them as simply worthless. Even today, there are some political milieux in which discussion is suppressed, and other situations in which people are more actively engaged and become used to hearing quite impassioned disapproval of others' ideas. Perhaps this was one reason I wrote a polemic meant to stimulate debate and stake out a position about gender and women's history, but it was not very satisfying, with discussants sometimes talking at cross-purposes. I was protesting the hierarchy being established between a superior gender history and a 'limited' women's history, while other commentators were criticizing what they saw as my rejection of 'diversification' of the field through the expanding categories associated with gender history.[133] Possibly some clarifications emerged that were useful, but in a small country that shuns argument, any debate can stall prematurely or become unproductively personalized.

Debates within feminism can be uncomfortable since we do not want to shut down all contacts, collaborations, and future invitations to discussion, and, for some women, this becomes equated with career issues. Why talk back or disagree, some may respond, when academic life — from publishing to jobs — hinges on maintaining good personal networks? Although I find this a depressing response, I recognize why the fear is there. Moreover, critique can seem a daunting prospect for all of us. Who wants to be criticized in print when our lives are so entangled with our writing, and when we invest so much of ourselves in our work? Who wants to be told that they had it 'wrong'? No one enjoys this, myself included. After all, a book is not just a job done: it's a labour of love. Interpretation and argument matter a great deal to us; they are not akin to fixing spelling mistakes in a memo, something we can leave at the office when we go home. We may also want to avoid conflict in order not to lose the sense of common purpose and female support networks that have sustained us as feminist scholars. Last, but not least, it would be naive to think that reprisals for criticism never occur in academic life.

In terms of generation and experience, some of us may have to accept that certain criticisms come with age (unfortunately we are not simply seen as 'wise women') as a newer group of historians, reared in a different political milieu, will identify things we neglected, or separate themselves from approaches they see as outdated — the inevitable "old fogey" quandary, as Veronica Strong-Boag put it[134] — though I suspect criticism will still be doled out to us disproportionately. No one enjoys being portrayed as a feminist dinosaur, a characterization I've seen directed against some fellow women's studies professors by students in our regular 'criticize the program' meetings. And no one enjoys being socially constructed, after even one academic debate, as "contentious," a "problem," and so on, with those adjectives seemingly glued to one's academic persona for life.

The solution to debatophobia, however, does not seem to me to be accommodation to a false consensus, which, as feminists found in political organizing, may actually result in one group claiming the high moral ground. Nor is it to resort to behind-the-scenes discussion (sometimes becoming gossip), which has a disproportionate impact in a small country. In academic life, there are many ways to establish a canon that excludes or diminishes without resorting to open criticism: by telling one's graduate students not to bother reading certain authors (or just leaving them off reading lists), by 'power citing' (using footnotes to exclude), and by typecasting a person's work according to their supposed politics or personality. These are all bad alternatives to a debate about what we actually *write*. They do not represent the type of engagement with ideas that we truly value; they do not reflect the intellectual excitement we feel as we puzzle through changing concepts; and they do not represent the reality that history is about interpretive and ideological difference. We can acknowledge the general contributions an author has made to the field, we can analyze the context in which they wrote, and we can make every effort not to misquote their words, but within those boundaries, critique is valid and necessary and, used effectively, it may help our collective project of developing an even richer, more complex, and exciting version of women's history.

Sharp debate may have seemed disloyal at a time when women's history was just finding its feet, but we are no longer standing on the margins, at least not simply because of our gender. True, we don't want to become too complacent, since there are sometimes backlashes and pockets of antifeminism to contend with, but we can still recognize the considerable shifts that have transpired in the practice of history. We must also concede that that having women integrated into the profession is not the same as social equality; those women marginalized by class, race, or sexual orientation, those who have no access to universities and no hope of other education, remind us that we are a relatively privileged group. Within the small circles of higher education, however, the field of gender and women's history has prospered, diversified, and expanded and can now boast a rich and varied history of its own. This should be cause for a celebration (not suppression) of our intellectual and ideological differences, which in turn can only tell new generations of historians that there is more work to be done, more arguments to question, more problems to solve. It is possible that our praxis will change over time, as we recognize how influential our ideas have become within the profession. Over the past thirty years, the impact of feminist organizing, thinking, and writing on scholarship has been significant; women are no longer 'nonentities' on the historical stage, and gender relations are seen as an important social category to integrate into our understanding of history. Innovative research that addresses new questions we never even thought about before, and that also revisits old problems we never solved, is appearing all the time. The more such work is published, the more debates about women's history see the light of day, the richer our praxis is, the richer our legacy for the next generation of feminist historians.

Notes

1 Sylvia Van Kirk, *Many Tender Ties: Women in Fur-Trade Society in Western Canada, 1670–1870* (Winnipeg: Watson and Dwyer, 1980); Constance Backhouse, *Colour-coded: A Legal History of Racism in Canada, 1900–1950* (Toronto: University of Toronto Press, 1999); Rusty Bitterman, "Women and the Escheat Movement: The Politics of Everyday Life on Prince Edward Island," in *Separate Spheres: Women's Worlds in the 19th Century Maritimes*, ed. Janet Guildford and Suzanne Morton (Fredericton: Acadiensis Press, 1994), 23–38.

2 I'm sure Ann Stoler thought we were picky, overly sensitive if not crazy Canadians when Bryan Palmer and I criticized her use of a Canadian book title to lead
off an article with virtually *no* Canadian content in it, although it was about
'North America.' It is true, however, that other American books use 'North
America' as a synonym for the United States and they do not understand why
we get exercised about this. Bryan Palmer and Joan Sangster, "Letter to the
Editor," *Journal of American History* 89, no. 3 (2002): 1185–86.

3 Judith Bennett, quoting Ellen DuBois and then noting Kathleen Canning in
History Matters: Patriarchy and the Challenge of Feminism (Philadelphia: University
of Pennsylvania Press, 2006), 163.

4 Beverly Boutilier and Alison Prentice, eds., *Creating Historical Memory: English-
Canadian Women and the Work of History* (Vancouver: University of British Colum-
bia Press, 1997); Cecilia Morgan, "Performing for Imperial Eyes: Bernice Loft
and Ethel Brant Monture, Ontario, 1930s–1960s," in *Contact Zones: Aboriginal and
Settler Women in Canada's Colonial Past*, ed. Katie Pickles and Myra Rutherdale
(Vancouver: University of British Columbia Press, 2005), 67–89; Edith Fowke,
Singing Our History: Canada's Story in Song (Toronto: Doubleday, 1984).

5 Janice Acton, Penny Goldsmith, and Bonnie Shepard, eds., *Women at Work:
Ontario, 1980–1930* (Toronto: Women's Press, 1974).

6 On the ccwh, see Veronica Strong-Boag, *Work to Be Done: The Canadian Committee on Women's History/Le Comité canadien de l'histoire des femmes* (Montreal: The
Canadian Committee on Women's History/Le Comité canadien de l'histoire
des femmes, 1995).

7 For two commentaries on feminist and working class history, see Bettina Bradbury,
"Women's History and Working Class History," *Labour/Le Travail* 19 (1987): 23–43;
Joan Sangster, "Feminism and the Making of Canadian Working-Class History:
Exploring the Past, Present, and Future," *Labour/Le Travail* 46 (Fall 2000): 127–65.

8 Johanna den Hertog, "What Did They Fight For, How Did They Organize?"
Kinesis (Sept. 1976): 13–17. Book reviews in *Kinesis* also reveal how little had been
written even by the late 1970s, as they often reviewed British books on topics
like the suffragettes, or more popular Canadian titles.

9 Sheila Rowbotham, *Hidden from History: Three Hundred Years of Women's Oppression
and the Fight Against It* (London: Pluto Press, 1973).

10 Barbara Roberts, "They Drove Him to Drink: Donald Creighton's Macdonald
and His Wives," *Canada: A Historical Magazine* 3, no. 2 (Dec. 1975): 51–64.

11 For example, the Irene Murdoch case concerning women's right to marital
property, or the legal fight for paid maternity leaves.

12 Andrée Lévesque, "Réflexions sur l'histoire des femmes dans l'histoire du
Québec," *Revue d'histoire de l'Amérique française* (RHFA) 51, no. 2 (1997): 271–84. On the

questions of 'victimization,' see also Micheline Dumont, "Histoire des femmes," *Social History/Histoire sociale* 21, no. 42 (1988): 319–45.

13 Nancy Christie and Michael Gauvreau, *A Full-Orbed Christianity: The Protestant Churches and Social Welfare in Canada* (Montreal: McGill-Queen's University Press, 1996).

14 Lévesque, "Réflexions," 277.

15 Ibid., 273.

16 There were some early biographies that could not just be dismissed as celebratory or un-analytical. See, for instance, Patricia T. Rooke and Rodolph L. Schnell, *No Bleeding Heart: Charlotte Whitton, A Feminist on the Right* (Vancouver: University of British Columbia Press, 1987). For a couple of examples of this recent use of biography, see Patricia Roome, "From One Whose Home Is Among the Indians: Henrietta Muir Edwards and Aboriginal Peoples," in *Unsettled Pasts: Reconceiving the West Through Women's History*, ed. Sarah Carter et al. (Calgary: University of Calgary Press, 2005), 47–78; Jennifer Henderson, *Settler Feminism and Race Making in Canada* (Toronto: University of Toronto Press, 2003). Biography has also been used more recently, either as a means of describing a remarkable woman's life in the context of her times or as a means of exploring the commemoration of certain women. On the former, see Faith Johnston, *A Great Restlessness: The Life and Politics of Dorise Nielsen* (Winnipeg: University of Manitoba Press, 2006), and on the latter, Colin Coates and Cecilia Morgan, *Heroines and History: Representations of Madeleine de Verchères and Laura Secord* (Toronto: University of Toronto Press, 2002).

17 It is also hard to define 'adding women' to history. Some more recent post-1995 books might seem to fit this bill too, yet they may well be excellent examples of the expansion of knowledge. For example, one could add or integrate women into the story of the political left through a biography, such as Johnston, *A Great Restlessness*, correct the history of Upper Canada by adding women in, as in Jane Errington, *Wives and Mothers, School Mistresses and Scullery Maids: Working Women in Upper Canada, 1790–1840* (Montreal: McGill-Queen's University Press, 1995), or add women to the history of a region in order to reconceive its history, as in *Unsettled Pasts: Reconceiving the West Through Women's History*, ed. Sarah Carter et al. (Calgary: University of Calgary Press, 2005).

18 Alison Prentice and Ruth Roach Pierson, "Feminism and the Writing and Teaching of History," *Atlantis* 7, no. 2 (1982): 37–46.

19 Joan Kelly, *Women, History and Theory: The Essays of Joan Kelly* (Chicago: University of Chicago Press, 1984); Gerda Lerner, *The Majority Finds Its Past: Placing Women in History* (New York: Oxford University Press, 1979), 174, 180; Judy Bernstein et al., "Sisters, Brothers, Lovers. . . . Listen," in *Women Unite: An Anthology of the Canadian Women's Movement*, ed. Canadian Women's Educational Press (Toronto: Women's

Press, 1972), 31–39. See also York University Archives, Toronto Telegram Collection, 197-001-354, file 2347, pictures of Toronto Women's Caucus demonstration.

20 Susan Stanford Friedman, "Making History: Reflections on Feminism, Narrative, and Desire," in *Feminism Beside Itself*, ed. Diane Elam and Robyn Wiegman (New York: Routledge, 1995), 14.

21 Ibid.

22 Ibid., 24–25.

23 Linda Gordon, "Comments on That Noble Dream," *American Historical Review* 96, no. 3 (June 1991): 685.

24 Wendy Mitchinson, "Gynecological Operations on Insane Women: London, Ontario, 1895–1901," *Journal of Social History* 15, no. 3 (Spring 1982): 467–84; Bettina Bradbury, "Pigs, Cows and Boarders: Non-wage Forms of Survival Among Montreal Families, 1861–91," *Labour/Le Travail* 14 (1984): 9–46. I have cited examples somewhat randomly, though many of these are articles that I remember students responding to especially well.

25 Gail Cuthbert Brandt, "Postmodern Patchwork: Some Recent Trends in the Writing of Women's History in Canada," *Canadian Historical Review*, 72, no. 4 (1991): 441–70.

26 Barbara Roberts, "A Work of Empire: Canadian Reformers and British Female Immigration," in *A Not Unreasonable Claim: Women and Reform in Canada, 1880s–1920s*, ed. Linda Kealey (Toronto: Women's Press, 1979), 185–202; Wayne Roberts, *Honest Womanhood: Feminism, Femininity and Class Consciousness Among Toronto Working Women* (Toronto: New Hogtown Press, 1976); Christina Simmons, "Helping the Poorer Sisters: The Women of Jost Mission," *Acadiensis* 14 (Autumn 1984): 3–27; Carol Bacchi, *Liberation Deferred: The Ideas of the English Canadian Suffragists* (Toronto: University of Toronto Press, 1983); Jean Burnet, *Looking into My Sister's Eyes: An Exploration in Women's History* (Toronto: Multicultural History Society of Ontario, 1986).

27 Meg Luxton, "Feminism Is a Class Act: Working-Class Feminism and the Women's Movement in Canada." *Labour/Le Travail* 48 (2001): 63–88.

28 For example, Margaret Conrad, *No Place Like Home: Diaries and Letters of Nova Scotia Women, 1771–1938* (Halifax: Formac, 1988); Eliane L. Silverman, *The Last Best West: Women on the Alberta Frontier, 1880–1930* (Montreal: Eden Press, 1984). A later examination of working women's life cycle is Gail Brandt, "The Transformation of Women's Work in the Quebec Cotton Industry, 1920–50," in *The Character of Class Struggle*, ed. Bryan D. Palmer (Toronto: McClelland and Stewart, 1986), 115–37.

29 Janet Guildford and Suzanne Morton, "Introduction," in *Separate Spheres: Women's Worlds in the 19th Century Maritimes*, ed. Janet Guildford and Suzanne Morton (Fredericton: Acadiensis Press, 1996), 12.

30   Suzanne Morton, "Gender, Place and Region: Thoughts on the State of Women in Atlantic Canadian History," *Atlantis* 25, no. 2 (2000): 123. It seems undeniable that in Canadian history more generally a concern with region is less evident today than it was thirty years ago. In some cases, this has been replaced by a concern with 'space and place,' a term that can be used anywhere in Canada.

31   For example, Carter et al., *Unsettled Pasts*, and *One Step over the Line: Toward a History of Women in the North American Wests*, ed. Sheila McManus and Elizabeth Jameson (Edmonton: University of Alberta Press and Athabasca University Press, 2008).

32   Ruth A. Frager, "Class and Ethnic Barriers to Feminist Perspectives in Toronto's Jewish Labour Movement, 1919–1939," *Studies in Political Economy* 30 (1989): 143–65; Varpu Lindström-Best, *Defiant Sisters: A Social History of Finnish Immigrant Women in Canada* (Toronto: Multicultural History Society of Ontario, 1988); Katherine Arnup, "Mothers Just Like Any Others: Lesbians, Divorce and Child Custody in Canada," *Canadian Journal of Women and the Law* 3, no. 1 (1989): 18–32; Andrée Lévesque, "Deviant Anonymous: Single Mothers at the Hôpital de la Miséricorde in Montreal, 1929–1939," *Canadian Historical Association Report* 19 (1984): 168–84; Joan Sangster, "The Communist Party and the Woman Question, 1922–29," *Labour/Le Travail* 15 (1985): 25–56.

33   Van Kirk, *Many Tender Ties*; Jennifer Brown, *Strangers in Blood: Fur Trade Company Families in Indian Country* (Vancouver: University of British Columbia Press, 1980).

34   Franca Iacovetta, "Gendering Trans/National Historiographies: Feminists Re-writing Canadian History," *Journal of Women's History* 19, no. 1 (March 2007): 211. "There are still Canadian women historians who, despite plenty of evidence to the contrary, say that more attention to gender will undermine a politically edged women's history. And that attention to race will mean abandoning women. . . . But only a few have publicly mocked efforts to build bridges across theoretical and generational differences" (210). No citation is given for these claims, which I think are not a fair reflection of the actual *writing*.

35   Marilyn Porter, "She Was Skipper of the Shore Crew: Notes on the History of the Sexual Division of Labour in Newfoundland," *Labour/Le Travail* 15 (Spring 1985): 105–23.

36   For example, on patriarchy, see Mary O'Brien, *The Politics of Reproduction* (Boston: Routledge and Kegan Paul, 1981), or on Marxist feminism, Sheila Rowbotham, *Woman's Consciousness, Man's World* (London: Harmondsworth, 1972); Michele Barrett, *Women's Oppression Today: Problems in Marxist Feminist Analysis* (London: New Left Books, 1980); Pat Armstrong and Hugh Armstrong, "Beyond Sexless Class and Classless Sex: Towards a Feminist Marxism," *Studies in Political Economy* 10 (1983): 7–43.

37   Susan Mann Trofimenkoff, quoted in Marlene Shore, "Remember the Future: The *Canadian Historical Review* and the Discipline of History, 1920–94," *Canadian Historical Review* 76, no. 3 (Sept. 1995): 449.

38 This tradition was drawn on by feminists like Sheila Rowbotham, *Women, Resistance and Revolution* (London: Penguin, 1975). For debates on capitalism and patriarchy, see Zillah Eisenstein, *Capitalist Patriarchy and the Case for Socialist Feminism* (New York: Monthly Review Press, 1979).

39 Two examples of political economists doing history are Gillian Creese, "The Politics of Dependence: Women, Work and Unemployment in the Vancouver Labour Movement before World War II," *Canadian Journal of Sociology* 13 (1988): 121–42; Alicia Muszynski, *Cheap Wage Labour: Race and Gender in the Fisheries of British Columbia* (Vancouver: University of British Columbia Press, 1996). Although there were some important literary-influenced studies, such as those by Carole Gerson, this genre seemed less influential than political economy, though it may well be increasing with books like Henderson, *Settler Feminism*. This increased significance could have something to do with an interest in poststructuralist literary theory.

40 For a brief summary of the areas affected, including notions of what is knowable, the self, metanarratives, structural explanations, etc., see Mary Maynard, "Beyond the Big Three: The Development of Feminist Theory in the 1990s," *Women's History Review* 4, no. 3 (1995): 259–81.

41 For example, Geoff Eley and Keith Nield in *The Future of Class in History: What's Left of the Social?* (Ann Arbour: University of Michigan Press, 2007) claim that Joan Scott's work "may have done more than any other single intervention to help bring the importance of feminist ideas from the barely tolerated sidelines of women's history into the central territories of the discipline and profession of history" (118). This is rather hyperbolic and ignores many other feminist historians with different politics whose work was important. For the argument that earlier connections between the New Left, Marxism, and women's history have been downplayed, see Sheila Rowbotham, "New Entry Points from USA Women's Labour History," in *Working Out Gender: Perspectives from Labour History*, ed. Margaret Walsh (Brookfield, VT: Ashgate, 1999), 12. For a critique of the conflation of women's history and poststructuralism, see Barbara Epstein, "Why Poststructuralism Is a Dead End for Women," *Socialist Review* 5 (1995): 83–119.

42 Mariana Valverde, "Some Remarks on the Rise and Fall of Discourse Analysis," *Social History/Histoire sociale* 33, no. 65 (May 2000): 64. The fact that this kind of unverifiable (and in my view wrong) historiographical statement has gone virtually unchallenged is a reflection of the problem of 'debatophobia' discussed below.

43 Franca Iacovetta and Wendy Mitchinson, "Introduction," *On the Case: Explorations in Social History* (Toronto: University of Toronto Press, 1998).

44 Eley and Nield, *The Future of Class*, 17. This is a sophisticated treatment of the theoretical debates, but ultimately the authors do favour poststructuralism over what they revealingly call the "myopia of materialism" (77).

45 For some who are critical, see responses by Frederick Cooper and Judith Stein, "Farewell to the Working Class?" *International Labor and Working-Class History* 57 (Spring 2000): 1–30.

46 Eley and Nield, *The Future of Class*, 77, refer to the "myopia of materialism."

47 Brandt, "Postmodern Patchwork," 467.

48 Brandt, "Postmodern Patchwork." Magda Fahrni suggests this is even more pronounced in Quebec, where other methods, such as quantitative work, have maintained more prominence. Fahrni, "Reflections on the Place of Quebec in Historical Writing in Canada," in *Contesting Clio's Craft: New Directions and Debates in Canadian History*, ed. Christopher Dummitt and Michael Dawson (London: Institute for the Study of the Americas, 2009).

49 See my discussion of book reviews in "Feminism and the Making" (146). This is only one example of this trend, however.

50 Moreover, even if gender is a focus for debate, it is possible that questions featured in Anglo-American debates may not be the same ones that 'take' in Latin America. Dutch feminist historian Mineke Bosch has similarly questioned the ways in which feminist historical debates are presumed to be 'international' in character. See Mineke Bosch, "Internationalism and Theory in Women's History," *Gender and History* 3, no. 2 (1991): 137.

51 Beverley Skeggs, *Formations of Class and Gender* (London: Sage Publications, 1997), 7. She notes: "Interestingly race is not dismissed as a structural dinosaur."

52 Matsuda, cited in Jennifer Nash, "Re-thinking Intersectionality," *Feminist Review* 89 (2000): 3.

53 Ibid. For a discussion of three different kinds of intersectionality writing, see Leslie McCall, "The Complexity of Intersectionality," *Signs* 30, no. 3 (2005): 1771–1800.

54 McCall, "The Complexity of Intersectionality," 1788.

55 Quotes from Nash, "Re-thinking Intersectionality," 5, 13, and Mieke Verloo, "Multiple Inequalities, Intersectionality and the European Union," *European Journal of Women's Studies* 13, no. 1 (2006): 211–25 (211); Nira Yuval-Davis, "Intersectionality and Feminist Politics," *European Journal of Women's Studies* 13, no. 1 (2006): 193–209.

56 See, for example, the special issue of *European Journal of Women's Studies* 13, no. 1 (2006), and Avtar Brah and Ann Phoenix, "Ain't I a Woman? Revisiting Intersectionality," *Journal of International Women's Studies* 5, no. 3 (May 2004): 75–86.

57 Hester Eisenstein, *Feminism Seduced: How Global Elites Use Women's Labor and Ideas to Exploit the World* (Boulder, CO: Paradigm Publishers, 2009); Nancy Fraser, "Feminism, Capitalism and the Cunning of History," *New Left Review* 56 (March–April

2009): 97–117. It seems facile to say this, but it does appear that the political and economic context, including the recent meltdown of global capitalism, may have helped to shift feminist thinking, even for some who previously offered the same critiques of 'metanarratives' that they are now reconsidering.

58 Obviously, other nation-states are not completely monolithic entities, and the international literature on nationhood has had an important influence on Canadian scholarship. As Fahrni points out, French literature on commemoration has had an influence in Quebec. See "Reflections," 7.

59 Arlene McLaren, "Introduction," *Gender and Society: Creating a Canadian Women's Sociology* (Toronto: Copp Clark Pitman, 1988), 11; Andrée Lévesque, "Réflexions," 278.

60 Christopher Dummitt and Michael Dawson, "Introduction: Debating the Future of Canadian History: Preliminary Answers to Uncommon Questions," in *Contesting Clio's Craft: New Directions and Debates in Canadian History*, ed. Christopher Dummitt and Michael Dawson (London: Institute for the Study of the Americas, 2009), xvii. They are referring to an article in the collection by Adele Perry. Even the endorsement on the book jacket from senior scholar Gerald Friesen notes wryly that this group gives 'short shrift' to their predecessors.

61 Again, one problem is that certain nations and points of view still dominate transnational histories: intellectual life is not immune to geopolitical power relations. Some borderland historians, for instance, question if these comparative projects will actually shake off the dominance of the English-speaking, Anglo-American academic world, and historians of the 'third world' rightly question whether transnational histories will unsettle the *hegemonies* of north-south, colonizer-colonized, 'the West and the rest,' and the prevailing structures of intellectual and cultural power. See Christopher Ebert Schmidt-Nowara, "Response to Borders and Borderlands," *American Historical Review* 104, no. 4 (Oct. 1999): 1226–28; Frederick Cooper, "Conflict and Contention: Rethinking Colonial African History," *American Historical Review* 99, no. 5 (1994): 1517.

62 On the benefits of transnational histories, see Sarah Carter, "Transnational Perspectives on the History of Great Plains Women: Gender, Race, Nations, and the Forty-ninth Parallel," *American Review of Canadian Studies* (Winter 2003): 565. The nomenclature of 'transnational' is itself contested, sometimes including (sometimes not) what we used to call comparative history. Comparative work has been very productive in terms of Aboriginal women: e.g., Jean Barman, "What a Difference the Border Makes: Aboriginal Racial Intermixture in the Pacific Northwest," *Journal of the West* 38, no. 3 (July 1999): 14–20; Victoria Freeman, "Attitudes Toward 'Miscegenation' in Canada, the United States, New Zealand and Australia, 1860–1914," *Native Studies Review* 16, no. 1 (2005): 41–70; Katherine Ellinghaus, *Taking Assimilation to Heart: Marriages of White Women and Indigenous Men in the United States and Australia, 1887–1937* (Lincoln: University of Nebraska Press, 2006).

63 Gerald Friesen, *Citizens and Nation: An Essay on History, Communication and Canada* (Toronto: University of Toronto Press, 2000); Ian McKay, "The Liberal Order Framework: A Prospectus for a Reconnaissance of Canadian History," *Canadian Historical Review* 81, no. 4 (2000): 617–45.

64 Phyllis Senese, "Weeds in the Garden of Civic Nationalism," in *Nations, Ideas, Identities*, ed. Michael Behiels and Marcel Martel (Don Mills, ON: Oxford University Press, 2000), 113–29. See also Himani Bannerji, *The Dark side of the Nation: Essays on Multiculturalism, Nationalism and Gender* (Toronto: Canadian Scholars Press, 2000); Sherene Razack, *Race, Space, and the Law: Unmapping a White Settler Society* (Toronto: Between the Lines, 2000).

65 Linda Kealey, Ruth Pierson, Joan Sangster, and Veronica Strong-Boag, "Teaching Canadian History in the 1990s: Whose National History Are We Lamenting?" *Journal of Canadian Studies* 27, no. 2 (1992): 123–31.

66 Micheline Dumont-Johnson et al., *L'Histoire des femmes au Québec depuis quatre siècles* (Montreal: Quinze, 1982).

67 Micheline Dumont, "Can Nationalist History Include a Feminist Reflection on History?" *Journal of Canadian Studies* 35, no. 2 (2000): 80–93; and "Histoire des femmes," *Social History/Histoire sociale* 22 (May 1990): 117–28. On the contradictions and collaborations of feminism and nationalism, see also Diane Lamoureaux, "Nationalism and Feminism in Quebec: An Impossible Attraction," in *Feminism and Political Economy: Women's Work, Women's Struggles*, ed. Heather J. Maroney and Meg Luxton (Toronto: Methuen, 1987), 51–68.

68 For two views of Quebec feminism, see Madeleine de Sève, "The Perspectives of Quebec Feminists," and Micheline Dumont, "The Origins of the Women's Movement in Quebec," in *Challenging Times: The Women's Movement in Canada and the United States*, ed. David Flaherty and Constance Backhouse (Montreal: McGill-Queen's University Press, 1992), 110–16 and 72–89.

69 Denyse Baillargeon, quoted in Fahrni, "Reflections," 7.

70 Fahrni, "Reflections," 17.

71 Jill Vickers, "Feminisms and Nationalisms in English Canada," *Journal of Canadian Studies* 35, no. 3 (2000): 128–43. I suspect the problem is also generational, for feminists politically active in the 1970s were more invested in the 'Quebec question.' When I pointed out to a younger scholar that Quebec was considered an issue of 'colonialism' in the 1970s, I was told that I needed to reflect on why I had "repressed" the real 'race' question of the time, i.e., whiteness.

72 Veronica Strong-Boag, Sherrill Grace, and Avigail Eisenberg, eds., *Painting the Maple: Essays on Race, Gender, and the Construction of Canada* (Vancouver: University of British Columbia Press, 1998).

73 Sherene Razack, *Dark Threats and White Knights: The Somalia affair, Peacekeeping, and the New Imperialism* (Toronto: University of Toronto Press, 2004).

74 Joan Sangster, "Robitnytsia, Canadian Communists and the Porcupinsim Debate: Reassessing Ethnicity, Gender and Class in Early Canadian Communism," *Labour/Le Travail* 56 (2005): 51–90.

75 Cynthia Wright, "Troubling the Nation: On Teaching Canadian History in the Women's Studies Classroom," *Atlantis* 25, no. 2 (Autumn 2000): 137–39.

76 See Ian McKay, "The Liberal Order Framework," and Gerald Friesen, *Citizens and Nation*.

77 Daiva Stasiulis, "Relational Positionalities of Nationalism," in *Between Women and Nation: Nationalisms, Transnational Feminisms, and the State*, ed. Caren Kaplan, Norma Alarcon, and Minoo Moallem (Durham: Duke University Press, 1999), 182–218.

78 Christopher Dummitt, "After Inclusiveness: The Future of Canadian History," in Dummitt and Dawson, eds., *Contesting Clio's Craft*, 98–122.

79 Friedman, "Making History," 35.

80 Dummitt, "After Inclusiveness."

81 Dummitt and Dawson, "Introduction," x.

82 Himani Bannerji, quoted in Radha Jhappan, "Post-Modern Race and Gender Essentialism or a Post-Mortem of Scholarship," *Studies in Political Economy* 51 (Fall 1996): 48.

83 It may appear that by calling for the continual reassessment of our interpretations and how they are constructed and justified, I am embracing a poststructuralist endorsement of 'indeterminacy.' I don't think so: one can continually interrogate all seemingly accepted truths while still holding to certain notions of advancement. This openness to constant reassessment, in fact, has been part of a historical materialist tradition. See E.P. Thompson, *The Poverty of Theory* (New York: Monthly Review Press, 1978). Nor I am suggesting that any explanation goes: there are better explanations, substantiated by evidence, that are a closer reconstruction of the past. See Joyce Appleby, Lynn Hunt, and Margaret Jacob, *Telling the Truth About History* (New York: Norton, 1994).

84 Jhappan, "Post-Modern Race and Gender Essentialism," 15–63.

85 Jane Roland Martin, "Methodological Essentialism, False Difference, and Other Dangerous Traps," *Signs* 19, no. 3 (Spring 1994): 630–57.

86 Miriam Glucksmann, "Airbrushing the History of Feminism: 'Race' and Ethnicity," *Feminism and Psychology* 18, no. 3 (2008): 405–9.

87 Janice Fiamengo, "Rediscovering Our Foremothers Again: Racial Ideas of Canada's Early Feminists, 1885–1945," *Essays on Canadian Writing* 75 (2002): 85–112.

88 Janice Fiamengo, "A Legacy of Ambivalence: Responses to Nellie McClung," in *Rethinking Canada: The Promise of Women's History*, 4th ed., ed. Veronica Strong-Boag, Mona Gleason, and Adele Perry (Don Mills, ON: Oxford University Press, 2002), 152–53. Where a piece of writing appears also matters a great deal. If it is in a reader used by hundreds of students over a number of years, this makes a difference.

89 Susan Mann Trofimenkoff and Alison Prentice, eds., *The Neglected Majority: Essays in Canadian Women's History* (Toronto: McClelland and Stewart, 1977); Linda Kealey, ed., *A Not Unreasonable Claim: Women and Reform in Canada, 1880s–1920s* (Toronto: Women's Press, 1979).

90 Fiamengo, "A Legacy," 153.

91 Ibid., 153–54. For example, she cites Wayne Roberts's writing as a possible exception to this emphasis on celebration.

92 "Review of *Gender Conflicts*," *Women's History Review* 3, no. 3 (Winter 1994); Enakshi Dua, "Canadian Anti-Racist Feminist Thought: Scratching the Surface of Racism," in *Scratching the Surface: Canadian Anti-racist Feminist Thought*, ed. Enakshi Dua and Angela Roberts (Toronto: Women's Press, 1999), 11.

93 Karen Dubinsky et al., "Introduction," *Gender Conflicts: New Essays in Women's History* (Toronto: University of Toronto Press, 1992), xiv, xvii.

94 Ibid., xviii.

95 Ibid., xvii.

96 Ibid., xvii–xviii.

97 Only one book was cited — a Marxist-humanist exploration of working-class Hamilton: Bryan D. Palmer, *A Culture in Conflict: Skilled Workers and Industrial Capitalism in Canada, 1860–1914* (Montreal: McGill-Queen's University Press, 1979).

98 Dubinsky et al., "Introduction," xvii.

99 For example, from the early period, see Joan Sangster, "The 1907 Bell Telephone Strike: Organizing Women Workers," *Labour/Le Travail* 3 (1978): 109–30; Bettina Bradbury, "The Family Economy and Work in an Industrializing City, Montreal," *Historical Papers* (1979): 71–96. For the later period, see Denyse Baillargeon, "La Crise ordinaire: Les ménagères montréalaises et la crise des années trente," *Labour/Le Travail* 30 (Fall 1992): 135–62.

100 One exception was Bryan D. Palmer, "Historiographic Hassles: Class and Gender, Evidence and Interpretation," *Social History/Histoire sociale* 33, no. 65 (May 2000): 105–44.

101 Lykke de la Cour, Cecilia Morgan, Mariana Valverde, "Gender Regulation and State Formation in Nineteenth-Century Canada," in Allan Greer and Ian

Radforth, eds., *Colonial Leviathan: State Formation in Mid-Nineteenth Century* Canada (Toronto: University of Toronto Press, 1992), 165.

102 Mariana Valverde, "Post-Structuralist Historians: Are We Those Names?" *Labour/ Le Travail* 25 (Spring 1990): 229, 236. It is important to note that she sees Riley more positively than she does Joan Scott, whose work she treats more critically, including Scott's failure to discuss problems with discourse analysis.

103 See the critique of 'scientific' Marxism by Thompson, *The Poverty of Theory*, 158, or two other discussions of Marxist methodologies: Martha Gimenez, "Capitalism and the Oppression of Women: Marx Revisited," *Science and Society* 69, no. 1 (Jan. 2005): 11–32; and Joseph Fraccia, "Marx's Aufhebung of Philosophy and the Foundation of Materialist Science of History," *History and Theory* 30, no. 2 (May 1991): 153–79.

104 These are two notable examples, but not the only ones. Carolyn Strange, *Toronto's Girl Problem: The Perils and Pleasures of the City* (Toronto: University of Toronto Press, 1995); Cecilia Morgan, *Public Men and Virtuous Women: The Gendered Languages of Religion and Politics in Upper Canada, 1791–1850* (Toronto: University of Toronto Press, 1996).

105 Joy Parr, "Gender History and Historical Practice," *Canadian Historical Review* 76, no. 3 (Sept. 1995): 355.

106 Ibid.

107 Michael Bliss, "Privatizing the Mind: The Sundering of Canadian History, the Sundering of Canada," *Journal of Canadian Studies* 26, no. 4 (1991–92): 5–17; J.R. Miller, "I Can Only Tell What I Know: Shifting Notions of Historical Understanding in the 1990s," in *Reflections on Native-Newcomer Relations* (Toronto: University of Toronto Press, 2004), 61–81. Because *so* much has been written on Bliss, I am concentrating here on the second piece, for which I have only the published version. I requested the unpublished one, but Jim Miller no longer has a copy. Note that while Parr uses words like "ferocious and hostile" to characterize critics generally, but not Miller and Bliss specifically, these are the only two historians cited.

108 Note that, in the published version at least, Miller does not quote von Ranke as his guide, but rather as an influence on historians. In Parr's piece, it is phrased this way: "He takes as his guide Leopold von Ranke" (358).

109 Parr, "Gender History," 356, 358.

110 Marlene Shore, "'Remember the Future': The *Canadian Historical Review* and the Discipline of History, 1920–95," *Canadian Historical Review* 76, no. 3 (Sept. 1995): 461.

111 Parr, "Gender History," 373.

112 Ibid., 362.

113 Ibid., 364. See also Joan Scott, "The Evidence of Experience," *Critical Inquiry* 17 (Summer 1991): 737–797. One indication of the changing interpretations of experience, to which I return in the last section of this book, is Parr's most recent book, in which experience is described differently. In her endnotes, Parr attributes the expression "meaning precedes experience" to Joan Scott. See Joy Parr, *Sensing Changes: Technologies, Environments, and the Everyday, 1953–2000* (Vancouver: University of British Columbia Press, 2010), 12.

114 Ibid.

115 Alex Callinicos, *Against Postmodernism: A Marxist Critique* (Cambridge: Polity Press, 1989); Ellen M. Wood, *The Retreat from Class: A New 'True' Socialism* (London: Verso, 1986); Bryan D. Palmer, *Descent into Discourse: The Reification of Language and the Writing of Social History* (Philadelphia: Temple University Press, 1990). The reception given to these books does differ outside of historical circles, which is why going to political economy or Marxist conferences is quite refreshing.

116 Karen Flynn, "Bridging the Gap: Women's Studies, Women's History, Gender History, and Lost Subjects," *Atlantis* 25, no. 1 (2000): 130–32.

117 Aijaz Ahmad, "Postcolonialism: What's in a Name?" in *Late Imperial Culture*, ed. Román de la Campa, E. Ann Kaplan, and Michael Sprinker (London: Verso, 1995), 11–32.

118 For a sympathetic but also critical take, see Paul Zeleza, "The Troubled Encounter Between Postcolonialism and African History," *Journal of the Canadian Historical Association* 17, no. 2 (2006): 89–112, and for more critical views, Arif Dirlik, *The Postcolonial Aura: Third World Criticism in the Age of Global Capitalism* (Boulder, CO: Westview Press, 1997), 163–85; Aijaz Ahmad, *In Theory: Classes, Nations, Literatures* (London: Verso, 1992).

119 In the words of one author, not only essentializing but 'tribalizing': Craig Ireland, "The Appeal to Experience and Its Consequences: Variations on a Persistent Thompsonian Theme," *Cultural Critique* 52 (Autumn 2002): 86–107.

120 Experience was a key focus of debates between Thompson and others, ranging from Louis Althusser to Stuart Hall. For a discussion of these, see E.P. Thompson, "The Politics of Theory," in *People's History and Socialist Theory*, ed. Raphael Samuel (London: Routledge and Kegan Paul, 1981), 396–408.

121 Eley and Nield, *The Future of Class*.

122 Sonia Kruks, *Retrieving Experience: Subjectivity and Recognition in Feminist Politics* (Ithaca: Cornell University Press, 2001).

123 Andrée Lévesque, "Historiography: History of Women in Quebec Since 1985," *Quebec Studies* 12 (1991): 82–90.

124 Judith Butler, "Merely Cultural," *New Left Review* 227 (Jan.–Feb. 1998); Nancy Fraser, "Heterosexism, Misrecognition and Capitalism: A Response to Judith Butler," *New Left Review* 228 (March–April 1998).

125 See Linda Gordon's review of *Gender and the Politics of History* and Joan Scott's review of *Heroes of Their Own Lives* and their responses in *Signs* 15, no. 4 (Summer 1990): 848–60.

126 Jill Vickers, Pauline Rankin, and Christine Appelle, *Politics As If Women Mattered: A Political Analysis of the National Action Committee on the Status of Women* (Toronto: University of Toronto Press, 1993).

127 Brian McKillop, "Who Killed Canadian History? A View from the Trenches," *Canadian Historical Review* 80 (June 1999): 269–99.

128 Bryan D. Palmer, "Of Silence and Trenches: A Dissident View of Granatstein's Meaning," *Canadian Historical Review* 80, no. 4 (1999): 676–86.

129 Dummitt, "After Inclusiveness," 106.

130 An example of the former might be Jack Granatstein's comments on women's history. See J.L. Granatstein, quoted in Michael Bliss, "Privatizing the Mind: The Sundering of Canadian History, The Sundering of Canada." *Journal of Canadian Studies* 26, no. 4 (1991–92): 5–17. An example of the latter is Bryan D. Palmer, "Historiographic Hassles." Note that Palmer, in the very same article, praises the "advances" made by other feminist authors. My view obviously differs from that of Franca Iacovetta, "Gendering Trans/National Historiographies."

131 Jhappan, "Post-Modern Race and Gender Essentialism."

132 Kenneth McNaught, "E.P. Thompson Versus Harold Logan: Writing About Labour and the Left in the 1970s," *Canadian Historical Review* 62 (1981): 141–68. For a discussion of the charged and contentious character of this debate, see Carl Berger, *The Writing of Canadian History: Aspects of English-Canadian Historical Writing, 1900–1970* (Toronto: Oxford University Press, 1976), 303–6; and Ramsay Cook, "The Meaning of Canadian Working Class History," *Historical Reflections/Réflexions historique* 10 (Spring 1983): 117.

133 See Joan Sangster, "Beyond Dichotomies: Re-assessing Gender History and Women's History in Canada," *Left History* 3, no. 1 (Spring/Summer 1995): 109–21, and the responses by Karen Dubinsky and Lynne Marks and by Franca Iacovetta and Linda Kealey in *Left History* 3, no. 2, and 4, no. 1 (Fall 1996): 205–20 and 221–37.

134 Strong-Boag, *Work to Be Done*.

DISCOVERING WOMEN'S HISTORY

Originally written in 1975 for a fourth-year seminar on labour history at Glendon College, "The 1907 Bell Telephone Stirke" is very much part of a moment of 'discovery' in Canadian women's history. Very little was written in Canadian women's history in the early 1970s, but by the end of the decade articles and monographs were appearing with increasing frequency, as we tried to address the silences, gaps, and malestream assumptions that had (mis)shaped history to date.[1] My treatment of the Bell Telephone strike reflected a fairly traditional historical training in terms of methodology: it drew on empirical research from sources such as government documents, personal letters, company files, and newspapers (both labour and mainstream), as a means of adding women to working-class history, which to date had concentrated more on male workers, particularly skilled ones. Unlike some of those contemporary studies of male workers, however, this article was less engaged with Marxist theory and was less concerned with questions of working-class culture.[2]

The article, like other women's history of the period, was both corrective and additive. The Industrial Disputes Investigation Act (IDIA), an important theme in this article (and in other writing on the state), had often been described with reference to strikes (by men) in resource industries and railways, while scientific management and welfare capitalism were also usually defined with reference to male workers. My purpose was not only to correct this gender bias vis-à-vis these concepts but also to try to understand the views and attitudes of women workers at a more human level — however naive that may now sound. How did they see their wage work? Did they garner a sense of collectivity and comradeship from their jobs? Why did they become so militant during the strike? Did they have a distinctive feminine working-class identity, different from that of middle-class women? While the latter question referred to gender and class relations, I would certainly now add questions about ethnicity and race.

At the time, simply locating women's actions and voices was presumed to be a valid goal for feminist historians, yet this still seemed a difficult endeavour when one relied so heavily on the records left by those with power, whether it was Mackenzie King (who seemed to reveal more of himself than anything else) or the medical experts he consulted, who saw women through their own ideological blinkers as weaker beings, seemingly ruled by their bodies — though at the time we were not speaking the language of 'body history.' I primarily saw the doctors' emphasis on protecting motherhood when I read their 1907 testimony, although Carolyn Strange would later delve into this same source with new analytical tools, pointing to the doctors' preoccupation with 'the mothers of the race' and explaining why this kind of medical knowledge became a source of important social power.[3] Recently, when I was researching the legal testimony in 1970s' court cases about flight attendants who wished to work during their pregnancies, I was struck by a sense of déjà vu, as women's 'vulnerable' bodies were still being interpreted for them by medical experts in a similar manner.[4]

Understanding gender ideologies, a theme being discussed in feminist writing at the time, was quite central to me. I was influenced very much by Wayne Roberts's fine work, which attempted to reconstruct working women as both classed and gendered subjects (in modern parlance) and which tried to understand the nature of exploitation as well as when, and why, women resisted the confining and exploitative conditions of their labour.[5] I started graduate school at McMaster in 1976, about the same time that Wayne was hired by Labour Studies there, and our debates and conversations about class and women's history were important in shaping my ideas, in pushing me to think about how to define gender oppression and class exploitation as different but overlapping and interconnected processes.

Even the language in this 1978 article reflected a particular historical and political moment. I felt it was important to name things like 'exploitation' rather than hiding behind more subdued, nonjudgmental language, for this meant politically identifying women's inequality, while terms like 'solidarity and sisterhood' were also commonly used in the late 1960s and early 1970s, even if, ironically, there was no unified women's movement at the time. Perhaps most telling, in a period — the 1970s — when socialist feminists (including those aligned with a Marxist-Leninist party and those not) were beginning to form separate organizations for working women, to engage in unionization campaigns, to set up separate women's unions, and to draw together coalitions of women within the labour movement, it is not surprising that I was preoccupied primarily with wage labour and especially with union organizing. In 1979, one of my housemates was a Canadian Labour Congress staffer trying to organize bank tellers, a campaign that, even in the context of unionized Hamilton, was very difficult. There were still some who claimed that women were 'hard to organize,' as if they were inherently conservative, yet I thought history suggested otherwise: that women might be mobilized, though they faced immense structural and ideological barriers to unionization. History did not offer up political solutions for the present, but it did at least suggest some of the questions we needed to ask.

While the approach, methodology, and language of this piece are shaped by this particular political moment of the 1970s, I believe there are some aspects of the article that remain relevant. For one thing, I don't think we should dismiss using very 'traditional' events like strikes as a focus for our research. They are moments of conflict that leave us rich sources and that may reveal far more than a chronology of events, indicating, for instance, key political debates and conflicting ideologies of the period. It is not the event but what we do with it that matters.[6] Second, I would still endorse the proposition that the labour movement of the time (including some labour feminists like May Darwin) had a deep sense of "ambivalence" about wage-earning women, sometimes supporting female workers' rights but also emphasizing an ideology of domesticity and motherhood. As Christina Burr would later argue, this idealized female domesticity stood in contrast to images of manly skill, breadwinning, and patriarchal protection, and these attributes were for many skilled workers also caught up in definitions of Anglo-Saxon superiority.[7]

Notes

1 One of the early books influencing me also reflected this view: Berenice Carroll, ed., *Liberating Women's History: Theoretical and Critical Essays* (Urbana: University of Illinois Press, 1976).

2 See, for comparison, Bryan D. Palmer, *A Culture in Conflict: Skilled Workers and Industrial Capitalism in Hamilton, 1860–1914* (Montreal: McGill-Queen's University Press, 1979).

3 Carolyn Strange, *Toronto's Girl Problem: The Perils and Pleasures of the City, 1880–1930* (Toronto: University of Toronto Press, 1995).

4 Joan Sangster, "Debating Maternity Rights: Pacific Western Airlines and Flight Attendants' Struggles to 'Fly Pregnant' in the 1970s," in *Work on Trial: Canadian Labour Law Struggles,* ed. Judy Fudge and Eric Tucker (Toronto: The Osgoode Society and Irwin Law, 2010), 283–314.

5 Wayne Roberts, *Honest Womanhood: Feminism, Femininity and Class Consciousness Among Toronto Working Women* (Toronto: New Hogtown Press, 1976).

6 One example of an excellent strike story is Jacqueline Dowd Hall, "Disorderly Women: Gender and Labor Militancy in the Appalachian South," *Journal of American History* 73 (Spring 1986): 354–82.

7 Christina Burr, *Spreading the Light: Work and Labour Reform in Late-Nineteenth-Century Toronto* (Toronto: University of Toronto Press, 1999).

In February of 1907 a dramatic strike of women workers took place in Toronto when over four hundred operators walked off their jobs with Bell Telephone. For days, the dispute between Bell and the "hello girls" captured front page headlines in the Toronto newspapers. The determination and militancy of the "pretty young girls in their tailor mades" in the face of Bell's intransigence created great public interest and aroused considerable sympathy.[1] The threat of a crippled phone service raised the issue of strikes in monopoly-controlled public utilities, an issue fresh in the public mind after a violent street railway strike in Hamilton only a few months earlier. As in Hamilton, public sympathy clearly lay with the strikers, since the monopoly-controlled utility was highly unpopular with the local citizenry.

The Bell strike was seen as an event of great importance by government and business leaders. Rodolphe Lemieux, the federal minister of labour, publicly pointed to the Bell Commission as a testing ground for the Industrial Disputes Investigation Act, legislation that provided for a cooling-off period and public investigation in utilities strikes. Privately, he declared that the Bell strike "marked the turning point of our future legislation."[2] The company also saw the strike as an event of some significance. Bell later claimed that the strike "brought an important new step in our labour relations thinking."[3] The operators' firm resistance to Bell's wage cutbacks and efficiency drive fostered the company's increasing awareness of the need for more refined scientific management and stimulated the introduction of consultation and welfare measures designed to enhance employee loyalty and diffuse unionization attempts.

As well as providing some insight into the mind of government and business, the strike furnishes an excellent picture of the working conditions, problems, and attitudes of women telephone workers. Unfortunately, the strike did not mark a significant achievement for the operators because they failed to obtain their wage demands, failed to gain significant changes in their working conditions, and failed to form a union. Nonetheless, the strike was characterized by a militancy and solidarity that contradicted the contemporary dictums about women's passivity and revealed the possibilities of protest against their exploitation.

By the turn of the century, operating had become a totally "female" occupation at Bell Telephone. After an experiment with women labour on both day and night shifts in 1888, the Bell had decided to switch from boy to women operators. Boys were found to lack tact and patience; unlike women, they were seldom polite and submissive to irate or rude subscribers but "matched insult for insult."[4] Furthermore, Bell said, boys were "hard to discipline" and were not as conscientious and patient as women.[5] Taking these qualities into account, as well as the important consideration that "the prevailing wage rates for women were lower," Bell hired only female operators by 1900.[6]

Bell demanded that their operators be physically fit in order to tackle the exacting work at the switchboard. Applicants had to be tall enough to reach the top wires, had to prove good hearing and eyesight, and could not wear eyeglasses or have a consumptive cough. Supervisors were instructed not to issue an application unless satisfied that the person was in "good health and physically well qualified."[7] An applicant was also requested to produce references, one from her clergyman, stating that she was "of good moral character and industrious habits . . . a person of truth and integrity, with intelligence, temperament and manners fit to be an operator."[8] With such qualifications Bell hoped to attract a "better class" of woman worker than was found in industrial employment. Early recruitment attempts stressed the occupation's white-collar characteristics: the clean workplace, "steadiness, possibility of advancement, shorter hours than factory work, and seclusion from the public."[9] The job specifications probably did result in a "better class" of employee. One early operator explained that she came to the Bell "while I was waiting for an appointment as a school teacher," while another commented that she became an operator because "few lines of work were open to women and these were not appealing, such as sales clerks."[10] Note was carefully taken of the "enunciation, education and penmanship" of all applicants.[11] This undoubtedly eliminated many immigrants and women with no formal education.

The Royal Commission revealed, however, that the operators' working conditions did not necessarily reflect their position as a "better class" of wage earner. In fact, the operator's shift work, close supervision, and ties to machinery made her job resemble blue-collar, rather than white-collar, work.[12] The operator's task was extremely exhausting, for great mental concentration, accuracy, and speed were essential. Each woman looked after 80 to 100 lines, with 6,041 possible connections, and placed about 300 calls an hour. Backless stools and a high switchboard, which some women could reach only by jumping up on the stool rungs, made the operators' work physically uncomfortable and tiring. If her own calls lagged, a worker was not allowed to relax, but had to help the operator next to her. In order to create a "business-like" atmosphere, the rules were strict: the women were instructed to line up five minutes before their shift entered the operating room, and when seated, had to "sit up straight, with no talking or smiling."[13] Supervisors who paced behind the operators inspecting their work were told to "nag and hurry the girls."[14] Other strains were added to the operator's rapidly paced work, such as the risk of physical injury and the knowledge that a monitor might be secretly listening in to check one's performance. Operators complained to the commission that heavy headgear could produce painful sores and that women sometimes fainted and occasionally became hysterical from the pressure of rapid work. Maude Orton, a supervisor and leader in the strike, claimed that women sometimes were pushed to nervous breakdowns, and that she was compelled to take nerve medicine. "I never knew what nerves meant until I started to work at the Bell," she commented.[15] The most dangerous work was on the long-distance lines, where operators sometimes received severe electrical shocks, which could send them into convulsions and lay them off work for weeks.

For such demanding work, the women received a starting salary of $18 a month, which after three years' service was increased to $25. Although this wage compared favourably with the hourly rate of many female factory workers, it fell below the monthly wage of the more skilled woman worker in industry, who could earn about $30 a month (and of course, it fell far below the male, skilled wage rate of $40 to $60 a month).[16] The immediate issue precipitating the 1907 strike, however, was not inadequate wages: the issue was an increase in hours. On 27 January, the Manager of the Toronto Central Exchange, K.J. Dunstan, informed the operators that, as of 1 February, their five-hour day would be lengthened to eight hours, and their salaries increased. Introduced originally in 1903, when noisy construction work made an eight-hour day at the switchboard impossible, the five-hour day was continued on as an experiment and then was "permanently" adopted in 1905 since management believed it to be a more efficient use of womanpower.

In late 1906, however, Dunstan became worried about the efficiency of the five-hour day. At the same time, the company decided to standardize the operators' hours of work in Toronto and Montreal, which still had an eight-hour day. In this period the policy of Bell Telephone President Charles Sise was to "eliminate all Bell's remaining competitors; to above all, give a better quality of service while keeping rates as low as possible."[17] Also at this time, American scientific management practices were adopted by some firms in Canada.[18] With the aims of increasing efficiency and raising productivity, programs such as cost and time studies, bonus systems, and job standardization were introduced into industrial establishments. Bell Canada, especially with its close branch-plant relationship to American Telephone and Telegraph, was influenced by these currents of thought. In late 1906, two expert engineers from AT&T were called in to make comparative studies of the Montreal and Toronto operating systems. In true scientific management style, the engineers performed stopwatch tests on the operators' responses, examined the quality of their answers, and from these calculated the speed and quality of operating.

Their reports agreed that the eight-hour system more efficiently used labour power, but their findings were not a conclusive indictment of the five-hour system, for one report called for "further investigation" and the other stressed the different personalities of the office managers in influencing the speed of operating.[19] Nevertheless, a decision was made to introduce an eight-hour day in Toronto when a new exchange was completed in the summer. In January 1907, however, Dunstan urged an immediate changeover because he knew that the self-supporting operators were becoming increasingly angry about their low wages. It was essential to raise the wages, he informed Sise, "and advisable that the increase in hours and wages coincide."[20]

Dunstan argued publicly that the changes were necessitated by Bell's inability to secure operators, "for our rates were too low and to attract more women we had to increase wages, therefore we had to increase hours."[21] He also contended that the change was made for the sake of the operators' health. "It is the pace that kills," he later told the commission.[22] The company's primary motive, however, was to reduce the "uneconomical" overtime being paid and to give increased service while keeping labour costs down. Company correspondence brought before the commission revealed that the new schedule was designed to "ensure the increase in wages would not equal that of hours and the cost per 1,000 calls should thus be lessened."[23]

The operators quickly realized that wages would not increase in relation to hours worked since the new schedule meant a reduction from approximately 21 cents to 16 cents an hour. For those operators who were entirely self-supporting, the salary changes were particularly disastrous. These women had previously worked extra five-hour shifts in order to pay for their board and clothing. Under the new system, such overtime would be impossible: their income would be drastically reduced. A small group of women, composed of supervisors and the more experienced operators, began to organize a protest against the new hours. With the help of Jimmy Simpson, a Toronto printer, and well-known activist in trade union and socialist circles, they formed the Telephone Operators, Supervisors and Monitors Association, and they engaged a lawyer, J. Walter Curry, to help them draft a petition of protest. Curry, a former crown attorney with strong Liberal connections, was active in the public ownership league formed in Toronto in February 1907. He donated his services to the operators free of charge, eager to aid in the fight against the Bell monopoly, and with the help of W.E. Maclean, editor of the *Toronto World*, started a public strike fund for the women.

Bell refused to meet with Curry or with the group of protestors whom Dunstan dubbed "a few firebrands and agitators stirring up trouble."[24] On 29 January, four hundred operators met at the Labour Temple to discuss their predicament. We have had grievances before, declared one operator, but never such good organization to back us up: "while it is the extension of hours we complain principally about now, it's the money too."[25] Faced by intransigent company officials who were unwilling to discuss the issue, the meeting voted to plan a strike. This vote had immediate results. Fearing disruption of telephone service, Mayor Coatsworth wired the federal government for assistance. Mackenzie King, then deputy minister of labour, hurried to Toronto, hoping to display his talents as a mediator. Bell, however, resolutely refused such "outside interference," and secretly made plans to bring in strikebreakers. Bell's head office in Montreal encouraged Dunstan's firm approach. Company President Charles Sise advised Dunstan to be "resolute . . . act with absolute firmness in rejecting consultation or compromise."[26] Not surprisingly, it was Bell that precipitated the crisis. On 31 January, the company demanded that operators either sign an acceptance of the new schedule or resign. The operators had no choice but to walk out; in a sense the confrontation was a lockout, not a strike.

That night, the women met again at the Labour Temple. The meeting, said the *Star*, "was militant and enthusiastic."[27] The women made an impressive show of solidarity and sisterhood. Strikers who lived at home contributed money for those independent women who had to make rent payments. Supervisors, monitors, and operators, all with different rank and salaries, joined together to protest the company's actions. Despite their higher salaries and positions of authority, the supervisors seemed to feel considerable concern for the operators' working conditions; perhaps these more experienced workers felt protective towards the younger women. The strikers were addressed by J. Lightbound, from the International Brotherhood of Electrical Workers (IBEW), who suggested that they affiliate with the union. The feeling of the strikers, reported the press, was strongly in favour of the idea.

Public sympathy bolstered the strikers' enthusiasm. Bell's monopoly made the company unpopular with Toronto citizens, who objected to the lack of competition and the arbitrary methods of fixing rates.[28] Shortly after the women had walked out, a crowd gathered at the Central Exchange and cheered on the strikers, while snowballing scabs entering the building and hooting at Dunstan when he came out to address the crowd. The company also had to ask for police protection for its strikebreakers, who were brought from Bell exchanges in Peterborough, Kingston, Ottawa, and Montreal. (The Montreal operators were promised an expense-paid trip and were given a $20 honorarium when they returned home.) The first day of the strike, the scabs were taunted by the picketers at the exchange door. "I hope you die of nervous prostration," shouted one irate striker.[29] Some of the Montreal strikebreakers had to be removed from their hotel when bellboys objected to their presence; other scabs complained of harassment over the telephone as they worked.

All the Toronto daily papers were sympathetic to the operators. A *Globe* editorial heartily endorsed the strike, criticizing Bell's selfish and inhumane treatment of its women workers. The company, however, was not censured for its use of strikebreakers, but rather for its neglect of the operators' health and mental well-being. In the York County Council a unanimous resolution was passed condemning Bell for its neglect of its employees' health; the company was described as "inhuman, a menace to business . . . and should not be tolerated in a free Canada."[30] On Sunday, 3 February, Reverend J.E. Starr, a local Methodist minister, held a church service for the strikers. His sermon, taken from St. Paul's words "I entreat thee also yoke fellow, help those women," condemned Bell's "tyranny over the weaker sex," and called for a more humane employment system that would not "strain women beyond their capacity and impair the interests of the unborn."[31]

Yet, despite such public sympathy, the strikers gained no ground. Moralistic sermons and editorials were not backed up with laws compelling Bell to negotiate with the strikers, nor were the women even unionized. The only real weapon the women had in the dispute was the withdrawal of their labour power, and that weapon had been quickly nullified by the use of strikebreakers. The Bell management was determined to avoid setting the precedent of discussing and negotiating working conditions with their employees: they were adamantly opposed to any semblance of collective bargaining. Charles Sise had made his ideological opposition to unions clear during a dispute with Hamilton linemen in 1900. In 1907 that opposition remained. Sise informed the Montreal press of his firm intention to lock out the women: "so far as we are concerned, the strike is over. The Company has all the new operators it requires."[32] Dunstan echoed this opinion, telling the Toronto newspapers that he might consider "on an individual basis only, any operator who wished to return to work on the eight hour schedule."[33]

The company did make some attempt to counter its unfavourable public image. In his interviews with the press, Dunstan stressed three arguments. First, he emphasized that the company's most important concern was its obligation to the community, justifying the use of strikebreakers by professing that Bell was interested only in continuing its service to the public. Secondly, Dunstan tried to prove that the strike was led by a few agitators and troublemakers, while the "majority would welcome the change and return to work."[34] Lastly, he claimed that compared to other women wage earners, operators were well off, and he pointed to the various "comforts" of the Toronto Exchange, such as restrooms and lockers, that were not found in most industrial establishments.[35] Bell's public relations efforts, however, did not include an offer to negotiate with the strikers. At a meeting on 31 January, the strikers had voted to accept an arbitrated settlement, believing that their cause was just. But Bell refused arbitration because the company anticipated that an arbitration board would rule against them.

Faced with this deadlock, Mackenzie King adopted a new tactic, advising the operators to request a public inquiry from the minister of labour. The operators were persuaded by their male advisors to return to work and accept the eight-hour day until the commission made its recommendations. Although hesitant to end the strike with no concrete gains, the strike committee decided to place their hopes for redress in an inquiry. The operators' male advisors encouraged them to view the commission with optimism. "I believe you will win," assured Curry, "for you have the public and the newspapers behind you."[36] The operators, reported one newspaper, were "jubilant, for they felt victory would emerge from the Commission"; enthusiastic cheering erupted when Simpson called for "No victory to the Company."[37]

The commission, however, was clearly not a solution to the operators' plight, for the company later refused to be bound by its recommendations. The strikers had now suffered a dangerous setback; they returned to work on the company's conditions, with no promise of negotiations on the issue of wages and working conditions. It is possible that King and Curry hoped public pressure would reverse Bell's decision and force concessions. On the other hand, there is abundant evidence that King's main aim in persuading the women to return to work was simply to bring peace and diffuse the conflict. There was quiet recognition by some trade unionists that the tactic of striking before unionization had been disastrous and that the strike was being crushed by the use of strikebreakers.[38] It is possible, therefore, that the women's advisors, foreseeing defeat, believed that the operators should regain their jobs as soon as possible. "They have fooled us," one disappointed operator realized, "we thought they couldn't get along for an hour without us, but they can."[39]

On 4 February, the operators returned to the exchange to offer themselves for re-employment. President Sise had informed Dunstan in a letter that "under no conditions should we take back an operator. Our strong point will be to show our utter independence of the disaffected operators."[40] Yet in a few days about 150 women were taken back, and after two weeks of commission hearings, the company announced it would make a concession and rehire all its former employees at their former salaries.

The royal commissioners were Mackenzie King and Judge John Winchester, a York county judge of Liberal persuasion with a record of sympathy on labour issues.[41] The sessions were well attended and thoroughly covered by the press. The operators, many of them still unemployed, were present in large numbers, and every newspaper commented on "the beauty show adorning the courtroom."[42] Reporters described the attractive array of millinery and dress at the enquiry, always distinguishing between the operators and the "men carrying on the serious business of the strike."[43] Some of the women, however, did manage to rise above their Dresden doll image: the committee of operators who initiated the strike advised their lawyer, Curry, throughout the proceedings, while other operators found themselves threatened with eviction from the courtroom when they interrupted Dunstan's testimony with loud protests.

The commission hearings concentrated on five main issues: the change in hours, the causes of the strike, the nature of the operators' work, medical opinion about the operators' workload, and lastly, the "listening board" issue that had come to light during the strike.

Bell's public image plummeted even further during the hearings. It was soon made clear that the company had made its changes in hours for commercial and business reasons only, despite previous assertions to the contrary. Also, Dunstan had claimed before the commission that Bell's new schedule would decrease the workload of each woman, but the evidence proved otherwise. All those operators who had been re-employed under the eight-hour schedule testified that there was no reduction in load: "the promised relief hasn't come; we are working just as hard."[44] The hearings further embarrassed Bell by revealing that the company had recently considered abolishing the workers' two-week paid vacation and that officials were aware that the operators' wages were inadequate. At first, Dunstan implied that many women came to Bell simply to earn "pin money," or that they spent their wages unwisely: "some women," declared Dunstan, "come to us just to earn a fur coat or something like that and leave to get married after two or three years."[45] But boarding-house rates were presented and self-supporting operators testified that without overtime they could not survive. Rent and food prices had escalated far beyond the reach of independent operators working only a five-hour day. The $18 a month received by a starting operator was quickly eaten up by board costs of about $12–14 and food costs of at least $4; overtime was necessary even to obtain the other essentials such as clothing, car fare, and laundry.[46] After these presentations, Dunstan conceded that for the 30–40 percent of the operators who were self-supporting, their normal wages were inadequate. Bell was also forced to admit to the arbitrary manner in which it had informed its employees of its intentions at the time of the schedule changes. Curry skilfully emphasized this testimony, trying to portray Bell as a monstrously rich and ruthless exploiter, a monopoly mercilessly grinding down its employees. He demanded to know why wages were not influenced by Bell's ever-rising profits. Horrified, Bell's Chief Office Manager, Frank Maw, replied that wages most certainly should not rise with profits: "after all, you pay the market price for your goods."[47]

The commissioners were especially concerned with the mental and physical hazards of telephone work. Testimony showed that operating was so rapidly paced and pressured that it resulted in unusually high rates of nervous strain and mental exhaustion. Supervisors testified that they were told to pressure the operators to quicken their pace: "I know that the girls are worked to the limit, but we are told to drive them."[48] Dunstan claimed that the five-hour day allowed many women to moonlight at jobs, such as housekeeping, while Maw argued that women came to work "already exhausted" from roller skating, one of the operators' favourite pastimes.[49] The strike leaders, however, vehemently denied these claims. After a day's work at the Bell, said Maude Orton, women could not moonlight anywhere: "they are only fit for bed."[50] The pressure of work, Miss Dixon continued, "doesn't allow young girls to enjoy themselves as they should, at roller skating or anything else."[51] Evidence also revealed that women often had to work extra relief periods for which they were never paid; extracting this free overtime labour was regular company policy. The most disturbing testimony, however, came from the long-distance operators who had suffered electrical shocks. One operator told the hearing that she was not informed about shocks when she took the job and in such an accident had lost the use of her left ear. Another woman who had suffered a severe shock and convulsion informed the commission that she was still too terrified to return to work.

The commission subpoenaed twenty-six Toronto doctors in order to obtain an objective view of the operators' conditions of work. All the medical experts agreed that the task of operating put exceptional strain on a woman's senses of hearing, sight, and speech, and that the result was "exhaustion, more mental and nervous than physical."[52] A consensus of medical opinion (with the exception of the company doctor) rejected the eight-hour day. Most doctors suggested a five-, six-, or seven-hour day with assured periods of relief. One helpful doctor observed that the weaker sex should not engage in such work at all: choosing between a five- and eight-hour day, he said, was like deciding "between slaying a man with a gun or a club."[53] The testimony of these medical experts reflected prevailing medical and social views of woman as the "weaker" sex. Young women, it was emphasized, were extremely susceptible to nervous and emotional disorders; "we are laying the basis of our future insane asylums with operating," warned one doctor.[54] Many doctors concurred with King's suggestion that women deserved the special protection of the state on matters regarding health and sanitary conditions in their place of work. One doctor added that it should definitely be medical experts who decided for the working woman: "they must be protected from themselves . . . . [T]he girls are not the best judges of how much work they should do."[55]

One other issue was investigated by the commission. When the strike first began, some operators had mentioned the existence of a listening board that could be used secretly to intercept a subscriber's conversation. Despite Bell's assurances that the listening board was only used to investigate technical problems, the press and public were not satisfied. For a time the striking operators were all but forgotten by the press, which denounced Bell for the irresponsible and arrogant use of its monopoly. "The public had been repaid for the inconvenience of the strike," said the *Globe*, "by gaining the important knowledge of listening boards . . . the opportunity for misuse is there."[56] Despite such fears, however, the hearings did not reveal that the opportunity had been taken. The newspapers' concentration on the listening board issue revealed how easily the operators could be forgotten. Many editorials and letters to the editor pointed to the strike as one more reason for nationalization of telephones and telegraphs. While disgust was expressed about the mistreatment of the operators, these proponents of public ownership were eager to use *any* argument, including threats to privacy and Bell's high rates, in order to buttress their case for public ownership.

On 18 February, the commission came to an abrupt end. The company's lawyers put forward a compromise solution that Curry and the operators accepted. A new schedule was proposed in which the operators were to work seven hours, spread over a nine-hour day. Extensive relief was to be given, with no consecutive period of work extending over two hours. Wages were to be those proposed under the eight-hour schedule, and a promise of no compulsory overtime was given. The operators were dubious about the offer, but decided in its favour after a conference with Curry and King. The women expressed fears that the load would not be reduced and announced that the "seven hour day was less injurious, but there was still too much strain."[57] Curry and King undoubtedly knew that the proposal favoured Bell, but at the same time believed that it was as much as Bell would surrender. It must have been clear that the company was largely unmoved by the condemning testimony of the hearings and by adverse public feeling. Bell officials realized that it was unlikely that special legislation would be introduced to enact such a short (five-hour) working day. They also knew that adverse public opinion would fade and that as a powerful monopoly, the company could withstand a great deal of adverse public feeling anyway. A letter sent to King almost two months after the settlement made it only too clear that the operators were the losers. Curry informed King that: "I learn from the young ladies that matters are not much improved from what they were before, that the only improvements are in the surroundings, not in the work itself."[58] The seven-hour schedule had not lessened the workload and had only reduced the amount of the wage cutback. The "compromise" agreement did little to solve the dilemma of the self-supporting operator. How was she now to pay for board and clothing when her wages still did not approximate her former five hours plus overtime salary?

Throughout the strike and the hearings Bell maintained a consistent attitude towards its women workers. First, the ocmpany insisted on complete control of its own labour policy: it was unwilling to give its employees any role in determining their working conditions and it abhorred government intervention. Secondly, Bell made extensive use of the largely unorganized, highly fluid female working force as a form of cheap labour and excused its low wages with the argument that women were not breadwinners, but were only working for "pin money" while awaiting marriage. This was the practice of many business concerns, but Bell's case seems particularly reprehensible, for as a stable company with rising profits and dividends, Bell clearly did not need to make wage cutbacks. Thirdly, Bell's claim that their employees' health was an absolute priority was pure rhetoric. Instead of establishing a workload compatible with the women's health, Bell sought to push them "almost to the breaking point."[59] The commission's report concluded that "one looks in vain for any reference that would indicate that the health or well being of the operators was a matter of any consideration."[60]

In a 1963 report on Bell's labour policy prepared for the company, G. Parsons concluded that some important lessons had been learned from the 1907 dispute. The company had decided that, as a monopoly, Bell was subject to closer scrutiny and thus must be more aware of "good grievances": if ignored, these grievances would be likely to gain a public hearing and would perhaps attract government intervention.[61] In the prewar period in the United States, Bell increasingly sought employee loyalty by developing employee associations that were to give some feeling of consultation and negotiation, by pioneering an employee benefit plan, and by making offices more pleasant workplaces (supplying lounges and cafeterias).[62] In Canada similar consultation and welfare programs were gradually introduced. After the strike, for instance, the company decided that attempts would be made to "foster better communications" with their employees, keeping them more closely informed of the company's plans and making some pretense of consultation.[63] Secondly, the office surroundings were improved; in the main exchange a matron was hired to bring the operators tea and coffee. A few months after the strike, Sise decided to supply a free medical examination for every operator. He privately informed the Hamilton manager that such examinations "may be desirable to save us trouble and expense inasmuch as we will avoid the training of useless operators who might be discharged because of unfitness."[64] Five years later, Bell introduced a health benefit plan to aid its employees in time of illness. These welfare measures were part of the broader scientific management program to increase efficiency and consolidate management control. By playing the benevolent paternalist, the company aimed to minimize dissatisfaction over wages, raise the prestige of the occupation, and discourage unionization. The 1907 strike was one impetus for the development of this welfare capitalist approach.

The strike not only acted as a mirror for Bell's labour policy; it also revealed Mackenzie King's approach to labour relations. King's view of women workers, of the governmental role in labour disputes, and his hopes for the Industrial Disputes Investigation Act were all exhibited in the hearings and the commission report. King's perceptions of the operators reflects a Victorian image of woman. As one of the latest commentators on King's personal "woman problem" has stated: "The image of woman in Christian society has revolved around the contrasting conceptions of Eve the Temptress and the Virgin Mary . . . at no time was this paradox more acute than in the Victorian age from whence King came."[65] King believed it was essential that a woman's maternal role be protected, not just for her own good but for the good of society as well. Thus, in the report he worried about the results of the nervous strain of operating upon a woman's future role: "the effects moreover upon posterity occasioned by the undermining or weakening [of] the female constitution cannot receive too serious consideration."[66] Women, however, could also be seen as Eves. In the hearings King interrogated Bell rigorously about its treatment of self-supporting operators: his concern was that the company's wage rates were inadequate to supply board in a "decent" home and thus women would be forced to turn to prostitution. It was King's first concern that predominated in his report. He expressed both privately and publicly his horror with the company's disregard for women's health. In his diary he wrote: "the more I go into the evidence the more astounded I am at the revelations it unfolds. The image is constantly before me of some hideous octopus feeding upon the life blood of young women and girls."[67]King's paternalism was revealed throughout the hearings and report. Because women workers were weak and "easily led," he later remarked, "to seek to protect this class is noble and worthy to the highest degree."[68] As woman's nature is particularly sensitive to physical and mental strain, he warned, her industrial working conditions must be regulated by medical experts and the benevolent state.

This view reflected a broader social attitude towards female labour often expressed by middle-class reformers. Doctors testifying before the commission shared King's concern for future mothers. Their greatest fear was that nervous strain would disqualify a woman from motherhood: "they [the operators] turned out badly in their domestic relations, they break down nervously and have nervous children; it is a loss to the community."[69] The press also criticized Bell primarily for its disregard for women's health; the use of strikebreakers, the payment of low wages, and the need for unionization were not considered the important issues. It was the moral, rather than economic, question of woman labour that was emphasized. As Alice Klein and Wayne Roberts have suggested, the impetus for middle-class reformers often came from fears that the femininity of women workers was endangered by their working conditions.[70] In order to ensure protection for women workers, King advocated cautious government intervention in industrial disputes. Later, in *Industry and Humanity,* he claimed to be particularly concerned with public utilities where an absolute or quasi-monopoly existed. In such situations, he said, "there exists an insistence on the part of the public of a due regard for the welfare of employees."[71] It is also clear, however, that King did not see the government's role as the primary or controlling factor in labour-capital relations: the government would intervene to legislate protective guidelines *only* if all other reform attempts failed. In the Bell report, King cited the need for protective legislation for women but he also pointed out the difficulty in securing it: "it is difficult to see wherein it is possible for the State to effectively regulate the speed of operating."[72] He concluded that the real hope for change lay in another area, namely a more enlightened attitude on the part of the company. This attitude was to be the outcome of an impartial investigation, the pressure of public opinion, and the company's own desire for efficiency.

King used the Bell dispute in his arguments for his Industrial Disputes Investigation Act (IDIA), which was presented for second reading in Parliament during the commission hearings. Both King and Lemieux tried to use the Bell dispute as a public testing ground for the IDIA principle and both cited it as an example for the success of that principle. The IDIA provided for a public investigation of all labour disputes in public utilities and a thirty-day prohibition of strikes or lockouts during the investigation. Although neither labour nor capital was legally obliged to accept the investigator's findings, King argued that the "pressure of public enquiry would force concessions and a settlement."[73] After the IDIA was presented for its second reading on 13 February, Lemieux informed King that: "I am very anxious to succeed re the telephone enquiry by all means settle the telephone strike *cum summia laude* [sic]. It marks the turning point of our future legislation."[74]

In the Commons Lemieux argued that the Bell Commission provided an excellent example of an impartial commission and public pressure bringing compromise to a labour conflict. "Due to the thorough scientific enquiry of the Commission," said Lemieux, "the Company has already compromised on its earlier policy, and agreed to rehire its former operators."[75] King used similar arguments to support the IDIA after the Bell inquiry was over. He maintained that a neutral inquiry and public opinion had been instrumental in bringing a settlement to the dispute. Writing to a Member of Parliament, King said:

> Take the case of the telephone girls in Toronto. What power had those girls, unorganized and unassisted, with no means of keeping up a strike. . . . When public opinion was brought to bear on the situation for the first time there was an approach to an equality between the parties.[76]

It is true that the investigation helped to end the dispute. The public hearings had brought some minor concessions from Bell, for the company agreed to reduce the amount of wage cutbacks and rehire all the strikers. (It is hard to imagine, however, that Bell could have continued indefinitely with out-of-town strikebreakers.) If peace was King's major objective, then perhaps the IDIA principle could be termed a "success." In his diary, King did optimistically claim that he thought the report would "mean a gain for workingmen and women."[77] Yet it is clear that his most important goal was immediate peace and *not* the kind of settlement the women received. Throughout the report, King pointed to Bell's insensitivity and to public opinion and to "its motives of business cupidity above all else."[78] How then could King have hoped for the company's enlightenment and reform? The contradiction between King's condemnation of Bell's greed and inhumanity and his hopes for its reform seems incredible.

Furthermore, King never replied to Curry's statement that the operators' working conditions had not improved; his willingness to ignore this letter seriously questions his expressed concern for the plight of the working woman. His delay in publishing the report also makes his concern for the operators suspect. In early April the operators and Curry pleaded with King to move as quickly as possible. "I had hoped," wrote Curry "to have attempted to get legislation here before the rising of the House [on 20 April]. It would seem to be almost impossible now to accomplish that purpose."[79] King replied that there was some "advantage in delaying the report a little for it has given the Company a chance to show what it can do."[80] The only advantage was to Bell, for when the report appeared six months after the strike, public interest had waned and over half the operators had left the company.

The Bell dispute did not prove the value to labour of the IDIA principle, but rather its dangers. The operators placed their hopes in redress through public investigation; yet Bell had been powerful enough to maintain wage cutbacks and arduous working conditions despite adverse public feeling. Public investigation, sympathetic editorials, and church sermons did not help the operators secure their demands. Better organization and an effective strike might have.

The issue of unionization was not central to the 1907 strike. After the strike had commenced, the operators passed two resolutions favouring an arrangement of affiliation with the International Brotherhood of Electrical Workers (IBEW), yet these plans did not materialize. The operators waited until 1918, when another major attempt to organize into the IBEW was initiated.[81] The failure to sustain a union after the strike in 1907 was the result of three factors: the hostility of Bell, the disinterest of the IBEW and other male labour leaders, and the particular problems encountered by the workers because they were women.

Bell's policy with regard to trade unions was clearly stated by Sise in 1900: "we have never recognized these unions in any way nor would we oblige ourselves to employ only union men."[82] This attitude remained firm in the 1907 dispute. Bell refused to rehire any of the strike leaders or picketers after the strike was over on 4 February. Even after the "amnesty" for strikers that the company announced on 13 February, women connected with the IBEW were asked to leave the union or resign from their jobs. Such anti-union victimization was obviously a major factor in discouraging unionization. The company's movement towards welfare capitalism and its attempts to "kill unionization with kindness" may have also successfully sidetracked the organization of the operators.

At the 4 February meeting of the operators a male labour leader admitted to a *Mail and Empire* reporter that "it was the general consensus of opinion that the girls have been beaten . . . it is too bad the way they were led into their present position by men without a stake in the contest."[83] Because the women were not unionized before going on strike, he said, the company had every advantage and the strikers no hope of sustaining a campaign of organization. It is questionable, however, how eager the IBEW was to organize the women. The IBEW had recently asserted its jurisdiction over telephone operators, but the union was showing little interest in organizing them. The IBEW had developed a strong tradition of inequality; in the United States, for instance, the few operators' locals existing before World War I were denied full autonomy and were given only half their voting rights. The brotherhood, its historians agree, was convinced that women made "bad" union members; it believed operators could not build permanent unions as "women were flighty and came to the union only when in trouble, then dropped out."[84] Behind these convictions lay other fears. The electricians claimed that unskilled operators might make foolish decisions on craft matters they did not understand. There was also strong apprehension about "petticoat rule": the large number of operators, it was feared, would come to control the union.[85] It is also possible that there was indifference to the operators simply because they did not threaten the earning power of other IBEW members. For all these reasons, the union executive most often refused requests to lend any aid to the organization of telephone operators. Such hostility was probably an important factor in the failure of the Toronto IBEW to sustain a campaign of organization.

The IBEW's hesitancy to organize women workers reflected a broader view of woman labour held by many trade unionists at this time. At the 1907 Trades and Labour Congress convention, the issue of unionizing the operators was not discussed, although a resolution was passed calling for protective legislation for women telephone workers. One of the TLC's expressed aims at this time was "to abolish . . . female labour in all branches of industrial life."[86] The views of many craft unionists were dominated by their belief that woman's role was primarily a maternal and domestic one. Apprehension about female strikebreaking and undercutting wages fostered and buttressed rationalizations about woman's role as wife and mother. "The general consequence of [AFL] union attitudes toward women," concludes Alice Kessler-Harris, "was to isolate them from the male work force."[87]

This thesis also seems relevant to the Canadian labour scene, as illustrated in the Ontario labour press. In the *Industrial Banner*, a London labour paper published by the Labour Educational Association, the telephone strike was not discussed. Some clues to the failure of male trade unionists to accept the need to unionize women workers are provided in the *Banner*, and in two earlier Toronto labour papers, the *Toiler* and *Tribune*.[88] Male craft unionists were concerned with protection and equality for women workers: decent working conditions and equal wages were always upheld as worthy aims.[89] But it was woman's contribution to the home, rather than her status as a worker, that was most often stressed in the labour press. In fact, concern that woman's wage labour would destroy the family was very strong.[90] Woman's contribution to the union movement, it was often maintained, could be made through her role as wife, mother, and manager of the family budget: she was to support the union label campaign and educate the family to union ideals.[91] In the eyes of male trade unionists women were hardly delicate and decorative appendages to be shunted to the sidelines of the class struggle, but their stay in the workforce was not a desirable thing, and was to be temporary, only an interlude before marriage and maternity. Thus, it was understandable that although some labour leaders momentarily encouraged the operators to organize, they were hesitant to follow up with the necessary further support. Their rather ambivalent attitude — of sometimes supporting female workers' rights, but usually emphasizing the home as woman's vocation — in fact discouraged the unionization of women. Stressing the maternal image, male trade unionists isolated women from the mainstream of the trade union movement and buttressed the employers' excuses for women's lower wages.

Reinforcing the hostility of Bell and the ambivalence of organized labour were the situations and the attitudes of the operators themselves. The great majority of operators were single women, about seventeen to twenty-four years old, who stayed less than three years with Bell. Most women left to marry, although some were promoted to clerical jobs in Bell, went on to other operating jobs, or returned home to aid their mothers. Occasionally, women were forced temporarily to bolster family finances due to sickness or unemployment, and when family circumstances no longer required extra aid, they gladly quit. This great fluidity of female labour obviously militated against successful unionization. By the time King's report was published in September 1907, half of the operators employed at the time of the strike had left, including the former president and secretary of the Telephone Operators Association. With personnel in perpetual motion, it was difficult to sustain educational and organizational work needed for effective unionization.

Despite the rapid turnover of operators, the physical setting of the Telephone Exchange did aid worker solidarity and organization. As Wayne Roberts has pointed out, many women workers at this time were concentrated in trades such as garment making and domestic service, which were highly decentralized and divided the workers from one another. Operating, however, did not present such communication barriers; in fact, the militancy and solidarity of the Bell workers were in part a result of a physical setting conducive to organization. On the other hand, Bell women were not protected by craft skills or effective organization.

Thus, strikebreakers from outside the city or inside the exchange could easily replace the Toronto operators. The technology of the switchboard allowed continued service, if only with half the usual workforce. Naturally, the nature of the Bell monopoly also worked against the women, for despite reduced service, Bell faced no loss of customers.

Another factor that may have handicapped effective unionization was the prevailing conception of woman's domestic and maternal vocation. Women workers like the Bell operators undoubtedly perceived their problems quite differently from the middle-class reformers who feared for the "working girl of delicate moral and physical viability, her womanliness endangered."[92] In the 1907 strike, the immediate issues of wages and hours, not their endangered maternity, were the concerns of the operators. Yet, while working women may not have assumed the decorative role imposed upon many Victorian middle-class women or perceived wage labour as threatening to their femininity, they probably did accept the Victorian sentimentalization of the home and family.[93]

During this period women's columns in the *Tribune* and *Toiler* show some of the same ambivalence towards female labour as did male trade unionists. In the *Tribune*, May Darwin's column for women called for women's social freedom, equal pay, and the unionization of female workers. Yet, later in the *Tribune*, as well as in the *Toiler*, the women's section was concerned with personal improvement and domestic issues, or, "recipes and fashions." Even feminist May Darwin stressed that women's contribution to the labour movement could best be made by buying union label goods, supporting her trade unionist husband, and educating her young to union ideas.[94] Such activities may have aided the development of women's trade union and working-class consciousness, but they still defined women's contribution in family-centred terms. This suggests that for many women workers such as the Bell operators, the family ideal was of considerable importance (although admittedly the working-class conception of the family may have differed considerably from the prevailing middle-class one). For the many Bell operators who "left to marry," such social values could not have aided the difficult process of unionization. The operators were part of a rapidly changing group of young women workers, who constituted a small minority of the female population: "they were isolated politically and socially . . . from their elder sisters, all of whom had returned to the home on marriage."[95] Their brief experience in the workforce preceding marriage "meant that they were deprived of a continuity of experience that might have allowed them to come to grips with the political economy of their experience."[96] The idealization of women's maternal and domestic roles must have dulled the development of a truly feminist working-class consciousness that recognized women's special oppression as workers. The tendency to define women in terms of husband, children, and home obscured a reality where women were also individual workers, sometimes breadwinners, needing adequate wages, job security, and unionization just like male workers.

The prevailing views on woman's maternal and domestic role were not, of course, the sole or primary causes for the operators' defeat in 1907. The Bell operators were severely handicapped by factors that impeded successful strikes and unionization for many male workers at this time. Most importantly, they were unskilled and lacked union protection; thus, their protest was easily and severely damaged by the importation of strike-breakers. Their cause was also injured when they were strongly encouraged to accept the bad tactic of abandoning their walkout and returning to work on the company's terms, placing their hopes in a royal commission. The commission was a dead end. Despite King's strong criticism of Bell, he could hide behind the qualification that labour legislation was primarily a provincial jurisdiction. The report came too late for such legislation, which probably would have been difficult to obtain anyway. Six months after the strike, public concern had waned and the workforce at Bell had drastically changed; half the operators employed in September had not even experienced the strike. Unfortunately for the operators, the 1907 dispute came after the peak of public feeling for public ownership of telephones in Toronto: the Laurier government had already made clear its opposition to nationalization.[97] Thus, as a testing ground for the IDIA, the strike had revealed the dangers of this legislation to labour's interests, dangers that later provoked calls for the IDIAs repeal. The "mythical neutrality" of King's IDIA was revealed in full: the main advantage of the principle of public investigation went to the company.[98]

For Bell, the strike was not without lessons. The company's attempt to streamline its service and to increase efficiency, while reducing wages, had not been accomplished without a major labour conflict. Bell had learned the necessity of refining its techniques of scientific management, of tempering its management control with negotiation and welfare measures designed to increase employee loyalty, to enhance the occupation's prestige, and to diffuse the desire to unionize. Bell's combination of benevolent paternalism and blatant victimization of union members was effective in delaying unionization for many years.

Faced with the hostility of the company, the ambivalence of organized labour, and the difficult realities of their working situation, it is not surprising that the Bell operators did not make impressive gains. Despite these barriers, the operators effectively formed a strike committee, lobbied for change within the company, then carried through a strike with impressive solidarity. "No surrender to the Company" was the enthusiastic and unanimous watchword of the strikers. The militancy of their protest contradicted the idea of passive femininity and indicated the potential for women workers' opposition to their economic exploitation.

Notes

1 *Toronto World*, 8 February 1907.

2 William Lyon Mackenzie King Papers, A. Lemieux to W.L. Mackenzie King, 15 February 1907.

3 G. Parsons, "A History of Labour Relations in Bell," unpublished manuscript, 1963, Bell Canada Historical Collection (hereafter BCHC).

4 Boy Operators file, BCHC.

5 Ibid.

6 Early Operators file, BCHC.

7 Circular to Supervisors re Hiring, Early Operators file, BCHC.

8 Ibid.

9 Newspaper clipping, Early Operators file, BCHC.

10 Early Operators file, BCHC.

11 Circular to Supervisors, BCHC.

12 See John Schacht, "Toward Industrial Unionism: Bell Telephone Workers and Company Unions, 1919–1937," *Labor History* 16 (Winter 1975): 10.

13 *Toronto Star*, 11 February 1907.

14 Ibid.

15 Ibid., 12 February 1907.

16 Bureau of Labour Report, Ontario *Sessional Papers,* no. 30 (1907): 100–113, 150–67. For example, the weekly wage of a female typographer was about $12, a boot and shoe worker $8, and a furrier $7. In the same occupations, male wages would be about $14, $14, and $15.

17 R.C. Fetherstonaugh, *Charles Fleetford Sise* (Montreal, 1944), 180.

18 See Craig Heron and Bryan D. Palmer, "Through the Prism of the Strike: Industrial Conflict in Southern Ontario, 1901–14," *Canadian Historical Review* 58, no. 4 (December 1977): 423–59. Heron and Palmer see the 1907 strike as an outcome of a managerial drive for efficiency, but this was only one factor behind the operators' protest. Other complaints, such as wage cutbacks, were crucial to the strike.

19 *Report of the Royal Commission on a Dispute respecting terms of Employment between Bell Telephone Company of Canada and Operators at Toronto* (Ottawa, 1907), 13–14 (hereafter *Report*).

20 Ibid., 15.

21 Dunstan in *Report*, 28.

22 Ibid., 63.

23 Ibid., 33.

24 *Toronto Star*, 30 January 1907.

25 Ibid.

26 Parsons, "A History of Labour Relations in Bell," BCHC.

27 *Toronto Star*, 1 February 1907.

28 See Canada, House of Commons, *Select Committee on Telephone Systems* (Ottawa, 1905), 1: 701–7.

29 *Toronto News*, 1 February 1907.

30 *Globe* (Toronto), 2 February 1907.

31 *Toronto Star*, 4 February 1907.

32 Ibid., 31 January 1907.

33 Ibid., 2 February 1907.

34 Ibid., 1 February 1907.

35 Ibid., 30 January 1907. Dunstan was later corrected by a striker who pointed out that the "comforts he speaks of are largely paid for out of our salaries" (*Toronto Star*, 8 February 1907).

36 Ibid., 2 February 1907.

37 Ibid.

38 *Toronto News*, 9 February 1907; *Toronto Star*, 16 February 1907.

39 *Toronto News*, 1 February 1907.

40 Sise to Dunstan, Labour Trouble file, BCHC.

41 Winchester chaired the Royal Commission on employment of aliens on Canadian railways in 1904. He sided with the workers and made scathing criticisms of the CPR. See Donald Avery, "Canadian Immigration Policy and the 'Foreign' Navvy, 1896–1914," Canadian Historical Association, *Historical Papers* (1972): 143.

42 *Toronto Star*, 5 February 1907.

43 *Mail and Empire* (Toronto), 5 February 1907.

44 *Toronto Star*, 9 February 1907.

45 Ibid., 5 February 1907.

46 One independent operator estimated that one-third of her salary had to come from overtime work. Operators' board costs ranged from $2.50 to $3.50 a week. Food costs were estimated by dividing family budgets presented in the *Tribune*, 17 March 1906, and Department of Labour, *Board of Inquiry into the Costs of Living, 1900–1915*.

47 *Report*, 35.

48 *Mail and Empire*, 12 February 1907.

49 *Toronto Star*, 7 February 1907.

50 Ibid., 12 February 1907.

51 Ibid.

52 *Report*, 60.

53 *Toronto World*, 15 February 1907.

54 *Toronto Star*, 15 February 1907.

55 *Report*, 76.

56 *Globe*, 5 February 1907.

57 Ibid., 19 February 1907.

58 Curry to King, 3 April 1907, Strikes and Lockouts file, Department of Labour Records.

59 *Report*, 96.

60 Ibid.

61 Parsons, "A History of Labour Relations in Bell," BCHC.

62 Schacht, "Towards Industrial Unionism: Bell Telephone Workers and Company Unions, 1919–37," 13.

63 Parsons, "A History of Labour Relations in Bell," BCHC.

64 Sise to Hamilton Manager, Early Operators file, BCHC.

65 R. Whitaker, "Mackenzie King in the Dominion of the Dead," *Canadian Forum* 55 (February 1976): 9.

66 *Report*, 95.

67 Library and Archives Canada, William Lyon Mackenzie King diary, 4 August 1907.

68 Canada, Parliament, Report of a Royal Commission into Cotton Factories, *Sessional Paper* no. 39 (1909): 11.

69 Canada, Parliament, Department of Labour, Report of the Deputy Minister, *Sessional Paper* no. 36 (1908): 129.

70 Alice Klein and Wayne Roberts, "Besieged Innocence: The 'Problem' and Problems of Working Women, Toronto, 1896–1914," in *Women at Work: Ontario, 1980–1930*, ed. Janice Acton, Penny Goldsmith, and Bonnie Shepard (Toronto: Women's Press, 1974), 212, 213, 226.

71 Canada, Parliament, Department of Labour, Report of the Deputy Minister, *Sessional Paper* no. 36 (1908): 121. See also W.L.M. King, *Industry and Humanity* (Toronto, 1973): 205–7.

72 *Report*, 98.

73 Canada, Department of Labour, *Annual Report*, 1908, 60.

74 King Papers, Lemieux to King, 15 February 1907.

75 Canada, House of Commons, *Debates*, 14 February 1907, 3009.

76 King papers, Memo re Bill 36, undated and MP unnamed.

77 King diary, 11 September 1907.

78 *Report*, 96.

79 Curry to King, 3 April 1907, Strikes and Lockouts file, Department of Labour Records.

80 King to Curry, 4 April 1907, Strikes and Lockouts file, Department of Labour Records. Allan Studholme, Labour MLA for Hamilton East, had suggested that a bill limiting the telephone operators to a five-hour day be introduced into the provincial legislature. The bill was never introduced.

81 In August 1918 the Toronto operators demanded a wage increase and organized into a local of the IBEW. After a Board of Arbitration sided with the operators, wage increases were given and Bell agreed to meet with operators from the union. After two years, however, the union's influence dwindled, and in 1920 it was reported that "the union of telephone girls had decreased to two score" (*Globe*, 11 April 1920). The problems of 1907 reappeared: company hostility, disinterest of IBEW officers, and lack of commitment by the operators. G. Parsons also notes that company welfare measures made the International less attractive. By 1921 the union was replaced by a company union, the Telephone Operators Association.

82 Sise, quoted in Parsons, "A History of Labour Relations in Bell," BCHC.

83 *Mail and Empire*, 4 February 1907.

84 Jack Barbush, *Unions and Telephones: The Story of the Communication Workers of America* (New York, 1952), 3. See also M. Mulcarie, *The IBEW: A Study in Trade Union Structure and Function* (Washington, 1923), 131.

85 Barbush, *Unions and Telephones*, 4.

86 Trades and Labour Congress of Canada, *Platform of Principles*, 1907.

87 Alice Kessler-Harris, "Where Are the Organized Women Workers?" *Feminist Studies* 3 (Fall 1975): 98.

88 The *Toiler*, an organ of the Toronto District Labour Council, was published from 1902 to 1904. The *Tribune*, edited by J.H. Perry, was published from 1905 to 1906.

89 See *Industrial Banner*, July 1907; *Toiler*, 16 October 1903.

90 See *Toiler*, 16 May 1902, 1 July 1904.

91 See *Industrial Banner*, April 1908; January 1909.

92 Klein and Roberts, "Besieged Innocence," 251.

93 For similar conclusions about British working-class women see, for example, Peter Stearns, "Working-Class Women in Britain, 1890–1914," in *Suffer and Be Still*, ed. Martha Vicinus (Bloomington, 1972): 112; and Dorothy Thompson, "Women in 19th Century Radical Politics," in *The Rights and Wrongs of Women*, ed. Juliet Mitchell and Ann Oakley (London, 1976), 138.

94 *Tribune*, 11 November 1905.

95 Wayne Roberts, *Honest Womanhood: Feminism, Femininity and Class Consciousness Among Toronto Working Women, 1893 to 1914* (Toronto, 1976), 11.

96 Ibid.

97 In 1905, agitation for more public control of telephones was appeased with the Parliamentary Select Committee to investigate telephone systems. After eight

volumes of testimony, the committee reported it was "impossible to come to any conclusions." William Mulock, who had voiced sympathy for public ownership, retired as postmaster general and was replaced by Allan Aylesworth, who had acted as counsel for Bell. The *World* and the *News* reported that Mulock had been driven out by Bell, which had already established close political relations with the Laurier cabinet. Sise had been reassured during the committee's hearings that the government had no intention of public ownership. See J.E. Williams, "Labour Relations in the Telephone Industry: A Comparison of the Private and Public Segments" (Ph.D. diss., University of Wisconsin, 1961), 83–85.

98 Whitaker, "Mackenzie King in the Dominion of the Dead," 153.

LOOKING BACKWARDS
RE-ASSESSING WOMEN ON THE CANADIAN LEFT

When Edward Bellamy wrote his famous utopian novel, *Looking Backward*, in 1888, his setting was the future in 2001. He would be disappointed to discover that we are not only far from a socialist utopia, but it seems we are travelling in the opposite direction towards unrestrained, "vampire" capitalism.[1] Even over the past thirty years, the strength and nature of socialist ideals have altered fairly dramatically: what seemed politically possible in 1975 was no longer so in 1995. Precisely because of the disappointing decline and fragmentation of the Left since the 1970s, I've probably reread and reconsidered the historiography relating to the Left more intensely than other writing.

Our views on politics and theory are shaped by the context in which we write, and this is particularly true of "The Communist Party and the Woman Question, 1922–1929," researched and written in the late 1970s and early 1980s as part of my doctoral dissertation, which was later revised as a book, *Dreams of Equality: Women on the Canadian Left, 1920–1950*. Abridged from an article published in *Labour/Le Travail* in 1984, this piece was written at a time when theoretical debates concerning capitalism and patriarchy and discussions about socialist-feminist political organizing were front and centre. During the 1970s and 1980s, many feminists were probing the relationship between class and sex/gender systems: the outpouring of writing on dual systems (i.e., capitalism and patriarchy) theory, (including critiques of dual systems theories), social reproduction, the domestic labour debate, women as a reserve army of labour (or not), sexing class and classing sex, and so on was quite remarkable.[2] Much of this writing attempted to use a revitalized, more flexible and open Marxism — the product of New Left and 'new' social history theorizing — along with feminist analyses to create Marxist-feminist theories. I found more than one strand of Marxist-feminist writing compelling: one was epitomized by Sheila Rowbotham's writing, which was in turn shaped by both feminism and the Marxist humanism often associated with E.P. Thompson,[3] while the other strand was a more structural fusion of Marxism and feminism represented by the work of Michele Barrett and Mary McIntosh.[4] Rowbotham's emphasis on women's experiences, human agency, and contradiction resonated with my own interests, on the one hand, while Barrett and McIntosh's discussion of the 'anti-social' family under capitalism, gender, ideology, and the family wage also had an impact.[5] Both these streams of writing addressed class relations and took a critical view of the male-headed family as it was experienced within capitalism; both suggested the need for radical social transformation. These critiques of the family were later criticized for being 'race blind,' as they certainly were, though I think some elements of the Marxist-feminist critique of the idealized nuclear family remain relevant today; moreover, they have been taken up and revised by a new group of Marxist feminists who pay far more attention to heteronormativity.[6]

The second impetus for this article, and likewise for my *Dreams of Equality* book, was the exciting expansion of socialist-feminist organizing, the latter designating a somewhat broader politic than Marxist-feminism, taking in those who had a critique of capitalism and who saw the goals of feminism and socialism as inseparable. In the late 1970s and into the 1980s, socialist feminists were active on multiple fronts. There had emerged a number of 'new communist' Marxist-Leninist parties, some of which were involved in the autonomous women's movement, while others were organizing women in the workforce. In Hamilton, Ontario, where I lived, the Revolutionary Workers League was involved in campaigns like Women Back into Stelco, as well as important labour movement support work, where our paths often crossed. Socialist-feminists were also active in more broadly based groups, such as Toronto's International Women's Day Committee (IWDC), Ontario Working Women, and Saskatchewan Working Women — to name a few. For a time, some of us established a Hamilton Working Women group, also dedicated to union support work. If Marxist-feminism was the 'theory,' all these efforts were the 'practice,' and they raised what we thought were key questions for socialists-feminists. Was social democracy à la the NDP worth supporting?

(We organized, not very successfully, Left caucuses within the party.) Was a vanguard party in fact the ideal way forward? (I admit I was influenced by some of the anti-Leninist writing of British socialist-feminists.) Was separate feminist organizing necessary to ensure that women's oppression would be a fundamental element of socialist politics? This conjuncture of theory and politics led to a curiosity about the history of women on the Left and a desire to connect past and present understandings of socialist-feminism. As I researched, I also began to question the dominant 'two wave' description of feminism that designated the period between 1920 and 1960 as something of a political trough, a model that seemed to be contradicted *by* the history of women on the Left.

Both this article and *Dreams of Equality* were written as overviews that did not focus intently on any one woman or delve primarily into any one issue (trade union work, for instance), or focus on one province or city, though there was a regional focus on Ontario and the West. My attention was concentrated on political parties, rather than the entire Left, and on what might be called programmatic and organizing issues: what were the changing perspectives on 'the woman question' in the organized Left, why did these particular priorities emerge, and how were they put into practice — or not? Given the Marxist-feminist debates at the time about the family wage ideal, I was also interested in women's perceived and expected role in the family, their domestic labour, and how the Left understood and negotiated the dominant ideas of family and female domesticity. And given the attempts, taking place around me, to recruit women into Left parties, I wondered what economic, intellectual, and social forces had drawn women to the earlier Left. That question necessitated attention to ethnicity as well as gender and class, since the Communist Party's three dominant cultural language groups were an integral part of its history. Without language skills and with only limited translations to rely on, my answers were underdeveloped, and it was only later, when I had access to more extensive translations of the Ukrainian paper for women, *Robitnystia,* that I could begin to talk about how important, and how closely intertwined, ethnicity, gender, class and culture were in communist history.[7]

There were also issues and approaches that I did not explore or stress at the time but that have come to the fore in subsequent feminist theorizing and historical writing. One was attention to image, representation, and literature. I found the pictures and cartoons in the CCF and communist papers fascinating, and there was some writing on socialist iconography at the time, but I did not analyze these representations at any length, even though they were a rich primary source that revealed much about the gendered nature of socialist discourses. Later writing, often drawing on modes of literary analyses, addressed representation and culture far more; some writing also explored the much broader literary Left that existed beyond the borders of Left parties.[8] Second, despite a concern with ethnicity, 'race' and imperialism were not central to my analysis, yet much could be said, for instance, about communist writing on imperialism, including its views on women in colonized countries, and much has been said about the CCF's understanding of Aboriginal peoples and colonialism.[9] Third, because I did not focus on any one woman, biography was not utilized as a window into the Left, nor did I explore in any depth key relationships between left-wing women, looking at how friendship and politics were intertwined: both these themes have been explored with great insight by subsequent authors.[10] I sometimes mourn lost opportunities in this regard. On the one hand, I think I should have asked more critical questions of some of my interviewees whom I was reluctant to challenge, most particularly communists who were already suspicious of my political motives. On the other hand, I wish I had done multiple interviews with women who deserve far more than they have received from posterity. Alberta's Nellie Peterson is just one example, and every time I see her in the film *Prairie Women* (which I regularly show to my women's history class) I feel moved, as I remember so vividly her intelligence, feistiness, and political integrity. Finally, my critical take on the Left's acceptance — or even idealization (to varying degrees, of course) — of the nuclear, male-breadwinner family and its inability to completely challenge patriarchal ideas did not explore heterosexuality and heterosexism, even though the nuclear, male-breadwinner family simultaneously denoted a heterosexual family. Despite some sympathy for alternative family forms and sexual innovation within the communist Left in the twenties, an acceptance, and sometimes an idealization of heterosexual relations came to characterize both the communist and social democratic Left to a great degree: this too still needs more exploration.

There are also some interpretive issues that remain contested in 2010, just as they were in 1980. In communist history, the relationship between the international movement (led decisively by the USSR after the mid-1920s), the national party, and local activities remains in dispute in both Canadian and American historiography, though the latter writing is more polarized on this issue. When I wrote in the 1980s, I was influenced particularly by (American) New Left reappraisals of the CPUSA that focused on single campaigns, issues, or organizing at the local level; these works were important attempts to move beyond the Cold War characterizations of the party as nothing but Moscow-controlled.[11] I attempted to do some of the same, but establishing a balanced understanding of this tripartite relationship as it shifted over time was difficult and was complicated by the lack of archival resources relating to the Comintern, some of which, in the aftermath of the implosion of the USSR, have now come to light. In retrospect, I think I too easily collapsed the issue of the Stalinization of the party with the issue of Moscow control — though they were connected, they were not one and the same.[12]

Interestingly, one current of recent scholarship still insists that we must focus primarily on the "local" communist scene,[13] a stance that not only airbrushes out some critical questions about how the party functioned at the centre but, more importantly, stunts a better understanding of how the triangulated relations of the international, national, and local operated. After all, in the interwar period discussed in the article below, the international movement, led by the USSR, and the central party apparatus played a role in determining how the issue of women's oppression was addressed — *along with* local conditions, cultures, and women's own efforts to interpret party directives. I wonder if the socialist vacuum that appears to reign across North America in our times has encouraged some historians to emphasize the 'best' side of the party, such as their militant unionization efforts and local organizing against unemployment and racism. This may also be one reason that the culture of the Popular Front, seemingly a period of some degree of unity and collaboration on the Left, is seen so positively.[14] In a recent article, one American historian calls for a "less partisan," more "detached" history of communism, placing its historical figures "into a world where everything is understood and all sins are forgiven" (are we *never* to be critical of the

Communist Party?). She caricatures those still interested in the party's actual program as "wounded participants," caught up in irrelevant Cold Wars; the superior approach, she asserts, with great certainty, would focus on topics such as the "culture" of the Popular Front.[15] It is fascinating that after so many years of poststructuralist writing that has sharpened our attention to the 'always political' discursive construction of history, authors like this assume other people's writing is partisan and political, while theirs somehow rises above this problematic burden. Her liberal argument for "detached" scholarship ignores the fact that one can't so easily separate the cultural and political in the history of the Left.

Writing on local manifestations and specific campaigns of communism on both sides of the border has enriched our understanding of rank-and-file activities, which were always more likely to encompass women, but dismissing political debates about party program and priorities as "intellectual quibbles" mysteriously depoliticizes historical actors who were profoundly political and who believed that these were key issues. Indeed, even when I interviewed people who had left the party, they were often still deeply engaged in debates about its programmatic platform.[16] Again, the current political context is likely influential in shaping these arguments. The emphasis on valuing the concrete, 'practical' (non-revolutionary) activities of local communists may reflect a certain left-liberal/social democratic sense of superiority (or even resignation) in current times, as well as a rejection of the so-called ultra-left of the sixties and seventies. In American writing particularly, Marxist-Leninist parties of this period are often stigmatized as the wild, unrealistic wreckers of a more diffuse, open, eclectic radicalism. They are portrayed as 'mistakes,' even in the words of some of their former members, including feminists who were understandably critical of the gendered power structures in vanguard parties.[17] What is quite puzzling, however, is how you can love the Popular Front but hate vanguard parties, which, however way you cut it, the CPUSA and CPC ultimately were. The intense hostility and disdain I have seen at academic conferences from self-designated progressives towards any person who appears to have retained a modicum of revolutionary commitment to socialism (most especially Trotskyists, whom everyone seems to resent, even though they did not establish any gulags) is very strong. This is an atmosphere rather different from that of the 1970s.

It would be simplistic if not erroneous to claim that Canadian debates about communist history are carbon copies of American ones (which are themselves often oversimplified).[18] Discussion about the relative roles of the local and the international in shaping the party, to take one example, is more polarized in the United States than in Canada, where more 'in-between' explanations have emerged. This likely reflects the presence of a far stronger 'spy' school of communist historiography in the US and perhaps also the successful cultivation of a more deep-seated fear of socialism, which seems ascendant at this point in time. As a result, left-leaning academics who fear the undue influence of the 'spy' school are less inclined to explore Leninism and the complicated history of the Comintern and more inclined to study local unemployment marches, antiracism, and rent strikes.

In Canada, Ian McKay has suggested a historical approach that looks at what many leftists shared in common, rather than simply what divided them, "writing generally about the Left."[19] This too may reflect a feeling, different from the mood of the 1970s, that in such bleak times of apparently unending neoliberal successes, we need to be Unitarians, welcoming any and all leftists who appear to object to the status quo or, as McKay puts it, all those who understand that humans should be able to "live otherwise"— a rather open-ended definition.[20] McKay's more recent writing has provided us with a detailed and rich account of early socialist organizations and ideas that preceded the Communist Party, but whether his suggested 'new' methodology of "reconnaissance" breaks from previous whig stories, hierarchies, and certainties, as he claims, is more questionable. Reconnaissance, according to McKay, is a "preliminary examination,"[21] a "scouting out" of the past that is more "provisional," questioning, and "heterogeneous," rather than dogmatic and sectarian.[22] Nor is it a "synthesis," for a synthesis browbeats us with its confining, "authoritative" form, often simply "fortifying" what we already know.[23] McKay contrasts his reconnaissance to the previous writing on the Left that assumed a "scorecard" approach, assigning to this or that author "stars and demerit points based on his or her present day politics."[24] How this is substantively (rather than rhetorically) different from McKay's reconnaissance, which he claims is a "political act of research,"[25] is not entirely clear. Invoking countless analogies and metaphors that denigrate previous writing as "ancestor worship," "polemics," "self-satisfied mystifications," "great man history"— to name a few — McKay suggests that a reconnaissance will liberate us from the "tiresome sectarianism and sentimentalism" that has hamstrung socialist historiography.[26] These negative characterizations of past writing, often with *no* citations as proof, set up a convenient straw historian against which to position his writing, though they seem to go against the grain of an open-minded 'reconnaissance.'

While I find McKay's exploration of new *themes*, including gender, very enriching, I do not think the *method* of a 'reconnaissance' offers us a radically new and useful way of reconceptualizing the history of women and the Left; at worst, reconnaissance can become an assertion of superiority rather than a method at all.[27] Can we really offer 'scout-like' observations about history, untethered from all judgments and hierarchies? McKay himself notes that historians must ascertain whether "some paths are more important than others,"[28] and like many of us writing about the Left, he too has some implicit 'scorecards,' though we do not need to use such a pejorative word for what are essentially evaluations of historiography and history. He establishes certain issues and thinkers he sees as central (putting immense emphasis on Spencer's influence); he positions his interpretation within his own 'liberal order framework,' which provides a synthetic framework for Canadian history; his assessment of other historians' works lays out more and less useful approaches;[29] and past socialists are also described in words that convey positive and less positive values.[30] One argument feminists in the 1980s put forward about knowledge production remains pertinent to these debates about how we reconstruct the Left: while committed to portraying, as much as possible, the "heterogeneity" of women's lives, they argued that we must also own up to the political values and priorities that animate our writing, rather than masking or disguising them, so that readers will be able to engage critically with our arguments.[31] An emphasis on heterogeneity and indeterminacy is not value-free, or somehow above other 'politically invested' approaches, for heterogeneity, too, is a politics of sorts, a way of looking at history that needs critical interrogation.

New questions, themes, and sources have deepened and broadened our understanding of the Left since I wrote in the 1980s, but this does not mean that all subjects and approaches we used in the past are passé. For

example, assessing communists' political program and their efforts to mobilize women will likely remain important to Left history. A program, after
all, was never an inert set of political slogans but rather a call to action, a set
of suggested values, an inspiration to organize, and sometimes a directive,
which may or may not have been followed. It was lived out, not only within
the strict bounds of the party, but also outside of it in sympathetic ethnic
organizations, grassroots arts groups, community protests, even within the
family. We also still need to ask what roles women assumed in the party,
and whether it promoted a vision of gender equality that differed from past
socialist ideas and from the dominant ideologies of the time, and if so, how
and why. Do I think that the party's abandonment of its support for legal
and free birth control in the early 1930s was a step backward? Actually I do,
even if that is a 'scorecard' approach. Contra Van Gosse's description of the
CPUSA in the 1920s as a party characterized by masculinist "workerism,"
"denying and denigrating" the familial, I think the CPC at this time made
some innovative efforts (however limited) to speak to working-class women,
addressing issues that had been largely avoided by previous Canadian
socialists — such as birth control.[32] This does not mean we need to judge
past actresses by current political standards, even if we are drawing on the
insights of present-day feminist theory. We need to understand how they
defined political issues and interpreted concepts like oppression, equality,
feminism, and socialism in the context of their times, even if those were
not the words they used at the time. In this regard, I think the term I used
two decades ago —'militant mothering'— remains a useful metaphor for
one current of left-wing organizing. The notion that women's maternal
and domestic work, responsibilities, and social roles shaped their outlook
and feelings, and thus their political needs and roles, was one component
of communist thinking and strategizing. 'Militant mothering' reflected
some aspects of the dominant, popular ideology of motherhood, but it also
reconfigured the popular ideal significantly, taking a different class form,
challenging notions of passive, apolitical, and 'home-centred' motherhood.
This is not to say that this is the only approach communists embraced, and
more recent biographies have also shown that some women leaders found
it a constraining and contradictory ideology.[33]

The problem with our analyses of various ideologies of maternalism,
later authors argued persuasively, was how loosely and widely the word

'maternalist' could be employed, taking in ideology, subjectivity, and tactics, stretching from fascist to communist women, and from those stressing biology to those who saw motherhood as socially constructed. We needed to hone our definitions and analysis of maternalism. Even within the Communist Party, women's maternalist statements drew on both essentialist and nonessentialist rhetoric, something that I needed to explore more fully. Molly Ladd-Taylor's suggestion that maternalism was an ideology about a "uniquely feminine value system based on care and nurturance" partially describes communist women, but they did not necessarily see all mothers "united across class, and race."[34] Still, I do not think we have to abandon the concept of maternalism entirely. Rather, we should avoid using it as a general paradigm, analyzing instead the very specific kinds of maternalist ideologies women developed, shaped by historical context, class and race relations, and political beliefs. Within the Communist Party in the 1920s, militant mothering was simultaneously a strategy of engagement developed by a male-dominated party and a deeply held belief on women's part concerning their important role in social reproduction and the need for communists to address family concerns.[35] And given the growth of Women's Labor Leagues in the 1920s, these two forces combined might actually work well, drawing women into the movement.

Notes

1 Marjorie Cohen, "From the Welfare State to Vampire Capitalism," in *Women and the Canadian Welfare State: Challenges and Change*, ed. Patricia Evans and Gerda Wekerle (Toronto: University of Toronto Press, 1997), 28–67.

2 For example, Zillah Eisenstein, *Patriarchy and Capitalism and the Case for Socialist Feminism* (New York: Monthly Review Press, 1978); Lydia Sargent, *Women and Revolution: A Discussion of the Unhappy Marriage of Marxism and Feminism* (Boston: South End Press, 1981). On domestic labour, Margaret Benston, "The Political Economy of Women's Liberation," *Monthly Review* 21 (1969): 13–27; Wally Seccombe and Bonnie Fox, eds., *Hidden in the Household: Women's Domestic Labour Under Capitalism* (Toronto: Women's Press, 1980). Political economists were central to the reconstruction of feminist and Marxist theory: Pat Armstrong and Hugh Armstrong, "Beyond Sexless Class and Classless Sex: Towards Feminist Marxism," *Studies in Political Economy* 10 (1983). To say that Marxist theory simply "saw the solution to women's oppression as including women in industrial

production" thus seems to me to simplify theoretical discussions of this period: Hester Eisestein, *Feminism Seduced: How Global Elites Use Women's Labour and Ideas to Exploit the World* (Boulder: Paradigm Publishers, 2009), 203.

3 Sheila Rowbotham, *Woman's Consciousness, Man's World* (London: Penguin, 1973), and *Women, Resistance and Revolution* (London: Penguin, 1973).

4 Michele Barrett, *Women's Oppression Today: Problems in Marxist Feminist Analysis* (London: Verso, 1980); Michele Barrett and Mary McIntosh, "The 'Family Wage': Some Problems for Socialists and Feminists," *Capital and Class* 11 (1980): 51–72.

5 Nancy Fraser, "Feminism, Capitalism, and the Cunning of History," *New Left Review,* 56 (Mar–April 2009), 110. Ironically, some scholars have recently suggested that feminists' political focus in the 1970s on 'tearing down' the family wage ideal unwittingly "provided a key ingredient of the new spirit of neoliberalism," namely the low wage, multi-earner family, an interesting but not unproblematic argument.

6 Rosemary Hennessy, *Profit and Pleasure: Sexual Identities in Late Capitalism* (New York: Routledge, 2000).

7 Joan Sangster, "*Robitnystia* and the Porcupinism Debate: Reassessing Ethnicity, Gender and Class in Early Canadian Communism," *Labour/Le Travail* 56 (Fall 2005): 51–89. A full treatment of this topic remains to be done, but there are now more discussions of ethnicity: Rhonda Hinther, "Raised in the Spirit of Class Struggle: Children, Youth and the Interwar Ukrainian Left," *Labour/Le Travail* 60 (Fall 2007): 43–76; Varpu Lindström-Best, *Defiant Sisters: A Social History of Finnish Immigrant Women in Canada* (Toronto: Multicultural History Society, 1992).

8 Candida Rifkind, *Comrades and Critics: Women, Literature, and the Left in 1930s Canada* (Toronto: University of Toronto Press, 2008). On the United States, see Charlotte Nekola and Paula Rabinowitz, eds., *Writing Red: An Anthology of American Women Writers, 1930–1940* (New York: Feminist Press, 1986); Paula Rabinowitz, *Labour and Desire: Women's Revolutionary Fiction in Depression America* (Chapel Hill: University of North Carolina Press, 1991); and a critique of her approach in Barbara Foley, "Women and the Left in the 1930s," *American Literary History* 2 (Spring 1990): 150–69.

9 See, for example, Laurie Barron, *Walking in Indian Moccasins: The Native Policies of Tommy Douglas* (Vancouver: University of British Columbia Press, 1997); David Quirling, ccf *Colonialism in Northern Saskatchewan* (Vancouver: University of British Columbia Press, 2004); Stephanie Bangarth, *Voices Raised in Protest: Defending North American Citizens of Japanese Ancestry, 1942–1949* (Vancouver: University of British Columbia Press, 2008).

10 Faith Johnston, *A Great Restlessness: The Life and Politics of Dorise Nielsen* (Winnipeg: University of Manitoba Press, 2006); Anne Toews, "For Liberty, Bread, and Love: Annie Buller, Beckie Buhay, and the Forging of Communist Militant Femininity in Canada, 1918–1939" (MA thesis, Simon Fraser University, 2009).

11   For example, Mark Naison, *Communists in Harlem During the Depression* (New York: Grove Press, 1984); Paul Lyons, *Philadelphia Communists, 1936–1956* (Philadelphia: Temple University Press, 1982).

12   Bryan D. Palmer, "Rethinking the Historiography of United States Communism," *American Communist History* 2, no. 2 (2003): 139–73.

13   Randi Storch, *Red Chicago: American Communism at Its Grassroots, 1928–1935* (Urbana and Chicago: University of Illinois Press, 2007), 230.

14   Michael Denning, *The Cultural Front: The Laboring of American Culture in the Twentieth Century* (New York: Verso, 1998). For a very sympathetic view of the woman question in the post–World War II period, see Kate Weigand, *Red Feminism: American Communism and the Making of Women's Liberation* (Baltimore: Johns Hopkins University Press, 2004). On communist unions and gender issues, Judith Stepan-Norris and Maurice Zeitlin, *Left Out: Reds and America's Industrial Unions* (Cambridge: Cambridge University Press, 2003).

15   Jennifer Uhlmann, "Moving On: Towards a Post-Cold War Historiography of American Communism," *American Communist History* 8, no. 1 (2009): 24.

16   Randi Storch, "American Communism and Soviet Russia: A View from Chicago's Streets," *American Communist History* 8, no. 1 (2009): 25.

17   One exception is Max Elbaum, *Revolution in the Air: Sixties Radicals Turn to Lenin, Mao and Che* (New York: Verso, 2002), though he only deals with Maoist parties.

18   Trying to squeeze historians, sometimes with different views, into two categories of "traditionalists" and "revisionists," for instance, is too simplified: Randi Storch, "American Communism." Repeating this categorization for Canadian history is quite problematic: for example, Stefan Epp, "A Communist in the Council Chambers: Communist Municipal Politics, Ethnicity, and the Career of William Kolisnyk," *Labour/Le Travail* 63 (Spring 2009): 80.

19   Ian McKay, *Rebels, Reds, Radicals: Rethinking Canada's Left History* (Toronto: Between the Lines, 2005), 24.

20   Ibid.

21   Ian McKay, *Reasoning Otherwise: Leftists and the People's Enlightenment in Canada, 1890–1920* (Toronto: Between the Lines, 2008), 1.

22   McKay, *Rebels, Reds, Radicals*, 95.

23   Ibid., 94.

24   McKay, *Reasoning Otherwise*, 1.

25   Ibid., 2.

26   Ibid., 82.

27 For a critical view of reconnaissance, see Gary Teeple, Review of *Reasoning Otherwise*, *B.C. Studies* 163 (2009): 122–29.

28 McKay, *Reasoning Otherwise*, 11.

29 To cite one example, he notes that Janice Newton's writing on early women socialists sets up unnecessary "dualisms" and that it "minimizes" women's contributions to the Left. Explanations with more "complexity and agency" are thus needed. Critical assessments like this are an essential part of history writing, but it is not useful to set up a dichotomy between this 'acceptable' critical commentary and the very 'bad' (whoever they are) scorecard historians of the past. See McKay, *Reasoning Otherwise*, 288.

30 For example, he is critical of atheists who offered "vicious" critiques of religion but sees those who did not as more tolerant (ibid., 248).

31 Nancy Adamson, Linda Briskin, and Margaret McPhail, *Feminists Organizing for Change: The Contemporary Women's Movement in Canada* (Toronto: Oxford University Press, 1980), 16–17.

32 Van Gosse compares this negative workerism to a positive "sea change" in discourse in 1930–31 concerning gender and the family. His comment may point to different communist histories in Canada and the United States, or it is possible it does not fully represent American communism in the 1920s (which in the US was also characterized by some lingering avant-garde views on sex and private life). This is another reason to be wary of assuming American historiography always fits in Canada. See Van Gosse, "To Organize in Every Neighborhood, in Every Home: The Gender Politics of American Communists Between the Two Wars," *Radical History Review* 50 (1991): 118, 124.

33 Johnston, *A Great Restlessness*.

34 For this definition, see Molly Ladd-Taylor, "Towards Defining Maternalism in U.S. History," *Journal of Women's History* 5 (Fall 1993): 110. Two other useful discussions are Seth Koven and Sonya Michel, eds., *Mothers of a New World: Maternalist Politics and the Origins of the Welfare State* (New York: Routledge, 1993); and Lynn Weiner, "Maternalism as a Paradigm: Defining the Issues," *Journal of Women's History* 5 (Fall 1993): 96–98.

35 Kathleen Brown makes this point about social reproduction in "'The Savagely Fathered and Un-Mothered World' of the Communist Party, USA: Feminism, Maternalism, and 'Mother Bloor,'" *Feminist Studies* 25, no. 3 (Fall 1999): 537–70. However, I think the Canadian example was different in terms of timing and the importance of a change in party priorities: I think women were drawn to the party as the Third Period thawed and the Popular Front emerged because the party line now encouraged more avenues for community organizing on family issues (i.e., on social reproduction) and eschewed denunciations of all other left-wing women (except for Trotskyists, of course, who were always the ultimate enemy), making coalitions easier.

THE COMMUNIST PARTY AND
THE WOMAN QUESTION, 1922–1929

The initial platform proclaimed by the nascent Communist Party of Canada in 1922 made no specific mention of gender inequality or woman's role in the revolutionary movement. Within two years, however, the Communist Party of Canada (CPC) had altered this oversight by setting up a Women's Department and spearheading the formation of a national organization for working-class women, the Women's Labor League (WLL). The Communist Party's approach to the woman question was conditioned primarily by its response to the advice of the Communist International, or Comintern, and secondly, by the party's own analysis of the needs of working-class women. In the last resort, the advice of Soviet Communists was refracted through the prism of local traditions, ideas, and realities. While the CPC's ethnic complexion and its emphasis on a class analysis of women's oppression signified continuity with the prewar socialist movement, Communists also sought to transcend their past, embracing a new social and sexual order that included the emancipation of women. And although the CPC remained a weak force within Canadian political life of the 1920s, its agitational work on women's issues did mark out new parameters of thought and action for Canadian socialism.

Admittedly, the woman question never became a central priority for the CPC, a consequence of internal party failings and external social pressures. Despite the Communists' connection to the "successful" Russian revolution, their vision of a new order for women remained marginal — even within their own movement. Although many noble convention resolutions declared the need to organize women, the party itself mirrored some of the formidable structures of inequality and oppression facing women in wider Canadian society.

International Advice and Canadian Responses

During the twenties, the influence of the Comintern on the Communist Party of Canada with regard to the woman question was very powerful, in part because the International was generally the guiding influence on its member parties, but additionally because reforms within Russian society appeared to herald major, inspiring advances towards women's emancipation. Soviet women were accorded political equality, registration of civil marriage was instituted, abortions legalized, and a new family law code established women's equal status in marriage. In 1919, the Soviet Communist Party set up the Zhenotdel, a women's section that attempted educational work — everything from literacy classes to conferences for working women — to draw women into political activity. The barriers to its work were immense: Zhenotdel workers had to contend with the economic chaos and poverty of postrevolutionary Russia; male hostility, even from within communist circles, to women's political activism; and firmly entrenched cultural barriers to women's emancipation, especially in the peasant villages and in the Muslim East. Despite these obstacles, the Zhenotdel waged a highly successful educational campaign, "achieving in its work, a major impact on Soviet society, especially in the cities."[1] Contemporary Bolshevik leaders, however, became increasingly alarmed at the Zhenotdel's "feminist tendencies," and in 1929, when the Central Committee Secretariat of the Party was reorganized, the Zhenotdel was effectively eliminated. Its demise, of course, was linked to the triumph of Stalinism and the liquidation of any organizations that might threaten the centralized party-state.

To North American Marxists and even to some socialists and liberals, who had been concerned primarily with transforming the productive process and according women political equality, the Russian example initially appeared to be a beacon of hope. Within the CPC, the Russian reforms stimulated new discussion of gender inequality and the organization of working women. From the *Communist International* and *Imprecorr*, Canadian Communist leaders gleaned information on Zhenotdel activities, conferences, theses, and Bolshevik resolutions on the mobilization of women. Directives from the International Women's Secretariat of the Communist International urged the establishment of a Communist women's organization in Canada, and Soviet reforms in marriage, divorce, and abortion laws fostered similar debates in Canada, opening up women's issues that had rarely been discussed by the prewar socialist movement and, indeed, were rarely discussed in the subsequent history of the Communist Party.

The recommendations for the organization of women made by the International Women's Secretariat essentially represented traditions already part of the Canadian Left: the unionization of wage-earning women and the establishment of support groups for working-class housewives. After the party decided to work openly in 1922, a Women's Department was set up to co-ordinate these activities. The first director, Florence Custance, remains a vaguely defined figure in Communist history, in part due to her early death in 1929. Born in England and trained as a schoolteacher, Custance immigrated to Canada with her husband, a carpenter, and she became involved in the labour movement as a leader of the Amalgamated Carpenters of Canada Wives Auxiliary. By the time of World War I she was deeply involved in the Socialist Party of North America, and in 1919 she was a participant in the secret Guelph Convention that established the CPC. In the 1920s she occupied strategically important party positions and headed the Canadian Friends of Soviet Russia. A somewhat reserved intellectual rather than an "agitational" leader, Custance also became the driving force behind the organization of the Communist women's movement. In May 1922, shortly before she left for the fourth Comintern Congress in Moscow, Custance's Women's Department announced its existence with a public meeting attended by about two hundred. *The Worker* sporadically carried news of the Women's Department until a regular women's column, coordinated by Custance and entitled "The Working Women's Section" began to give more frequent coverage to the woman question. Finally, in 1926, Custance initiated *The Woman Worker,* a separate newspaper written by and for the Women's Labor Leagues.

Following repeated directives of the International to set up a working-class women's organization to be guided by the party, Custance turned her energies also to the Women's Labor Leagues (WLLS). The labor leagues followed in the tradition of the prewar SDPC Finnish sewing circles and took their name directly from existing WLLS, which had been established as adjuncts to labour parties and socialist groups, sometimes with links to the trade union movement.[2] Gradually, Custance and other Communist women began to join and form their own WLLs, and in 1924 a federal WLL apparatus for the growing movement was established at a conference in London, following that year's Trades and Labour Congress convention. Elected national secretary at that conference, Custance announced that the leagues would enjoy some local autonomy, although they would be guided by the general goals of the larger Federation of WLLs.

Much to its chagrin, the federation was denied formal affiliation to the TLC, supposedly because its members, as housewives, were not "producers." Custance drew strong applause from women delegates when she retorted that male trade unionists "lived in the Middle Ages" and should "wake up" to the fact that WLL members "are women who cook, sew, wash, scrub, and who perform duties necessary to the whole process of production."[3] The presence of Communists like Custance on the WLL executive, however, was likely the true reason for some TLC members' hostility to the leagues. Rejection of the WLLs by the TLC was a disappointing setback for Custance, for affiliation had been part of the party's larger United Front scheme to work within and influence the labour movement. At the local level, some WLLs had more success with this strategy. In 1924, for example, the Toronto WLL affiliated with the Toronto and District Labour Council, and over the next three years it earned praise from trade union men. But in 1927 this amiable relationship ended abruptly with the WLL's expulsion from the council. A campaign against the league was led by socialist Jimmy Simpson, who had heartily endorsed the WLL in 1924 but now objected to its Communist membership.[4]

The Women's Labor Leagues, like the larger CPC, also tried to play a role in the young Canadian Labor Party (CLP). In the early 1920s labourites participated in some local WLLs and contributed to *The Woman Worker*. WLLs in turn attended Labor Party conventions and successfully lobbied for resolutions on issues like "no cadet training in the schools," which most socialists and labourites alike supported. Only in 1927, however, were Communists able to dominate the resolutions agenda, and this was a shallow victory, as labourites had decided to abandon the CLP, leaving Communists to occupy its shell. In the West, the WLLs also participated in the Western Women's Social and Economic Conferences, initiated by labourite Beatrice Brigden in 1924. In the first few years, the WLLs easily carried motions from their own program, such as demands for better minimum wage laws. But by the late 1920s, Communist women became increasingly disturbed by the conference's reformist viewpoint and its paternalistic concentration on issues like sterilization of the "feebleminded." Unable to mould a majority that was Marxist and Communist in outlook, the WLLs eventually withdrew from active participation.

By 1927, the WLLs had become predominantly Communist in outlook. Only a minority of WLL women were party members, but most were willing to accept political guidance from the CPC's Women's Department. As the number of Labor Leagues grew to thirty-seven at the end of 1927, they also came to reflect the ethnic strengths of the Communist Party, with Finnish leagues outnumbering the English-speaking ones. Jewish, Ukrainian, and Finnish women were also organized through their respective ethnic organizations: the Jewish Labor League, the Finnish Organization of Canada, and the Ukrainian Labour-Farmer Temple Association. Finnish and Jewish women, however, participated in Labor Leagues that were loosely, sometimes closely, linked to the Party's Women's Department. Ukrainian women, on the other hand, belonged to the Women's Section of the ULFTA, answered to ULFTA's Central Committee, and usually had less contact with the English WLLs.

Organizing Women Workers

Whatever the organizational differences based on ethnicity, there was basic agreement on the overall perception of the woman question. Capitalism, emphasized the first WLL constitution, had created two kinds of labour: "household drudgery and wage labour . . . both of which were essential to the maintenance of capitalism."[5] Revolutionaries, Custance argued, must therefore fight for women's right to organize and for equal pay, as well as for the protection of mothers and children. Moreover, "working class women must struggle for equality along with men of their own class, refusing to be used as scabs or wage-reducers" and unswayed by the false arguments of the feminist movement. Sex, it was stressed, was "a minor question compared to the class struggle . . . we must first take up the struggle against capitalist tyranny which keeps our husbands chained to uncertainty and us to worry and desperation . . . and our children to want."[6]

Throughout the 1920s these basic tenets — the economic exploitation of women and the imperative of unified revolutionary action — were stressed again and again. Prewar socialist parties had taken a similar approach, but the Communist Party was distinguished by its new emphasis on the woman question and by a measure of sympathy for women's *particular* oppression within capitalism. *Worker* articles, for instance, emphasized the necessity of bringing the "most oppressed" group — women — into revolutionary politics, to help them "work out their own emancipation."[7] *The Woman Worker,* unabashedly political, proclaimed its intention to forgo all the traditional "fashions, recipes and sickly love stories" of other women's papers. It kept its promise and concentrated on women's struggle for "equal duties and rights with men" as well as women's specific "fight against customs, traditions, and superstitions which have kept them chained to passive roles and conservatism."[8]

The WLLs were the centerpiece of the Communist Party's attempts to put its theory on the woman question into practice and were intended to join together women in the home and women in the workforce, a task the party immediately found problematic. Young and/or single women cadres, with their greater freedom to travel, were more likely to be active as organizers for the Young Communist League (YCL) or as industrial agitators, while it was the married "Party wives," tied closely to home and family, who concentrated on the support work associated with the WLLs. The Labor Leagues, explained one Finnish woman, were made up of women like her mother who "mainly did fund-raising and social affairs" along with an "important attempt at political education."[9] That "the WLLs were for the housewives, not the women in the factories" became the common perception.[10] Ironically, in keeping with predominant social norms, many homemakers might be charged, especially in the absence of their travelling revolutionary husbands, with the difficult tasks of feeding and clothing the family, but not with the task of political and labour organizing. In Britain, one historian argues, a very sharp separation existed between the "cadres" and the "Party wives," with the latter held in some contempt by the former.[11] In contrast, the Canadian WLLs occasionally did draw both groups together, but even though the two groups were not hostile, differences *did* exist. And clearly, the party lamented the housewife composition of the WLLs, for according to advice from Moscow, as well as traditional Marxist thinking, the mobilization of wage-earning women should have priority.

To facilitate this work with wage-earning women, the CPC's Women's Department studied the economic, legal, and social status of working women and published its findings in the founding WLL leaflet. The vast majority of wage earners, the WLL document declared, laboured in unskilled jobs, often without even the protection of the minimum wage. Low wages, long hours, and unsafe working conditions were convincing indications of the necessity to unionize these women: a Comintern directive was hardly needed to encourage revolutionaries' disgust with the lot of Canadian women workers.

Desperate working conditions, however, do not necessarily make unionization an easy prospect. Custance believed there were four substantial obstacles to the party's work with wage-earning women, including the influence of religious, social, and pacifist organizations like the YWCA, which "pose as protectors of the working girls"; the organized welfare programs of factories; to a certain extent the misleading protection of the minimum wage laws; and, lastly, the fact that "women do not take wage-earning seriously" but see it as a "temporary necessity" before marriage.[12] Whatever the presumed consciousness of working women, the structural realities of their work lives — seasonal and unskilled work, small workplaces, and a high turnover — did mitigate against their organization. Furthermore, women could draw little aid from the established trade union movement, for the conservative TLC, weakened by the 1921–22 depression, membership losses, and employer overtures and offensives, had little or no time for the concerns of working women.

The party's initial trade union strategies, however, also tended to exclude women. In the early 1920s the Red International of Labor Unions (RILU), a Comintern organization, urged its member parties to work within established trade unions. Women's marginal status in the union movement meant that they were easily bypassed by these strategies, which concentrated on areas of established radical support, such as mining and lumbering. Other suggestions for organizing wage-earning women were similarly inappropriate: the Comintern's repeated advice to initiate "mass delegate meetings from the factory nuclei" of activist women belied the Canadian reality of an extremely weak radical presence in most women's workplaces.[13] Finally, organizing new locals of unions was a time-consuming and expensive enterprise that the small, poorly funded Women's Department was ill-equipped to pursue on its own. Ultimately, if the wage-earning woman failed to take herself seriously, so, too, did the CPC. In its self-criticism, the party openly admitted its efforts with working women were lacking: "The material at the disposal of the Party to carry on this," reported Custance in 1927, "has been up to the present limited and weak. Therefore, much that could have been done has been left undone."[14]

Despite these failures, the Women's Department did give attention to the plight of working women in its own press. The "Working Women's Section" and later *The Woman Worker* abounded with personal and second-hand descriptions of the day-to-day existence of working girls and women, often followed by an analysis of women's wage labour under capitalism written by Custance or perhaps by Becky Buhay, a young organizer quickly growing into a party leader. The problems of working women were also debated in *Kamf*, *Vaupaus*, and *Robitnysia*. The *Kamf's* Women's Section, for example, printed the tale of a Jewish garment worker describing the speed-up and unhealthy conditions in her Montreal factory. In reply, Buhay pointed out that terrible conditions could only be effectively combated with a union, and that the "false consciousness" of the author's fellow French-Canadian workers should be faced squarely with gentle reprimands for their frivolous ways. Sometimes advice like this lectured working women, telling them, for instance, to eschew "charm and personality" courses at the YWCA and "thoughts of catching Prince Charming" and instead to educate themselves to the class struggle.[15] Still, letters were not always greeted with paternalism; they were given encouraging, though simple advice: keep on fighting for your rights, organize a union, and find support in the revolutionary movement.

The Women's Department also developed a campaign to expose the violations and inadequacies of the minimum wage laws, thus "showing the ineffectiveness of government protection as compared with that of unions."[16] In the fall of 1924, for instance, the Toronto WLL pursued evidence that the Willard Chocolate Company, which had prosecuted girls for stealing fifty cents worth of candy, was falsifying its time cards and that the Minimum Wage Board had only taken steps when the workers secured a lawyer. Even then, the board urged no publicity, supposedly for the sake of Willard's. This famous 'Chocolate Case' became a labour *cause célèbre*, but despite WLL and Labour Council pressure, public hearings did not produce a conclusive conviction of the employer. Nevertheless, the CPC continued to press home the message that the Minimum Wage Board was essentially afraid of business, and that the government was hardly a "neutral" body acting to protect women. The Women's Labor Leagues produced evidence at the annual board hearing to show that the suggested "minimum" wage could barely support a working woman, and that it often became the "maximum" wage for women. Across Canada, newly organized WLLs also took up cases of minimum wage abuse; the campaign was visible in Vancouver, Montreal, Winnipeg, and Regina, where an Employed Girls Council, initiated by the WLL, had some small successes in pressuring the government to close loopholes in the legislation. Florence Custance played a pivotal role in the Ontario effort, making useful alliances with local Labour Councils and the Canadian Labor Party. Her effort even earned her praise from the labourite paper, the *People's Cause*, which commended Custance's stubborn persistence in tracking down employers who were ducking the law.[17]

Finally, in the later 1920s, a few WLLs were also able to spark the creation of social and support groups for young working women. In such cities as Sudbury and Toronto, for instance, Finnish Communists established organizations for Finnish maids. Though not officially trade unions, these organizations did aim to improve the work lives of domestics, while also offering social and recreational activities. Once an economic downturn set in, they tried to prevent "unscrupulous" employment agents such as an infamous Lutheran minister in Toronto, from taking advantage of unemployed Finnish women by offering them jobs at low wages. "Maids," cried out one circular in *Vapaus*, "join the membership of Finnish maids organization, where you have no bosses, no clerical hirelings, only yourselves . . . we will strengthen our mutual enterprises and act for our education, and amusement too."[18]

Organizing Housewives

The second aim of the CPC's Women's Department was to mobilize women in the home by setting up housewives' auxiliaries that would aid men's struggles and concurrently develop women's revolutionary consciousness. Communists strongly believed that working-class women were a conservative influence on their families; like Lenin, they saw women, isolated amidst domestic drudgery, as easy prey for the illusory myths of a capitalist society. "Women," wrote Custance in a Women's Department report, "are almost entirely under capitalist class influence, through the church and the newspapers."[19] Nowhere was this more boldly stated than in the Ukrainian press, which claimed that women were poorly educated, sometimes illiterate, their class consciousness low, and their knowledge of politics in general and Marxism in particular almost nonexistent. Indeed, ULFTA set up a separate newspaper for women, *Robitnysia (The Working Woman)*, specifically as an educational tool to "bring women up to the level of men." Unlike the Finnish or English Communist papers, *Robitnysia* saw illiteracy as a major obstacle in its work among women, indicating that Ukrainian women did have more serious barriers to political involvement than many other party women. *Robitnysia* was concerned not only with teaching women to read, and the fundamentals of Marx, but also with basic scientific education. A popular science section including articles such as "Charles Darwin" and "Where Did Man Come From?" was designed to wean women away from superstitious and religious interpretations of natural phenomena.

Communists were especially concerned that wives of trade unionists be made sympathetic and active supporters of their husbands in struggle, for "women can determine the fate of a strike, make, or mar men's morale."[20] While the party recognized the essential role that women played in labour struggles, it also projected a simplified view of working-class women that placed women at polar ends of the political spectrum. Women were supposedly suspicious of social change and socialism, but when their revolutionary consciousness was raised they became militant fighters, even more militant than men. "Will women speed the liberation of society or be the bulwark of reaction?" was the classic question asked by the Communist press.[21] As Dorothy Smith notes, "working-class women are portrayed either as 'backward' or as salt of the earth heroic figures; both are polar positions along a single dimension."[22]

How do we explain this extremely prevalent view of women's "innate" conservatism? It is possible, first, that women's apathy or cynicism was interpreted as conservatism or, second, that this view of women as "backward" was simply the product of strong male prejudices that female party leaders, such as Becky Buhay, were not hesitant to criticize. Ukrainians, she once charged, "have the old peasant attitudes on this question [of women]. . . . They say a woman talks too much and can't be trusted. . . . In Lethbridge . . . they even suspended a woman from the meetings."[23]

At the same time, it is possible that women were less interested in politics because of the material realities of their lives and the powerful ideological message that women "belonged in the home." If Ukrainian women lacked the opportunity to learn how to read, if Jewish women were shut out of union drives, if Finnish and English women were pressed to finish their domestic work in the home — by definition a never-ending job — then it is hardly surprising that they had little time for the party.

Despite fears of female conservatism, women, it was believed, *could* be radicalized. Housewives were reminded of the limited material conditions of their lives, the drudgery of endless domestic labour, the meagre wages of their husbands, and the limited opportunities facing their children. In a short story published in *The Worker,* two working-class housewives talk over the fence about the effects of war and unemployment on their homes. The narrator's husband, a veteran, is unemployed: the "British Vampire," his wife explains, "took his best and left him no will to fight."[24] The story's final message is clear: the role of a housewife was to bind her husband and family together despite and against an unjust, exploitative capitalist society. Stories and poems, some of which were made into plays, were also found in *Robitnysia,* depicting arguments to drive home the realities of class and the need for homemakers to join in the fight against injustice. In one story a housewife demonstrates to her husband that his unwillingness to let her join a women's organization plays into the hands of the bosses; other stories portrayed the suffering of mothers who could not feed their children, whose sons were exhausted by work, or whose daughters had to resort to prostitution to make ends meet.

Communists assumed that women in the home did understand in a personal way the consequences of unemployment, low wages, and rising prices. Thus, the task of the party was to "make the personal, political," and to this end, homemakers were frequently appealed to on consumer and peace issues. The Communist press reflected the prevailing notion that men were the breadwinners, while women supervised the family budget; rising consumer prices were therefore seized on as a potentially radical issue for homemakers. Similarly, articles on peace, which had a high profile in *The Woman Worker,* tried to personalize international issues by appealing to women on the basis of their maternal instincts. The peace appeal also attempted to expose war as a consequence of capitalist economics and imperialist expansion, but the materialist theme was intertwined with the maternal one. Not only will you lose your sons, these articles pointed out, but you will lose them in a war that will bring you hunger and capitalists greater profits.

While *The Woman Worker* urged its readers to reject the liberal pacifism represented by the United Nations Organization and the Women's International League for Peace and Freedom (WIL), it shared the WIL's emphasis on maternalism, though shaping it into a class-conscious mould. Associated with the antiwar cause was the campaign to remove military training from the schools, thereby eliminating the capitalist and militarist indoctrination of working-class youth. In keeping with United Front tactics, the WLLs tried to link forces with other reformers on this issue, and Custance attempted herself to run for the Toronto School Board, including "no cadet training" in her platform.[25]

As well as appealing to working-class women on issues of bread and peace, the party encouraged women's active support for the labour struggles of their men folk. Though women sometimes played a crucial role in strikes, it was difficult to sustain their involvement in ongoing political organizations, so *The Worker* and *The Woman Worker* used their columns to publicize numerous examples of wives' militancy, and to encourage their further political action. During a cross-country tour for *The Worker,* Becky Buhay found herself in the midst of a coal miners' strike in Alberta. She helped the wives organize a support group that clashed more than once with police. After the most violent exchange on the picket line, eighteen women were injured, one suffered a miscarriage, and many were jailed and sentenced on charges of rioting. *The Worker* followed their cases, which Buhay used as inspiring evidence that women, when aroused, could be excellent revolutionary fighters: "The women's defiant attitude was the greatest surprise to the authorities who expected tears, supplications and general weakness, but they discovered before long that women were made of sterner stuff."[26]

The Family and Reproductive Rights

Although economic issues, especially the family wage and the workplace, were central to the Communist Party's approach to work among women, it did not totally ignore reproductive issues or women's subordination in the family. Some party leaders, but particularly Custance, were aware of the important writings of Bolshevik Alexandra Kollontai on love, marriage, and the family, though Kollontai's ideas were probably reinterpreted or dismissed by the end of the decade, as she fell out of favour in Russia. In their discussion of women's role in the family, Canadian Communists wrestled with lingering patriarchal traditions and new revolutionary ideas. Working-class women were idealized and commended for their selfless devotion to home and motherhood, but Communists also criticized a society that tied women to "household drudgery" and argued that to be truly free, women had to be relieved of the degrading labour of "providing services to others, . . . living by the sufferance of one's husband."[27] "Complete freedom is impossible as long as men are the privileged sex," continued another article on this topic, and women were advised to "break through their bonds of timidity and through self assertion help to achieve their own emancipation."[28]

Canadian Communists were certainly sympathetic to Leninist conclusions about the need to liberate women from domestic toil, but it was never clear *how* that would happen. As late as 1925, after most Russian communal kitchens had closed, they were referred to positively in the Canadian Communist press. By the end of the decade, however, they were largely forgotten; the socialization of domestic labour never became a major point of discussion for the party.

The CPC also wrestled with the issues of birth control and abortion. A call for mothers' clinics, which were to dispense birth control, was part of the first WLL platform, though Communists always carefully placed the demand for birth control within a class analysis, rejecting neo-Malthusian justifications for control of working-class births. Poverty, Florence Custance reminded her readers in *The Woman Worker,* was not due to the size of the population but to the distribution of wealth, and fewer births would not solve the poverty problem.[29] The party's approach to reproductive issues was also influenced by the example of the USSR, which had legalized abortion and birth control to provide immediate economic and physiological relief for working-class women. Like the Soviets, the CPC stressed the health benefits to working-class wives, rather than presenting birth control as the inalienable right of every woman, though the latter view may have been held by some Communist women. Statistics showing maternal ill health and a high incidence of maternal and infant mortality, for example, were often used to buttress the WLL's arguments for mothers' clinics. Emma Goldman's more radical libertarian perspective on birth control was resolutely rejected; in 1927, her Canadian speeches on birth control were ignored by the Communist press. Rather, the party promoted its own class analysis, which stressed the right of the working-class family to make their own decisions about family size, and working-class wives' need for relief from the physical burdens of constant child bearing.

While quite different from the contemporary feminist rationale for reproductive control, the Communist Party's support for mothers' clinics was still a small crack in the wall of silence existing in Canadian society in the 1920s. Unlike the United States, Canada had not yet produced a birth control movement of any substance, and given the persisting medical, clerical, and legal opposition to birth control, the subject was largely taboo. Despite the illegality of disseminating birth control information, women were eager, even desperate, to obtain this information, and abortion was sometimes attempted as the last resort in fertility control. Pressure from rank-and-file women was clearly one impetus to the party's discussion of the subject. Immediately after an article on birth control appeared in *The Worker,* an Alberta comrade responded by insisting that birth control was "an essential information for working-class women in the here and now... an indispensable psychological aid to working-class marriage," and he urged the party to devote more space to the subject.[30]

In the columns of *The Woman Worker* the issue was even more hotly debated, and Custance noted that concern with birth control was a major drawing card for women's interest in the WLLs.

Rank-and-file letters to *The Woman Worker* indicated the wide parameters the birth control debate assumed. In its first issue *The Woman Worker* reprinted a speech given to a Vancouver WLL, which took the radical line "that every woman should have the right to decide when to have children."[31] The subsequent responses of readers, however, revealed the persistence of more conservative eugenicist ideas within the WLLs, paralleling their strength in the wider society. One Toronto member challenged religious objections to birth control but then went on to argue for a "scientific view," saying "we can no longer breed numerically without thinking about intelligence and quality of offspring."[32] The most extreme eugenicist wrote in, warning that forcing women into child bearing might "breed race degeneracy." The writer drew proof for her contention from the "fact" that the "priest-ridden Poles, Slavs and Italians have weak and sickly children."[33] Although these views were printed in *The Woman Worker,* editorials tended to downplay eugenics, and they completely rejected any hint of neo-Malthusian support for birth control.

In terms of political action, some local WLLs pressed city government for mothers' clinics and lobbied the Canadian Labour Party to place birth control in its platform. While the Labor Leagues were successful in making mothers' clinics part of the CLP policy, they were less successful in gaining wider public attention or government sympathy. Toronto League members described being literally "laughed at" by local government officials during one lobbying attempt; the issue, tersely commented a WLLer, "is not supported by the Establishment."[34] But even within the party, there was some hesitancy to embrace the birth control cause. *Robitnysia* simply avoided the issue, and after the establishment of *The Woman Worker,* so, too, did *The Worker.* Though *The Worker* editors may have felt that birth control was a "woman's issue," this meant that there was little wider party discussion and recognition of the seriousness of WLL demands for mothers' clinics.

The issue of abortion was also dealt with by the party, though in a secondary, quiet manner. Abortion, too, was analyzed from a materialist perspective that stressed the immediate needs and social reality of working-class women. Readers were sometimes reminded of new access to abortion in the Soviet Union, and similar liberalization was recommended for Canada. But abortion was described as an unpleasant and unfortunate practice, resorted to only in capitalist societies or a Communist society in transition. The author of a rare article on abortion maintained that "we are for less and less abortions; they could be reduced to a minimum with birth control information made available."[35] Still, the writer continued, the laws should be reformed, for they were routinely disobeyed by doctors and women, to the danger of women's health and life. Although different in content from later feminist arguments stressing women's right to choose, the CPC's occasional calls for liberalization were very radical in a time when church, state, and the medical profession would barely countenance discussion of the topic. This intense opposition, along with the party's own ambivalence, may be the reason that the year 1927 saw the last major discussion of abortion in the CPC press for many years.

International Mentors and Local Opponents

Articles in the Communist press dealing with abortion, birth control, and women's role in the family often drew dramatic comparisons between the oppression of Canadian women and the constantly improving lives of Russian women. While the Communist press primarily pointed to women's equal political status and economic independence in the USSR, attention was also given to women's new sexual autonomy and the emergence of an egalitarian family life. Marriage laws, "no longer made only to benefit men," and the accessibility of divorce were destroying the patriarchal family, the press claimed. With the disappearance of sexual inequalities, the double standard, and economic dependence, Russian women were said to "feel like they are real human beings . . . equal to male workers."[36] Reports of Soviet life were especially vocal about the new Russian motherhood: "with the availability of birth control, aid to pregnant women and modern creches, we have abolished women's subordination," declared one optimistic author.[37]

It is difficult to assess how thoroughly these optimistic views of Soviet life were assimilated by Communist women. Certainly, leaders like Becky Buhay displayed an intense admiration for Soviet life, even in private letters written during her visits to the USSR.[38] Surely, however, romantic pronouncements on the USSR also served to obscure the complexity of women's oppression and the extent to which it was embedded in both Russian and Canadian society. Of course, one-dimensional *Worker* articles may not have reflected Communists' private experience of altered sex roles and the family.

Within the party, new forms of relationships and family arrangements were accepted, although only to a limited extent. In the prewar socialist movement, Finnish women had turned a critical eye to marriage, and Finnish Communists were known to opt for common-law liaisons rather than legal marriages. They made a political point of rejecting church-sanctioned relationships: "we didn't believe in that religious hocus pocus," remembers one Finnish comrade; "when we were married our friends gave us a party. . . or you might put an ad in the paper with our friends' greetings and congratulations."[39] As a result of such experimentation, some members must have experienced the difficulties of living out female "independence" in a sexist society. The rejection of traditional relationships potentially had a tragic side: dominant social norms in the 1920s still saw such relationships as immoral, and in their defiance of these norms women could be hurt.[40] Moreover, not all ethnic groups in the movement shared a positive view of sexual experimentation. The Ukrainian press had little sympathy for alternative relationships: the women's paper made it quite clear that one rationale for women's self-organization was the creation of "a new morality" to "root out habits of darkness . . . [including] promiscuity."[41]

Overall, information on women in the USSR still had a substantial impact on Communist Party members, creating feelings of international solidarity and party loyalty. Building on a long-established tradition of internationalism within the socialist movement, the CPC helped to galvanize anger about women's exploitation abroad, draw lessons about women's opposition to capitalism, and create hope and support for Communist movements of resistance. The struggles of Communist women in the Third World, the United States, and Europe figured highly in the press: stories of American textile workers battling southern police or of impoverished Chinese workers became rallying points for Communist loyalty, forging a definition of the movement as just, militant, and destined to victory.

In Canada, International Women's Day was used to enhance international solidarity and to publicize the struggles of Canadian women. In the 1920s this day became a major event, celebrated in public meetings that were themselves international in character, encompassing one, two, or three language groups. From small towns like Blairmore, Alberta, to urban centres like Toronto, Finnish, Ukrainian, Jewish, and English women's groups created International Women's Day events that combined rousing political speeches, solidarity greetings, and musical entertainment. In Sudbury, reported one account, the "lady comrades worked ceaselessly on an inspirational program in English, Ukrainian and Finnish." The evening festival began with a march to the stage by the women comrades, showing "how women in a united mass step forward to demand their rights." Then the women sang "that ravishing workers song, the Internationale, in different languages," and there followed a program including Ukrainian mandolin orchestras, choirs, solos, Finnish poetry readings, and speeches given in each language, detailing the rise of women in Russia and the women's movement in Canada.[42] These meetings often publicized a list of women's demands coincident with the party program, stressing the organization of women workers and the need for mothers' clinics and better minimum wage laws.

The tasks of Communist women were not only set out in the framework of an international struggle but were counterposed to the unacceptable political aims of Canadian middle-class feminists. By the 1920s, the resolution of the suffrage issue had dispersed much of the prewar feminist movement, but such women's religious and reform organizations as the YWCA and the National Council of Women [NCW] were still active. The Communist leadership feared the influence of these groups on working-class women, who, they believed, might be easily patronized and swayed by their social "betters" and thus have their attention deflected from class issues. Rank-and-file Communists shared these worries. Finnish WLLer Mary North complained to *The Woman Worker* that working-class women in her Alberta mining town too naively accepted the opinions expressed in bourgeois women's magazines, which pandered to women with articles on fashion and movie actresses, while Glace Bay activist Annie Whitfield bemoaned the local church's influence on working-class women. *Robitnysia*, in particular, addressed what it believed to be the dangerous religiosity of working-class women. These fears were grounded, in part, on realistic observations of women's participation in nonpolitical groups and on the numbing influence of antisocialist and antifeminist popular magazines and movies in the 1920s. At the same time, many of the warnings about women's participation in middle-class culture again embraced the old adage that women's natural deference made them easy prey to counter-revolutionary influences.

To counter the danger posed by middle-class organizations, the Communist press tried to expose the misguided, bourgeois views of women's reform groups. In 1927, The Woman Worker ridiculed the NCW's efforts to have women senators appointed and denounced the NCW's attack on socialist Sunday schools and its resolution to "investigate communist education" in Canada.[43] In 1925, at a large Toronto meeting initiated by the WLL to discuss the "protection of womanhood," Florence Custance laid out the WLL's case for the unionization of women workers. The Worker contrasted Custance's comments with those of Mrs. Huestis, a former suffragist, who claimed that prostitutes made an "immoral" choice of occupation, having already "succumbed to the lure of commercialized entertainment and pretty clothes." It was clear, retorted The Worker, that middle-class women were interested in moral reform and "protection for the feeble-minded," but they did not understand that for working girls the real issues were good wages and unionization.[44] There was little to quibble with in The Worker's characterization of the paternalistic attitudes of reformers like Mrs. Huestis, but its biting comments didn't solve the CPC's basic problem of many women joining nonpolitical or moderate reform organizations rather than the WLL.

Hence, following the party's United Front strategy of limited, but critical, participation in non-Communist groups, the Women's Department occasionally included news items on women's reform groups in The Woman Worker and, most importantly, tried to maintain contacts with women in labourite, farm, and peace organizations in the hopes of drawing them into the Communist movement. The Women's Labor Leagues, for instance, were interested in linking up with women's farm organizations, although they were hesitant to support farm women already allied to local Councils of Women. The National Council of Women, The Woman Worker tried to convince Saskatchewan women in the United Farmers of

Canada, was "well-intentioned" but was basically anti-labour and patronizing to working girls.[45] The *Woman Worker* did print a reply from the farm women, which argued that the Local Council was its "only contact with urban women" and assuring *The Woman Worker* that farm women still had "independence of action."[46] But Custance made sure that she had the last word, once again counselling the dangers of alliances with privileged middle-class feminists unaware of the daily realities of exploitation suffered by farm and working women.

The Women's Labor Leagues

As the WLLs were slowly influenced by the Comintern Congress of 1928, their opposition to women's reform groups sharpened. Until 1930, however, and the immersion of the Labor Leagues in the Workers Unity League, the WLLs comprised a unique experiment in Canadian Communist history. Although generally controlled by the party, they constituted an organization separate in name and identity from the CPC, with a membership that went beyond party members and a structure that allowed a degree of local autonomy. When the Federation of WLLs was founded in 1924 it was far from assured that the leagues would prosper. Custance's task was not an easy one: she depended on local party officials for organizational aid, and few district functionaries had the time or inclination to organize Women's Labor Leagues. In 1924, Custance later noted, there was pessimistic speculation about the WLLs' future, and for two years they made slow progress, gaining little support from "our men in the labour movement."[47] The leagues' failure to gain affiliation to the TLC probably made them even less important in the eyes of many Communist labour leaders.

Despite this apathy and pessimism, the WLLs expanded from ten to thirty-seven in 1927 and, according to the *The Woman Worker,* to sixty in 1929. This expansion can be attributed in large part to Custance's organizational skills and hard work, and also to the existence of a stimulating and provocative women's newspaper, for, as Custance noted, *The Woman Worker* sustained and extended the Labor Leagues with its wide selection of fiction, educational material, and the inspirational reports from sister leagues. The highly ethnic character of the Communist movement also pointed to the essential role that the CPC's sibling associations, the Finnish Organization of Canada and the Jewish Labor League, played in encouraging WLL activity. As Mary North pointed out, *The Woman Worker* was sold and read concurrently with the Finnish-American equivalent, *Toveritar (Woman Comrade)*. The Finnish leagues, influential because of their sheer numbers, drew on strong traditions of women's self-organization rooted in the prewar socialist movement. During the 1920s they also had their own organizer, Sanna Kannasto, a socialist orator and writer from the Lakehead area, who had worked as an organizer for the Socialist Party of Canada and Social Democratic Party of Canada. Kannasto, "a small bit of a woman, with piercing eyes" and a "fiery" orator's tongue, was even viewed with some trepidation by the local WLLers, who saw her militant style as a marked contrast to that of many women, especially the "cool, undemonstrative Finns." Kannasto did education work for the FOC, even taking in promising young female comrades for intensive study. One such student spent two weeks at Kannasto's farm, trying to learn public speaking and socialist theory: "A lot of the Theory," she later quipped, "went right over my head."[48]

The Finnish leagues critiqued their own failure to break out of their ethnic enclaves, though overall the Finnish and Jewish leagues had closer contact with the Women's Department than did Ukrainian women, who were primarily tied to ULFTA. Before World War I, few Ukrainian women were full-fledged members of the Ukrainian Social Democratic Party. The Russian Revolution and the founding of ULFTA, however, stimulated new interest in women's organization, and out of Ukrainian Women's Committees to Aid Famine Victims in the Soviet Russia grew the first locals of the "Workingwomen's Section of the Labour-Farmer Temple." By 1923, there were fourteen such women's locals, and the following year *Robitnysia* was launched. This women's paper was edited by male leadership from the ULFTA, who naturally set the political agenda and provided the ideological framework for the discussion of the woman question. Indeed, when it was first established, there were frequent reader complaints that some *Robitnysia* articles were simply reprints from the *Ukrainian Labor News*. *Robitnysia's* own editors, in turn, muttered that they were expending too many columns teaching uneducated women the most basic questions about how to build a women's organization. Despite evidence of paternalistic control, the paper began to gradually provide an outlet for women anxious to express their political views, often for the first time.

All these varieties of Women's Labor Leagues consisted largely of housewives and were firmly structured around language groups. When directives came from the Comintern in the mid-1920s to "Bolshevize" the party, that is, establish membership around factory rather than language groups, they had little impact on the WLLs. Becky Buhay noted that CPC work among women should be conducted in "purely proletarian circumstances," perhaps a critical reference to the WLLs' failure to change their language orientation.[49] It was a failure that could only reinforce the CPC leadership's lack of interest in the WLLs.

Yet the WLLs did serve a necessary purpose: based on a socially acceptable auxiliary model, they answered the needs of women who were less proficient than male party members in English, who were not eligible for trade union membership or welcomed as party cell members. Most Labor Leagues divided their time between self-education and fundraising. They held euchres and bazaars, sponsored May Day dances and anniversary festivals for the Russian Revolution, donating their proceeds to local Communist causes or to organizations like the Canadian Labor Defence League (CLDL), which looked after the legal defence of radical trade unionists and Communists. In fact, the WLLs were encouraged by the CPC to affiliate to the CLDL, perhaps because the CLDL was eager to use the WLLs' proven fundraising talents. The Saskatoon Ukrainian women's local, named after Alexandra Kollontai, spent a major portion of its time on basketball events, dances, and raffles, raising as much as $1,000 a year, a substantial sum in the 1920s.[50]

Also in the auxiliary tradition, the Women's Labor Leagues initiated summer camps, usually organized along language lines, for Communist youth. Women's involvement in this work was partly the consequence of housewives' flexible work schedule during the summer, but it was also linked to the strong identification of women with the maternal task of socializing the youth for the future. "We are growing older," *Robitnysia* reminded its readers, and we "must replace today's comrades . . . and where will they come from, if we do not raise them ourselves?"[51] This identification of women with maternal roles did circumscribe women's role in politics, just as the earlier maternal feminism had limited the parameters of women's political participation. Nonetheless, youth education was important: the party needed to augment its ranks, and youth camps helped to counter values taught in the public schools with an alternate ideology that could sustain the loyalty of party children, perhaps even draw in new recruits.

Internally, league activities were directed towards their members' own education: the women spent time reading books, discussing current events, and improving their understanding of socialism. In northern Ontario a travelling library of radical books was circulated among towns, while the Ladysmith branch of the women's section of the FOC attempted to initiate its own in-house, handwritten newspaper, *Kipinä (Sparks)*. Though the editors sometimes had trouble gathering articles, the women could look on their dilemma with humour; at the next meeting, they once reported, "the *Kipinä* paper will be read even if it does not have one article in it."[52] The Ladysmith branch also sponsored internal discussions on a wide range of topics. As members carefully sewed crafts to sell at fundraising events, they debated: "Does woman belong at home or in politics?" or, more revealing, "Does the marriage law secure women their livelihood or oppress them as slaves?" In both cases, apparently, the women affirmed the latter proposition.[53] Some leagues rotated their officers every three months so that all members could gain leadership experience; others offered oratory lessons to develop the skills of women reluctant to speak in public. By meeting weekly to discuss books, commented one member, "we have been able to develop our own understanding and skills: we are no longer asking our men how we should think."[54] For women living in families where men's activities and opinions were considered of primary importance, this self-confidence was an achievement.

Although party officials sometimes commended WLL work, they more frequently lamented the leagues' failure to recruit wage-earning and English-speaking women. At the same time, they were at a loss as to how to change the WLLs, especially when women's work was not high on their priority list. Party leader Jack McDonald claimed that "for two years, the Central Executive Committee never devoted one meeting to discussion of work among women. The Central Committee gave absolutely no attention to women's work."[55] Ironically, the large proportion of housewives in the leagues, which so concerned the CPC leadership, contradicted their stereotype of "housewife conservatism." Interestingly, although *The Woman Worker* did echo the fear that housewives were "backward," it also contained alternative opinions voiced by rank-and-file WLLers. One correspondent pointed out that women's educational opportunities —"their opportunities to learn the truth — were fewer, and that working-class men, too, were conservative, due to the influence of the press, school, and church."[56]

A similar response came from some Ukrainian women in reaction to the "porcupinism" debate that raged in the pages of *Robitnysia* in the late 1920s. The term "porcupinism" was taken from the name of an author, Tymko Izhak, who penned a fierce diatribe in the paper against women's organizations, claiming that women, who were weak, un-intellectual, and unproductive in the economy, should simply concentrate on being "man's helper."[57] Porcupinism, an apt synonym for male chauvinism, was actually endorsed by many letters from self-confessed porcupines, which the editors chose not to print, indicating how entrenched stereotypes of female backwardness were in some sections of the party. The article, however, was likely composed deliberately to provoke women's opposition, and it did just that. Women readers responded in anger to Izhak's accusations. One group of letters accepted the label of female backwardness, but then tried to turn it to advantage, to argue for women's release from their isolated, domestic imprisonment. It was precisely because women were so behind ideologically, they said, that they needed to become active in their own organization and thus "develop confidence and enlighten themselves." "To be in the same organization as men," wrote another, "would be again to subordinate our thoughts and wishes to men."[58] Women readers were even more critical of Izhak's claim that women's work was unproductive. They provided long lists of women's crucial labour to the family; "at the end of the day," concluded one miner's wife, "you, my husband have worked your shift and for this you have your pay, but you, woman, where is your pay?"[59]

These Ukrainian women, like the WLL correspondents, were attempting to express their female experience of the world within a class perspective. Although *Robitnysia* and *The Woman Worker* never deviated from an overall emphasis on class struggle, they did provide a forum for the voices of working-class women who felt they were accorded an inferior status, treated "like toys or slaves" by their men folk.[60] Some even implied that women were the scapegoats for class and patriarchal relations: "women are forced into an authority relationship with husbands who have grown to think they are the bosses in the home, and boss wives, as bosses boss them."[61] Florence Custance offered some sympathy for women suffering within marriage, but she immediately counselled them not to misdirect their anger against men. In the long term, she tried to show, "there are no easy cures for sexual inequality in marriage . . . we must see the basic causes of inequality . . . [capitalism] . . . . Thus, if women want more than a truce, if they want true freedom, the struggle against capitalism must take precedence."[62]

Social issues like prostitution and alcoholism were also presented within a class analysis, yet with some reference to the immediate suffering of women. Very occasionally, writers in *The Woman Worker* would refer to the white slave trade as "an outlet for male licentiousness."[63] More often, though, editorials attributed prostitution to poverty and low wages. Similarly, alcoholism was often portrayed as a consequence of the alienating capitalist work world, although its tragic effects on working-class households, and especially on women, were noted. In *Robitnysia*, some references were even made to wife battering, a phenomenon middle-class reformers had usually linked to alcoholism but the left-wing press rarely mentioned. There was not complete consistency in readers' assessments of such issues as alcoholism; but overall, such "moral" issues never assumed the focal position in the WLLs that they had taken in the prewar women's movement.

Although the Women's Labor Leagues generally followed the views of the CPC on social and economic issues, they did develop a small measure of autonomy, just as recommendations of the International Women's Secretariat were modified to fit Canadian conditions. In the coal-mining districts of the Crowsnest Pass, WLLs existed in close alliance with the Communist-dominated Mine Workers Union of Canada (MWUC). Wives and daughters of miners made up the bulk of Labor League membership, for, as Mary North pointed out, "naturally . . . we are housewives for jobs here are only in mining and are hardly even accessible to the man."[64] The Crowsnest leagues concentrated on building an auxiliary to the MWUC and, for a while, on raising money for the Labour Party of Alberta. Their numerous social and fundraising endeavours cited in *The Woman Worker* had political as well as financial importance, for union picnics and May Day dances were crucial stimulants to Communist solidarity; the atmosphere created by the women provided a social glue that helped to cement and sustain political allegiances.

In the northern Ontario WLLs, members were often the wives of primary resource workers or single domestics drawn in by the Finnish connection. As in the Crowsnest Pass, birth control was not an important public issue, indicating that *The Woman Worker*'s vocal stance on birth control did not reflect the views of all the WLLs. "Our members," recalled one woman from the Lakehead, "were extremely embarrassed when Sanna Kannasto insisted on talking about sexuality and birth control to the Finnish women's meetings."[65] The BC Finnish leagues also pursued activities linked to their ethnic identification; in Vancouver, they organized Finnish domestics, while in Sointula, once a Finnish utopian socialist community, they helped run the local co-operative store. Isolated by the Rockies, the BC WLLs held regional conventions, passing resolutions that were then pressed on the local Labour Party or on civic and provincial governments. Particular local and ethnic concerns were evidenced by calls for legislation permitting civil marriage, a reflection of the anti-church views of the Finnish leagues.

Alberta and northern Ontario WLLs sometimes sponsored regional conventions as well, but this practice was often forgone by the larger urban leagues of Toronto and Montreal, with their higher membership numbers and easier access to the party's organizational machinery. In Toronto, the WLLs had a major hand in editing *The Woman Worker* and, during Custance's illness in 1928–29, kept the magazine going. The Toronto leagues were active in union support work but lacked the single-union emphasis of an area like the Crowsnest Pass; they helped with a boycott campaign during a bakers' strike, as well as a YCL effort to organize York Knitting Mills. In keeping with its urban setting, the Toronto WLLs, like those in Montreal and Regina, spent a large amount of time on the minimum wage campaign, and in Toronto they lobbied for mothers' clinics. Urban leagues also had greater opportunities to join with other Communist organizations, co-sponsoring rallies and demonstrations, such as the large defence meeting the Montreal WLL held for Sacco and Vanzetti.

The measure of local autonomy enjoyed by the WLLs was in part a consequence of the Women's Department's flexibility and concern for local conditions. But it was also the result of party indifference and default. Communication problems arising from language differences, geography, and party disorganization were all factors creating the diversity of the league experience. After the 1929 CPC convention, questionnaires were sent out to the Labor Leagues to ascertain their membership and activities; the central office apparently had scanty records of the WLL network. This was partly a result of disarray in the wake of Custance's unexpected death, as Custance had been compelled to run a "one woman department."[66] In the final analysis, though, it was also a reflection of the peripheral status of the woman question within the party.

Conclusion

Within the Communist agenda, the woman question remained a secondary priority; nevertheless, its significance had increased since the time of the prewar left. The CPC's new initiatives in work among women were primarily inspired by the example of Soviet Russia and directives from the Comintern. To Canadian Communists, the impressive transformation of women's status in Russia implied both the value of the USSR's strategic suggestions and, if imitated, the possibility of similar successes. The party attempted to build a Marxist and Leninist women's movement that was firmly rooted in the same political goals as the revolutionary movement, stressing economic issues and the primacy of class-based political action. The Women's Department focused its agitational efforts at the unique exploitation of women under capitalism, and while some party goals, such as the unionization of women, were never fulfilled, other initiatives, like the minimum wage campaign, were more successful in exposing women's inequality under capitalism. By the end of the decade, the party had grown, though women still constituted a small minority of the membership, and the WLL members tended to be party wives, not the desired newcomers from the factories.

Although economic issues formed the core of the Communist program, birth control and family life were not ignored, partly because of the impact of Soviet reforms, but also because of the keen interest of

Canadian women in reproductive control and sexual autonomy. In lobbying for mothers' clinics or in doing their auxiliary work, the WLLs were involved in the socialist movement at a different level, and sometimes with a different rationale, than male members. WLLs provided women with a separate space to build their confidence and explore socialist issues from a woman's perspective. Their auxiliary work gave important support and sustenance to the movement; unfortunately, it also kept women in a sex-stereotyped domestic role that isolated them from power and perpetuated women's secondary status in the party. With the notable exception of Florence Custance, and later Becky Buhay and Annie Buller, women were not represented in the Communist Party's seats of power. In fact, if only one family member could buy a party card, it was to the "head of the household." As one comrade remembers, "Woman's place was in the home. It's all right to organize women, men would say, but not my wife! So, when it came to going to a meeting, the men would go. It was more important. The men were the 'brains.' The women were in the kitchen. But they still supported so many causes."[67]

At the same time, domesticity was used as a radicalizing tool: demands for bread and peace were rallying cries used to mobilize women in their socially accepted roles as wives and mothers. Because Communists largely adopted the ideal of a family wage, women's political consciousness was interpreted in the context of their domestic activities. Women's domesticity, of course, was a double-edged sword. It might lead women to radical politics; but it was also perceived as the cause of their conservatism. Though it is true that women were less likely to join the party, their "reactionary" mentality did not keep them tied to the kitchen, as the "porcupines" claimed. Women's leap into sustained political activity was precluded by illiteracy, material impoverishment, family responsibilities, the unwelcoming attitudes of male party members, and the same anti-socialist pressures that kept working-class men from joining the party. Moreover, women may have been radicalized on issues like birth control, while men were drawn in by trade union concerns. However, the party's peripheral interest in such women's issues as reproductive control — a direct consequence of the CPC's brand of Marxist-Leninism, as well as persisting patriarchal prejudices — inevitably gave men's issues the weight of prestige and importance within the party.

Although woman's role in the family was seen as crucial to her political understanding, it was not analyzed as critically as her role in production, nor was it judged to be central to her oppression. While the problems of working-class housewives were sympathetically explored, in the final analysis, women's maternal role was accepted, even sentimentalized. *The Woman Worker* did not embrace a dogmatic economism that rejected *all* issues of women's sexual subordination; but the solution to sexual oppression was always seen in class terms. This emphasis on the necessity of revolutionary working-class solidarity would soon become of paramount importance to the organization of women during the next period of the CPC's evolution.

Notes

1 Richard Stites, *The Women's Liberation Movement in Russia* (Princeton, 1978), 344. On the transformation of woman's status in Russia, see also Dorothy Atkinson, ed., *Women in Russia* (Stanford, 1977); Gregory Massell, *The Surrogate Proletariat: Moslem Women and Revolutionary Strategies in Soviet Central Asia, 1919–1929* (Princeton, 1974); Barbara Clements, "Working-Class and Peasant Women in the Russian Revolution," *Signs* 8, no. 2 (Winter 1982); Alix Holt, "Marxism and Women's Oppression," in *Women in Eastern Europe and the Soviet Union*, ed. Tova Yedlin (New York, 1980).

2 On the prewar WLLs, see Carol Lee Bacchi, *Liberation Deferred?: The Ideas of the English-Canadian Suffragists* (Toronto, 1982), chap. 8; Linda Kealey, "No Special Protection, No Sympathy: Women's Activism in the Canadian Labour Revolt of 1919," unpublished paper, 1987.

3 *London Free Press*, 18 September 1924; Report of the Conference of Women's Labor Leagues, 17–18 September 1924, London. Ontario.

4 Although the WLLs were technically expelled because of a constitutional amendment, anticommunism was the most important force behind their expulsion. See the *Toronto Star*, 4 November 1927; *The Woman Worker*, December 1927.

5 Public Archives of Canada (PAC), Finnish Organization of Canada Collection, MG 28 V 46, vol. 141, "Program and Constitution of the Canadian Federation of Women's Labor Leagues."

6 *The Worker*, 1 May 1922.

7 Ibid., 13 June 1925.

8 *The Woman Worker*, July 1926.

9 Taime Davis, interview with Joan Sangster and Karen Teeple, 14 July 1982.

10 Lil Himmelfarb, interview with Joan Sangster and Karen Teeple, 30 January 1983.

11 Sue Bruley, "Women in the Communist Party of Great Britain, 1921–1939" (Ph.D. diss., University of London, 1980).

12 University of Toronto Rare Books Room (hereafter U of T), Kenny Collection, Box 3, "Our Tasks Among Women," Central Executive Committee Report, Fifth Convention, 1925, 64.

13 *Imprecorr*, 4, 71 (6 October 1924); ibid., 6, 69 (26 October 1926).

14 U of T, Kenny Collection, "Our Tasks Among Women," 63.

15 Reprinted in *The Worker*, 15 November 1925.

16 U of T, Kenny Collection, "Our Tasks Among Women," 64.

17 *The People's Cause*, 26 April 1925. On the Willard Chocolate case, see Margaret McCallum, "Keeping Women in Their Place: The Minimum Wage in Canada, 1910–1925," *Labour/Le Travail* 17 (Spring 1986): 29–56.

18 *Vapaus*, 22 November 1933. *Vapaus* charged that a "heavenly agent [i.e., a Lutheran minister] was hovering about unemployed maids," taking advantage of their economic desperation by acting as an employment agent but finding them low-paid jobs.

19 U of T, Kenny Collection, "Our Tasks Among Women," 64.

20 PAC, FOC Collection, "Program and Constitution of the Canadian Federation of Women's Labor Leagues."

21 *The Worker*, 1 May 1922.

22 Dorothy Smith, *Feminism and Marxism* (Vancouver, 1974), 4.

23 Becky Buhay and unknown party member, quoted in Donald Avery, *Dangerous Foreigners* (Toronto, 1979), 127.

24 *The Worker*, 1 May 1922.

25 Custance was prevented from running because she could not fulfill the property qualification.

26 *The Worker*, 1 February 1923. See also M. Ann Capling, "The Communist Party of Canada in Alberta, 1922–29." (MA thesis, University of Calgary, 1983), chap. 2.

27 *The Worker*, 7 November 1925.

28 Ibid., 21 March 1925.

29 On the Left and birth control, see Angus McLaren, "What Has This to Do with Working-Class Women? Birth Control and the Canadian Left, 1900–1939," *Social*

History/Histoire sociale 14 (November 1981): 435–54. See also Angus McLaren and Arlene Tigar McLaren, *The Bedroom and the State: The Changing Practices and Politics of Contraception and Abortion in Canada* (Toronto, 1987).

30 *The Worker,* 20 June 1925.

31 *The Woman Worker,* July 1926.

32 Ibid., September 1927. The rationale that fewer births would produce "better children" remained popular in the interwar period among feminist and medical proponents of birth control. See Linda Gordon, *Woman's Body, Woman's Right: A Social History of Birth Control in America* (New York, 1974), chap. 10.

33 *The Woman Worker,* December 1927.

34 Ibid., April 1928.

35 *The Worker,* 4 June 1927.

36 Ibid., 2 May 1925 and 2 November 1924.

37 Ibid., 21 March 1925.

38 Buhay's letters were written during and after trips to Russia in the early 1930s and in the 1950s. See ibid., 30 August and 6 September 1930, for a description of Buhay's first trip to the Soviet Union, and U of T, Kenny Collection, Box 41, for letters written during her stay in the 1950s.

39 Interview with Taime Davis. On prewar Finnish socialist women and marriage, see Varpu Lindström-Best and Allen Seager, "*Toveritar* and the Finnish Canadian Women's Movement, 1900–1930," unpublished paper, 1985, 9.

40 For example, see references to Communists' personal lives in Lita-Rose Betcherman, *The Little Band* (Ottawa, 1982): chap. 11. Allen Seager, "Finnish Canadians and the Ontario Miners Movement," *Polyphony* 3, no. 2 (Fall 1981): 35–45, also points out how unmarried women could be punished by people outside the Communist movement. After the Hollinger mine disaster of 1928, the company refused to compensate the Finnish widows because they had not been legally married.

41 *Robitnysia,* 15 December 1925.

42 *Vapaus,* 9 March 1933.

43 *The Woman Worker,* April 1927.

44 *The Worker,* 18 July 1925.

45 *The Woman Worker,* October 1927.

46 Ibid., February 1928.

47 Ibid., October 1927.

48 Interview with Taime Davis.

49 *The Worker*, 22 August 1925.

50 *The Voice of the Workingwoman* (a precursor to *Robitnysia*), January/February 1922. $1,000 was donated to Soviet famine relief; $328 went to the ULFTA in Saskatoon.

51 *Robitnysia*, 1 April 1924.

52 PAC, FOC Collection, MG 28 V 46, vol. 4, file 11, Minutes of the Ladysmith's Finnish Women's Branch of the Communist Party of Canada, 17 December 1925.

53 Ibid., 19 February 1925 and 28 May 1925.

54 *The Woman Worker*, February 1927.

55 Public Archives of Ontario (PAO), Communist Party of Canada Collection, Report of the 6th National Convention, 31 May–7 June 1929.

56 *The Woman Worker*, September 1927.

57 *Robitnysia*, 1 April 1928.

58 Ibid., 15 May 1928.

59 Ibid., 1 June 1928.

60 *The Woman Worker*, March 1928.

61 Ibid.

62 Ibid., April 1928.

63 Ibid., December 1927.

64 Ibid., July 1927.

65 Interview with Taime Davis.

66 PAO, CPC Collection, Report from Sudbury District Executive Committee of the WLLS to Exective Committee of the Federation of WLLS, 5 February 1930.

67 Interview with Taime Davis.

MANUFACTURING CONSENT
IN PETERBOROUGH

The following three pieces emerged from research on Peterborough working women, and they may reflect the times in which they were written, in the sense that I had moved, by the mid- to late 1980s, from writing about the hope of socialist opposition to writing about the reality of criminalization and class incorporation. They did, in a peculiar way, reflect my feelings about life in Peterborough: it might be a city, but it had a small-town feel to it; it might have been considered a 'working-class town,' but it exhibited residual strains of paternalism and conservatism. This small-town sensibility was signified for me in some of my interviews with retired working women, who worried that any and all information spread quickly in a small city, and who expressed as strong a feeling of commonality with managers as with other workers, as the former were their neighbours, living "just down the street."

"The Softball Solution" grew out of my book on Peterborough, *Earning Respect: The Lives of Women in Small-town Ontario,* which was intended to be a case study but not a local study: using one city as my focus, I wanted to address broader debates in feminist history and sociology about the sexual division of labour, work culture, the unionization of women, and the interconnectedness of family and work relations. These topics may be seen now as more 'traditional' forms of labour history, in which the workplace, production, and unions take centre stage, and this is quite true. However, I would argue that there is still much to be written on these 'traditional' women's labour history topics in Canada, and that they remain of critical importance, even though we might approach them quite differently in 2010. At the time, I was influenced by British studies on the factory life and the work process by Miriam Glucksmann, by Susan Porter Benson's and Louise Lamphere's writing on work culture, by Ruth Milkman's discussion of different union regimes, and by feminist theorists still interested in developing a materialist feminist analysis[1] — the interviews, largely done in 1989, thus inevitably reflected these academic questions. Alice Kessler-Harris's suggestion that historians needed to conceptualize gender as a process rather than a structure — as E.P. Thompson had described class — also influenced my thinking. By integrating gender into our analysis of all aspects of working class life, including home, community, union, and work, she argued, we can better understand the process of class formation, including the fractured nature of class consciousness, and working-class accommodation to capitalism.[2]

Both "The Softball Solution" and "Pardon Tales" drew on a range of sources, but each article looked more intensely at one in particular, oral history in the case of "The Softball Solution," and the narratives proffered by women in court in "Pardon Tales." I don't think I would have been able to write "The Softball Solution" without those oral histories, and it was not only women's words, but the *feeling* they conveyed when I talked to them that mattered. What the women told me in the interviews was sometimes a surprise: I did not expect the women who had worked at Westclox to be so (apparently) supportive of its paternalist management style, or the male managers to be so forthcoming about how a moralistic paternalism was cultivated. Nor did I expect to find so many women I interviewed urging me to "seek out the ballplayers." Finding the unexpected in our research is often very productive, because it pushes us to rethink our initial assumptions, and sometimes shifts the focus of our inquiry: in the case of Westclox, I was led inevitably to new queries about working-class accommodation and consent to capitalist social relations. This necessitated an analysis of the deeply gendered culture of the paternalist workplace, in which masculinity and femininity were constructed and reconstructed over time — and not only in relation to the work process or division of labour, as I might have imagined. Of course, oral histories are no panacea for the silences of history, and the personal encounter may also inhibit discussions of violence, conflict, or divisions between women or within the working class.[3] Were I to interview the same women now, I would pose some questions differently, and also probe more concertedly about ethnic and cultural identity, and about the religious divisions of Catholic and Protestant, which were not explored in the book.

Understanding how working-class people are incorporated into capitalism, justifying rather than questioning it, is the flip side of understanding why they develop a critique of capitalism, as my earlier socialist and communist women did. Yet the two positions are not simply mirror opposites, with a more advanced versus a more naive political outlook facing off against one another. Both views may co-exist, overlap, or appear at different times, in a person or in a group; this seemed particularly true when I interviewed women about the 1937 strike, the focus of the "Telling Our Stories" article. Accommodation and resistance are both part of a complex ideological process, in which ideology is not a seamlessly unified and homogeneous system of beliefs, values, and practices, but rather is fragmented, uneven, and contradictory — and it may appear particularly meaningful and 'real' to working people precisely for these reasons.

Other sociologists had explored the 'manufacturing of consent' in the workplace,[4] but Antonio Gramsci's writing on hegemony, employed productively by a number of social historians at the time,[5] seemed a particularly useful way of understanding the complex of social and cultural relations that governed working women's lives both on and off the job. Hegemony — the way in which those with power are able to secure support for the prevailing social order, *their* social order — involved both consent and coercion (though in some writing the former only is discussed), which in the workplace meant the blunt threat of no job at all, as well as the more subtle practices, values, and traditions that legitimated unequal and hierarchical social relations. Hegemony encompassed a broad cultural process on the one hand, but on the other hand, it also seemed to explain, at a more micro level, the 'internalization' of capitalist values by individuals. Yet these individuals were not merely passively imbibing ideologies not in their interest — with ideology a mere "bad dream of the infrastructure"[6] — for ideology became 'common sense' precisely because it was woven into the fabric of daily life and social practices.

The concept of hegemony also allowed for negotiation and resistance, for there was always the possibility of oppositional, subaltern, emergent ideologies as well as dominant ones. In both articles, I wanted to give readers a sense of women's agency, whether it was the Westclox ballplayers taking advantage of their status to secure better working conditions, or the more impoverished women in court trying to escape a criminal charge levied against them. In the latter case, I had never intended to write on crime, but faced with so little archival material on Peterborough labour, I decided to comb every possible primary source I could, from School Board minutes and Mothers Allowance files to local prison registers and court columns in the newspaper. The latter were such an unbelievably rich source that I was hooked on them, and after sharing the material with a friend who was an actress and playwright, we collaborated with a musician to produce a piece of musical theatre, *Under the Law*, about two women from the rural 'Badlands' of Peterborough — one an accused murderer and the other an accused moonshiner — who became entangled in the criminal justice system.

While women's courtroom stories are analyzed in "Pardon Tales" as constructed narratives, I do not see them *only* as constructions or discursive strategies, for there often seemed to be some small 'kernel of truth' about their lives that was uncovered or revealed in their testimony. Women's stories were thus shaped by the dominant ideologies of the time, but they could not be disconnected from the material and social context that made them possible, and indeed, perhaps made them probable. This was one reason to show the quantitative results of my prison register research in the article as well, for these charts and graphs visibly reinforced the argument that criminality could not be considered apart from class as well as gender relations.

The use of oral histories was well established in labour and women's history by the time I wrote "Telling Our Stories." In the 1970s and 1980s, interviews were seen as an important source that might counter the lack of documentary and archival records about the lives of those with less power in society, less likely to leave detailed written records. Some labour oral history and autobiography projects in Canada were done with the double objective of creating new scholarship and contributing to the labour movement.[7] Similarly, women's historians saw their research as a scholarly *and* feminist enterprise that would counter the dominant 'malestream' history, encouraging a reappraisal of women's experiences, roles, contributions, and struggles in Canadian history.[8] Historians of ethnicity and immigration were also deeply involved in oral history.[9] It is true that there was more inclination in the 1970s and early 1980s to assume we could recreate women's experiences from listening to their words, but looking back, I don't think we should overemphasize a sharp disjuncture between an earlier period in which oral history was marginal, unreflective, and celebratory versus a later, more sophisticated discussion of oral history, something my article too easily suggests in its opening pages, and a claim made more bluntly in a recent essay by Steve High. His suggestions that oral history was initially "greeted with anger and sarcasm" by the profession and that the New Social History framing early oral history practice "did not change our relationship to the past or the public," but made us "more inward looking than ever" seem rather dubious.[10] Also, queries about the construction of memory were introduced in some early scholarly pieces, although it is undeniable that this conversation proliferated and intensified considerably as the method of oral history was interrogated critically, and with the advent of poststructuralism.[11]

"Telling Our Stories" and "Pardon Tales" thus both reflected some of the shift taking place in feminist theory by the mid-1990s. When I did the research for *Earning Respect*, there was still some interest in materialist and Marxist feminisms, but by the early to mid-1990s, poststructuralism was transforming historical thinking and debate. This may seem rather 'late' in terms of international debates, especially those circulating in literary theory; Joan Scott, after all, published her manifesto on discourse analysis and working-class history in 1987.[12] The linguistic turn, however, did take time to trickle through the profession: in the late 1980s and early 1990s, many books in Canadian women's history either had not absorbed, or did not reflect this 'turn.'[13] (Nor were those feminists sympathetic to poststructuralism simply followers of Scott.)[14] Despite the trickle-down effect, I sometimes felt as if I was just getting through my reading list on one theoretical debate when it was already surpassed by another.

By the mid-1990s, the challenges posed by poststructuralism to women's and labour history had to be considered. "Telling Our Stories" thus engaged with poststructuralist writing on oral history that challenged positivist assumptions about this methodology, questioned its 'authenticity' as a more direct means of understanding women's experience, and called for a decentring of the power of the interviewer. While some of these works gave me new ideas about the construction of women's memories, I did not see this construction as infinitely variable. Rather, women's memories were shaped not only by their individual stories, but also by the dominant ideologies of the time and the productive and reproductive relations framing their lives. In the cases of both women's memories and their courtroom tales, it was important to try and understand how *and why* certain discourses came to dominate, while others remained alternative and marginal. The notion, embraced by some feminists, that one could really 'share authority' with an interviewee also seemed problematic, an idealization that ran the risk of masking our influential role in shaping the interview and our academic investment in it.

Notes

1 Miriam Glucksmann, *Women Assemble: Women Workers and the New Industries in Inter-war Britain* (London: Routledge, 1990); Ruth Milkman, *Women, Work, and Protest: A Century of US Women's Labor History* (Urbana: University of Illinois Press, 1987); Louise Lamphere, *From Working Daughters to Working Mothers: Immigrant Women in a New England Industrial Community* (Ithaca: Cornell University Press, 1987); Susan Porter Benson, *Counter Cultures: Saleswomen, Managers and Customers in American Department Stores, 1890–1940* (Urbana: University of Illinois Press, 1987); Rosemary Hennessy, *Materialist Feminism and the Politics of Discourse* (New York: Routledge, 1993); Pat Armstrong and Hugh Armstrong, "Beyond Sexless Class and Classless Sex," in *The Politics of Diversity: Feminism, Marxism and Nationalism,* ed. Roberta Hamilton and Michele Barrett (London: Verso Press, 1986), 208–39.

2 Alice Kessler-Harris, *Gendering Labor History* (Urbana: University of Illinois Press, 2007), 131.

3 Although I found women reluctant to talk about this, other historians have sensitively uncovered the history of violence in other contexts. See, for example, Marlene Epp, "The Memory of Violence: Soviet and Eastern European Refugees and Rape in the Second World War," *Journal of Women's History* 9, no. 1 (1997): 58–88.

4 Michael Burawoy, *Manufacturing Consent: Changes in the Labor Process Under Monopoly Capitalism* (Chicago: University of Chicago Press, 1979).

5 For a discussion of this in the international literature, see Geoff Eley and Keith Nield, *The Future of Class in History: What's Left of the Social?* (Ann Arbor: University

of Michigan Press, 2007), 143–44, and, for a good Canadian example, Ian McKay, *The Quest for the Folk: Antimodernism and Cultural Selection in Twentieth-Century Nova Scotia* (Montreal: McGill-Queen's University Press, 1994).

6 Terry Eagleton, *Ideology: An Introduction* (London: Verso, 1991), 117.

7 For example, the oral histories and autobiographies published by the Canadian Committee on Labour History were intended to appeal to the labour movement as well as academics. See, for instance, Bryan Palmer, ed., *A Communist Life: Jack Scott and the Canadian Workers Movement, 1927–1985* (St. John's: Committee on Canadian Labour History, 1988). Other oral histories and working-class remembrances were produced in accessible, pamphlet form for the labour movement, such as Wayne Roberts, *Where Angels Fear to Tread: Eileen Tallman and the Labor Movement* (Hamilton: McMaster University Labour Studies Programme, 1981); *A Miner's Life: Bob Miner and Union Organizing in Timmins, Kirkland Lake and Sudbury* (Hamilton: McMaster University Labour Studies Programme, 1979); *Organizing Westinghouse: Alf Ready's Story* (Hamilton: McMaster University Labour Studies Programme, 1979).

8 Eliane Leslau Silverman, *The Last Best West: Women on the Alberta Frontier, 1880–1930* (Montreal: Eden Press, 1984); Sara Diamond, "Women in the B.C. Labour Movement," *Canadian Oral History Association Journal* (1983). Works on Indigenous women's oral narratives were also prominent: Margaret Blackman, *During My Time: Florence Edenshaw Davidson, A Haida Woman* (Seattle: University of Washington Press, 1982), and Julie Cruikshank, *Life Lived Like a Story: Life Stories of Three Native Yukon Elders* (Lincoln: University of Nebraska Press, 1990).

9 This is clear when you look over all the early articles in the *Canadian Oral History Association Journal*, now available online through its new incarnation, *Oral History Forum*, http://www.canoha.ca/.

10 One might question the whig claims-making in this article. High writes that the "cultural turn . . . has challenged all of us to take a more explicitly political and critical perspective," adding that this turn "tends to unite younger researchers in opposition to an older generation of social historians." I am not so sure that generational writing is that 'united,' and the idea that critique and politics were made more explicit by the cultural turn is questionable. See "Sharing Authority in the Writing of Canadian History: The Case of Oral History," in *Contesting Clio's Craft: New Directions and Debates in Canadian History*, ed. Christopher Dummitt and Michael Dawson (London: Institute for the Study of the Americas, 2009), 22–23.

11 For an early positive article on oral history from a Canadian political historian, see Bernard Ostry, "The Illusion of Understanding: Making the Ambiguous Intelligible," *Oral History Review* 5 (1977): 7–16. Issues of power imbalances and power sharing were especially evident in the feminist literature by the 1990s. See Susan Geiger, "What's So Feminist About Women's Oral History?" *Journal of*

Women's History 2, no. 1 (1990): 175, and the articles in Sherna Berger Gluck and Daphne Patai, eds., *Women's Words: The Feminist Practice of Oral History* (New York: Routledge, Chapman and Hall, 1991).

12 Joan Scott, "On Language, Gender and Working Class History," *International Labor and Working-Class History* 31 (1987): 1–13.

13 Veronica Strong-Boag, *The New Day Recalled: The Lives of Girls and Women in English Canada* (Markham, ON: Viking Press, 1988); Wendy Mitchinson, *The Nature of Their Bodies: Women and Their Doctors in Victorian Canada* (Toronto: University of Toronto Press, 1991); Ruth Frager, *Sweatshop Strife: Class, Ethnicity and Gender in the Jewish Labour Movement, 1900–1939* (Toronto: University of Toronto Press, 1992); Jane Errington, *Wives and Mothers, School Mistresses and Scullery Maids: Working Women in Upper Canada, 1790–1840* (Montreal: McGill-Queen's University Press, 1995). The obvious exception was Mariana Valverde, *The Age of Light, Soap, and Water: Moral Reform in English Canada, 1885–1925* (Toronto: McClelland and Stewart, 1991).

14 For example, Mariana Valverde, "Poststructuralist Gender Historians: Are We These Names?" *Labour/Le Travail* 25 (Spring 1990): 227–36.

THE SOFTBALL SOLUTION
FEMALE WORKERS, MALE MANAGERS, AND THE OPERATION OF PATERNALISM AT WESTCLOX, 1923–1960

I always said that we didn't need a union there because we were treated so well. It was a nice place . . . I had nice friends. . . . Plus we were fairly well paid. A lot of today's troubles come from unions.

Management had the whole picture; they knew the situation best.[1]

These retrospective observations of former workers at a Peterborough clock factory reflect common characterizations of this workplace by women who once assembled the minute, inner workings of the famous Westclox alarm clocks and watches. Their positive memories of Westclox and the view that workers there owed their managers "respect" were repeated by many other former workers in interviews. Their collective character-ization of Westclox must be analyzed in the context of the operation of paternalism in the Westclox plant for a period of over thirty years. Within this small Ontario manufacturing city, no other factory with hundreds of employees could claim as effective a management strategy, or as loyal and respectful a workforce. While this cannot be measured 'objectively' through statistics such as workplace longevity, it can be measured subjec-tively through the way in which former Westclox workers construct their memories, endorsing the familial metaphor promoted by the company.[2]

It is my intention to examine the rise and decline of paternalism in this factory, exploring both managerial intentions and worker responses to paternalism, with special emphasis on women's understanding of the workplace hierarchy. A long chronology of varied paternalisms, based on the axes of race, class, and gender, has been documented in North Ameri-can labour history.[3] As recent studies have argued, we need to pay close attention to historical specificity in our analyses of industrial paternalism;

local studies like this one may thus provide clues to the common processes creating consent in the workplace, and to the seemingly tenacious persistence of class and gender inequalities in the workplace.

Attention to the material context and economic pressures, as well as the ideological mechanisms sustaining paternalism, is essential if we are to address these broader questions. Westclox's initial success in this ethnically homogeneous, small Ontario city emerged from its overlapping strategies of nineteenth-century paternalism and twentieth-century welfare capitalism, made possible by the distinct material and cultural conditions in this workplace, industry, and locale. Secondly, paternalism was a managerial strategy that embodied a gender ideology of male dominance; its operation was intertwined with and aided by a gender hierarchy found in family, wider community, and the workplace, which ultimately supported women's secondary status as daughters in the Westclox family.

Finally, women's own memories of work at the Westclox illuminate the way in which workers understood, utilized, negotiated, and eventually repudiated paternalism; their recollections suggest a more complex relationship between manager and worker than mere rebellion against, or sycophantic acceptance of, the company's aims. In trying to map out workers' responses to paternalism, oral history is especially useful as a means of probing the subjective areas of experience and feeling.[4] (See Appendix A for a description of the interviews.) The structure of memory and the emphasis, tone, and language of interviews provide insight into how experience and ideology shaped the outlook and choices of women workers, and thus how accommodation operated in the factory. If we are to comprehend working-class support for the economic status quo, and attempt to theorize about consent in the workplace,[5] then we must also listen to the voices of the workers who embraced or at least tolerated paternalism as part of their daily efforts to survive the difficulties of wage labour.

Paternalism and Welfare Capitalism

Often applied to nineteenth-century industrial experiments, the term paternalism conjures up images of a single entrepreneur who "ruled his works and his workers directly from some large baronial home overlooking the industrial village."[6] Drawing on previous forms of deference within the church, the community, or especially the household, the factory owner attempted to incorporate these social relations into the factory regime. British and American historians have explored the way in which an employer, playing a visible role on the factory premises, tried to create the feeling of an 'organic community,' often by equating the factory with an actual or imagined family. Paternalism was intended to avoid labour unrest, preserve managerial authority, and satisfy a patrician sense of philanthropy.[7] Paternalism has also been designated a form of patriarchy,[8] for it sustained a hierarchical system in which older men dominated younger men, women, and children; it was premised on a conception of "mutual rights and duties connected to the unequal relations of authority . . . found in the household."[9] Despite these common patterns in paternalist experiments, there was also considerable diversity; recent American studies have shown how paternalism was shaped by the material and cultural factors conditioning production and profit in the industry, by distinct local, cultural, and political contexts.[10]

The twentieth century supposedly inaugurated a 'professionalization' of paternalism with the introduction of welfare plans and a trained workforce of welfare and personnel specialists.[11] Replacing the fatherly factory head was the corporate practice of organized, efficient welfare capitalism, which still contained some of the basic principles of paternalism: the familial metaphor, the endeavour to create a company culture of consensus, deference, and accommodation, attempts to maintain a loyal, long-lasting, and of course, un-unionized workforce. American historians have debated the success of welfare capitalism with workers in the twentieth century, as well as its chronology of rise and decline; while many see this strategy as a 'top down' attempt to shape and control the workforce,[12] more recent interpretations present welfare capitalism as a negotiated relationship between Capital and Labour.[13] Canadian case studies, while few in number, have argued that some Canadian businesses in the early and mid-twentieth century achieved a limited measure of success with welfare capitalist strategies to "manufacture consent"[14] in the workplace. Welfare capitalism, they also caution, usually offered workers the "velvet glove," combining coercion with the 'carrot' of welfare benefits; moreover, many of these benefits offered little of real material "substance"[15] to improve workers' lives. Unfortunately, some discussions of Canadian welfare capitalism have either concentrated on the picture from perspective of the employers[16] or assumed Canadian business strategies followed a trajectory similar to that of American welfarism, moving in a linear manner from scientific management to welfarism to a postwar labour/capital contract.[17] In actual fact, companies followed a number of distinct paths to and from welfare capitalism, which were not "happenstance"[18] as much as reflective of varying regional, industrial, and political influences. Some of these Canadian experiments failed amidst the Depression,[19] while others, such as Westclox, persisted throughout the thirties and forties, and even beyond. Moreover, more than one managerial strategy could be attempted at the same time:[20] in the Westclox case, the introduction of welfare capitalism and modern personnel management did not preclude the persistence of some nineteenth-century forms of paternalism: the two existed together.

In examining the operation of paternalism (a term I use to include both traditional paternalism and organized welfare capitalism), two interlocking power relationships must be highlighted. First, paternalism was a relationship premised on fundamentally unequal economic relations, though there were also possibilities of negotiation and bargaining embedded in these power relations. To see paternalism as only a form of clever managerial social control is to simplify its operation and render the workers in such a system passive, malleable, and without agency. While the labour movement was understandably suspicious of welfare capitalism, some workers were sympathetic to it, and their outlook cannot be dismissed as simply 'false consciousness.' Not only does this obscure the multi-layered and contradictory nature of consciousness (for consent and class consciousness may well coexist) but it also overlooks the fact that struggle between groups with unequal power may proceed on many levels, and that "class conflict may involve those with power avoiding confrontation with those without it,"[21] and those without power bargaining in sporadic, informal, even unconscious ways.

Nonetheless, the subtle but powerful process of ideological hegemony sustaining paternalism must still be highlighted.[22] In order to interpret their workplace experiences, workers inevitably drew on the ideological resources at their disposal, and the dominant ideology — experienced as lived, habitual practice, interwoven throughout the culture, discerned as 'common sense' — justified existing corporate leadership and the 'natural' existence of gender and class stratification.[23] One manifestation of the ideological hegemony of those with social and economic power, paternalism encouraged consent to economic hierarchy as an inevitable part of daily life: in a Gramscian sense, it successfully "universalized ruling class interest with community interest."[24]

Paternalism was also a power relationship based on notions of gender difference and structures of gender inequality. Feminist historians have argued persuasively that we need to understand the ways in which the family and the workplace were interlocking hierarchies of dominance and negotiation, with class and gender constructed simultaneously.[25] Nineteenth-century paternalism, argues Judy Lown, did not simply draw superficially on familial metaphors; rather, male dominance was an "organizing principle"[26] of paternalist workplace relations. Similarly, the Westclox example demonstrates the centrality of gender ideology to paternalism, and consequently, the need for a feminist analysis of the material and ideological processes behind its operation.

Establishing the 'Westclox Way' in Canada

The Western Clock Company was established in 1895 by entrepreneur F.W. Matthiessen, who located his first clock factory near his zinc smelter in LaSalle, Illinois. Variously known as the Western Clock Co., Westclox, and after a number of mergers and takeovers, as General Time Instruments, the enterprise remained a family company until the 1930s when it expanded considerably and was listed on the New York Stock Exchange. Westclox built a Canadian branch plant in Peterborough in 1923 that grew alongside the American parent company: in 1926, it employed 180, by the late 1930s approximately 400, and during World War II, its payroll hit an all-time high of 800. Although male employees outnumbered women in the company's infancy, women soon became a majority of about 60 percent (and during the war years their numbers, as well as their percentage of the workforce, rose even higher). Protected by the Imperial tariff in the 1930s, the company maintained fairly good health even in the Depression, and business grew during World War II, when both clock and munitions work proved extremely profitable. In the immediate postwar period, sales remained strong, but signs of trouble were apparent by the mid-1950s: consumer sales were sagging, despite attempts to move into new fields such as computer and missile timing devices. New plants in Mexico and the Virgin Islands, and the transfer of business from the flagship LaSalle factory to Georgia by the early 1960s offered the writing on the wall: the corporation was relocating its large plants into low-wage areas of the United States and elsewhere. Despite a takeover by new management, the Canadian Westclox closed in the 1970s.

Until the 1960s, however, Westclox was seen as a stable Peterborough employer that had a "complete manufacturing operation,"[27] including design, industrial engineering, and accounting as well as assembly. One person dominates the history the Canadian Westclox: its general manager, later president, J.H. Vernor. Until his retirement in 1953, Vernor was a guiding force of company personnel policy,[28] though company administration was also strongly influenced by the American parent, which trained many Canadian administrators in managerial exchange programs. Vernor saw himself in the terms familiar to paternalist enterprise: as the concerned but disciplinarian father. He was referred to in the community as "Mr. Westclox,"[29] a term he actually promoted. In their recollections, employees repeat this nickname, and some clearly adopted, at some level, the familial analogy of Vernor watching over his employees 'like a father.' One even mused that because Vernor was childless himself, he invested inordinate interest and energy in his surrogate children, his employees.

Indeed, it is revealing that many employees have constructed their memories of the company around a narrative theme that stresses the rise and decline of the family — like an epic saga — at Westclox that roughly (though not completely accurately) coincides with the company's financial success and decline.[30] In this narrative theme, the 'family' and the business enterprise have merged, their fate tied to the story of a man whose health and spirit went downhill along with the factory: the economic vigour of the factory and workers' job security clearly help to shape the collective script of their stories.[31] In this script, Vernor, the young, dashing executive, popular with most of his employees, ages rapidly in the postwar years as the closely knit family becomes more troubled, stressed, and less cohesive and congenial. In some oral accounts, unionization in

1952 symbolized the inauguration of a new era and the rejection of the older family, along with its father. "The union broke Vernor's heart — Westclox was his family" commented one employee.[32]

It was not simply Vernor's use of the familial metaphor, however, that kept Westclox from unionizing until relatively late, prevented any strikes, and produced a paternalistic workplace. First of all, paternalism was necessarily constructed on the edifice of unequal economic power: material constraints should not be minimized in the paternalist equation, for they provided the essential backdrop for the factory's authority structure. As Patrick Joyce notes, "power relations are a precondition for [paternalism] . . . vulnerability sows the seeds of deference."[33] The Westclox factory was quite tightly controlled by managerial prerogative: until after World War II, a number of managers and foreman were influential in hiring, firing, and in assigning work duties. Hiring, remembers some former workers, seemed personal and arbitrary: one worker remembers Vernor talking to him briefly, "making a few scratchy notes," then saying "you're hired."[34] In 1945 a separate personnel department was set up at the urging of the parent company, which feared that its unorganized workforce would be stirred by the wave of unionization sweeping North America. Even after this, Vernor and other managers took a personal interest in hiring, with recommendations of family and friends carrying weight in their decisions. As a former manager put it, "there were names that immediately boded well for you, but others that meant instant disaster . . . forget this talk about nepotism . . . it was just a form of reference."[35]

Securing jobs for kin, keeping a job during the Depression, choosing where one wanted to work within the factory: these were the economic pressures that employees had to consider when interacting with their superiors. Because jobs were often secured through family, women also developed a sense of 'debt' to their employer, particularly during the Depression; as Joy Parr argues in her case study, workers felt "they owed their jobs to their patrons."[36] During the worst of the Depression, the factory reduced the work week and instituted job sharing in order to keep people at least partially employed, a measure that accentuated a sense of obligation to the company. Indeed, in comparison to often-cited American example, the Depression could actually give paternalism a new lease on life.

The regulation of the work process also provided clues to the operation of paternalism. At first glance, the work process, especially for the women, appeared tightly controlled. Although some skilled men, like the tool and die makers, exercised considerable authority over their work conditions, women were primarily assigned to repetitive jobs in assembly line work that were often compensated through piece work or production targets. In the office, women's work was closely supervised and their polite demeanour noted when it came to promotions and raises, which were individually assigned, as no clear job posting system existed until the 1950s.

The 'blue-collar' women at Westclox worked on an assembly line characteristic of the new 'mass industries' of the twentieth century, in which a carefully engineered, continuous flow work process produced mass goods for a growing consumer market.[37] Women's work was characterized by machine pacing of the job, by "indirect assembly"[38] (as opposed to direct servicing of machines), and by the extensive use of some kind of piece work or incentive pay. Moreover, some of the assembly line work at the plant was extremely fine work, for which women were given finger dexterity and eyesight tests (though it was also claimed that dexterity and careful attention to detail were inherently female attributes). Within this fairly rigid structure, however, there existed a small degree of flexibility that assisted the company's efforts to "manufacture consent"[39] by mitigating the inherent alienation of wage labour. For one thing, the range of jobs (however monotonous each one was) was greater here than in local factories like the textile mill, and management allowed women some mobility within the factory. Even more important was the degree of autonomy and respect built into the system of supervision. When former women workers describe why they stayed at Westclox they often emphasize the atmosphere, nature of supervision, and flexibility on the shop floor. Supervision and the practice of paternalism interacted on one another, with the paternalist philosophy of the company creating the precise shape of authority relations in the workplace. Women, for example, might be allowed to 'sneak out' a few minutes early to catch their train home for the weekend, workplace joking and socializing were given fairly elastic boundaries, and the continuous-flow assembly work, though seen as taxing and difficult, was not continually and arbitrarily pushed to its limit with speed-ups — at least not in the early years before Westclox's financial problems became visible.[40]

Foremen were also trained to listen and mediate, rather than reject complaints, and especially not to embarrass or humiliate women workers. Almost every female interviewee commented positively on the manner in which their male foremen dealt with conflict and grievances. "We were taken aside, never embarrassed in front of others on the line," remembers one woman. "I learned *never* to dismiss a complaint," recalls a former manager, "J.H. [Vernor] once took a strip off me for brushing off a complaint . . . I listened, even if the complaint didn't seem [justified]."[41] Some women claimed to prefer this conciliatory method to later union practices, as the latter tended to be more confrontational, drawing attention to the griever as "the union was always looking for an issue to hold over the company's head."[42] While an analysis of women's work culture indicates that they had their own code of behaviour and sense of solidarity that was not simply equated with company interest, Westclox's labour relations were still compared very favourably to shop floor relations in other factories. Westclox's "laissez-faire supervision" thus tended to "mystify labour/capital relations";[43] it was construed by women workers as evidence of the company's familial style of management.

Managers were encouraged to deal with men under them in a somewhat different manner, with an eye to creating a feeling of male partnership, even though the workers knew this to be something of an illusion. In one meeting a foreman was severely "chewed out" by a manager in front of his peers, a humiliating experience. His response was to pull a different kind of rank on the manager — that of moral superiority and reference to the comradeship preached by the company. "I might be a farmer's son and you a university grad," he replied, "but you can't treat me that way, and if you do, I'm quitting."[44] The manager backed down, and the foreman's tactics were applauded by his colleagues, who had absorbed the Westclox message that class differences could not, at least, be flaunted, and that all workers deserved respect. As Gerald Zahavi argues, workers' loyalty could not be extracted without a price; in return for accepting the company paternalism, male workers manipulated the company's rhetoric to secure working conditions they wanted.[45]

While styles of supervision were important to workers, material rewards were also part of the paternalist bargain: Westclox's early attempts to establish good pay and benefits compared to other industries in Peterborough helped create an informal peace treaty with labour. By paying one or two cents more an hour than other factories and providing paid vacations, the company hoped to procure better-educated workers, increase productivity, and secure a stable workforce. Because this was not a one-company town, Westclox management felt it had to compete for skilled male labour, but they also extended this strategy to include female workers. When J.H. Vernor first established female wage rates that were one or two cents more than the larger Canadian General Electric, claims a former manager, a prominent GE manager "stormed up the hill" to demand a rollback. Vernor argued that, in order to recruit a workforce from scratch, Westclox needed some tangible economic inducements.[46] The company also persuaded community members of the superiority of its white-collar work. When looking for new secretarial help, the personnel manager would call the head commercial teacher at the local high school and ask him to send over the top three or four women in the graduating class for interviews: the teacher obliged.[47] The company's investment in welfare capitalist policies was clearly motivated by a desire to avoid unionization, but to young women seeking jobs in the thirties and forties, this goal did not worry them.[48] Time and again, women remember the sense of competition for the few openings at Westclox. One woman climbed the hill day after day to ask if there was a position; another, lacking a family member there, babysat for a foreman and persuaded him to speak for her.

While many companies assumed women were not interested in these material benefits, women did consider these part of the allure of employment at Westclox.[49] On top of paid vacations, available after five years of service (one of the most attractive benefits), there was also a group insurance plan, instituted from the beginning, which the employer paid. From the 1930s on, employees could also contribute to a jointly paid sick leave plan, but a pension plan didn't appear until 1940. There were also a number of less costly benefits, though ones that the company loudly advertised, such as a cafeteria with cheap hot meals, tennis courts on the grounds, and an infirmary.

Compared to those at other large Ontario companies, these were good, but by no means outstanding benefits. A 1927 study done for the Ontario government on the physical, recreational, and financial benefits offered by businesses revealed that many companies offered cheaper benefits like recreation and cafeterias, while fewer offered more costly employer-paid vacations, sickness insurance, pension plans, and so on.[50] Later analyses of welfare plans by the Canadian Manufacturing Association in the 1930s indicated that, in comparison to large enterprises such as Imperial Oil, Westclox was now lagging behind.[51] Still, it is important to compare Westclox to other Peterborough industries;[52] in contrast to the low wages and no benefits offered by the large woollen mill, the longer work week at Quaker Oats, and the notoriously authoritarian management style at CGE, Westclox "looked great"[53] to prospective workers. Even after monetary rewards improved elsewhere by the 1950s, Westclox could ride on its existing reputation, aided by its public relations campaign, already successful in the community.

While many of the benefits offered by the company were standard ingredients of welfare capitalism, an important element of the company's paternalism was the personal and discretionary way that benefits were imparted: nineteenth-century paternalism thus overlapped with twentieth-century welfarism. In a confidential survey returned to the Ontario Department of Labour in 1927, the company revealed that in "deserving cases, money was sometimes lent on the quiet for house buying," but at the same time the survey recorded that "Vernor hates anything paternal."[54] While understanding the pejorative connotation of the word, he was still willing to apply its principles.

Until a union contract of 1952 there was no official bereavement leave and pay; before that, management created, on an ad hoc basis, similar benefits for some employees. One long-time blue-collar employee, whom Vernor knew well, remembered the situation when her father died. Not only was she was given time off, but Vernor lent the family his car for the funeral and when he came to pay his respects, he shook hands and discreetly left a $20 bill behind — a personal contribution to funeral expenses that families sometimes found hard to meet. While most women report similar instances of sympathetic paternalism, a former secretary noted that when her mother died, the company sent for her at the funeral home to come and finish some special typing only she had done in the past; paternalism, in other words, was arbitrarily applied.

These discretionary benefits were important for they reinforced ties of loyalty and obligation between boss and worker, sometimes so successfully that workers began to *interpret* legal rights as personal gifts. Even after a sick benefits plan was introduced, Vernor told woman office worker to "let him know if she needed time off because there was sickness in the family"[55] so he could arrange it, an incident then translated as evidence of his flexibility and concern. Another blue-collar employee praised Vernor for his concern with the personal safety of his female employees who had to be taxied home after midnight shifts during the war years. Although she was very vaguely aware that this was required by law, she primarily saw Vernor's hand in it: "the taxi driver had to wait until we were in the door... and if he didn't, we were supposed to notify Mr. Vernor about [it]."[56]

While many Canadian managers claim that the company's benefit schemes emerged from the personal and 'fatherly' concern of the Matthiessen family for their employees,[57] Westclox's paternalism evolved as a more complex amalgam of corporate planning and worker responses. The company's paternalism was also aided by the social structure of this small city in which management's prestige was confirmed by their prominent social status in the 'town below' the factory on the hill. More than one interviewee pointed to the elite family connections or important community stature that certain managers (or their wives) enjoyed, thus reinforcing patterns of paternalism already forged at work.[58]

Women and Men in the Westclox "Family"

When former workers offered positive interpretations of company paternalism, most did not employ a language of worker deference as much as they used familial metaphors that were intimately connected to the sexual division of labour in the plant, and to notions of female respectability and male breadwinning. Westclox promoted a sexual division of labour that was characterized by women's exclusion from supervisory positions, apprenticeships, and heavy work in shipping and automatics, and their concentration in assembly line work and clerical work. Women's relegation to these job ghettoes was rationalized on two bases: the male breadwinner ideology and women's 'natural' physical differences, especially their nimble fingers and ability to tolerate fine eye work. While a former manager claimed that the company simply "hired for the job," he also saw some impermeable gender boundaries: "you wouldn't hire a man to knit would you? his fingers were too big and clumsy. . . . girls are much more adaptable to assembly work."[59]

Explanations for this sexual division of labour were often interwoven with descriptions of paternalism in the factory; accounts of why and how the sexual division of labour existed are characterized by a familial discourse within which women workers assume the role of daughters and maiden aunts, while men assume the role of sons. The latter role, of course, was constructed in a particularly patriarchal manner, with younger men under the control of older ones, but always with the prospect of advancing themselves into positions of power.

Westclox strongly encouraged internal advancement of its male employees into supervisory and even management positions. J.H. Vernor's keen eye for potential foremen and managers, and his use of corporate training plans to promote them, meant that some men were offered opportunities at Westclox not available elsewhere, ensuring their indebtedness to the firm. Not only were men promoted internally, but the bonds of male solidarity were also cemented by perks like a clubhouse for foremen and managers on the Westclox property, and by men's social events such as golf stags, poker nights, and Vernor's annual foreman's picnic held at his cottage on Buckhorn Lake. Here, male camaraderie was reinforced with activities like fishing derbys, horseshoes and cards, and, one assumes, drinking as well, as Vernor was not known as an abstainer. Indeed, some of the men who Vernor came to know well helped to 'protect' his public image by buying his scotch for him; after an impaired driving charge in 1954, while preparing for one of his cottage stags, however, Vernor's reputation became more public.[60] A sense of shared masculinity thus temporarily superseded class hierarchy, even though Vernor always made it clear that respect for his title should take precedence within the factory. Fraternal organizations may also have played a role in cementing these male ties: both Vernor and the (later) General Manager Cranford were active Masons, as were some of the workers on the shop floor.

What role did women's labour play in this family? As with domestic labour, women's wage labour sustained the enterprise but was also undervalued, and did not lead to possibilities of significant advancement and power. The distinction between the paternalism directed towards men and women was the way in which sons might prosper in the family, but women could only maintain their secondary roles. As daughters primarily interested in temporary wage work and ultimately marriage, women were assumed to be satisfied with smaller wage packets, a view many women, even some single career women, remember endorsing. The one way that women could use the company's emphasis on internal promotion and discretionary paternalism was to advance from blue- to white-collar work, which offered better working conditions, more interesting work and higher status, if not better wages. Though this promotion ladder was truncated compared to men's, it was appealing to some working-class women, especially those whose education had been cut short during the Depression.[61] An idealized notion of a family wage underpinned different job options for men and women. The hiring of single women only was the policy until World War II. "My thinking," explained one manager, using a revealing familial metaphor, "was if two girls came up, one married and one single, you should hire the latter for she had been kept, clothed by the family until then, so why not give her a job and take her off her father's hands."[62] Even after the marriage bar had been disrupted by the war, a 'maternity bar' remained in the postwar years, becoming the new rationalization for a family wage for men and secondary salaries for women.

The one group of women who did not fit into this familial model were single, unmarried 'career' women who chose to pursue wage work rather than marry. Interestingly, these women are sometimes described with metaphors that suggest their role as 'spinsters' or maiden aunts — as determined, unusual, even eccentric women — or alternatively, as dutiful daughters, who in their own way, were also playing the appropriate familial roles by caring for aging parents. "You *must* talk to Susan," I was told by one manager, "you know she was really a 'good girl'. . . she worked all her life, lived at home and looked after her mother until she died."[63] This is not to say that women all placidly internalized the familial models of daughters' temporary work and spinsters' self-sacrifice: they saw their roles shaped by a more complex web of choices and necessities, and a few identified the discrimination involved in the existing sexual division of labour, though they also tended to see it as insurmountable reality.

Even after women were allowed to work after marriage, the paternalism accorded men and women remained a feature of factory life. By rationalizing its hiring decisions and the gendered division of labour with appeals to innate sexual abilities and the male breadwinner ideal,[64] the company incorporated gender ideology directly into its managerial strategy; these assumptions reinforced the notions that women were less concerned with autonomy and control over their work, less suited to supervise and that women's wage work was secondary to domestic duties.

The incorporation of paternal assumptions into the dominant characterization of white-collar work was especially noteworthy: the attributes of a good white-collar worker underlined a paternal relationship between female worker and male supervisor. Good work habits — punctuality, preciseness, politeness, pleasant personality — were essentially seen as 'female' attributes, and as Margery Davies points out, the very language used to describe the ideal secretary — as adaptable, deferential, a good listener, and nice-looking — in fact, "cast her in a female role as office daughter/wife."[65]

Such assumptions both reflected and were bolstered by the prevailing gender ideology of the time. Women workers recall accepting the 'natural' placement of men over women on the job, and blue- as well as white-collar women spoke of the need to respect male supervisors because of their greater experience, skill, and knowledge. Women's accommodation to the gendered hierarchy at work was reproduced not only through the daily practice of a sexual division of labour, but also through the notions of masculinity and femininity, and the gendered meanings of experience, skill, and the right to work that women absorbed from the wider cultural context. Gender ideology thus assisted the acceptance of male authority as 'natural' and inevitable and helped create the paternal — and patriarchal — workplace. Earlier research argued that both male and female workers were "rendered childlike" by paternalism, which also "undermined [men's] sense of identity as breadwinners,"[66] but this obscures paternalism's inherent rationalization of gender divisions within the factory. As in a patriarchal family, some men could assume control, at least in theory, over women. The same was true for Westclox sons, but obviously not for its daughters.

There were other differences between the treatment of sons and daughters: one of the most important was the moral protection of women by the company. It is often assumed that such moral paternalism — a form of industrial moral regulation — did not persist past the Progressive era, yet at Westclox quite the opposite was true.[67] Although the image of what a respectable working girl's social life was like did change after 1920, with activities like dancing increasingly taken for granted, anxiety about sexual morality and marriageability remained a subtext of concern at Westclox. Many veiled references to sexual respectability, to the 'better class' of girl who was hired in the 1930s and 1940s, especially before the company went 'downhill' in the 1960s, indicates how the theme of sexual propriety of the daughters was also tied into the narrative theme of family decline. Other local factories were contrasted to the Westclox: the textile mill, which employed many women, was referred to as "tough, you know, you had a tough name if you worked there. My wife lived near there, *but her father wouldn't let her get a job there.*"[68] The way that the word 'nice' was used made it clear that moral respectability was at issue. As one manager commented: "We hired very nice girls [at Westclox]. We were careful about that, to hire good girls, respectable girls. You could be a preacher's daughter and work at Westclox you know."[69] Former workers made the same connection, implying that it drew in a more educated, and thus respectable class of women: "we took the cream of the crop . . . we even had school teachers there. . . . But after the war, it was harder to find people and we had to take some we didn't really want."[70]

Extremely revealing is the incident involving a woman who had already been interviewed and offered a job in the postwar period only to be phoned back and told there were no openings available; a male worker who had witnessed part of the interview had informed a manager that she was living immorally with a married man. Notwithstanding the many implications of this episode — including the masculine solidarity evidenced and how easily 'small-town' gossip can ruin a woman's reputation — the message was quite clear: she was promiscuous and therefore should be denied the job. "If you hire a few like that," one male interviewee commented, then "all the girls are tainted with the same brush."[71] In a similar vein, one correspondent for the in-house newspaper, *Tic Talk*, was told in no uncertain terms that the paper would not print a gossip item that implied a married man had been parking "up on a hill" with another woman from work: "[that] had to [be] edited out; we had to be careful about what went in [the paper] after all, that would have caused him trouble at home [if his family had read that]."[72]

Respectability was a particular concern of the factory patriarch, J.H. Vernor. One former worker remembers a lecture he delivered on the state of the woman's washroom (which he had apparently inspected after hours); another recalls his admonishments on 'ladylike' dress. A softball story highlights well his self-designation as paternal overseer of his daughters' decency. After one out-of-town game, some of the players went into a bar for a drink. Others, who still saw bars as a place where women were 'picked up,' went elsewhere. When Vernor found out, the coach was reprimanded for letting the players be seen in a bar. It was never to happen again. We had to be ladies, you see . . . he insisted on that,"[73] explained a former team member.

The company's attempt to champion the morality and respectability of its women workers was not entirely unwelcome with female employees in the 1930s and 1940s. This dimension of paternalism offered women, especially those in the plant, some reciprocal psychological benefits, by countering a prevailing image of the 'tough' factory girl, which many women workers resented. Women who worked in other heavier industries in the city like General Electric and Outboard Marine lamented that factory women were viewed as less feminine or 'refined': tough and rough were the two words commonly used. Apprehension about blue-collar work was symbolized in the references to cleanliness and dress: the sight of coveralls, even during the war, carried with it fears of endangered femininity. Women who worked at Westclox, on the other hand, constantly cited their clean workplace and the fact that they could wear what they wanted as evidence of their better class of employment, especially in comparison to the "dirty, dark"[74] GE. Other historians have pointed to the symbolic importance of dress for working women as signs of their "orderly,"[75] successful, or respectable character: for Westclox women, dress, cleanliness, and an impeccable reputation offered them a modicum of respectability that they felt was denied them by prevailing images of factory workers.

This appeal to a sense of respectability may have been shaped by ethnic homogeneity and exclusivity as well. Like the city itself, the plant was predominantly Anglo/Celtic in character.[76] Although there was occasional

Catholic/Protestant rivalry in the plant, women were ultimately drawn together more a sense of being 'upright' and respectable than they were separated by religious differences. Even the religious differences that did occasionally surface had been tempered by the company's conscious personnel strategy of hiring Catholics in proportion to their numbers in the city and opening up skilled positions "elsewhere under control of the Masons" to Catholic men. "I remember our priest saying how good [Vernor] was to East City" remembers a male worker. "He praised J.H. up and down for hiring Catholics."[77] By carefully attending to religious tensions, Vernor was able, again, to bolster his image as fair-minded and generous to the local community.

Company Sports and Newspapers

It was not only through the provision of material benefits and support for notions of respectability that Westclox sustained its paternalism. The company's onsite clubhouse, tennis courts, and its careful maintenance of extensive gardens and lawns (and its advertisement of its civic awards for the best-kept industrial workplace) were all designed to create a 'homelike' atmosphere. Company rituals, especially those geared to Westclox children, such as picnics and Christmas parties, and those geared to long service, such as retirement dinners and the Quarter Century Club events, were also very important. Many who attended the Quarter Century Club and retirement dinners characterize these events as lavish affairs, which they see as evidence of the company's magnanimity. One employee proudly repeated, in her interview, word for word, the acceptance poem she delivered when she received her twenty-five-year award.

Other initiatives were probably more important: one of those was the encouragement of recreation and athletics for employees. J.H. Vernor supported the creation of industrial league teams for both men and women and donated money to rent the YWCA for team sports, sometimes personally passing on the cheque through an employee. Westclox's community name, however, was best known for its women's softball team. Indeed, when I began to interview employees, I was repeatedly urged to seek out the women ballplayers.

Women workers were sometimes ballplayers scouted out by coaches concerned more with team needs than with manpower needs in the plant. One woman remembers that even before she finished high school "they were hot and heavy after me to play softball for them . . . but my mother put her foot down as she wanted me to finish my business training."[78] When another teenager was approached by the coaches before her sixteenth birthday, her parents were also consulted, a sign not only of her youth, but also of the company's desire not to interfere with traditional family authority. One woman was recruited by her sister, already a Westclox athlete: "I went there to play in the sports. I think you'll find a lot of the girls did the same thing. They got jobs to play softball, basketball. My sister got the job first, then Mr. Vernor, who was the president, needed another player [so I was hired]."[79]

Women on the Westclox team practised regularly, competed fiercely, and did well: in 1945 they were runner-up for the provincial championship. The company outfitted the women with uniforms, paid for buses to transport them across the province, and although the women were not supposed to get extra perks at work, some lateness might occasionally be accepted when they were playing for championships out of town. When one ballplayer sprained her ankle, Vernor sent a truck to pick her up every day so that she could make it to work.

Sports were meant to create a sense of company loyalty, suggesting competition with the outside, but team effort inside; they were supposed to create a loyal, disciplined and committed workforce that strove to give its best performance on and off the job. Anxious to cash in on the popularity of amateur sports in the interwar years,[80] the company also saw sports teams as a good source of advertising: they made the Westclox name known outside of Peterborough, and reinforced a positive view of the company inside Peterborough. Nor did this end with World War II; if anything, an emphasis on sports increased in the 1940s.[81] Contrary to the sweeping claim by one sports historian that by the mid-1920s employer-established recreational sports were disappearing, unable to compete with programs offered by radical sports groups, company sports remained an attractive option in many small towns and cities.[82]

American historians examining company sports often assume their primary goal was to build manly "character" amongst its male employees, especially the "middle class values of sobriety, thrift and industriousness."[83] Conversely, feminist analyses of women's sports in the interwar period have been critical of the ways in which male medical and educational experts attempted to control women's bodies, preserving traditional notions of female physical weakness, while business interests marketed women's teams in a voyeuristic way as 'attractive [sexualized]' entertainment.[84] Yet listening to women's subjective memories of industrial sports suggests a different perspective: the actual meaning sports had for players might differ from the intentions of team promoters.[85] Women who played on Westclox teams enjoyed the physical competition and public visibility involved. When a woman from the Westclox basketball team remembered her exhibition game with the famous Edmonton grads, she noted how exhilarating it was to play in front of a large crowd, if only to lose to such competitive, top-notch players. Ballplayers recall with pride the spectators who filled the stands; there was no mistaking the sense of public presence articulated by one woman who told me "that [baseball diamond] at [Riverside park] *belonged* to us girls . . . then later, the men took it over."[86] "Years later," a star player remembered nostalgically, "someone would come up to me on the street downtown and say, 'I remember you pitching for Westclox!'"[87]

Women's teams drew together a "specially bonded"[88] female community, and at Westclox united office and plant workers, who rarely socialized in other companies. Teams also became a way for married women to continue work and friendly contacts that homemaking denied them after they left the company. One woman, self-described as "ball crazy,"[89] continued to play and tour after she left work to have children; she used to take her children to practices, and another Westclox friend looked after them. The strong identification of these women with sports may well point to a class dimension missing in the feminist analysis of Canadian sport: Veronica Strong-Boag has suggested that working-class women were perhaps "less intimidated by stereotypical assumptions" about femininity and thus uniquely placed to take advantage of new team opportunities.[90] The early experience of many of these women playing ball in the streets and fields with brothers and friends, and their later hearty embrace of sports, indicates this to be true. Working-class women's attitudes towards team sports also suggests that medical and educational experts were not entirely unsuccessful in promoting a passive and delicate image of femininity: rather, the Westclox women believed they could combine 'being ladies' on the field (i.e., not swearing, drinking) with being excellent, competitive, assertive ballplayers. As Kate McCrone has argued for an earlier period, emancipatory possibilities for women could emerge from even the most limited and male-defined extension of women's sports.[91]

To the company, of course, promotion of these teams was a form of boosterism, a means of encouraging company loyalty and keeping good workers. Some women ballplayers remained for years with the company; once established there, the existence of benefit and pension plans encouraged one's decision to remain. And while workers who participated in sports may not have directly shared in the company's goals, their sports playing still had a positive influence on their attitude towards their employer. Moreover, for some women, excellence in sports seemed to provide a source of personal identification that helped to overcome the limitations of the glass ceiling encountered at work: women came to identify their enjoyed sport and leisure time with their workplace; as a result, 'the softball solution' did aid the company's effort to manufacture consent in the workplace.

If team sports supplied one glue to cement the Westclox family together, another was the company publication, *Tic Talk*. As Stuart Brandes has argued, company publications were a well-planned strategy to persuade the worker that she had a stake in the company's success, that the company had the economic sense to run the show and also cared about their personal goals and family life.[92] Westclox introduced an all-Canadian version of *Tic Talk* in the late 1930s, when Peterborough's GE also inaugurated its own in-house newspaper. Although GE boasted in the *Financial Post* about its success in "spreading the news"[93] through its paper, few GE employees seem to have read it, whereas many Westclox employees wrote for *Tic Talk* and remember reading it; even union activists often offered to lend me copies they had saved.

Like other in-house publications, the Westclox one attempted to create support for company objectives. Basic lessons in economics were standard fare: the hazards of running a profitable business were stressed and concepts like capital formation were made familiar with comparisons to homes and gardens; "capital formation . . . is just [the same] as when you set up a garden, you buy the necessary tools, fertilizer. . . . It is what every company or country needs to provide jobs for *all of us* [my emphasis] in the coming years."[94] The Horatio Alger myth was also a staple theme, as was the company's goodwill and connections to the community, its commitment to full employment, and especially its concern for health and safety (though accidents, it was stressed, were invariably the result of individual failings). Changes in company structure were rationalized, particularly downsizing exercises, increasingly accompanied by veiled warnings that the company was "vulnerable" because its "high costs of assembly," especially wages, were too high.[95] Finally, the company's fate, it was stressed, lay in the response of "Joe Customer" to the quality of its product.[96] Workers were simultaneously encouraged to see themselves as consumers, thus making the point that workers were the architects of their own employment fate.[97] Indeed, the theme of consumerism ran throughout the publication; the company included ads for its own products and gossip columns abounded with notices of workers' consumer purchases: "Ethel . . . came in all smiles this morning," noted one writer for *Tic Talk*, "her hubby has given her a new radio and hi fi. Add to this the new automatic dryer she got recently and she isn't doing badly!"[98] That Ethel's own wages had been used to make these purchases is not noted.

Tic Talk also promoted a vision of Westclox as a family, and in doing so, reinforced certain images of women's and men's gendered work and family roles: for instance, women's domestic and mothering duties were lauded approvingly, while biographies of long-time employees often confirmed their status as 'good family men.' Family ties were often mentioned as a theme underlying plant relationships; as Father's Day approached one year the editor urged everyone to have a very special "Westclox Fathers Day" celebration because so many kids had "followed their dads into the plant."[99] During the war, sections of the company were encouraged to adopt Westclox boys overseas, sending them collective presents. In turn, their letters of thanks were reprinted for the employees (largely female) to read: in one, addressed "Dear Mother," the soldier notes how much the Westclox present meant: "You know it was being a kid on Christmas morning . . . it was like receiving my first toy."[100]

Nowhere are distinct gender roles more clearly accented than in the extensive gossip columns sent in by worker-writers. The births, deaths, and marriages columns were obviously meant to reinforce a sense of community and overcome the impersonal alienation of factory life. But it was the mating and dating game that clearly drew most reader interest. Here, the dominant social prejudices of the period are replicated with little or no critical comment. Women are supposedly consumed with mating impulses and bliss is achieved when a diamond ring appears. Especially after the war years, women come close to being man hunters: "She may not be in the RCMP, but she got her man!"[101] Once mated, a woman was then "out of circulation,"[102] no longer fair game for other interested bachelors. Male reporters were almost as concerned with romance, ridiculing fellow workers who were smitten with the "love bug" and would soon lose their manly independence to the trap of marriage.[103] Particular relish is shown for in-house romances, which then become a focus for further teasing. Once official, engagements are followed by a number of rituals: departmental showers, parties, and a public gift giving. With marriage, it is assumed that "women will now retire to take up another job, homemaking,"[104] while men will continue to work at the plant. Few references to married working women are made, save for one reporter who notes that the married women are easily noticed by their "weary faces,"[105] a rare comment on the double day. Until the 1960s, one image of the family is made to seem natural and inevitable in these columns: the nuclear, home-owning, mother-at-home, father-at-work family.

The sexes are bound together by dating and mating, and ultimately, "marriage comes highly recommended,"[106] but at the same time, men and women are oceans apart in character and ability — an implicit justification for a division of labour. Women are concerned with beauty and appearance, men with technical knowledge and physical strength. Women's 'known' love of shopping is mentioned frequently, while fishing and hunting are clearly pursuits which preoccupy male departments. Cars are a man's joy, but women are "the plague of our highways."[107] While car ownership is clearly offering some women new independence by the 1940s, depictions of women's car trips and vacations often carried a punchline describing mishaps or teasing about the potential perils of female independence.

Tic Talk's use of graphics and pictures also exhibited the familial theme: not only were company events showing workers and managers happily playing together profiled, but many employees sent in their own pictures of family and fellow Westclox friends. Again, the contrast with the GE publication is stark: while GE pictures were often posed for plant photographers, the Westclox ones were submitted by the workers themselves. Pictures are off-centre, sometimes ill-focused and completely home-grown: it is this lack of professionalism, ironically, that characterized *Tic Talk*'s success, for a feeling of active involvement in the publication, rather than company manipulation, was created, consciously or not, by this 'family album' approach.

Although *Tic Talk* columns were occasionally edited, they were also the product of shop floor banter that many workers clearly enjoyed. One of the ways in which workers cope with the workplace, Louise Lamphere argues, is to create their own social networks that celebrate life rituals, offer mutual support, and break down the anonymity of the factory.[108] These social networks may be particularly important to women because they reproduce care-giving roles learned in the family and because women's wage work, which is characterized by little control and autonomy, needs a strong antidote of sociability on the shop floor. By integrating these social networks into its own publication, Westclox was able to promote the image of a humane workplace, concerned with workers' lives outside the factory. While the company calculated this as a means of securing worker satisfaction and loyalty, workers participated for different reasons: to alleviate boredom, engage in daily gossip (surely one of the most important social staples of our lives), connect with other people. Women who are asked in interviews about the *conditions* of work often quickly move into discussions of these *social networks*; the connection in their memories says much about the way in which women wanted to 'socialize' the workplace to make it as livable and human as possible. At the same time, by participating in the company magazine, by endorsing images of male breadwinner and female dependent, male competence and female technical scatterbrain, workers were also legitimizing the division of labour and the existing hierarchy in the factory and in the household. While trying to make the workplace livable, they were unconsciously reproducing its gendered hierarchy.

Conclusion: Paternalism in Decline

Westclox's paternalism was, from the very beginning, part of a conscious strategy to avoid unionization, but the company was ultimately unable to defeat a powerful postwar trend, and in 1952, after more than one union attempt, the plant chose the International Union of Electrical Workers (IUE) as their bargaining agent. Still, the office workers consistently resisted unionization, the plant never went on strike, and the union was considered 'moderate' by others in the vicinity.

Plant workers became sympathetic to unionization when they saw the material benefits of paternalism seriously eroding. As other major Peterborough plants secured good benefit packages, Westclox's former generosity began to look deficient. Once the gap between the promise of paternalism and the reality became quite wide, disappointment set in, perhaps even more strongly because of previously raised hopes of fair dealing on the company's part.[109] With more economic pressure on the company, the shop floor also became more pressured by the 1960s and the previous bargain of flexibility in work relations deteriorated. Unionization was perceived as a necessary (and by some, even unfortunate) last resort to defend the benefits initiated by the company in earlier decades. Finally, as the parent company restructured and eventually threatened to move (to low-wage Nova Scotia), the union was seen as a means of protection in the face of the company's disintegration.

Unionization was an indication that the negotiated partnership and paternalist bargain fostered in the 1920s, 1930s and 1940s, had begun to erode. As Gerald Zahavi points out, workers tried to use paternalism for their own ends, extracting certain economic and moral obligations from the employer in return for their loyalty.[110] Women and men at the Westclox plant used the rhetoric of paternalism, and obtained their own rewards, as much as possible, from the company. Men could benefit from a degree of autonomy on the shop floor, hope of upward mobility, a sense of masculine privilege and camaraderie, and reinforced identification with the image of the male breadwinner. Women could also try to use paternalism to make their workplace more human, less confrontational and flexible, to provide mobility within female job ghettos, and also to reinforce a sense of dignity secured through their status as moral working women.

For some individuals, like the favoured softball players, there were other sources of pride and compensation. Thus, even if paternalism seemed to symbolize deference to one's employer, a more negotiated accommodation was involved. While the paternalist bargain meant acquiescence, at least to some extent, to economic inequality, and acceptance of a gendered hierarchy at work, a distinct notion of *dignity owed* to workers and the respectability of their aspirations and lives — though differently defined for men and women — was promoted and defended by the workers.

The resilience of paternalism at Westclox, well into the twentieth century, is explained by the specific material and local conditions in which the factory was embedded, the economic pressures encouraging conformity in the workplace, and the influence of powerful, dominant ideologies that offered a meaningful rationale for the 'natural' hierarchy and justice of paternalism. For many years, Westclox successfully synthesized favourable local and international economic conditions with a policy of moderate benefits and discretionary paternalism. Unlike the local textile firms employing women, the clock factory was able to pay slightly higher wages and remain competitive. As an astute executor of Westclox's management strategy, J.H. Vernor's apparently charismatic and convincing role as patriarch should also be noted. Westclox's overlapping tactics of nineteenth-century paternalism and twentieth-century welfarism were also likely aided by Peterborough's overwhelming ethnic homogeneity, and by the size of the city, with its 'small-town' atmosphere. The spatial proximity of worker and manager in some neighbourhoods and churches, close knowledge of family networks within the city, and a stable social hierarchy bolstered the ideological hegemony operating within the factory, creating the illusion of an 'organic community' in which class and community interest were one and the same. Earlier work has suggested that class consciousness could be "reinforced by the community solidarity of small towns,"[111] but the Westclox example suggests that the social relations of small cities might also inhibit class conflict. Furthermore, Peterborough's distinct labour history, in particular the failure of an industrial strike in textiles in 1937, and the inability of industrial unions to make significant inroads until the later 1940s, also meant that workers did not have at hand institutional or ideological alternatives to the paternalist bargain.

Finally, the resilience of paternalism must also be explained by the ideological creation of consent. Already existing, dominant notions of 'natural' economic hierarchy and inevitable gender differences were diffused through daily workplace practices, company symbols, and rituals. Gender was not peripheral, but rather central to this ideological hegemony. Paternalism was sustained by its assimilation and reproduction of a gender ideology that reinforced an image of female transience and marriageability, male independence and camaraderie, female obedience, and male authority. The workplace hierarchy was fused with gender roles supposedly found in the household and given strong sanction by society. A familial language justified *both* the gendered division of labour in the plant *and* the paternal placement of male managers over female workers; notions of sexual difference explained why males might go from being sons to fathers, while women remained forever daughters.

However, decent benefits and wages were always part of the 'deal' that the company fashioned with its workers. If the company let down its part of the bargain, workers felt justified in shifting their allegiance as well. Significantly, when the company called for a rollback in wages in 1969, it targeted *only* the women workers. When the union appeared to waver on the issue, one female union executive had to write an indignant letter to the union negotiator warning him that women workers were upset about reported 'secret negotiations' between the (male) union and management, and that women would not tolerate union leaders making a backroom deal to sell the women out.[112] When the General Time Empire began to fold in Canada, Westclox women were first asked to pay the price and become even more dependent on the 'father' with lower wages. The fact that women refused indicates that the paternalist bargain, while appealing, always had its limits.

Appendix: A Note on Methodology

This article is part of a much larger study of working women in Peterborough from 1920 to 1960. While government documents, newspapers, and manuscript collections have been used as research tools, I have also used oral histories of former workers and managers as a basis for my conclusions. This was particularly important in the Westclox case, as the company denied me access to any of their records.

From the larger sample of Peterborough interviews, those with former Westclox employees number twenty-nine: twenty-one of these were with female white- and blue-collar workers, and the remaining were male managers, workers, and foremen. While the blue-collar women made up roughly two-thirds of the female group, it is difficult to precisely characterize women by occupation as there was quite a bit of movement from the factory floor into the office.

The interviews were usually two or more hours in length and were sometimes followed by phone conversations to clarify issues. The interview sample was a 'snowball' sample; many of the women and men were referred to me or called me after an article in the local newspaper described my research. Some responded to flyers posted in the local library and museum, or were referred by family, neighbours, or members of the labour movement who eventually heard of my work.

All of the women interviewed began work at Westclox in a twenty-year period between 1933 and 1953; 50 percent began before World War II and 50 percent began after 1940. Approximately half, again, were 'long-time' employees, working at Westclox over ten years, with the other half shorter-term employees, working under ten years (with about one-quarter of the women very short-term employees, working approximately three to four years). The majority of the men were longer-term employees.

This sample thus favours longer-term employees, although Westclox also claimed that it was particularly successful in keeping workers and offered some statistics to prove this. The observations of the longer-term employees were also important, for these workers often periodized the history of the company: many referred to the 'early years,' which usually meant the period up to the immediate postwar years, and the 'later years,' which meant the period from the 1950s, and especially the 1960s, on.

Notes

1   Westclox Interviews #18, Feb. 1990, and #1, July 1989. I have deliberately chosen one quote from a blue-collar worker and one from a white-collar worker.

2   Without access to company records (which I have been denied), I cannot produce such statistics, though by reading articles and biographies in the company's in-house publication, I could get a sense of how many employees were rewarded

for long service. At one company dinner, a manager claimed that 40 percent of those employed in 1931 were still with the company twenty-five years later. Oral history *can* measure people's perceptions that there were many people who stayed with the company for a long period of time. Conclusions about the nature of people's memories of Westclox were reached after comparing Westclox interviews to those with workers from other companies in the city, particularly the three other largest businesses at this time.

3 Eugene Genovese, *Roll, Jordan, Roll: The World the Slaves Made* (New York, 1976), provides one of the classic arguments for paternalism in race relations. A more recent essay that looks at class, gender, and race and the operation of industrial paternalism is Dolores Janiewski, "Southern Honour, Southern Dishonour: Managerial Ideology and the Construction of Gender, Race, and Class Relations in Southern Industry," in *Work Engendered: Toward a History of American Labor,* ed. Ava Baron (Ithaca, 1991). This paper primarily makes reference to works on industrial paternalism. See note 8 below.

4 On oral history as a methodology, see Ronald Grele, *Envelopes of Sound* (Chicago, 1975), Michael Frisch, "The Memory of History," *Radical History Review* 25 (1981), or, more recently, Sherna Gluck and Daphne Patai, eds., *Women's Words: The Feminist Practice of Oral History* (New York, 1991).

5 As Ava Baron points out, in working-class history "while women's resistance has been documented, their 'consent' to oppression, like that of men, remains undertheorized." See Ava Baron, "Gender and Labor History: Learning from the Past, Looking to the Future," in *Work Engendered,* ed. Baron, 16.

6 Craig Heron, *Working in Steel: The Early Years in Canada, 1883–1935* (Toronto, 1988), 100.

7 On Britain, see Patrick Joyce, *Work, Society and Politics* (London, 1980), and, more recently, Judy Lown's *Women and Industrialization* (London, 1990), which addresses the question of gender as a central part of her thesis. See also Donald Reid, "Industrial Paternalism: Discourse and Practice in Nineteenth Century French Mining and Metallurgy," *Comparative Studies in Society and History* 27 (1985); Charles Dellheim, "The Creation of a Company Culture: Cadburys, 1861–1931," *American Historical Review* 92, no. 1 (Feb. 1987). American studies range from those starting with the mid-nineteenth century textile mills to those extending their focus into the twentieth century. See Philip Scranton, "Varieties of Paternalism: Industrial Structures and the Social Relations of Production in American Textiles," *American Quarterly* 36 (Summer 1984): 235–57; Jacqueline Dowd Hall, *Like a Family* (Chapel Hill, 1987); Frances Couvares, "The Triumph of Commerce: Class, Culture and Mass Culture in Pittsburgh," in *Working-Class America,* ed. M.H. Frisch and D.J. Walkowitz (Urbana, 1983), 123–52; Tamara Hareven, *Family Time and Industrial Time* (New York, 1982); Stephen Meyer, *The Five Dollar Day: Labor Management and Social Control in the Ford Motor Company, 1908–21* (New York, 1981);

Stanley Budner, *Pullman: An Experiment in Industrial Order and Community Planning* (New York, 1979); the best recent book is Gerald Zahavi, *Workers, Managers and Welfare Capitalism* (New York, 1988).

8   Judy Lown, "Not So Much a Factory, More a Form of Patriarchy: Gender and Class During Industrialization" in *Gender, Class and Work*, ed. Eva Gamarnikow (London, 1985). Lown argues that "paternalism is only one of many and varying forms of legitimation that holders of patriarchal power adopt" (35–36).

9   Lown, *Women and Industrialization*, 3.

10 See Philip Scranton's distinction between "formal, familial and fraternal" paternalism in the textile industry alone in "Varieties of Paternalism." The local context is also stressed in works such as Hall, *Like a Family*, and Zahavi, *Workers, Managers and Welfare Capitalism*.

11 Stuart Brandes, *American Welfare Capitalism, 1880–1940* (Chicago, 1976); Daniel Nelson, *Managers and Workers: Origins of the New Factory System in the United States, 1880–1920* (Madison, 1975); David Brody, *Workers in Industrial America: Essays on the Twentieth Century Struggle* (New York, 1980). Nelson, for example, sees paternalism and welfare capitalism as distinct and claims that in some situations traditional paternalism "deterred" the adoption of welfare work (115).

12 Brandes and Couvares suggest that workers were suspicious of welfarism, but Brody claims it was having some successes until the Depression revealed its inherent problems. Sanford Jacoby, *Employing Bureaucracy: Managers, Unions and the Transformation of Work in American Industry, 1890–1945* (New York, 1985), suggests that interest in welfare capitalism was waning by the late 1920s.

13 Zahavi, *Workers, Managers and Welfare Capitalism*.

14 Robert Storey, "Unionization Versus Corporate Welfare: The Dofasco Way," *Labour/Le Travail* 12 (1983): 7. See also Bruce Scott, "A Place in the Sun: The Industrial Councils at Massey-Harris, 1919–29," *Labour/Le Travail* 1 (1976); James Naylor, *The New Democracy: Challenging the Social Order in Industrial Ontario, 1914–25* (Toronto, 1991), chap. 6; Craig Heron, *Working in Steel*, 98–111; Margaret McCallum, "Corporate Welfarism in Canada," *Canadian Historical Review* 71 (1990). The one Canadian book that deals with the question of gender and paternalism is Joy Parr, *The Gender of Breadwinners* (Toronto, 1990). Overviews of Canadian business, such as Michael Bliss, *A Living Profit: Studies in the Social History of Canadian Business* (Toronto, 1974), and *Northern Enterprise: Five Centuries of Canadian Business* (Toronto, 1987), are remarkably silent about paternalism and welfare capitalism.

15 Heron, *Working in Steel*, 110; Naylor, *The New Democracy*, 177.

16 Margaret McCallum has offered a useful view of welfare capitalism drawn from *Industrial Canada* and the Labour Gazette, but her article does not intend to analyze workers' reactions to this managerial strategy.

17 Neil Tudiver, "Forestalling the Welfare State: The Establishment of Programmes of Corporate Welfare" in *The "Benevolent" State: The Growth of Welfare in Canada*, ed. Allan Moscovitch and Jim Albert (Toronto, 1987).

18 McCallum, "Corporate Welfarism in Canada," 47.

19 As Michael Earle pointed out to me, in Sydney, the meagre attempts to attempt paternalist strategies at DOSCO (e.g., setting up things like Works Councils) *did* flounder with the Depression, thus replicating the pattern that some American labour historians have pointed to.

20 See Daniel Nelson and Stuart Campbell, "Taylorism Versus Welfare Work in American Industry: H.L. Gantt and the Bancrofts," *Business History Review* 46 (Spring 1972): 1–16.

21 Genovese, paraphrased from Jackson Lears, "The Concept of Cultural Hegemony: Problems and Possibilities," *American Historical Review* 90, no. 3 (June 1985).

22 Recent writing has shied away from the very word 'ideology,' influenced by poststructuralist critiques of the concept and understandably wary of a very traditional Marxist categorization of 'false' or illusory ideology mystifying the 'true' picture of society. Instead of jettisoning the concept, it may be useful to use it, in a Gramscian and feminist manner, as one means of understanding how class and gender inequalities become 'naturalized' and universalized, in the workplace and in larger society.

23 My thinking here is indebted to interpretations of Gramsci by both labour historians and social theorists: three examples are Robert Gray, *The Labour Aristocracy in Victorian Edinburgh* (Oxford, 1976); Anna Pollert, *Girls, Wives, Factory Lives* (London, 1981); Terry Eagleton, *Ideology* (London, 1991).

24 Carl Boggs, *The Two Revolutions: Gramsci and the Dilemmas of Western Marxism* (Boston, 1984), 160.

25 For workplace studies incorporating this perspective, see, for example, Mary Blewett, *Men, Women and Work: Class, Gender and Protest in the New England Shoe Industry* (Champaign, IL, 1988); Patricia Cooper, *Once a Cigar Maker: Men, Women and Work Culture in American Cigar Factories* (Urbana, IL, 1987); Cynthia Cockburn, *Brothers: Male Dominance and Technological Change* (London, 1983); Parr, *The Gender of Breadwinners*.

26 Lown, "Not So Much a Factory," 34.

27 "The Westclox Story," company pamphlet, c. 1978, personal copy.

28 Although financial and production management was guided by others, including long-time manager, Newfoundland-born Herbert Cranford.

29 "Mr. Westclox Dies," *Peterborough Examiner*, 20 July 1966.

30 Of the interviews with blue- and white-collar workers, about half made reference to the congenial, family atmosphere. Others, while they did not describe the workplace in familial terms, made observations such as: "Westclox was a wonderful place to work when I started. . . . Management and employees got on so well; I could hardly wait to get back to work the next day": Westclox Interview #22, July 1989. A minority certainly saw this simply as a job like any other; these were more often shorter-term employees.

31 On such workplace 'scripts,' see John Bodnar, "Power and Memory in Oral History: Workers and Managers at Studebaker," *Journal of American History* 75, no. 4 (March 1989): 1201–21.

32 Quote from Interview #2, June 1989. Although this was a manager speaking, similar observations were made by other white- and blue-collar employees, though they did not describe the situation quite so tragically.

33 Joyce, *Work, Society and Politics*, 94.

34 Westclox Interview #9, 10 April 1991.

35 Westclox Interview #23, July 1989.

36 Parr, *The Gender of Breadwinners*, 35.

37 Miriam Glucksmann argues that women were the primary — and crucial — workforce in many mass-production industries making food and small appliances; this resulted not from a de-skilling process, but rather from the initial, conscious decision of management to hire cheaper female labour. See Miriam Glucksmann, *Women Assemble: Women Workers and the New Industries in Inter-war Britain* (London, 1990).

38 Glucksmann, *Women Assemble*, 154.

39 This term is taken from Michael Burawoy, *Manufacturing Consent: Changes in the Labor Process Under Monopoly Capitalism* (Chicago, 1979). Burawoy concentrates on the manufacturing of consent on the shop floor through the organization of the labour process — through game playing, lateral displacement of conflict, etc. Although some of his conclusions are useful for an analysis of the work process at Westclox, I have chosen to concentrate on other means of manufacturing consent in this paper.

40 After the company's increasing economic problems in the 1960s, however, some long-time blue-collar employees found the atmosphere less hospitable, in part due to increasing cost cutting and speed-ups.

41 Westclox Interview #6, 27 June 1989; Interview #23, July 1989.

42 Westclox Interview #6, June 1989. It is possible that women's own methods of conflict resolution learned in the family, or even their different sense of privacy, made them appreciate this mediated approach. This is not an ahistorical claim that women are, by nature, 'conciliatory,' but rather a suggestion that,

in this time period, women often learned mediating roles in the family and community. While labour historians have documented women's different work cultures and different approaches to resistance, there is less research on women's 'accommodation' in the workplace. More recent feminist literature on women's methods of organizing have suggested that our gendered experience, as well as feminist ideology, produces different methods of organizing. See Jeri Wine and Janice Ristock, eds., *Women and Social Change: Feminist Activism in Canada* (Toronto, 1991). It is worth noting that a contemporary study of activist women draws different conclusions about the relationship between family and work than I do: see Karen Sachs, *Caring by the Hour: Women, Work and Organizing at Duke Medical Centre* (Urbana, IL, 1988).

43 Kate Purcell, "Female Manual Workers: Fatalism and the Reinforcement of Inequalities" in *Rethinking Social Inequality,* ed. David Robbins (London, 1982), 49.

44 Westclox Interview #9, 10 April 1991.

45 Zahavi, *Workers, Managers and Welfare Capitalism.*

46 Westclox Interview #2, June 1989.

47 This practice seemed to persist into the 1950s.

48 It is also important to note that the city as a whole was largely un-unionized until the later 1940s.

49 Women's attitudes towards benefits were also shaped by their age and longevity of employment. Still, many industries made generalizations about all women workers. For example, General Electric in the United States assumed that women were interested in "sociability not security." See Ronald Schatz, *The Electrical Workers: A History of Labor at General Electric and Westinghouse, 1932–60* (Urbana, IL, 1983), 22.

50 Archives of Ontario (AO), RG 7-57, Dept. of Labour, Miss Finlay's report, 1927. Westclox's paid vacations were the most expensive and attractive of its benefits. In the 1927 study only about one-third of the companies surveyed had paid vacations.

51 *Industrial Canada,* June 1935; Sept. 1935; Oct. 1935; Aug. 1936.

52 It also needs to be compared to industries of other size and wealth. Companies like Imperial Oil were much larger and able to sustain expensive benefits. As Nelson points out for the United States, only the larger minority of companies ever became really involved in welfare plans; many smaller companies continued to deal with unions in a different way — with active intimidation. See Nelson, *Managers and Workers,* 116.

53 Westclox Interview #4, 12 Dec. 1990.

54 AO, RG 7-57, Dept. of Labour, File: Industrial Relations, pre-1936. It is revealing that other Peterborough industries listed in the same file indicated similar

patterns. Quaker Oats, for instance, said there "was no pension plan, but the company takes care of needy and deserving cases. No one is allowed to suffer."

55 Westclox Interview #18, 8 Feb. 1990.

56 Westclox Interview #20, 22 Aug. 1990.

57 Ralph H. Matthiessen, claim former managers, also evidenced paternal concern for his employees. This manager cited an example, not witnessed, but rather part of oral tradition, that Matthiessen approved wage increases in the Depression, despite falling profits, as a measure of the company's moral debt to its workforce. Interview #21, 18 July 1989.

58 Even if they didn't actively participate in city government or social organizations, some managers were perceived as 'well-connected,' respected community leaders. Westclox managers in these years were less visible than GE ones in civic politics. Vernor never became openly involved, perhaps because he was American. His wife, however, was associated with appropriate charities, like the YWCA, and he was involved in fraternal organizations, as was his second-in-command, Cranford. Evidence of the 'respect' held for some of these managers is well illustrated in the number of times I had to turn the tape recorder off rather than reveal any fact that might be interpreted negatively.

59 Westclox Interview #2, June 1989.

60 *Peterborough Examiner*, 1 Dec. 1954.

61 On department stores' successful use of paternalism, including the encouragement of upward mobility of women into white-collar jobs, see Gail Reekie, "'Humanising Industry': Paternalism, Welfarism and Labour Control in Sydney's Big Stores, 1890–1930," *Labour History* 53 (Nov. 1987): 1–19.

62 Westclox Interview #2, June 1989.

63 Ibid.

64 As other authors have noted, companies' promotion of the ideal of a family wage also provided ideological and economic reinforcement for women's role in unpaid domestic labour. See Martha May, "The Historical Problem of the Family Wage: The Ford Motor Company and the Five Dollar Day," *Feminist Studies* 8, no. 2 (Summer 1982): 399–424. See also Linda Frankel, "Southern Textile Women: Generations of Survival and Struggle," in *My Troubles Are Going to Have Trouble with Me: The Everyday Trials and Triumphs of Women Workers*, ed. Karen Sachs (New Brunswick, NJ, 1980), for the argument that "paternalism . . . depended on women's continued responsibility for domestic life" (46).

65 Margery Davies, *Woman's Place Is at the Typewriter: Office Work and Office Workers, 1870–1930* (Philadelphia: 1982), 155.

66 Brandes, *American Welfare Capitalism*, 140.

67 From the chaperoned boarding houses of Lowell to lessons in culture at Heinz, employers utilized various tactics to create the impression that, under their tutelage, working-class women would be better able to maintain their pure character and thus become respectable and sought-after wives. On distinct programs for women, see Nelson, *Managers and Workers*. On nineteenth-century paternalism and the protection of women's 'respectability,' see Parr, *The Gender of Breadwinners*, chap. 2. In *Workers, Managers and Welfare Capitalism*, Zahavi argues that Endicott Johnson defended the morality and respectability of wage-earning *mothers*, primarily because these women's labour was needed in his factory — indicating the malleability of paternalism according to the needs of capital. In the context of the Peterborough labour market, married women were not a crucial necessity to the company (at least until the war years), and so the company could endorse the family wage and ignore the issue of wage-earning mothers.

68 Westclox Interview #2, June 1989.

69 Ibid.

70 Westclox Interview #1, 10 July 1989.

71 Westclox Interview #23, July 1989.

72 Westclox Interview #2, June 1989.

73 Westclox Interview #20, 22 Aug. 1990.

74 Westclox Interview #4, 12 Dec. 1990.

75 For discussion of how dress, image, and gesture were used to express gender identity for working-class women, see J. Dowd Hall, "Disorderly Women: Gender and Labor Militancy in the Appalachian South," *Journal of American History* 73 (Summer 1986): 354–82; and Kathy Peiss, *Cheap Amusements: Working Women and Leisure in Turn-of-the-Century New York* (Philadelphia, 1986).

76 Census material from 1921 to 1941 confirms this characterization. For example, Canada, Census of 1921, vol. 1, table 28, shows those listing British racial origins to be 92% of the city's population. Canada, Census of 1931, vol. 2, table 34, shows 91% of the population listing British racial origins; table 47 shows that 80% of the population was born in Canada and 16% born in the British Isles. Canada, Census of 1941, vol. 1, table 34, indicates that 90% listed British origins; table 45 indicates that 83% were Canadian born and 12% were born in Britain. This was a stable and predominantly Anglo city.

77 Westclox Interview #9, 10 April 1991.

78 Westclox Interview #12, July 1989.

79 Westclox Interview #7, Sept. 1989.

80 Carl Betke, "The Social Significance of Sport in the City," in *Cities in the West*, ed. A.R. McCormack and I. Macpherson (Ottawa, 1975). American sports historians

point to the commercialization of sports in this period, but this was not so visible in a smaller community. See Mark Dyreson, "The Emergence of Consumer Culture and the Transformation of Physical Culture: American Sport in the 1920's," *Journal of Sport History* 16, no. 3 (Winter 1989): 261–81.

81 On the increasing use of recreation programs by companies in World War II, see "Industrial Recreation, Canadian Style," *Recreation*, Dec. 1944. For a revisionist view which suggests that American companies renewed their interest in welfare capitalism during the war, see Elizabeth Fones-Wolf, "Industrial Recreation, the Second World War, and the Revival of Welfare Capitalism, 1934–60," *Business History Review* 60, no. 2 (Summer 1986): 232–57.

82 Ronald Melchers, "Sports in the Workplace," in *Not Just a Game: Essays in Canadian Sport Sociology*, ed. Jean Harvey and Hart Cantelon (Ottawa, 1988).

83 Wilma Pesavento, "Sport and Recreation in the Pullman Experiment, 1880–1900," *Journal of Sport History* 9, no. 2 (Summer 1982): 38–62. See also John Schleppi, "'It Pays': John H. Patterson and Industrial Recreation at the National Cash Register Company," *Journal of Sport History* 6, no. 3 (Winter 1979): 20–28. On Canada, Morris Mott, "One Solution to the Urban Crisis: Manly Sports and Winnipeggers, 1900–14," *Urban History Review* 12, no. 2 (1983): 57–70.

84 Helen Lenskyj, *Out of Bounds: Women, Sport and Sexuality* (Toronto, 1986). See also her "Femininity First: Sport and Physical Education for Ontario Girls, 1890–1930," in *Sports in Canada*, ed. Morris Mott (Toronto, 1989).

85 Melvin Adelman, "Baseball, Business and the Workplace: Gelber's Thesis Reexamined," *Journal of Social History* 23, no. 2 (Winter 1989): 285–301.

86 Westclox Interview #20, 22 Aug. 1990.

87 Westclox Interview #12, July 1989.

88 *Peterborough Examiner*, undated clipping, 1990. This term was used by a woman interviewed about her memories of wartime industrial softball leagues.

89 Westclox Interview #7, 20 Sept. 1990.

90 Veronica Strong-Boag, *The New Day Recalled: Lives of Girls and Women in English Canada, 1919–39* (Toronto, 1988), 31.

91 Kathleen McCrone, *Sport and the Physical Emancipation of English Women, 1870–1914* (London, 1988).

92 Brandes, *American Welfare Capitalism*.

93 "How GE Spreads Its News," *Financial Post*, 2 April 1955.

94 *Tic Talk*, June 1954.

95 By the 1960s these warnings were hardly veiled. In *Tic Talk*, Dec. 1966, the paper asked, "Do these names mean anything to you?" It offered names of plants

that had gone out of business in Peterborough and then concluded: "The key to job security is in your hands."

96 *Tic Talk*, Dec. 1956 and Dec. 1962.

97 At GE, interestingly, it was *Mrs.* Consumer who was featured in their paper. For a discussion of companies like GE that deliberately pursued promotion of consumerism amongst its workers, see John T. Cumbler, *Working-Class Community in Industrial America: Work, Leisure, and Struggle in Two Industrial Cities, 1880–1930* (Greenwood, NJ, 1979).

98 *Tic Talk*, Dec. 1959.

99 *Tic Talk*, June 1954.

100 *Tic Talk*, June 1944.

101 *Tic Talk*, Dec. 1956.

102 *Tic Talk*, June 1954.

103 *Tic Talk*, June 1966. The humour relating to marriage in these columns bears a striking resemblance to themes presented in James Snell, "Marriage Humour and Its Social Functions, 1900–39," *Atlantis* 11, no. 2 (1986).

104 *Tic Talk*, Dec. 1966.

105 *Tic Talk*, July 1966.

106 *Tic Talk*, Sept. 1959.

107 *Tic Talk*, Sept. 1959.

108 Louise Lamphere, "Bringing the Family to Work: Women's Culture on the Shop Floor," *Feminist Studies* 11 (Fall 1985): 519–40.

109 There is also an argument to be made that the experience and age cohort of women working in the plant by this time made them more sympathetic to unionization. There were probably more women with long experience in the plant and slightly more married women with dependents by the early 1950s.

110 Zahavi, *Workers, Managers and Welfare Capitalism*.

111 Craig Heron and George de Zwaan, "Industrial Unionism in Eastern Ontario: Gannoque, 1918–21," *Ontario History* 77, no. 3 (Sept. 1985): 159–82. It is important to note that many of the businesses (except for GE) in this city were, like Westclox, small enough to facilitate the cultivation of paternalism.

112 Library and Archives Canada, IUE Collection, 28-I-264, vol. 83, P. Drysdale to George Hutchens, President, Canadian IUE, 15 Sept. 1969. This issue is taken up by other women outside the factory who write to the Ontario Women's Bureau complaining that such a rollback would be "discriminatory": AO, RG 7, Dept. of Labour, Women's Bureau Correspondence, Series 8, Box 1.

In 1929 a group of men and women faced Peterborough's magistrate after police had intervened in a particularly loud and raucous party. Charged with being found in a disorderly house, the men and women tried to convince the magistrate to be as lenient as possible. The men based their pleas for tolerance on their status as wage-earning, respectable married men with families to support, and this being a first offence in an otherwise moral life. The magistrate, however, enforced fines, pointing out that mere attendance at a party where there was alcohol and young single women signified their "neglect of duty" to their families.[1] For the young women, the image of the hard-working family man didn't promise leniency; instead, their pleas were based on mercy, naïveté, and repentance. Claiming they had never been in such an embarrassing situation, and they were "very sorry and would never do it again,"[2] the women were allowed to go after a stern lecture on morality from the magistrate. These disorderly house arrests illustrate how men and women employed different defences to prove their innocence or justify their crime, and how the court responded with judgments shaped by the dominant social definitions of normal and proper gender roles. An analysis of the women most likely to come before Magistrate's Court, the court's claim to 'knowledge' about women's crimes, and women's own interpretations and defences of their crimes are the three themes of this article.

While a quantitative analysis of women arrested in the period from 1920 to 1950 emphasizes both the economic and social marginality framing these women's lives, and the importance of changing policing concerns to the very definitions of crime, the knowledge of women's criminality claimed by the magistrate and other legal experts exposes competing discourses, one stressing the environmental causes, the other the inevitable seeds of immorality behind female law breaking. Legal experts' explanations for women's criminality were shaped by shifting class and gender power relations, by cultural traditions and moral anxieties. Although these definitions did alter over these decades, they consistently reflected social, economic, and gender expectations rooted in the established power relations of class and patriarchy.

Finally, women's own interpretations of their law breaking are of special interest. Though sometimes represented by counsel, many others spoke alone, and even women with lawyers helped to construct their defences.[3] And while newspaper accounts offer a slanted version of their stories, fashioned for the paper's respectable readership, women's own voices and agency are still visible, often revealing women's attempts to actively shape the court's agenda. Indeed, the very subjectivity of women's stories may offer us the richest insights into how women perceived, and tried to control, the magistrate's justice meted out to them. As Natalie Zemon Davis argues for women defendants in an earlier time period, women "shaped and moulded" their stories with "careful choice of language, detail and order to present an account that seemed meaningful and explanatory."[4] In many cases, women's stories incorporated accepted themes of femininity and repentance, implying the need for leniency and a second chance. Fewer women, though quite aware of what was expected, mocked, or even rejected the knowledge of experts. Their challenges to the court speak to a current of resistance often forgotten in the history of women and crime.

Female Arrests and Male Magistrates

Previous examinations of women and crime in Canada have focused on women in conflict with the law in large urban centres in the nineteenth and early twentieth centuries, and sometimes on pivotal trials in the higher courts.[5] My intention is to refocus our sights on women from a small city and its rural hinterland, who are brought before Magistrate's Court in the mid-twentieth century. For over 90 percent of the Ontario women arrested at this time, justice started and ended with the magistrate,[6] who tried almost all summary offences, as well as some felonies, and drafted indictments for cases destined for a higher court.

In Peterborough, the court also absorbed the responsibility for juvenile and family matters until a Family Court was established in the late 1940s. The magistrate worked closely with both the police and with agencies like the Children's Aid Society and the Police Matron; they provided the magistrate with information on their suspects and clients, and often followed up with surveillance after sentencing.

Peterborough's combined city and county Magistrate's Court ruled a relatively stable rural and urban area, with an established manufacturing and service economy, an ethnically homogeneous population of Anglo/Celtic descent, and very little immigration in this period. Nonetheless, the city and county still experienced severe economic crisis during the Depression, as well as the upheavals of World War II, and local social reformers shared other Canadians' fears of crime and social disorder in their midst.

Indeed, these definitions of disorder, and subsequent policing priorities, rather than law breaking itself, are made most visible through the surviving arrest statistics. Nonetheless, an extensive debate about the worth of such quantitative sources[7] indicates the value of arrest statistics, if only as guideposts for changing policing concerns and as indicators of the social background of those who stood before the law. As European theoretical fashions place more analytical emphasis on the discourses constructing criminality, the stark picture offered by quantitative sources may be a useful reminder that those constructions had roots firmly planted in patterns of poverty and social marginalization.[8]

Women who found themselves before the magistrate were predominantly poor and working-class;[9] in the interwar period, a majority, representing numbers far greater than their presence in the local population, were domestics, whose work was characterized by low pay, low status, isolation, and transience.[10] In the 1920s, domestics accounted for 52 percent, housewives 25 percent of all charges; these two occupations continue to dominate, with housewives becoming the larger group (45 percent), and domestics second (25 percent) by the 1950s, a reflection of the decline of domestic service, but the continued marginalization and dependence of women working within the household. Factory workers ranked a more distant third for arrests, and by the 1950s, the growing number of women in clerical occupations were just as noticeable as their blue-collar sisters (see figure 1).

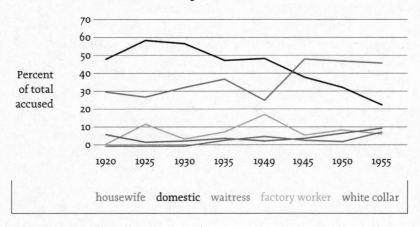

FIGURE 1. Occupations of Accused

Percent of total accused

housewife **domestic** waitress factory worker white collar

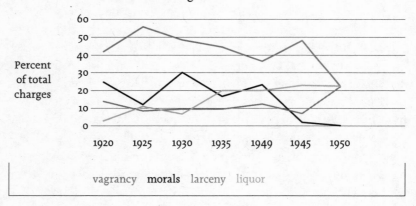

FIGURE 2. Charges

Percent of total charges

vagrancy **morals** larceny liquor

Most men in the jail cells were also poor and working-class, but their arrests stood in stark contrast to women's: men outnumbered women by 9 to 1,[11] and were more likely to be charged with theft and robbery, violent and sexual crimes, and extremely frequent liquor offences. Sixty-nine percent of all women's arrests,[12] conversely, were for three offences: small thefts, 'moral' crimes such as prostitution, and especially vagrancy (see figure 2). A vagrant was defined as any "loose, idle or disorderly" person who was begging, without financial support, loitering, destitute, or a "common nightwalker or prostitute."[13] Vagrancy, in other words, could be interpreted broadly by the police and magistrate to deal with women who stepped outside prescribed roles as private, domestic and mannerly citizens.[14] Women's lower arrest rate than men and their incarceration for different crimes have been attributed to their socialization, opportunities for crime, and distinct cultural, social, and economic roles; the legal system, moreover, literally defined crimes (such as prostitution) with reference to gender norms.[15]

Women's arrests reflected changing social anxieties and definitions of crime: until World War II, vagrancy consumed a vast amount of the police and magistrate's time, but by the postwar period, it was women's alcohol offences. In the 1920s, more women were arrested for making and selling, than drinking liquor, and in the Depression, moonshining could still result in a miserable three months in the county jail. By the 1950s, however, consumption of alcohol, not its sale, is the perceived problem, not because every bootlegger had gone out of business,[16] but because the possibility of obtaining cheap beer had cut into the trade. Whether women's actual drinking patterns had changed, a possibility given the fading memory of the temperance movement and the relative freedom of the war years, there is no doubt that authorities were enforcing a new concern with women's public, disorderly conduct while under the influence of liquor.[17]

Political or economic crises also highlighted new 'problems' for the authorities to tackle. During the war years, for example, when there was increasing panic over venereal disease, more local women were sent to the reformatory for treatment of VD. The cycles of the economy undoubtedly had an effect on types of offences committed, although not producing a simple cause and effect of all offences increasing during hard times, for charges could skyrocket in prosperous times, such as the late 1920s.[18] The effects of the Depression, however, were still visible in the increasing arrests for prostitution at the very beginning of the decade, though one of the most significant effects of Depression may have been an increasingly harsh magistrate whose sentencing reflected his fears that the economic crisis was causing social disruption, producing 'bad girls in a bad time' (see figure 3).[19]

TABLE 1. Arrests by Decade

Charge	1920s	1950s	1940s	1950s
		(in percent)		
Vagrancy	51.3	46.5	41.7	19.6
Vagrancy/prostitution	9.4	18.1	7.4	—[a]
Bawdy/disorderly/morals	6.0	4.7	6.1	—
Theft	10.3	9.4	9.8	16.3
Intoxication	1.7	10.3	21.5	27.8
Selling liquor	6.8	4.7	0.6	—
Suicide/insanity	6.8	4.7	0.6	3.3
Assault/manslaughter	0.9	0	4.3	7.7
Other	6.8	1.6	8.0	25.3[b]
Total	100	100	100	100
Number of charges	117	127	163	209

[a] Any prostitution arrests came under vagrancy in this decade.
[b] Of these charges, 21% came under the Child Welfare Act, 19% were public disturbance/obstructing police, 15% were false pretences/forgery, 13% came under the Juvenile Delinquent Act, 5% were perjury/material witness, and the rest were single charges for various crimes. Overall, child welfare charges would have been 5% of the total charges in this decade.

TABLE 2. Outcome of Arrests by Decade

Outcome	1920s	1930s	1940s	1950s
		(in percent)		
Discharge	36.8	17.3	7.4	24.6
Suspended sentence	7.6	11.8	12.9	13.1
Acquitted	0.9	6.3	17.8	1.4
Fine paid	1.7	3.1	16.0	19.8
County jail	13.7	40.9	31.3	16.0
Provincial jail	30.8	16.5	8.0	15.4
Hospital	5.9	1.6	6.1	8.7
Other	2.6	2.4	0.5	1.0

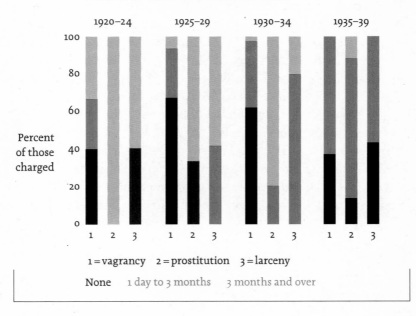

FIGURE 3. Sentences: Interwar Years

1 = vagrancy   2 = prostitution   3 = larceny

None   1 day to 3 months   3 months and over

Policing concerns were focused sharply on youthful offenders. Women in their teens and twenties made up the about two-thirds of the arrests, with women in their twenties slightly ahead of their teen sisters, save for the Depression years.[20] Overall, teens accounted for at least half of the theft and prostitution charges; the majority charged with streetwalking and vagrancy were also young, single women, with older and married women more likely to be charged under the disorderly and bawdy house sections of the Criminal Code. Middle-aged women in their thirties and forties were often taken in for vagrancy, with prostitution and theft increasingly displaced by alcohol as their cause of arrest. Age and occupation clearly played a role in overdetermining women's likelihood of being arrested, although aged women and widows, with known high levels of poverty, remain a small a percentage of arrests. Their absence might be explained by the concern of the authorities with very visible signs of poverty and public rejection of appropriate sexual and social roles — hence their concentration on young women in the streets.[21]

Given reformers' views that it was imperative to resocialize wayward girls at a young age, the strict sentencing of these women becomes understandable. More women were sent to Mercer for prostitution than for any other crime, and for young women, incarceration was an especially strong probability.[22] From 1920 to 1949, 75 percent of the teens arrested on morals charges went to jail, and 56 percent of them had sentences of over three months, more severe terms than for theft charges. These young women were sent out of town, to be removed from the source of their corruption, to the provincial Mercer Reformatory (or the Catholic alternative). As Carolyn Strange argues, by the 1920s local magistrates were heeding the advice of Mercer's superintendent, who claimed that, with flexible, indeterminate sentences, she might have an opportunity to reform the younger women — though not the older, experienced criminals.[23]

Unlike age and occupation, religion was not a notable variable in arrests, save for the slight over-representation of Pentecostals and Salvation Army women for moral offences in the 1930s.[24] Significantly, Irish Catholics, highly visible in nineteenth-century studies,[25] are not noticeable here: largely early settlers in the area, Irish Catholics may have assimilated well enough to the social order that they were less marginalized by poverty than their earlier cohorts. The notion that the Irish were more prone to crime, however, was still a feature of the social imagination, as evidenced by the police recorder who wrote in unusually large letters "Irish" beside the rare jail entry who claimed such a birthright. Though absent from arrest numbers, religious tension was displayed in the local court: one judge's confidential justification of his controversial sentencing of a Protestant/Catholic couple, for instance, rationalized that to treat either husband or wife differently would "raise the old cry of Catholic versus Protestant [which] we have had enough of [here]."[26]

Local judges and police also publicly claimed that crime was imported into Peterborough, yet the majority of arrests were native-born Canadians and resident Peterboroughians. The minority of women from outside the county were more likely to be vagrants, appearing more frequently after the transiency of the second world war years. Moreover, the crown attorney's claim that the rural hinterland — with some townships nicknamed the Badlands — nurtured immorality and crime was also suspect, as least in terms of women's misdemeanours.[27] In tandem with rural depopulation, the proportion of county women arrested declines, though the urban/rural locale consistently shaped differences in arrests. It is not surprising that rural housewives were more likely to be arrested for making illegal liquor — one of the few examples of the female crime 'entrepreneurs' found in large cities[28] — and that the county also sported few disorderly and bawdy houses: they were so obvious that local township councils passed public resolutions demanding that certain addresses be "cleaned up."[29]

Even Peterborough did not claim a major prostitution problem. After a flourish of concern in the Victorian and Edwardian era, newspapers' and reformers' interest in prostitution declined. By 1930, in fact, law enforcement officers reassured local citizens that prostitution had virtually disappeared as the city's "houses of ill fame" had been "cleaned up."[30] Since this is unlikely, it is possible that public scrutiny of the issue had declined as prostitution became a scattered enterprise, dominated by streetwalkers, with no fixed and glaring red light district in the city.[31] Prostitution could also have been more marginal because of the close proximity of the city of evil: Toronto. Given the possibilities of anonymity, and a more supportive work culture, many women might have opted for the big city over what became known later as 'PeterBOREough.' This may also account for the extremely low rate of prostitution charges for three-, four-, and five-time repeaters.[32]

Strict sentencing for moral offences remained a constant throughout the reign of two magistrates, though for other crimes incarceration did decrease by the postwar period. In the 1920s and 1930s, 44 percent and 57 percent of women were sentenced to some time in jail, even for crimes as innocuous as vagrancy, but by the mid 1940s more women were paying fines for all their crimes (especially alcohol offences), and walking out of court. A simple equation of increasing leniency over time, however, is misleading. Even though the magistrate was more likely to acquit or give suspended sentences to women by the postwar years (perhaps reflecting their use of attorneys) almost one-third still spent time in the county jail, and provincial jail terms could be one or two years.

Very few women who came before the court needed a second lesson. The majority (60 percent) of women arrested were first-, and one-time offenders, most likely cautioned or sometimes treated to an unpleasant stint in the county jail. Offenders with three or more offences were a small minority, recidivists with five offences a mere nine over four decades. Women with long histories of trouble with the law may have left for other cities, as the reigning magistrate came to know his clients, and a clear pattern of increasing severity of sentence, and more likelihood of confinement to the ancient and depressing county jail, existed with repeat offenders. Given the types of offences most recidivists were arrested for, almost exclusively vagrancy and liquor abuses,[33] it is clear that the majority of women in constant trouble with the law were often poor, homeless, sometimes alcoholics whose need was financial aid, perhaps family support, detoxification, and housing.

These, then, were the women who had to face magisterial justice. The majority were one-time offenders who made temporary transgressions of the law, and most came from backgrounds where they lacked economic security and social comfort. Many were housewives, unemployed, unskilled, or domestic workers. Born into a system characterized both by economic inequality and patriarchal power relations, women's confrontations with the courts were indelibly shaped by their location within that system.

The men who dispensed justice to these women in Magistrate's Court also shared similar backgrounds. The Peterborough Court was presided over by O.A. Langley, until the mid-1940s, when W.R. Philp, who also became the Family Court Judge, took over.[34] Both were university-educated, highly respectable community members, with close ties to legal circles, fraternal organizations, and churches in the community. Langley, a QC, who presided over the court for more than thirty years, came from an established Lakefield family; his long reign as a "strict" magistrate earned him the nickname of "thirty days or thirty dollars Langley."[35] Trained as lawyers, both men lacked the infamous Colonel Denison's contempt for the profession, but like him, they were less concerned with the intricacies of law than with the context of the defendant's misdemeanour and her moral character.[36] They saw their role as a composite of a judge, social worker, and arbitrator, and their pronouncements as emblems of morality for the community.

Perhaps their direct, moralistic pronouncements and speedy dispensation of justice facilitated the court's acceptance by the working class.[37]

Working people did bring their conflicts to the magistrate, though some-times as a last resort, or in an attempt to shame their adversaries: women transferred their children's neighbourhood fights to the court, landlord and tenant disputes were aired for revenge (during World War II, a boarder was charged with biting her landlord over a rationing dispute), and more than one dance or party that finished in physical brawl ended up in court.[38] At the same time, women's brushes with the law for moral offences or theft contravened notions of working-class respectability, distancing them from their own community. One distraught mother, for instance, wrote to the Mercer Reformatory, pleading that her daughter's presence there be kept a secret; otherwise, "if she returns home it will be hard to reform her if this small community finds out."[39]

The magistrate manoeuvred with considerable flexibility, wielding both formal and informal authority as he settled cases. Although women were dealt with speedily once in court, they could be remanded a week or more after arrest, while authorities renewed their surveillance, collected information, or gave them time to repent. Women might be bailed out or released on their own recognizance, though the magistrate, fearing flight from town, could also keep them in jail. Even more important, in the interwar period especially, many cases never made it to court. A 1926 *Peterborough Examiner* article, "A Day in Police Court," which charac-terized the court's offerings as "Justice, Mercy and Humour," noted that many cases, especially family disputes, were settled informally: "what is not generally known to the public is that hundreds of infractions of the law are never aired" in court. Police Chief Sam Newall often held his own informal "receptions" in his office or the courtroom, where a per-sonal lecture was the only sentence. This method was perceived to be useful as a first warning to young offenders and as a means of shielding "respectable citizens" from a court record. "Unofficial all this," breezed the reporter, but one of the "best" aspects of the administration of justice in Peterborough.[40] This reporter's disclosures also laid bare the process that women faced during the weekly court hearings. The first thing the prisoner saw, when she was escorted into the building, pos-sibly from a dreary jail cell, was the "the Magistrate, Chief of Police, and the Crown Attorney and several lawyers and policemen, chatting and swapping stories in the Chief's office in the lobby,"[41] a scene that could only confirm her fears that the authorities represented a united, antagonistic opponent. Once in court, she might also face spectators and the press. Located within the old city hall, near the city centre's market square, the court was conveniently placed for the casual as well as the dedicated observer.

Like the nineteenth-century police court, this one was represented in the local press in a manner that "affirmed" for the better off "their comfortable" and justly deserved place in the existing social hierarchy;[42] court reporting reminded the middle classes of the gulf between the respectable classes and the criminal, and warned the working class against falling from respectability into crime. In the interwar years, the comical, melodramatic, and salacious depiction of defendants was sometimes evident in the local newspaper, though by the 1940s, this long tradition of portraying the court as popular theatre was declining, and fewer spectators crowded the court.[43] Nonetheless, the embarrassment of exposure — particularly evident in a small town — still existed for women before the court.

In contrast to the spectacle of the court was the authority invested in the magistrate. For defendants and spectators, the symbols, rituals, and structure of the court reinforced the idea that the magistrate's knowledge was 'just and right, thus endowing it with great power.'[44] When the female prisoner entered the courtroom, she found dignified rituals that stressed the authority of the magistrate, who sat on a raised platform, was addressed as Your Honour, and whose comprehensive knowledge of the law endowed him with further authority. Looking down on the defendant, he consulted with the police beside him, whose advice was clearly valued more than the stories of the women defendants. Defendants were forced to recount personal aspects of their lives in this public forum, and they sometimes spoke without counsel's aid, interpreting the perplexing procedures of the court as best they could. This "coercive control of scene, scheduling, staging and ritual," concludes Pat Carlen, legitimizes the justice handed out in Magistrate's Court, "suppressing the incongruity between abstract law and the realities" of women's stories displayed in court.[45] Those stories were also given their own particular interpretation by the magistrate and other experts surrounding him; like the women defendants, they too constructed tales of female crime.

The pronouncements about women lawbreakers made by the magistrate, the legal profession, social workers linked to the court system, and other experts presented a picture of women's criminality from the top down that, as it was created, justified, and circulated, became a set of accepted truths shaping the responses of police, judges, and social workers to women, and ultimately, also affecting women's responses to their own situations.

The views of these experts could differ: social workers, for instance, increasingly used psychological models to understand and reform women criminals, while police remained wedded to analyses shaped by the imperatives of preserving law and order. Nonetheless, in both their private assessments and their public pronouncements a common theme emerges: the experts spoke two languages, one of structural causes and cures, and another of irretrievable victims of character failure, with the latter, darker view tending to dominate. These competing discourses paralleled the contradictory thinking of twentieth-century criminologists who utilized a scientific language of bad environment, structural causes, and possible cures for women's crime, yet paradoxically linked women's law breaking to deep-rooted psychic deficiencies originating in their biological makeup.[46] Characterized by a deep pessimism and embodying a rationalization for the existing class and gender hierarchy, the second discourse saw women lawbreakers — and especially repeaters — as morally deficient in an unalterable way. As late as the 1940s, a magistrate's report on a young female offender with repeated convictions for incorrigibility concluded that she was just "no good," a young woman "at war with society."[47]

Many social service workers and attorneys argued that, since women became criminals because of the deleterious effects of family life, they should be accorded a second chance. Even repeat female offenders, argued the Police Matron, who was ideologically positioned close to the Children's Aid Society (cas) in the interwar years, needed repaired family lives, "love and charity" to correct their behaviour. Paradoxically, though, the matron added a more pessimistic view: women offenders, she said, were "of low mental calibre and indifferent home surroundings," and were often "diseased," as they exercised "very little [sexual] self control." Although she noted that some local families were too poor to support their children, she concluded with the observation that "wickedness and immorality were rampant" in a "certain class" in the city. One of her solutions to female crime was sterilization of the feeble-minded.[48]

The matron's double vision of structural causes and character flaws causing women's crime was shared by some members of the CAS. In the interwar period, the CAS Board, dominated by local clergymen, middle-class housewives, professionals, and law enforcement officers — Police Chief Sam Newall, *and* at one time his wife, were on the board — expressed concern that poverty, especially of single-mother families, would lead to crime. Yet once they perceived signs of immorality, sympathy quickly disappeared. Judgment was severe for women who were not "living on the straight and narrow"[49] — women deemed sexually promiscuous — and delinquency was still attributed to "lazy careless mothers."[50] By the late 1930s and war years, professionally trained social workers increasingly emphasized diagnoses shaped by psychology (later psychiatry) case work, and an understanding of the "emotional roots" of delinquency and crime.[51] This emerging discourse of psychology and its consequent forms of regulation stressing personality rather than moral alteration, however, can also be seen simply as new means of "pathologizing women in a disciplinary society."[52]

Furthermore, well into the 1940s, the themes of immorality and character weakness causing crime characterized the views of some CAS officials. In a rural area near Peterborough, the CAS advertised its work by presenting standard tales of crime and neglect in order to gain financial and volunteer support. Analyzed according to their narrative structure — their setting, fixed villains and heroes, and resolution — these stories presented the CAS as saviour, suggested the possibility of resocializing children, but also incorporated images of hopelessly debased adult women. The hillbilly tale, for example, described an isolated, rural family where "no one knew what a bath was"[53] in which neglect and violence prevailed. The children were rescued, bathed (perhaps saved by this symbolic cleansing), then adopted. An urban tale focused on the criminal effects of economic and moral mismanagement by parents, with one wartime variation of this tale highlighting the delinquent, immoral girl caused by the absent, materialistic working mother. "Show me a home where the inmates go to Sunday School or where there is a nice clean wash out on Monday morning" said one CAS official (indicating the emphasis on *women's* moral responsibilities) "and there will be no problems."[54] A pessimistic theme of character failure thus remained a subtext in the tales, even as other social workers were trying to establish a counter-discourse of structural causes and logical psychological cures.

Social workers' fears of endangered morality were focused primarily on the poor. While middle-class crime was mystified as a rare, "particularly tragic" occurrence, or dismissed as unbelievable,[55] the poor were seen as uncommonly prone to moral lapses. Obviously, class differences often separated social workers from their clients: the CAS, capturing this in language, referred to its volunteers as "the ladies" and its clients as "women." A similar association between crime and poverty, combined with a strong sense of social distance, was evident in the commentary of lawyers: in a public speech in the 1940s, a well- known local lawyer explained to his middle-class audience that the magistrate's job was to "understand the *other* half of the world and how they live."[56]

Accompanying these class distinctions came an image of the alien, the outsider, the foreigner, that sometimes encapsulated the meaning of criminality for the police and judiciary. In 1933, for instance, County Court Judge Huycke lectured the Quarter Sessions about the current incidence of "repugnant, beastly crimes" and warned almost hysterically of an accelerating Depression "crime wave." Combating crime was a "patriotic" duty, he concluded, because it was primarily the result of "immigrants from foreign countries [especially the United States] who bring their vices with them."[57] These narratives reinforced a polarized view of 'them and us': the image of outsider, the 'other' was a comforting explanation for crime that obscured a critical examination of the existing social structure.

Nowhere was the association of poverty and immorality, and the externalization of crime, more dramatic than in the Badlands report of 1916. Asked to examine the "degenerate and wretched" conditions that a judge and the crown attorney believed were causing escalating criminal acts in the outlying areas of Peterborough county,[58] the grand jury duly reported — over the vigorous protests of some rural community leaders — that extreme poverty had resulted in a "careless and degenerate" people predisposed especially to sexual crimes. Like the pronouncements of the Police Matron, the report embodied two messages: on one hand, it blamed "*not* the people but the conditions of securing a livelihood"[59] in the area; on the other, it presented images of a people hopelessly lost to immorality and lust. Replete with veiled warnings of race suicide, including the proliferation of "idiocy" in the population, the report defined public perceptions for years to come, becoming a species of folklore about hillbillies similar to the stereotypes associated with white Appalachia.[60] Ten years later, a Toronto expert was still urging the Ontario government to clean up this "foul canker" of immorality, where "men live like animals . . . and low class women . . . reject legal marriage."[61] Ironically, a domino effect of externalizing crime existed: while Peterborough legal authorities denounced the immorality in the rural Badlands, Toronto government officials privately criticized the same Peterborough authorities for being too lax on their rural hinterland.[62]

Within the circle of experts commenting on women's criminality, the magistrate occupied a position of critical significance, and not only because he handed out sentences. By establishing standards of appropriate behaviour and by justifying them with moral principles and public lectures, in the courtroom and the later in the press, the magistrate was creating powerful knowledge about women and crime, which carried with it messages about respectability, sexual morality, and proper gender roles; his pronouncements became part of the dominant discourse on criminality. Like social workers and legal practitioners, the magistrate indicated sympathy for the structural causes of women's crimes, but also condemnation of women's moral and character failure. The latter theme was especially discernible in his public pronouncements, which must be read, in part, as intended morality lessons.

The magistrate's awareness of women's crime, drawn from his class background and social milieu, his experience with the legal system, and the prevailing views of other experts in law and criminology, led him to judge a woman in relation to her social stature in the community, her sexual morality, and her role in the family. In his deliberations on women's sexual morality, the magistrate or 'Cadi' was assisted by the police and, by the 1940s and 1950s, by more social workers and doctors. In the interwar period especially, the Peterborough police chief had a network of local contacts who passed on information on his suspects' whereabouts, actions, and friends. In his sentencing report for one woman, Langley suggested the prison might obtain better information from Police Chief Newall, "who has a pretty full and accurate knowledge of her doings for some time past."[63] In court, the police chief might lean over and offer an observation that although the woman appearing had never been charged before, "he had seen her . . . she was a troublemaker," for she was on the streets, living with a married man and refused to get a job or return home to her family.[64] The magistrate would heed his allegation.

A woman's moral character was defined in terms of whom she kept company with, and her placement on the sexual purity/promiscuity continuum. While vagrancy could be a fairly innocuous crime, it depended on where, when, and whom you were arrested with. Women picked up at night in the company of men were immediately suspect. In the thirties two young women found themselves stranded near Lakefield after their "chance dates" took off on them.[65] They found refuge in the Lockmasters building, but were arrested for vagrancy and spent time in jail, a severe price to pay for being stood up.

Women's sexual morality was so important that it could influence the magistrate's deliberations on charges other than vagrancy and prostitution. When a twenty-one-year-old rural woman, Eva, and her mother, Amy, were arrested in 1921 for theft and possessing stolen goods from nearby cottages, the daughter's sexual morality was put to trial as well, for she had married a younger man of seventeen without securing a divorce from her previous marriage. Despite the fact that the whole family was first accused of theft, charges were soon limited to the two women. Because it was household items such as blankets that were stolen, the men argued they would not have recognized them, not being acquainted with housekeeping matters. Even more damning for the women was Eva's illicit relationship, which both the mother and daughter were supposed to take responsibility for. Langley implied that he would send Eva to Mercer even if she was acquitted for theft: "rather than permitting you to live in immoral condition in your parents' home."[66] Both mother and daughter ended up in the Mercer Reformatory. The men stayed home, presumably to look after the household.

Concerns about women's sexual morality were linked to racist fears of miscegenation. Any implication of white women's intimacy with non-white men was cause for concern. In 1940s, when a woman was picked up for vagrancy, Chief Newall opened the courtroom discussion by telling the Cadi that "she is associated with a local Chinese [which] is not a desirable condition"[67] Another woman imprisoned by Langley for vagrancy was accused of "misbehaving with the Indians out on the Reserve"[68] as well as staying out late with men. Women found with Chinese men were immediately suspected of prostitution. During World War II the magistrate had to chastise the police for bringing a vagrancy case against a Chinese man, despite a complete lack of evidence, but the white women found in his company were still charged with prostitution, and despite denials of guilt, they were fined.[69]

The magistrate's understanding of crime was also shaped by a woman's economic status. Most women charged with theft pilfered small items — like the young women who stole swimmers' clothes from Inverlea beach or the bowling-alley clothes thief apprehended during the Depression. A destitute, poverty-stricken defendant might elicit sympathetic comment from the magistrate, who saw a connection between poverty and crime, but this did not mean he excused her actions. Economic circumstance could play a role in the magistrate's sentencing, but he still registered his moral disapproval in his courtroom lecture. Theft indicated a weakness of character: the fact that you were poor didn't mean you had to steal, in his view.

Women's status within their families and their acceptance of prescribed roles of daughterly obedience, domesticity, and motherhood were also important to the magistrate. Legal authorities made sense of a woman's actions in terms of the familial and domestic role she had played, or the one she promised to play in the future.[70] Like the CAS, the magistrate believed that a lack of parental and especially patriarchal control could lead to young women's crimes. A suspended sentence was found for one young woman, provided she "return to her father's home until her husband can provide a new one for her."[71] Almost a decade later in 1938, Langley informed a rebellious teen who tried to "bolt" from the courtroom that she would have to face jail because she had "to learn she can be dealt with" by "authority" figures, including her parents.[72]

The theme of parental authority is often played out in another way:

some distressed parents requested the magistrate's intervention when their daughters were misbehaving. In one case in the thirties, a father removed his daughter from a house where she was drinking and partying with older men and took her to the police. Fifteen years later another father told the court that his paroled daughter was "uncontrollable," staying out all night and that "he didn't want her back."[73] Parents often tried to use the court system in their struggle to maintain economic and moral control over their rebellious daughters.[74] The magistrate, though sometimes troubled by the knowledge that women were trying to escape unhappy families, still saw the reconstitution of the nuclear family, with a male breadwinner, domestic mother, and obedient daughter, as the best solution. An emerging emphasis in the 1940s on family therapy as a form of rehabilitation may have simply institutionalized this solution through the informal means of "socialized justice."[75]

Finally, demeanour was also considered when the police and the magistrate assessed a woman. One woman, accused more than once of selling liquor illegally, entered the court after "a minor riot scene in the chief's office in which two languages were used — English and profane." The court reporter noted that she was "pressured" to plead guilty (with threats that more charges would be laid because some of her customers were minors) and was sent to the most unpopular place where the magistrate punished non-reformables: the county jail.[76] Demeanour was taken to an almost ridiculous length in 1949 when the crown attorney, in dealing with a complicated assault case materializing out of a dance fight, suggested that the two women who were chewing gum in court were probably the guilty ones because nice women didn't engage in such "crude" behaviour.[77]

One's class and social circumstances, role in the family, and feminine demeanour — connected by the themes of sexual purity, morality, and domesticity — were all part of the magistrate's understanding of both the prevention and cure for crime. That women could be condemned so severely, for crimes such as having premarital sex, or stealing a dress, should offer a sobering antidote to any sweeping charges of paternalism within the justice system.[78] Like other experts, the magistrate spoke more than one language: while he voiced sympathy for the economic problems experienced, for example, by single mothers, he also censured those whose moral character failed them. Ultimately, it was the second language that took precedence and endowed the court with tremendous authority. As Ann Worrall, drawing on Foucault, argues, the appearance of coherence, the denial of contradiction between discourses, gave legal authorities the authority to 'know' the women before them.[79] Whether that knowledge was based on the letter of the law or on common-sense notions about morality and human nature, it came to define an understanding of crime that denied its basis in power relationships and placed its origin in moral failures. Women who came before the court had to justify their stories with reference to this authority, though occasionally they also attempted to mock, reject, or subvert it.

Pardon Tales from Magistrate's Court

Silence and physical rebellion were the responses of some women brought before the magistrate. As one woman listened to her sentence for theft of some clothing and a small amount of money from the house where she was staying, she "hung her head, trying to hide from view." Don't hide, Magistrate Langley chided her, and humiliating her even more, added: "I've seen prettier girls than you."[80] Others indicated their renunciation of the process by lashing out with violence, even against themselves: the woman charged with biting her landlord was so incensed she smashed the toilet in her holding cell, while another woman turned her anger inward, and tried to swallow a bottle of ink at the police station.[81] Once imprisoned, women might remain silently unco-operative; a pregnant teenager, ostracized by her family, was sent to Mercer in the early thirties for vagrancy but she couldn't answer questions about her place of residence when admitted to hospital for the birth (as they wanted to bill the family). Prison officials were quick to assume her "mental deficiency" (as they did in other cases); one wonders whether her silence actually signified trauma, anger, or rebellion.[82]

Women's attempts to explain, deny, or excuse their crimes indicate that a minority of defendants did not accept the court's definition of immorality or their own criminality. Many more began by arguing their innocence, but seeing the power of the court to define the situation, then explained the reason for their crime or professed repentance. They appealed to the court's mercy, or even its sense of humour, but rarely to principles of justice. In telling their version of the crime, women often interpreted their actions in ways that "established their status as moral beings,"[83] for example, as dutiful daughters or virtuous mothers. Women's courtroom tales may therefore represent both an affirmation of court's power over women *and* a form of defiance. While their stories were used to secure release, they may have also reinforced those very discourses ensuring women's social regulation by patriarchal ideology.

In the 1920s and 1930s some women played on the theatrical and comic traditions of the court, especially for vagrancy and alcohol offences. As the theatrical image of the court declined, fewer women adopted such roles, and as alcohol offences became more routine, the magistrate was less interested in hearing about women's extenuating circumstances. In the 1930s, however, "Bridget," a woman apparently well known by the authorities, seemed to purposely fabricate stories to explain her latest arrest for public intoxication, at the same time that she mocked deference to the legal authorities. After one arrest, she denied the charge, then turned about-face to pretend that an honourable policeman's word could not be doubted: "If he says I was drunk, I must have been for a policeman never lies" she told the Cadi. Playing along, the crown attorney thanked her profusely and added that her word was "one of the highest tributes the police could receive." Bridget then explained how she became drunk: "I was doing a heavy wash," she explained, "putting coal oil and washing soda in the clothes to whiten them, when the fumes overtook me." Seeing the magistrate's doubt, she added a second story: "I went out to pick beans in the garden and the sun struck me so much that I can't remember any more." When neither story was accepted, she responded to her sentence of ten days or ten dollars by saying she couldn't pay the fine; moreover, during her last stint in jail, her house was robbed, so that the police would have to do extra duty guarding it for her — as if to imply it wasn't worth the court's time and money to lock her up.[84]

The press relished her stories as examples of the day's entertainment in the prisoner's dock; at the same time, it is clear that Bridget is participating in the performance, perhaps even hoping for a sympathetic ear from the magistrate with her image of the industrious washerwoman, so intent on producing a white wash that she became drunk in the process.

Other women, though less inventive than Bridget, also tried to persuade the magistrate that their alcohol offences were trivial, requiring no punishment. They usually implied that their crime was out of character; as one women pointed out, she was working and supporting an aged mother, surely a sign of a moral and dutiful daughter, and her "celebration" with alcohol simply "carried her" away "because she was so happy" to have a job. A county resident, she was offered a discharge if she left the city.[85]

Occasionally, a vagrant told her story with humorous disdain, only to receive the magistrate's obvious disapproval: Langley's temper was roused when a young female Depression hobo, arrested for hitchhiking near Peterborough, treated her court appearance as a joke, and confidently referred to her long travels across the provincial highways. She was treated to a stiff sentence in Mercer and could only secure satisfaction by impertinently feigning a "Thanks Judge" to the magistrate as she left the courtroom.[86] Other vagrants were luckier, especially if they promised to make themselves scarce; in some cases, this was part of an informal deal to 'git out of town before sundown,' thus saving the municipality money for jail time. One such woman promised she would immediately "return to Montreal on the noon train accompanied by the local man who was with her."[87]

Some one-time offenders used stereotyped images of femininity, such as women's concern with their appearance, in their tales. One woman arrested for drunkenness, for instance, inquired if she could be released to go shopping and get her hair done. The magistrate asked whether she might lose her way on the way to the hairdresser and end up in a beverage room, but she assured him not. She was eventually released. Another woman, accused in the 1950s of taking part in a brawl at a gas station, based part of her defence on the kind of shoes she was wearing. I couldn't possibly have kicked down that glass door, she protested, because I was wearing my toeless shoes and I would not have been silly enough to purposely break my toes.[88] Feminine deportment could also be utilized in women's defences: those who "broke down and wept," who told the magistrate of "all their recent trials and tribulations,"[89] or who pleaded their cases contritely, implied the court reporter, were viewed more leniently than those who swore at the magistrate.

Considering that many women arrested were out of work or laboured in low-wage jobs, it is not surprising that they claimed poverty as their rationale for theft. It is hard to imagine a more pathetic tale than that told in the early Depression, when an unmarried seventeen-year-old mother working as a servant admitted that she stole some baby clothes and a paltry amount of cash from her employer. Though the court reporter was sympathetic, the magistrate still gave her a short jail term, probably because it was her second offence.[90] Similarly, one woman sent to jail in the 1940s for selling moonshine as well as collecting welfare was severely sentenced, even though she tried to argue that "welfare only paid $8.00 a month, not enough to live on." Her sentence was undoubtedly shaped by the fact that her husband was a repeat offender, and because of suspicions passed on to the magistrate that she was also engaging in prostitution.[91]

Sympathy for economic tales declined quite obviously after the Depression, although stealing to literally feed one's family might result in the dispensation of mercy. In 1942 a young mother was let go after she took some tea from a store; she persuaded the magistrate that "her family was destitute" because her unemployed husband "had finally found work, but had not yet received a pay check."[92] When there were no such heart-rending circumstances, the penalty could be stiffer. In another petty theft case, the magistrate announced he "didn't believe"[93] the defendant's carefully constructed alibi when she was charged with stealing bottles of perfume from a store. He noted that she was living with a man in a hotel room, a sure sign of immorality; moreover, her theft of a luxury item did not elicit his sympathy. Lacking evidence, though, the frustrated magistrate could not convict her.

Perhaps becoming aware of the magistrate's predilection to look askance at poverty as an excuse, women tried other strategies, such as blaming it all on one's accomplice, as *both* women employed in a hotel purse heist tried to do,[94] or claiming a misunderstanding, as did a woman charged with passing a bad cheque, who declared "she intended to pay the rest and didn't expect the merchant to take her to court."[95] In trying to decide how much destitution to claim and how much moral guilt to assume, women were in a difficult quandary. If it was a crime unprecipitated by obvious destitution, an open confession might be the best strategy. For example, two women, one with alcohol problems, executed a common female robbery: drinking with, then stealing from a man once he passed out. On the advice of counsel, they pleaded guilty, but one justified her actions by explaining that the man's constant boasting and flaunting of all his money before them simply told her that "they had a greater use for the money than him."[96]

While defendants like Bridget tried to play into the theatrical context of the court, some crimes, such as prostitution or child neglect, were viewed too seriously to contemplate such a tactic. Women who defended themselves against charges of bad mothering needed more than poverty to explain how they could reject this 'natural' impulse. During the World War II, one distraught woman, for example, tried to explain her infant daughter's abandonment in a tale that wove together destitution, isolation from familial protection, and her status as an abandoned soldier's wife. She tearfully recounted how she had been on relief before the baby was born, then left to work to work outside the city as a domestic for six dollars a week, "not enough to send back money for the baby." She wasn't allowed to go back to her father's house, nor could she find lodgings allowing a child. "They say I'm to blame, but I wasn't," she concluded.[97]

Women must have also been aware that charges for prostitution could have serious consequences. It is not surprising that young women — sometimes mere teens whose "precocious sexuality"[98] was defined as criminal by parents and police wedded to the view that premarital sex for women was immoral — who were arrested on morals charges implied that sexual liaisons had never been consummated, even if they had stayed out all night with a man. One young woman tried to convince the magistrate she had only camped out in a friend's car. Once jailed, those charged with prostitution might indicate remorse; one such woman "thanked God for sending" her to jail to "teach her a lesson" and change her ways, though even this could have been a strategy to win early release.[99]

Some women, though, were quite unrepentant. Although prostitution cases were not well covered in the press, there is evidence that the moral suppositions of the law were repudiated by those accused. One illustration is the story of a convicted woman's ongoing battle with the magistrate and the CAS to have her children returned to her. After a term in Mercer she tried to regain her children, despite the opposition of the authorities, who saw her as a bad mother because of her prostitution charge. Her rejection of their assessment and her determination to retrieve her family, even if it meant a public fight with the CAS, suggest that this woman did not see her own actions as immoral.

Women charged with prostitution also pointed to the hypocrisy of those charging them. In one case, "Amy," a woman incarcerated in Mercer for keeping a bawdy house, tried to enlist the support of her recently released accomplice, to pay back the police. In letters obtained by the prison authorities, Amy tried to persuade her friend to go public with joint claims of police corruption and thus "put the chief out of a job." You "know we received whisky" in the police station, she wrote, "and also more than that took place . . . we were fools." She claimed one policeman in particular, promised early parole in exchange for a confession, a ruse that successfully aided their conviction.[100] Whether her charges were true or attempts to garner revenge cannot be stated: her letter is characterized, however, by a strong sense that the authorities were the real criminals.

Women recognized only too well that their sexual morality was being scrutinized by the authorities — even if they did not sit in the defendant's seat. In the late 1930s, when Myrtle L. brought a charge of common assault against a man for "throwing her down and kicking her" after an evening out, she was put on the defensive in court. She admitted that she had gone to a show with the accused, Joe, and afterwards to her brother's house. A fight ensued, she testified, over who would take her home and she was assaulted by her date. Perhaps realizing that she might be suspected of enticing her date to the house, Myrtle made an effort to assert her own morality, denying that she had even kissed Joe, as "I am quite fussy about whom I kiss."[101] She then produced a story that incorporated themes from well-known white slave stories. Joe, she said, purposely gave her a funny cigarette in the movie that made her confused and dizzy. She claimed he had "doped" her, and that she was subsequently unable to account for her actions. Given her age, it is likely that Myrtle had heard some of the white slave scenarios of the 1910s and 1920s; her own account seemed to incorporate some of plot twists from these tales. Drawing upon such cultural codes may well have been unconscious on the part of women as they utilized well-known storytelling devices or metaphors to relay their own experiences. In the end, however, her tale of deception was rejected and the charge against Joe dropped.

Women also utilized themes of familial protection and duty in their court presentations.[102] Both men and women cited responsibilities to other family members such as aging parents as evidence of good character, or as a rationale for suspended sentence, but women were more likely to point to their child care duties, for instance, to offer a reason for a lenient sentence. And in many respects, women were in a more vulnerable position than men: they were more likely to be faced with an unwanted pregnancy or child care crisis, including loss of custody. These were not fabricated tales: they reflected women's own economic and social responsibilities.

At the same time, women might play to the court's view of the family as a place of control, good behaviour, respect for authority, and hence rehabilitation. One woman may have tried to get out of her sentence for theft by assuring him that she was getting married soon; another tried to explain her clash with the law in the context of her abandonment by both her husband and her father. For young women, the acceptance of parental authority was a prudent strategy. In one case of teenage theft, a suspended sentence was granted when the girl agreed to "obey her parents," pay back the small sum of money, and "place herself under the authority of the Salvation Army Police Matron."[103] Her sentence was more lenient than the teen vagrant who, after being charged with begging, refused to take a job the matron found for her. "I can find my own jobs," she retorted defiantly. She was sent to the Reformatory.[104]

This script of familial protection was still unpalatable to some women: for them, the family itself may have been the problem, not the solution. Parental control was not the lesser but the greater of evils for "Gertrude," a teen who in 1940 ended up in jail after disobeying the magistrate's orders "to stop smoking, staying out late and disregarding her parents' rules."[105] One young woman even used a peculiar form of self-sentencing to remove herself from her family: she ran away to Toronto, and made up a very convincing, long story about being orphaned; her heroic father was supposedly killed at Vimy Ridge, while her mother died tragically afterwards. Once discovered, rather than go home, she turned herself in to the Catholic Reformatory for Girls in Toronto.[106]

While both men and women might employ familial ideology in their presentations, there was no equal to women's elastic utilization of the theme of motherhood. Motherhood was an unstable image that could be used to secure compassion, but could also be turned against women. For those who did not measure up to the dominant norms of respectable mothering, the court might show little sympathy.[107]

That motherhood could be used in different ways both by the defendant and the court is well illustrated by two cases that came from the Badlands. May Hill was a well-known figure in Magistrate's Court, for she had married into a notorious family in Dummer township, the heart of the Badlands, around which violent feuds (especially unneighbourly cattle poisoning) had occurred since the turn of the century. Men in the Hill family, including May's husband, had also been charged with assaults against women. May had to stand up to her violent in-laws, raise eleven children, and in the face of her husband's absences, support the family. To do the latter, she took over the Hill's moonshine operation. Her business became infamous: in 1927, after one of her customers recklessly drank too many bottles and died, she faced a coroner's inquest; after another RCMP investigation, her neighbours developed sudden amnesia on the witness stand, rather than risk testifying against a member of the Hill family.[108]

In the thirties she continued to appear before the court and, far from being intimidated by the magistrate, May was actually quite defiant and mocking. During one 1933 court appearance, she tried out a number of stories out on the magistrate. First, she denied that the barrel found in her barn contained liquor: it was merely chicken mash, she claimed, full of feed, dishwater, and other unappetizing ingredients. When faced with a lab analysis she abandoned that course and admitted guilt, but her lawyer argued that she should be given a suspended sentence because of her mothering duties. While sympathetic to her child care problems before, Magistrate Langley had lost patience: "I have seen this woman before me for ten years, I am not about to let her go."[109] May, however, was not prepared to serve time in the county jail. When she returned for sentencing, she had concocted a scheme that drew upon her role as mother. She entered her youngest baby in the county fair's beautiful baby contest, and when he won a prize, she brought him, and his newfound fame, along to court. "How can you put me in jail," she asked the magistrate, when I will have to take this "beautiful, bouncing baby boy"— a prize winning baby at that — to county jail?[110] May was unsuccessful in escaping a term in jail, but her reputation (and perhaps her business) was, if anything, enhanced. She had used the pride of motherhood, framed in a context of humour and 'pulling a fast one on the judge,' that the newspapers, and probably the public, rather enjoyed.

Women charged with more serious crimes could not follow May's example. In 1927, Mary Dwyer was charged with the manslaughter of her twelve-year-old stepchild, John. Her case reveals the severe suspicion of women who appeared unnatural mothers, as well as the determining effect of one's social and economic status, exemplified here by residence in the Badlands, in shaping public and judicial perceptions of women charged with crimes. In the face of these odds, it was questionable whether any story Mary told could have satisfied the magistrate.

Although an autopsy showed meningitis as the cause of John's death, his emaciated body and indications of physical abuse led to charges of manslaughter against Mary, and then later, against the boy's natural father, George Dwyer. Initially, newspaper reports were more concerned with lauding George Dwyer's honourable war record than investigating family abuse.[111] On the other hand, the crown attorney and magistrate seemed determined to make Mary morally, if not legally responsible for the incident, even if she was not the boy's legal guardian.

The magistrate heard testimony from doctors, neighbours, and extended and close family, and complicated charges and counter-charges of physical abuse came from both Mary and George's kin. Mary, who initially appeared extremely composed in court — demeanour immediately deemed suspicious by newspaper reporters[112]— related a tale of poverty and fear of her violent husband. She claimed she "did her best with the little food" they had, and that her own children were better fed because they were sent to her parents for food. Moreover, she lived in "daily fear" of her husband and was too frightened to disobey him when he forbade a doctor for the sick child.

The crown attorney was skeptical, if not mocking, and the press too was initially doubtful. Evidence of the father's violent domination of family seemed at first less palatable than the image of the evil stepmother who favoured her own children and starved her husband's. Only after collaborative testimony was her tale of abuse given more credibility. Residence in the Badlands also condemned her. The press resurrected the most lurid sections of the Badlands report, and a local doctor suggested it was time prominent citizens led a "clean-up" of this "plague infested" area,[113] conjuring up images of a morality posse heading out into the sunset.

After the charges were reduced to neglect, and the mother related her story to a jury, she was found not guilty. The father was found guilty of neglect by a judge, but given a suspended sentence. County Judge Huycke noted that the father's "valiant war record" entitled him to respect, and that he undoubtedly loved his children; nor could he support them if he went to jail. He commented that he liked the father's story "with respect to his wife very little," but the mothers "story with respect to her husband *even less*." Nonetheless, he suggested the family "reunite" and begin anew.[114] While Mary's husband was offered public respect for his status as an honoured military man, Mary was ultimately offered little more than pity in the public courtroom. Her tale of poverty, initially suspect because of her residence in the Badlands, was later accepted; her maternal morality and respectability, however, remained dubious to the legal authorities.

Conclusion

More than one perspective may be necessary to analyze women's criminality in this period. Quantitative sources serve as a stark reminder that certain economic and social conditions overdetermined women's chances of arrest; women's economic dependency and their lack of social power accounted, at least in part, for their conflicts with the law. Women's alienation as unhappy members or outcasts from the family, their addiction, homelessness, and other factors creating social marginalization also shaped their likelihood of arrest or their decision to engage in the risk of crime. As Pat Carlen argues for women today, "they have chosen crime, but under conditions not of their own choosing."[115]

Quantitative sources also suggest the importance of changing policing concerns: the increasing incarceration of women during the World War II for venereal disease and the changing seriousness of alcohol offences were two examples noted here. Police preoccupation with crimes protecting property and regulating female sexuality, through vagrancy and prostitution arrests, also indicate that the laws most stringently enforced served to mediate and control social relations already premised on social inequality and gender hierarchy. Thus, while the definition of women's disorderly behaviour and how to reform it may have altered over time, the class and patriarchal power relations underlying the operation of the law remained a consistent theme.

In court, women faced a powerful body of knowledge about their lawbreaking that was produced, circulated, and justified though the letter of the law, the processes and rituals of the court, and the dominant discourses about how and why criminality occurred. Shaped by the social distance separating the experts and the defendants, this knowledge came to exert tremendous power by "disqualifying other interpretations"[116] and claiming its roots in moral principles, justice, and eventually science. The experts, who both objectified and truly wished to help the women before them, offered an explanation for women's predicament incorporating a language of structural causes and environmental cures, but also a more pessimistic rhetoric of immorality and inevitability. Both these discourses existed in the interwar period, though dark metaphors of disease and degeneracy sometimes dominated.

By the end of the 1940s, there were changes, not only in the theatre of the courtroom, but in the knowledge circulated about women lawbreakers. Increasing use of social work and medical assessments, including psychiatric ones, was evident, and a stronger language of environmental causes outpaced a rhetoric of immorality, but new ways of understanding female lawbreakers also became methods of pathologizing them. Furthermore, women's economic and social vulnerability still framed their likelihood of arrest, and women in trouble with the law were still assessed according to their placement on the purity/promiscuity continuum, their demeanour, and their willingness to accept appropriate domestic roles. At the end of the 1950s, women admitted to Mercer were scrutinized on their tidy hair, willingness to wash dishes, and sexual morality.[117]

Conceptions of women's moral, then later personality 'failure' were grounded in existing power structures and in a complex externalization of crime, which obscured its roots in the existing social and gender hierarchy. The understandings of crime conveyed by these experts were not one of many discourses, any one of which could have been chosen: certain discourses came to dominate precisely because they reflected class and patriarchal power, justifying the existing social order and pathologizing the experiences of the marginalized. The moral lectures of the magistrate were an ideological articulation of those power relationships and they assumed hegemony for precisely that reason.[118]

How were women to defend themselves? Accounts of their crimes are conveyed to us through distorting mirrors of expert commentary, or newspapers, which made them more melodramatic, entertaining, or stereotypical. Yet women may have utilized these same conventions to effectively tell their stories. The tales they told were justifications, interpretations, strategies, and for a few women, small rebellions against the court. Simply by explaining their crimes, they were sometimes contradicting the knowledge of experts and society about their lives. Placing their thefts in the context of want and poverty contradicted the claim that it was greed or weakness of character that led to property crime; rejection of the immorality associated with prostitution was an affront to dominant notions of femininity. Rebellion, for other women, involved rejection of parental authority and the healing powers of the family. For a few, silence may have been a protest shaped by their awareness that their own lives and values had been a priori condemned. Even May Hill's humour, though playing to the court, also made fun of it.

Yet for most women, staying out of jail, not challenging the court, was probably their primary goal, and to do this, they had to translate their crimes into images that validated "their status as moral beings."[119] As Patricia Spacks points out, "the stories we tell about our lives are shaped in part from the suppositions of stories we are supposed to tell."[120] This is not to dismiss women's stories as contrived fiction; rather, they encapsulated women's reactions to their difficult material and social circumstances, but were shaped by dominant cultural motifs and astute perceptions of the posture designed to release them from the court's clutches, in the same way that the women described by Natalie Zemon Davis carefully shaped their pardon tales to obtain the king's mercy. Women's stories reflected their own lack of power, but also their attempts to utilize elements of restrictive gender ideology to secure their freedom. That so many inventive tactics and rebellious justifications could be located within the court of a small town speaks to the agency of women often portrayed as victimized and controlled. These women may have sensed the paradoxes of paternalism in a patriarchal society. It is revealing that mercy and humour, rather than justice, were invoked as they faced the magistrate. Did they know, only too well, that the justice of courts was a far cry from social justice?

Notes

1 *Peterborough Examiner* (hereafter *Examiner*), 30 Dec. 1929.

2 Ibid.

3 When I know a lawyer is involved, I always note this.

4 Natalie Zemon Davis, *Fiction in the Archives: Pardon Tales and Their Tellers in Sixteenth-Century France* (Stanford, 1987), 3.

5 Sources are obviously better for the higher courts. Even overviews of female offenders, such as D. Owen Carrigan, *Crime and Punishment in Canada: A History* (Toronto, 1991), chap. 5, tend to stress sensational trials. Most studies focus on the late nineteenth and early twentieth centuries, drawing on quantitative sources or records left by reformers. Some also examine the familial and cultural background of criminals. For the latter, see Judith Fingard, *The Dark Side of Victorian Halifax* (Porters Lake, NS, 1989), and Carolyn Strange, "The Velvet Glove: Maternalistic Reform at the Andrew Mercer Reformatory for Females, 1874–1927" (MA thesis, University of Ottawa, 1983). Other Canadian literature includes: B. Jane Price, "Raised in Rockhead, Died in the Poor House: Female Petty Criminals in Halifax, 1864–90," in *Essays in the History of Canadian Law*, vol. 3, *The Nova Scotia Experience*, ed. Philip Girard and Jim Phillips (Toronto, 1990); Elizabeth Langdon, "Female Crime in Calgary, 1914–41," in *Law and Justice in a New Land: Essays in Western Canadian Legal History*, ed. Louis Knafla (Toronto, 1986); Indiana Matters, "Sinners or Sinned Against? Historical Aspects of Female Juvenile Delinquency in British Columbia," in *Not Just Pin Money: Selected Essays on the History of Women's Work in British Columbia*, ed. Barbara Latham and Roberta Pazdro (Victoria, 1988); André Lachance, "Women and Crime in Canada in the Eighteenth Century," in *Crime and Criminal Justice in Europe and Canada*, ed. Louis Knafla (Waterloo, 1985); For serious and violent cases, see L. Fee, "Women on Trial: Serious Female Crime and the Assize Court in Grey, Halton and Peterborough Counties, 1880–1930" (MA thesis, University of Guelph, 1988); E. Stoddard, "Conflicting Images: The Murderess and the English Canadian Mind, 1870–1915" (MA thesis, Dalhousie University, 1991). On rural areas, see Karen Dubinsky, "Sex and the Single Industry Community: The Social and Moral Reputation of Rural and Northern Ontario," paper presented at the Canadian Historical Association

conference, Kingston, 1991. On women and the law, see Constance Backhouse, *Petticoats and Prejudice: Women and Law in Nineteenth-Century Canada* (Toronto, 1991).

6   After the 1874 Speedy Trials Act, magistrates could try summarily, with the consent of the defendant, offences previously tried at the Quarter Sessions (a higher court). For 90 percent figure, see Dorothy Chunn, "Maternal Feminism, Legal Professionalism and Political Pragmatism: The Rise and Fall of Margaret Patterson, 1922–34," in *Canadian Perspectives on Law and Society,* ed. Wesley Pue and Barry Wright (Ottawa, 1988), 97. See also Margaret Banks, "The Evolution of the Ontario Court System, 1788–1981," in *Essays in the History of Canadian Law,* vol. 2, ed. David H. Flaherty (Toronto, 1983).

7   On the use of statistics for the nineteenth century, see V.A.C. Gatrell and T.B. Hadden, "Criminal Statistics and Their Interpretation," in *Nineteenth-Century Society: Essays on the Use of Quantitative Methods for the Study of Social Data,* ed. E.A. Wrigley (New York, 1972), and Harvey Graff, "Crime and Punishment in the Nineteenth Century: A New Look at the Criminal," *Journal of Interdisciplinary History* 7, no. 3 (Winter 1977): 477–91. Studies that use and defend quantitative data include Eric Monkkonen, *The Dangerous Class: Crime and Poverty in Columbus, Ohio, 1860–1885* (Cambridge, MA, 1975); George Rudé, *Criminal and Victim: Crime and Society in Early Nineteenth-Century England* (Oxford, 1985); and John Weaver, "Crime, Public Order and Repression: The Gore District in Upheaval, 1832–51," *Ontario History* 78, no. 3 (Sept. 1986): 175–207.

8   The statistics for this section were drawn from an analysis of 616 arrests from 1920 to 1960. For most cumulative calculations I have used statistics from three decades, 1920–50, because the data from the 1950s is shaped by new variables (including the operation of a family court) and altered record taking, particularly for vagrancy/prostitution arrests. I have used numbers from all four decades only where noted.

9   On the economic causes of crime, see Peggy Giordano, Sandra Kerbel, and Sandra Dudley, "The Economics of Female Criminality: An Analysis of Police Blotters, 1890–1975," in *Women and Crime in America,* ed. Lee Bowker (New York, 1981).

10 Domestics were a far greater proportion of the arrests compared to the numbers of women over fifteen, the numbers of women wage earners, or even the number of women in personal services noted in the censuses of 1921, 1931, or 1941. To use only one example: in the 1930s domestics were 49 percent of arrests, while female servants were 10 percent of the female workforce (Canada, Seventh Census of 1931, vol. 7). These numbers may be augmented by the fact that some unemployed women listed themselves as domestics.

11 This is an estimate drawn from a five-year count of men's and women's charges in the Registers, as well as data from Ontario, Legislative Assembly, Report of the Inspector of Prisons, later Report of Prisons and Reformatories, later Report of the Dept. of Reform Institutions.

12 In the 1920s, these categories comprised 77 percent of arrests, in the 1930s, 66 percent, and in the 1940s, 65 percent.

13 See Revised Statutes of Canada, 1906, c. 146, s. 238, for the full definition. I have differentiated between those arrested as prostitutes under the vagrancy act (streetwalking) and other vagrants. When I refer to morals charges, I have combined streetwalking charges with those laid under the bawdy and disorderly house sections of the Criminal Code.

14 On vagrancy laws, see Jim Phillips, "Poverty, Unemployment and the Administration of the Criminal Laws in Halifax, 1864–90," in *Essays in the History of Canadian Law*, vol. 3, ed. Girard and Phillips, and Jim Pitsula, "The Treatment of Tramps in Late Nineteenth-Century Toronto," *Canadian Historical Association Papers* (1980).

15 On the latter, see Carol Smart, *Feminism and the Power of the Law* (London, 1989).

16 See the assault case involving a bootlegger in the *Examiner*, 8 June 1955.

17 Charges for intoxication went from a mere 2 percent of charges in the 1920s to almost 30 percent of all charges in the 1950s, only a few of which were linked to drinking and driving.

18 Arrests go up from 32 in the first five years of the decade to 81 in 1925–29; arrests do not reach this level again until the 1940s, and there is no apparent change in policing at this time. Crime in times of prosperity has been attributed to rising material expectations and more risk taking. See T. Thorner and N. Watson, "Patterns of Prairie Crime, 1875–1939," in *Crime and Criminal Justice in Europe and Canada*, ed. Knafla.

19 County Court Judge Huycke's comments, noted later in this article, assumed that crime was intensifying during the Depression. Similarly, a Grand Jury's report on the Mercer Reformatory assumed economic decay was translated into moral decay. See Archives of Ontario (AO), Vanier/Mercer Records, RG 20, vol. 35, Grand Jury Reports, 1934.

20 In the 1920s teens were 29 percent of arrests; women in their twenties 39 percent of arrests; in the 1930s teens were 41 percent and women in their twenties 28 percent; in the 1940s teens were 29 percent and women in their twenties 40 percent.

21 It is not possible to tell how many women arrested had children, as only marital status is given. It is *possible* that women with familial responsibilities were protected from arrest as the authorities also had to face the problem of who would care for their children. Still, married women do not receive a disproportionate number of discharges, nor do they have a substantially lower conviction rate, and they are only slightly more likely to pay fines and avoid a jail sentence than single women.

22 Over three decades, 78 percent of those arrested for streetwalking and 87 percent of those arrested under the bawdy house/disorderly house clauses were convicted, and 75 percent of the teens who were charged with prostitution spent some time in jail, compared to 45 percent for theft, or 40 percent for vagrancy.

23 Strange, "The Velvet Glove," 62–65.

24 In the 1930s these women comprised a fairly high 20 percent of the arrests for prostitution offenses. This may be related to the socio-economic background of these sects, or even to the possibility that they claimed that some 'rescued' women subsequently had relapses.

25 Weaver, "Crime, Public Order and Repression."

26 AO, Attorney General's Papers, RG 4-32, file 509, Judge to Attorney General's Staff, 30 Nov. 1926.

27 Arrests for violent crimes *against* women by men are slightly higher in the county, compared to the city, in the 1920s.

28 Alan Block, "Aw, Your Mother Is in the Mafia: Women Criminals in Progressive New York," in *Women and Crime in America,* ed. Bowker.

29 *Examiner,* 16 Nov. 1926.

30 *Examiner,* 18 Feb. 1930. Comparisons with the earlier period made from Marg Phillips, "Women and Crime in Peterborough County, 1879–1909," unpublished Honours paper, Trent University, 1990.

31 While most bawdy houses operated in an area near the downtown core, there is a decline in the number of bawdy house arrests by the 1930s and 1940s.

32 On prostitution, see Constance Backhouse, "Nineteenth-Century Canadian Prostitution Law: Reflection of a Discriminatory Society," *Social History/Histoire sociale* 18 (1985): 387–423; John McLaren, "Chasing the Social Evil: Moral Fervour and the Evolution of Canada's Prostitution Laws, 1867–1917," *Canadian Journal of Law and Society* 1 (1986): 125–66; D. Nilsen, "The Social Evil: Prostitution in Vancouver, 1900–1920," in *In Her Own Right,* ed. B. Latham (Victoria, 1984); Andrée Lévesque, "Le Bordel: Milieu de travail contrôlé," *Labour/Le Travail* 20 (1987): 13–31. The high representation of domestics in prostitution arrests in Peterborough in the interwar years corresponds to conclusions of Nilson's earlier study.

33 Of three-, four-, and five-time offenders, the majority of arrests were for vagrancy and liquor consumption (58 percent and 16 percent, respectively). For five-time offenders, seven of nine women had no arrests for prostitution on their records, which were predominantly liquor and vagrancy arrests.

34 Philp came from Colbourne but practised in Peterborough before becoming a magistrate. He was active in the local Historical Society, the CAS, the Masonic

Lodge, and the United Church. See *Examiner*, 27 March 1971. The nearby magistrate from Lindsay, E.A. Gee, also occasionally sat in Peterborough.

35 Personal information from Langley's descendants.

36 For an endorsement of this view, see Judge E. Coatsworth, "A Model Magistrate's Court," *Canadian Bar Review* (June 1929). On other magistrates: Gene Homel, "Denison's Law: Criminal Justice and the Police Court in Toronto, 1877–1921," *Ontario History* 73, no. 3 (1981): 171–84; T. Thorner and N. Watson, "Keeper of the Kings Peace: Colonel G.E. Sanders and the Calgary Police Magistrate's Court, 1911–1932," *Urban History Review* 12, no. 3 (1984): 45–55.

37 As an extensive debate on the legitimacy of the law has demonstrated, the courts, despite their discriminatory focus on the crimes of the poor and working class, secured a degree of consent and approval from these very groups for complex ideological reasons. See Douglas Hay et al., eds., *Albion's Fatal Tree: Crime and Society in Eighteenth-Century England* (New York, 1975). For Canadian commentary, see Greg Marquis, "'A Machine of Oppression Under the Guise of the Law': The St. John Police Establishment, 1860–1890," *Acadiensis* 16 (Autumn 1986): 58–77; Paul Craven, "Law and Ideology: The Toronto Police Court," in *Essays in the History of Canadian Law*, vol. 2, ed. Flaherty.

38 For example, after one square dance a woman was fined $25 for assault after a clumsy husband caused a fight by trampling on another woman's feet: *Examiner*, 24 Oct. 1945.

39 AO, Andrew Mercer Reformatory Records (Mercer), Case File 9291.

40 *Examiner*, 10 April 1926. In 1927, the police matron claimed that Newall saw about 500 juveniles informally that year, while she saw 150: *Examiner*, 20 May 1927.

41 *Examiner*, 10 April 1926.

42 Craven, "Law and Ideology: The Toronto Police Court, 1850–80," in *Essays in the History of Canadian Law*, vol. 2, ed. Flaherty, 295.

43 Even in the interwar period, reporting was changing: the local paper claimed it had decided not to use the names of those involved in domestic disputes, though the reporter sometimes couldn't resist, as in one case involving Italians, where ethnic stereotypes were resorted to.

44 My description of the court is based on a reading of the *Examiner*, but it is heavily indebted to Pat Carlen's ideas in *Magistrates' Justice* (London, 1976).

45 Carlen, *Magistrates' Justice*, 23, 100.

46 Dorie Klein, "The Etiology of Female Crime: A Review of the Literature," in *Women, Crime and Justice*, ed. Susan Datesman and Frank Scarpitti (Oxford, 1980); Carol Smart, *Women, Crime and Criminology* (London, 1977).

47 AO, Mercer, Case File 10154.

48 *Examiner*, 20 May 1927.

49 Peterborough CAS Records (hereafter CAS), Board Minutes, 14 Feb. 1922.

50 Ibid., 21 Feb. 1928.

51 Ibid., 28 April 1949.

52 Smart, *Feminism and the Power of the Law*, 10.

53 CAS, Victoria Haliburton Report, 1942.

54 CAS, Board Minutes, 25 April 1940.

55 See the Knox suicide-murder (*Examiner*, 19 Feb. 1928). It was deemed unlikely that a middle-class, model member of society had killed a woman and then himself. Metaphors of degeneracy were not employed in cases like the CAS orphanage head dismissed for "mistreatment" of the children (*Examiner*, 22 Feb. 1928). On the under-policing of middle-class crime, see D. Owen Carrigan, *Crime and Punishment; A History* (Toronto, 1991), or Pat Carlen, *Women, Crime and Poverty* (Philadelphia, 1987).

56 *Examiner*, 19 Sept. 1944; emphasis mine.

57 *Examiner*, 13 Dec. 1933. Few Americans were ever arrested in Peterborough.

58 AO, Attorney General's Correspondence, RG 4-32, "Report of Certain Conditions Existing in a Part of the Northern District of the County of Peterborough," presented by Grand Jury, 1916.

59 Ibid.

60 See James Klotter, "The Black South and White Appalachia," *Journal of American History* 66, no. 4 (1980): 832–49.

61 AO, Attorney General's Papers, RG 4-32, file 509. Eugenic concerns were very clear. See Angus McLaren, *Our Own Master Race: Eugenics in Canada, 1885–1945* (Toronto, 1990), 12–3, 117–26.

62 Admittedly, domestic violence in the Badlands was not merely an invented problem. The question is a complex one and will be discussed in a subsequent article. See also Karen Dubinsky, "Sex and the Single Industry Community: The Social and Moral Reputation of Rural and Northern Ontario," paper presented at the Canadian Historical Association conference, Kingston, 1991, 32.

63 AO, Mercer, Case File 7628.

64 *Examiner*, 7 July 1931 and 2 Oct. 1931.

65 *Examiner*, 26 Sept. 1930.

66 *Examiner*, 19 Feb. 1921.

67 *Examiner*, 10 June 1940.

68 AO, Mercer, Case File 7628.

69 *Examiner*, 15 June 1944.

70 Once they were incarcerated, training for domesticity was seen as an important part of women's 'rehabilitation' — in contrast to the emphasis on the reform of boys through work, order, and military discipline. See Paul Bennett, "Taming 'Bad Boys' of the Dangerous Class: Child Rescue and Restraint at the Victoria Industrial School, 1887–1935," *Social History/Histoire sociale* 41 (May 1988): 71–96.

71 *Examiner*, 26 Jan. 1929.

72 *Examiner*, 10 May 1938.

73 AO, Mercer, Case File 113170.

74 Mary Odem, "Single Mothers, Delinquent Daughters and the Juvenile Court in Early 20th Century Los Angeles," *Journal of Social History* 25, no. 1 (1991): 27–43. In Odem's study, parents were primarily motivated by need for their daughters' wages. In this case, parents appear especially concerned with control of their daughter's sexuality. Women's economic contribution to the household was the concern of some families, who wrote asking/demanding women's release from prison so they could return to help support the family.

75 Dorothy Chunn, *From Punishment to Doing Good: Family Courts and Socialized Justice in Ontario, 1880–1940* (Toronto, 1992).

76 *Examiner*, 26 Jan. 1929.

77 *Examiner*, 4 May 1949.

78 The concept is often used in relation to women's violent crimes. But paternalism, when it existed, fluctuated according to a complex relationship between the defendant, the crime, and its context; moreover, the 'protection' it offered also had its harsher, discriminatory side. See Etta Anderson, "The 'Chivalrous' Treatment of the Female Offender in the Arms of the Criminal Justice System," *Social Problems* 23 (1976):349–57; N.E.H. Hull, "The Certain Wages of Sin: Sentence and Punishment of Female Felons in Colonial Massachusetts," in *Women and the Law: A Social and Historical Perspective*, vol. 1, ed. D. Kelly Weisberg (Cambridge, 1982).

79 Ann Worrall, *Offending Women: Female Lawbreakers and the Criminal Justice System* (London, 1990), 29–30.

80 *Examiner*, 30 July 1926.

81 *Examiner*, 28 Dec. 1940.

82 AO, Mercer, Case File 6323.

83 Patricia Myer Spacks, "Women's Stories, Women's Selves," *Hudson Review* (Spring 1977): 33.

84 *Examiner*, 15 July 1934.

85 *Examiner*, 30 April 1936.

86 *Examiner*, 21 Nov. 1933.

87 *Examiner*, 11 Sept. 1935. At least 50 percent of those arrested for vagrancy were discharged with no sentence.

88 *Examiner*, 3 Feb. 1956.

89 *Examiner*, 6 May 1929.

90 Stealing small items from one's employer was quite common. In the 1930s, 50 percent of all theft charges were levelled against domestics. The consequences could be severe: only 25 percent got off, and 75 percent were convicted.

91 AO, Mercer, Case File 7830.

92 *Examiner*, 27 Nov. 1942.

93 *Examiner*, 13 Nov. 1944.

94 *Examiner*, 18 Jan. 1950.

95 *Examiner*, 28 Sept. 1949.

96 AO, Mercer, Case File 10786.

97 *Examiner*, 5 Jan. 1943.

98 On the arrest of young women for 'promiscuous' behaviour, which is ignored for young men, see Steven Schlossman and Stephanie Wallach, "The Crime of Precocious Sexuality: Female Juvenile Delinquency in the Progressive Era," in *Women and the Law*, vol. 1, ed. Weisberg.

99 AO, Mercer, Case File 5383. Carolyn Strange also argues that some younger women *were* more likely to respond to the superintendent's intense program of character alteration.

100 AO, Mercer, Case File 5383.

101 *Examiner*, 2 May 1938.

102 In *Justice for Women?* Mary Eaton argues that familial ideology in pleas of mitigation is still used differently by men and women, with the court's response shaped by women's adherence to conventional family roles.

103 *Examiner*, 24 Oct. 1940.

104 *Examiner*, 18 July 1955.

105 *Examiner*, 10 June 1940.

106 *Examiner*, 19 Nov. 1928.

107 On the contexts within which juries showed leniency towards mothers accused of infanticide, see Constance Backhouse, "Desperate Women and Compassionate Courts: Infanticide in Nineteenth-Century Canada," *University of Toronto Law Journal* 34 (1984): 447–78; Mary Ellen Wright, "Unnatural Mothers: Infanticide in Halifax, 1850–1875," *Nova Scotia Historical Review* 7, no. 2 (1987): 13–29.

108 *Examiner*, 23 Sept. 1932.

109 *Examiner*, 13 Oct. 1933.

110 Ibid.

111 Judith Allen, *Sex and Secrets: Crimes Involving Australian Women Since 1880* (Sydney, 1990), discusses the use of 'the honourable military man' defence plea in the interwar period. It was often used in this court as well.

112 *Examiner*, 4 March 1927.

113 *Examiner*, 4 March 1926.

114 *Examiner*, 12 June 1926. Emphasis is mine.

115 Carlen, *Women, Crime and Poverty*, 163.

116 Smart, *Feminism and the Power of the Law*, 14.

117 AO, Mercer, vol. 36, Sampled Case Files, 1958–59. Staff commented on a willingness to learn and help with domestic tasks, posture, manners, and morality. One, for example, sarcastically criticized an inmate: "hair resembled a bird's nest, in fact a crow's nest."

118 See Stuart Hall, "The Toad in the Garden: Thatcherism Among the Theorists," in *Marxism and the Interpretation of Culture*, ed. Cary Nelson and Lawrence Grossberg (Urbana, IL, 1988), on hegemony. I declare my crime of "bringing back the concept of ideology through the back door after discourse analysis threw it out the front door." See Mariana Valverde, "The Rhetoric of Reform: Tropes and the Moral Subject," *International Journal of the Sociology of Law* 18, no. 1 (1990): 61–73.

119 Myer Spacks, "Women's Stories, Women's Selves," 33.

120 Ibid.

TELLING OUR STORIES
FEMINIST DEBATES AND THE USE
OF ORAL HISTORY

When people talk about their lives, people lie sometimes, forget a little, exaggerate, become confused, get things wrong. Yet they are revealing truths. . . . the guiding principle for [life histories] could be that all autobiographical memory is true; it is up to the interpreter to discover in which sense, where, and for what purpose.[1]

For almost two decades, feminist historians have played an important role within the profession stimulating new interest in, and debate surrounding, oral history.[2] The feminist embrace of oral history emerged from a recognition that traditional sources have often neglected the lives of women, and that oral history offered a means of integrating women into historical scholarship, even contesting the reigning definitions of social, economic, and political importance that obscured women's lives. The topics potentially addressed through oral history, the possibilities of putting women's voices at the centre of history and highlighting gender as a category of analysis, and the prospect that women interviewed will shape the research agenda by articulating what is of importance to them all offer challenges to the dominant ethos of the discipline. Moreover, oral history not only redirects our gaze to overlooked topics, but it is also a methodology directly informed by interdisciplinary feminist debates about our research objectives, questions, and use of the interview material.[3]

Although both popular and scholarly historical works have increasingly embraced oral history as a methodology able to expose ignored topics and present diversified perspectives on the past, there lingers on some suspicion that oral sources may be inappropriate for the discipline. As one labour historian recently pointed out, it would unthinkable for historians to host a conference session asking "written sources: what is their use?"[4] yet one still finds that question posed for oral history. Consideration of whether oral sources are "objective," it appears, still worry the profession — even for those using oral history.[5]

While the biases and problems of oral history need to be examined — as do the limitations of other sources — my intention is not to retrace these older debates, but rather to examine some of the current theoretical dilemmas encountered by feminist historians employing oral history. Rather than seeing the creation of oral sources as biased or problematic, this process can become a central focus for our research: we need to explore the construction of women's historical memory. Asking why and how women explain, rationalize, and make sense of their past offers insight into the social and material framework within which they operated, the perceived choices and cultural patterns they faced, and the complex relationship between individual consciousness and culture.[6]

For feminist historians, two other questions are pressing: what are the ethical issues involved in interpreting other women's lives through oral history, and what theoretical approaches are most effective in conceptualizing this methodology? The latter question is especially timely in the light of recent poststructuralist skepticism that we can locate and describe a concrete and definable women's experience, separate from the cultural discourses constructing that experience.[7]

I wish to explore these three interrelated issues using examples from my own oral history research on the lives of wage-earning women in the large factories of Peterborough, Canada, from 1920 to the end of the Second World War. By exploring in some detail a concrete example — women's memories of a major textile strike in 1937 — I hope to highlight our current theoretical dilemmas and argue for an oral history enhanced by poststructuralist insights, but firmly situated in a materialist and feminist context.

Oral History and the Construction of Women's Memories

If we are to make "memory itself the subject of study,"[8] our interviews must be carefully contextualized, with attention to who is speaking, what their personal and social agenda is, and what kind of event they are describing. We need to unearth the underlying assumptions or 'prob-lematic' of the interview, and to analyze the subtexts and silences, as well as the explicit descriptions in the interview.[9] We need to avoid the tendency, still evident in historical works, of treating oral history only as a panacea designed to fill in the blanks in women's or traditional his-tory, providing "more" history, compensating where we have no other sources, or "better" history, a 'purer' version of the past coming, unadul-terated, from the very people who experienced it.[10] The latter approach erroneously presents oral histories as essentially unmediated, ignoring the process by which the researcher and the informant create the source together and the complicated questions of how memory is constructed, to what extent oral sources can ever reveal the objective experience of people, and whether oral histories should be seen as expressions of ide-ologies — whether dominant, submerged, oppositional — given to us in the form of personal testimony.

It is also crucial that we ask how gender, race, and class, as struc-tural and ideological relations, have shaped the construction of histori-cal memory. The exploration of oral history must incorporate gender as a defining category of analysis, for women often remember the past in different ways than men. Some studies, Gwen Etter-Lewis points out, have found that "women's narratives" are more liable to be characterized by "understatements, avoidance of the first person point of view, rare men-tion of personal accomplishments and disguised statements of personal power."[11] Similarly, a French oral historian noted that the women she interviewed were less likely to place themselves at the centre of public events than men; they downplayed their activities, emphasizing the role of other family members in their recollections.[12] Furthermore, women's "embeddedness in familial life" may also shape their view of the world, and even their very consciousness of historical time.[13] In my study, for instance, many women reconstructed the past using the benchmarks of their family's life cycle — as does Amelia, described below, whose recol-lections of a major textile strike are woven around, and indeed are cru-cially influenced by, her memory of her wedding.

Class, race, and ethnicity, other writers have shown, create significant differences in how we remember and tell our lives; in some instances, these influences overshadow gender in the construction of memory.

Cultural values shape our very ordering and prioritizing of events, indeed our notions of what is myth, history, fact, or fiction.[14] In my study, class shaped people's recollections in stark as well as subtle ways. Not surprisingly, managers remember history differently than workers; a manager in one factory described the period when the company explored relocation to other cities in search of lower wages as "an interesting"[15] time of travel and experimentation, as he knew his job would be salvaged. But workers in the plant who faced job loss remember that same period as a "stressful"[16] and uncertain. On a more subtle level, in this workplace, the reticence on the part of many women to speak forcefully as critics of, or experts on, their workplace contrasted markedly to managers' strong sense of pre-eminence on these issues; these contrasting styles reflected the confidence shaped by both class and gender inequalities.

One's past and current political ideology also shapes the construction of memory. Women who were more class-conscious, militant trade unionists did not hesitate to criticize managers, and they presented workplace conditions in a more critical light than other workers. Interviewees' knowledge of my ideological sympathies, combined with their own, could also shape the interview. A male trade union official I interviewed tended to remember his life story around the theme of himself as a progressive socialist, battling more conservative unionists. Suspecting I was a feminist, his role vis-à-vis the defence of women's rights in the union became aggrandized in his interview, beyond my own reading of the written record.

The influences of class, gender, culture, or political worldview on memory may reveal themselves through both content and the narrative form of the interview. While recent writing on oral history draws heavily on poststructuralist theory to explore narrative form and the way in which subjectivity is created, similar themes have preoccupied oral history theorists for some time. Almost twenty years ago, Ronald Grele suggested we uncover the theme that suffuses the life history, the 'script' around which an informant shapes the presentation of their life. Amelia, for instance, though now comfortable, grew up in the 1930s in a poor farming family; at fifteen, she was forced to leave school to work in a textile mill. Throughout the interview, she criticized current social values, often by contrasting her youth — characterized by hard work and selfless dedication to her family — to the current selfish, affluent youth. Whether or not she was influenced by a conservative philosophy that distrusted modern trends, or whether she wished to understand her relative success as a result of hard work, or whether she was hurt by the seeming neglect by the younger members of her family — or all of the above — the point is that this critical world view came to colour her description of the working conditions she had seen in the textile factory.

Oral history may also illuminate the collective scripts of a social group, revealing, for instance, how and why people's memories of their workplaces or communities are created.[17] Many workers I interviewed who were employed at a factory that embraced paternalism as a labour relations strategy emphasized the "family-like"[18] atmosphere at the plant, and the way in which the patriarchal and charismatic company head saw himself as a father figure. Their descriptions of the rise and decline of the firm were recounted in the form of an epic family drama, with the eventual economic decline of the factory actually compared to a family breakup. Their way of remembering indicates the assimilation, at some level, of the familial metaphors employed by the company to promote its paternalism.

Other ingredients of the narrative form, such as expression, intonation, and metaphors, also offer clues to construction of historical memory. When I asked one woman how her family survived during the time she and her father were on strike in 1937, she couldn't remember. It is possible, first, that the family went on welfare but that she has forgotten because it was a humiliating experience for some people. Later in the interview, however, she made a casual aside, noting that her mother "sewed at home for extra money."[19] Her mother may have supported the family during the strike, but her work in the informal economy (like that of many women) was undervalued, remembered as an afterthought, indeed almost forgotten.

Revelations may also come from silences and omissions in women's stories.[20] The realization that discrimination based on religion is not socially desirable led many women I interviewed initially to deny any religious rivalry in their workplaces; yet one such woman, when describing a different issue — the foreman intervening in a bitter dispute on the line — admitted that severe Catholic and Protestant taunting had initiated the disagreement. One of the most telling examples of silences is the way in which women reacted to the subject of violence. In response to questions about sexual harassment at work (often I didn't begin by using that modern term) or about women's freedom on the streets after work, women seldom spoke of women's vulnerability to violence. Others purposely contrasted the absence of violence when they were younger to contemporary times: in their youth, they claimed, women could walk home alone at night, they were not bothered at work, and that violence against women was rare.

Yet, from other sources and research, I knew that violence in the streets, and in women's homes, was very much a part of daily life. I came to understand women's silence in a number of ways: for one thing, a few women's veiled and uncomfortable references to harassment indicated that some working women, especially in the 1930s, saw harassment as an unfortunate but sometimes obligatory part of the workplace that one couldn't change and didn't talk about. Secondly, it is not only that feminism has made us more aware of harassment and thus provided us with a vocabulary to describe it, but also that similar experiences were labelled differently in the past, often with the term 'favouritism.' Third, a denial of violence was sometimes an externalization of women's ongoing painful fears about violence, and a comforting means of idealizing a chivalrous past in contrast to the more visible violence of today.

Finally, in order to contextualize oral histories, we also need to survey the dominant ideologies shaping women's worlds; listening to women's words, in turn, will help us to see how women understood, negotiated, and sometimes challenged these dominant ideals. For example, perceptions of what was proper work for young women are revealed as women explain the images, ideas, and examples upon which they constructed their ambition and work choices. Ideals of female domesticity and motherhood, reproduced in early home life, the school, and the workplace, and notions of innate physical differences, for instance, were both factors moulding young women's sense of their limited occupational choices in both blue- and white-collar work in the 1930s.[21] Interviews may also indicate when women questioned these dominant ideals, as a few notable women described how and why they made the unusual decision not to marry, to work after marriage, or to attempt a nontraditional job.

Understanding the ideological context may help to unravel the apparently contradictory effects of ideology and experience. Why, for example, when I interview women who worked during the Second World War, do they assume that the war had a liberating effect on women's role in the workplace, even when they offer few concrete examples to substantiate this? As Ruth Pierson points out, sex segregation and gender hierarchy persisted in the Canadian wartime workforce, despite rhetoric to the contrary. Why this contradiction between women's positive memory of new opportunities during the war, and the reality of persisting discrimination?[22] One answer may have been the powerful and hegemonic influence of a popular and mystifying ideology of 'the people's war'— the notion that women were breaking down gender roles — on the very construction of women's memory.[23] Secondly, oral history may reveal women's own definitions of liberation, which may actually diverge from those utilized by historians. In this small city, women saw the wartime abandonment of the marriage bar in local factories as a small revolution for working women. Historians, on the other hand, have based their assessments of continuing inequality on the maintenance of a gendered division of labour during and after the war.

In using oral history as a means of exploring memory construction, then, careful attention to the processes of class and gender construction is needed, as is an understanding of ideological context shaping women's actions. In order to understand the formation of women's gendered consciousness and memory, however, we must also acknowledge our *own* influence on the shape of the interview.

Ethical Dilemmas: For Historians Too?

It is important to acknowledge how our own culture, class position, and political world view shapes the oral histories we collect, for the interview is a historical document created by the agency of *both* the interviewer and interviewee. Many of us originally turned to oral history as a methodology with the radical and democratic potential to reclaim the history of ordinary people and raise working-class and women's consciousness. As feminists, we hoped to use oral history to empower women by creating a revised history *"for* women,"[24] emerging from the actual lived experiences of women. Feminist oral history has often implicitly adopted (though perhaps not critically theorized about) some elements of feminist standpoint theory in its assumption that the distinct material and social position of women produces, in a complex way, a unique epistemological vision that might be slowly unveiled by the narrator and the historian.[25]

'Representing the world from the standpoint of women,' while a laudable feminist aim, may still be difficult to accomplish. As well as the thorny theoretical question of our ability to adequately locate women's experience — discussed below — there are two other concerns. Are we exaggerating the radical potential of oral history, especially the likelihood of academic work changing popular attitudes? Even more important, are we ignoring the uncomfortable ethical issues involved in using living people as a source for our research?

Some years ago, feminist social scientists mounted a critique of interview relationships based on supposed "detachment" and objectivity, but in reality on unequal power and control over outcome. As a solution, sociologists like Ann Oakley proposed the laudable aim of equalizing the interview, making it a more co-operative venture.[26] Yet in attempting this, we may be simply masking our own privilege. While a detached objectivity may be impossible, a false claim to sisterhood is also unrealistic. As Janet Finch has argued, a romanticization of oral history research that ignores the fact that we are often "trading on our identity — as a woman, a professional"[27] — to obtain information is not useful. Judith Stacey also argues that feminist research is inevitably enmeshed in unequal, intrusive, and potentially exploitative relationships, simply by virtue of our position as researchers and that of other women, with less control over the finished product, as 'subjects' of study.[28] I agree. Nor will renaming these relationships with terms implying a sharing of power completely erase our privilege.[29] After all, we are using this material for purpose of writing books that are often directed, at least in part, to academic or career ends. I gained access to women's memories not as a friend, but as a professional historian.

These ethical issues are visibly highlighted through the conflicting interpretations that may be embraced by my informants and myself. By necessity, historians analyze and judge, and in the process, we may presume to understand the consciousness of our interviewees. Yet our analysis may contradict women's self-image, and our feminist perspective may be rejected by our interviewees. Would women who worked in the paternalist factory I studied agree to the very word 'paternalist' as a description of their relationship to management? Would workers in low-paid textile work accept language like subordination or exploitation to describe their status in the family or workplace? The answer to the latter two questions might be 'no.'

While I had every intention of allowing women to speak about their *own* perceptions, if my interpretation and theirs diverged, mine would assume precedence in my writing. We can honour feminist ethical obligations to make our material accessible to the women interviewed, never to reveal confidences spoken out of the interview, never to purposely distort or ridicule their lives, but in the last resort, it is our privilege that allows us to interpret, and it is our responsibility as historians to convey their insights using our own — as the opening quotation to this article indicated. Even feminists like Judith Stacey and Daphne Patai, who offer trenchant critiques of the unequal interview relationship, do not recommend abandoning this methodology; in the last resort, they see the potential for feminist awareness and understanding outweighing the humbling recognition that it is currently impossible to create an ideal feminist methodology that negates power differences.

These debates have usually taken place between sociologists and anthropologists, less often with historians' participation. Why? Is it related to the fact that, as Ruth Pierson argues, until recently, we have undertheorized our work?[30] Is it possible that our traditional disciplinary training — especially an emphasis on empirical methods and a tendency to objectify our sources, but also the preference of the discipline *not* to work with living subjects — has obscured these questions from our view? We might be less concerned about imposing our interpretations on women's voices if we were dealing with a written source; we are particularly sensitive about judging women because of the personal relationship — however brief — established between ourselves and our interviewees. But this is not necessarily positive, for it may lead us to shy away from critical conclusions.

Other limitations in our historical training may also obscure these ethical questions. Is the study of people of different time periods, cultures, and classes so taken for granted that we have not questioned the power inherent in writing across these boundaries? As Pierson notes on the current, troubling question of who has the 'right' to write whose history, if historians cannot study women of different backgrounds who have less power, we may be reduced to writing autobiography.[31] Perhaps the mere fact of historical time — again, inherent in the discipline — helps to distance us, if only in an illusory way, from the issue of unequal relationships. When I interview wage-earning women about their experience in the 1930s, the age gulf allows both of us detachment from the subject we are discussing, which then sanctions the licence to interpret and judge.

In the last resort, I wonder how much soul searching is useful: is endless debate self-indulgent, sometimes an ex-post-facto justification of our work, and does our concern with interviewing women from other backgrounds sometimes take on a condescending tone?[32] Perhaps it is important not to definitely answer, but rather to be ever aware of these questions: we need to continually analyze the interview as a interactive process, examine the context of the interview, especially inherent power imbalances, and always evaluate our own ethical obligations as feminists to the women we interview.

Theoretical Dilemmas

While it is important to explore the interview as a mediated source, moulded by the political and social worldview of the author and subject, I think we should beware of recent trends that see oral history embodying innumerable contingencies and interpretations. When more traditional historians questioned the reliability of oral sources, suggesting that interviews are more fiction than fact, they may not have realized that they were echoing the tenets of some poststructuralist analyses that explore the relationship between language, subjectivity, and the construction of cultural meanings and social organization.

While linguistic theories are far from new in the interdisciplinary field of oral history, the more recent turn to poststructuralism suggests a more intensive concern with both linguistic structure and cultural discourses determining oral narratives, as well as a skepticism about any direct relationship between experience and representation. This theorizing has enriched our understanding of oral history, but it may also pose the danger of overstating the ultimate contingency, variability, and 'fictionality' of oral histories and the impossibility of using them to locate a women's past that is "real and knowable."[33]

Since the mid-1980s, oral historians have increasingly examined language "as the invisible force that shapes oral texts and gives meaning to historical events."[34] This approach is evident in the recent *Women's Words*, whose editors urge us to consider "the interview as a linguistic, as well as a social and psychological event."[35] While the books' contributions range widely in their perspective, substantial attention is paid to narrative form and language; one author urges the embrace of "deconstruction" rather than mere "interpretation" of the text.[36] In other works, the emphasis on language has been taken to more extreme conclusions, resulting in the denigration of historical agency; one such writer claims that the "narrative discourses available in our culture . . . structure perceptual experience, organize memory . . . and purpose-build the very events of a life." Our life stories then come to "reflect the cultural models available to us," so much so that we become mere "variants on the culture's canonical forms."[37]

Practitioners of oral history have been more visibly influenced by the poststructuralist turn in anthropology and by some literary theory than by similar historical debates. In anthropology, life histories are being re-evaluated as poststructuralist voices emphasize the power-laden, complex process of constructing the oral narrative; one author suggests that life histories "provide us with a conventionalized gloss on a social reality that . . . we cannot know. . . . We may be discussing the dynamics of narration rather than the dynamics of society."[38] Similarly, works like *Writing Culture* have stressed the creation of an indeterminate reality by the observed and the observer, well summed up by the conclusion that we can only hope for "a constructed understanding of the constructed native's constructed point of view."[39]

Of course, poststructuralism has also stimulated debate in historical circles, with feminists apparently sympathetic or at least divided, and some working-class historians more critical.[40] Feminist historians have been understandably attracted to the challenge to androcentric epistemologies, critiques of essentialism, concerns with language and representation, and the analysis of power suggested by some poststructuralist writing.[41] Nonetheless, critics have cautioned against the inherent idealism in some poststructuralist theory and the abandonment of the search for historical causality and agency, not to mention a sense of political despair when the very notions of exploitation and oppression are deconstructed so completely as to be abandoned.[42]

These debates — which cannot be explored in detail here — have important implications for the way in which we interpret our interviews, confront the ethical questions of the power-laden interview, and consider the concept of experience. New attention to language and the way in which gender is itself shaped through the discourses available to us can offer insight as we analyze the underlying form and structure of our interviews. Reading our interviews on many levels will encourage us to look for more than one discursive theme and for multiple relations of power based on age, class, race and culture as well as gender.

On the ethical question of the inherent inequality of this methodology, however, poststructuralist writing is less useful. As Judith Stacey persuasively argues, the postmodern strategy of dealing with ethical questions in ethnography is inadequate because it highlights power imbalances we knew to exist, but does not suggest any way of acting to ameliorate them. Poststructuralist anthropologists, for instance, suggest the process of "evoking" rather than describing narratives through "co-operative" dialogue, or fragmentary or polyphonic discourse,[43] as an alternative to their own power of authorship. As critics point out, however, these tactics can also veil and deny power: they can involve "self reflection, perhaps self preoccupation, but not self criticism."[44] Privilege is not negated simply by inclusion of other voices, or by denial of our ultimate authorship and control. Solutions that disguise power are not helpful to the historical profession in particular, which still needs to face and debate the question of power inherent in historical writing.

Finally, there is also the troubling and seemingly unsolvable problem of experience. Exploring and revaluing women's experience has been a cornerstone of feminist oral history, but the current emphasis on differences between women — in part encouraged by poststructuralist writing — has posed the dilemma of whether we can write across the divides of race, class, and gender about other women's experiences, past or present. In the case of oral history, Ruth Pierson implies that we should be "as close as possible" to the oppressed group being studied, preferably a member of that group. Secondly, we should concentrate on the exterior context of women but avoid with "epistimal humility" a presumption to know women's interiority.[45] This raises troubling questions for me: just how close should we be to our subjects we are interviewing? Across the boundaries of sexual orientation, race, ethnicity, disability, class, and age, can we score two out of six and still explore subjectivity: where are the boundaries and under what circumstances can they shift? Secondly, separating exterior context from inner lives is extremely difficult. Does my assertion that women's ambition was social constructed not emerge from precisely that presumptuous supposition about the relationship between context and interior life? Will we not impoverish our historical writing if we shy away from attempts to empathetically link women's inner and outer lives?

Also, is experience itself a construction of the narratives available to us in our culture? The concept of experience is not without its problems in history and feminist theory; it has been used to justify essentialism and to create a homogeneous 'woman' whose existence is enigmatic.[46] But what are the consequences of ignoring a concept that allows women to "name their own lives"[47] and struggles, and thus validates a notion of real, lived oppression that was understood and felt by women in the past?

Related concerns were voiced over a decade ago by Louise Tilly, in her critique of oral history shaped by literary theory and used to study subjectivity, and her counter-endorsement of a materialist oral history, used to study social relations.[48] But can these two aims be so easily separated? Can the interview not be interpreted with a keen materialist and feminist eye to context, and also informed by poststructuralist insights into language? The cultural construction of memory would still be a focus of inquiry, posed within a framework of social and economic relations and imperatives. While is it important to analyze *how* someone constructs an explanation for their life, ultimately there are patterns, structures, and systemic reasons for those constructions that must be identified in order to understand historical causality.[49] Polarities between subjectivity and social relations, or between a dated "older" generation of women doing oral history who supposedly naively accepted the "transparency" of their interviewees' accounts and the new, 'complex' approach influenced by theory[50] may not be justified — and ironically create precisely the kind of "conceptual hierarchy which poststructuralism is supposed to decentre."[51]

It has been suggested that historians may be able to extract techniques and insights from poststructuralist writing, yet still critique other premises of poststructuralist theory. One way to explore some of the current theoretical dilemmas of feminist historians utilizing oral history, and indicate a useful reconciliation of these debates, is to take an in-depth look at the process and outcome of my interviews with working women who participated in a major strike at Peterborough's largest textile mill in 1937.

Five Strike Stories

In this small city, a variety of factories offered women employment, but one of the largest was a textile mill, the Bonnerworth, owned by a large absentee corporation, Dominion Woollens. In 1937 men working at another local Dominion Woollens mill initiated unionization and strike action in pursuit of better wages, and the Bonnerworth women immediately joined the strike. Part of a larger Canadian pattern of revolt in the textile industry at this time, the Bonnerworth strike was characterized by anger and violence on their picket line, which came to dominate press coverage as well as governmental concern and action. In the city's labour history, this textile strike has been portrayed within two dominant themes: as the first, and ultimately unsuccessful, attempt to organize industrial unions, which had a negative effect on organizing for some time, and as a rare example of violent class conflict polarizing the community.

By the time I interviewed former Bonnerworth workers, I had already presumed the themes listed above to be historically significant — a fact that did shape the interview process. As Susan Geiger notes, our preconceived notions of what is important or marginal privileges certain voices and obscures unexplored themes.[52] One of my first aims, for instance, was to find Edith, a well-known leader in the strike and union. Yet other women had very different memories than Edith, downplaying, or even forgetting (what I had considered) important parts of the strike, such as union organizing or picket line violence.

Women's strike stories varied significantly, despite similarities in their biographies: the five women described below all came from working-class families; by fifteen, they were working in the mills, usually as spinners and twisters; they contributed their pay to the household economy; and they all left the mill by the early 1940s for married life. Their stories highlight a long-standing problem for historians: how do we reconcile different interpretations of the past, in this case, all seemingly based on first-person experience? As their diverse accounts emerged, I reassessed my a priori assumptions about the strike and began to question the existence of an identifiable, common experience or class consciousness on women's part. Would I be reduced to emphasizing 'individual' experience — surely a pluralist retreat with little explanatory force? Perhaps the poststructuralists were right: there could be no 'truth' or 'reality' outside of our multitudinous constructions of them! What then were women's strike stories? Five short samples taken from a much larger study follow.

Rosa was a second-generation Italian immigrant who had to leave school at thirteen, despite the fact that she was very clever. She went to work at the Bonnerworth mill, and became a trusted, versatile employee, a talented machine operator often moved around to difficult jobs throughout the plant. When the strike began, she stayed out for a day or two, but she was soon back at work, crossing the picket line. "It wasn't very nice going to work . . . I tried to find different ways of going, but you were always called a scab." she remembers. "The police were always there . . . you couldn't go home for lunch." Extremely revealing is Rosa's claim that her close friend also continued to work; yet other glaring evidence (her friend's arrest notice in the paper, confirmed by a family member) says otherwise.

Initially guarded and defensive when talking to me about the strike, she slowly explained that her parents had influenced her stand, telling her to ignore the strikers and "mind my own business." Moreover, the demand for more money was not a compelling enough reason to walk out; though acknowledging "the money wasn't good" she also felt she was "getting by" and that she owed her boss, whom she liked, some loyalty. Overall, Rosa played down the strike in the history of her work life, de-emphasized its importance and conflictual nature, was critical of strikers' tactics, and spent more time describing work dynamics in the mill, in particular her encounter with a woman who "wanted the [better] job" Rosa was on and tried to convince the foreman she "could do it better."[53]

I believe that her memory of the strike was influenced by her need to justify her decision to cross the line and deal with the discomfort of this difficult event — being denounced as a scab is not something we all want imprinted in our memories for the rest of our lives. Her memory lapse about her friend probably reflects precisely this process of self-justification. Her loyalty to her boss becomes more understandable in the larger context of her life history. Living in a dominantly British city that was often ambivalent to immigrants and coming from an unskilled working-class family, she was understandably pleased to have the managers recognize and respect her intelligence and talents. She felt pride in this recognition and was not willing to throw it away just to join others on the picket line, especially the same woman who "wanted her job."[54] While many other Italian workers supported the strike, Rosa did not: her memory reveals her very particular and individual efforts to cope with structures of economic and ethnic discrimination.

A second strike story told by June downplayed the strike even more dramatically. This young woman, from an English working-class background, had been working at the Bonnerworth for a year, since she was fourteen, when the strike began. She described the strike as an abrupt, puzzling event, that the women in the mill did not create: she simply went to work one day and found a picket line set up. Along with a group of friends, she became involved in strike aid, making sandwiches for the night picketers, collecting funds, and helping at the union office. But her attitude towards the union was less than dedicated; when fellow workers elected her shop steward after the strike, she said, laughing, "I was [so surprised] . . . I nearly flipped." Drawing on her father's advice "not to become involved," she declined and never attended a union meeting.

As she told her story to me, I was struck by June's deprecation of the seriousness of this event, and by her denial of any leadership role in the strike. She distanced herself from a woman union leader whom she saw as both politically and morally 'radical'; alternatively, she presented her own role as a social diversion for the summer. "During the strike, it was an opportunity for us to go downtown together . . . the girls I chummed with weren't bitter about it . . . it was almost a heyday. . . . we had street dances. I don't remember any tear gas. Us kids didn't know what [the] strike was about."[55]

Portraying a strike that included tear gas, arrests, and violence as a heyday was not something I had expected. Her memory, however, was influenced by her youth at the time, her position in the household, and her later, more conservative political views, which became apparent during the interview. Because of the latter, she had no desire to assume the persona of a working-class militant. Secondly, for the young women workers — mere teenagers — the strike could have been 'a lark,' a rest from the long, hot hours in the factory. If the family had other wage earners (as hers did) and could scrimp by, then why not enjoy this unexpected vacation? Because these young women did not have a strong say in the union, they understandably downplayed their agency in creating the strike. The tear gas is forgotten either because June missed those picketing days or because overall, these details don't fit in with her narrative script of the strike as a 'heyday.'

The third story is told by Amelia, a farm girl from who began work at fifteen. Like many other farm families, hers saw high school as an unattainable luxury, and so she dutifully followed her sister into the textile mill. When she moved into an inspector's position, she had a slightly less arduous job. This, along with a strong feeling that she owed her employer honest, hard work, led to her ambivalence about the strike. Though Amelia recognized that her pay "was very low," she did not want to be seen as a complainer by management. She didn't openly oppose her striking workmates, though their rejection of authority seemed outrageous and "brazen" to her; instead, she simply avoided picket duty. She told the union she lived too far from the mill, but to me she noted her choice was also political: "I wasn't much of a politician then, and so I just went with them [the strikers] because I didn't want to be seen [as] against the strike."

What was more memorable for Amelia, however, was the relationship between the strike and a more important event in her life: her wedding. She was disturbed about being off work because she was "saving up for [my] wedding and I wasn't saving anything on strike." Indeed, strike events become lost amidst her remembered concern with her trousseau and her wedding: "I remember being fretful about going on strike . . . there was a settlement suggested in August when I was getting ready for my wedding . . . Yes, I knew it ended before I got married because I [used my] back pay to buy new curtains for my home. . . . I guess I missed the violence, but I was really preoccupied with my upcoming plans."[56]

A fourth story moves closer to the images of class conflict portrayed in the press and government reports. Margaret also started in the mill at thirteen, but by 1937, she had been there ten years. She was not involved in the union or strike planning but she was forthright in her support. Arrested for assaulting a police officer, she both denied the charge and later joked about her respectable family's horror at her notoriety.

Margaret, despite this upsetting incident, tried to assess the strike from a number of perspectives, even offering a sympathetic interpretation of strikebreakers: "maybe they . . . needed the money more than we did." Never concentrating only on her own story, she related the strike and its consequences to the lives of her workmates, friends, and family — a common characteristic of women's narratives. Margaret also avoided a depiction of her role as heroic or militant. She spoke of her horror at being arrested, but in retrospect couches the episode in humour, characterizing her day as a "jailbird" as an aberration in an otherwise law-abiding life. While embracing an interpretation of the strike as a just cause precipitated by exploitative working conditions, she avoided placing the many actors, including herself, into polarized or one-dimensional roles.

Finally, Edith, a leader in the strike, did remember it as tragic struggle between an unethical employer, aided by the police, and exploited workers. What was the strike about, I asked? "Wages, the whole thing was wages . . . They paid starvation wages, and everybody knew that," was her response. Edith came from an extremely large working-class family, many of whom had worked at the mill at some time. She was determined to create a life better for herself and her children, indicating to me that she purposely had fewer children than her mother. She had worked at the plant for some time, even after her marriage, and this longevity, along with a streak of rebelliousness, earned her a reputation for "talking back" to managers and standing up for other workers. She took some pride in her prominent role in the strike and saw it as a just cause waged between the forces of greed and the right to basic decency and survival.[57] In Edith's words, I had I finally found a voice that replicated the official version of the strike as unmitigated class conflict. As a labour historian I could readily identify with Edith's method of presentation, as it approximated a long tradition of 'strike histories' in the discipline!

But other women's voices, in all their diversity, also had to be explained. One possibility was to abandon the attempt to write "one true story,"[58] looking instead at the structure of each narrative, uncovering the script being played out, contradictions in the narrative, and the cultural discourses disclosed. Poststructuralist writing on oral history is useful in thinking through the deconstruction of these interviews. A close examination of narrative form helps to uncover layers of meanings in women's words, the simultaneous stories that were being played out, and the script around which the interview was moulded. Even the metaphors, tone, and silences of women were significant: June's repeated laughter denoting her deprecation of the strike; Edith's use of resolute, cut-and-dried juxtapositions to convey images of class conflict; Rosa's significant silences on the question of her strike breaking.

Secondly, attention to the construction of the text by myself *and* the women interviewed was also valuable. How did I help to shape the interviews? It is possible that by appearing with newspaper clippings of strike battles, I actually encouraged Edith and Margaret to remember it as a conflictual event? And did my assumption that the important story was one of unionization lead me to ignore the effect of the strike on young women marginalized from the union? Finally, the attempts of recent feminist (including poststructuralist) writing to challenge class reductionism encouraged me to contemplate how a woman's gendered and class identity is created within a number of discourses, possibly producing a contradictory and fragmented consciousness: women's understandings of the strike were shaped by more complex influences than predetermined notions of class conflict I had previously read into the event. Indeed, these strike stories evocatively point to the variability of working-class women's experiences and the way in which — even in the crucible of conflict — working-class consciousness may be oppositional, accommodating, or even a mixture of both.

While these insights are useful, the narrative form and the construction of these women's identities must still be related to evidence from other historical sources. Some women's denial of conflict and violence, for instance, might have led me to conclude that the strike was less conflictual than subsequent history claimed; but I could not ignore the stark pictures of violence presented in the newspaper. Secondly, women's diverse understandings of the strike must be situated within the economic, social, and political context of women's lives at this time.

The material structures of class and the dominant gender ideals, as well as women's struggles to deal with these realities, must also be used as interpretive frameworks. The social relations of power in the family and society, the economic limits and possibilities of women's lives, and their own reactions to those possibilities were all significant. All these women were expected to contribute to the family economy for basic survival; many were subject to parental authority on pain of losing the roof over their heads; and they were influenced by the dominant political ideology, which feared communism and radical union activity. Even their individual negotiations of these realities can be partly understood by looking at the possibilities that emerged from existing social constraints: some young women did not entirely agree with parents' admonitions not to become involved, but they felt they had few choices, as "there was none of this leaving home like there is today."[59]

If we examine the power relations of age, gender, ethnicity, and class, as well as the dominant gender ideals of the time, these apparently diverse stories assume more discernible patterns. Rosa, who crossed the picket line and has suppressed her recollections of her best friend's different position, and in fact has constructed a life script stressing acceptance and achievement, is telling us something about her difficult status as a member of an ethnic minority in a WASP city and her purposeful memory of a hard-won battle to achieve respectability in the workplace. Like other women interviewed, Rosa is also telling us how difficult it was for young women to contradict the power of parental authority.

Amelia's preoccupation with her wedding reveals much about dominant gender ideals of the time that stressed women's private, marital, and family lives. The expectation that women would marry as a natural part of their life course was firmly embedded in Canadian culture at this time;[60] Amelia's memories reflect the priority given to the ritual of marriage and investment in an ideal of domesticity as a fitting end to women's time in the labour force. This is underscored in many other interviews, including one where a woman remembered the "bitterness"[61] after the strike in only one way: she was denied the ritual wedding present by her fellow workers because she had crossed the picket line.

Perhaps the strength of these gender ideals helps to explain in part why some of the younger women like June did not remain interested in the union. At the same time, though, June's testimony also speaks to the male-dominated, exclusive power relations of union politics. Younger women were not adequately integrated into the union, seldom informed of strategy or considered potential leaders; the result was their lack of interest in the union. June's story also made me aware of my tendency to view the motivations of women strikers through presentist glasses, and the need for a historical view of age differences and their meaning in different material and social contexts. The strikers were often teenagers: they were not women with immediately dependent families, older, with more workforce experience (except, significantly, the female leader), like those often visible in recent strikes.[62] I had to ask myself if I was ready for serious political commitment, or just out for a "heyday," at sixteen? My answer made me cognizant of the importance of June's age and position in the household in shaping her role in the strike.

Finally, the role of political ideology in shaping memory is also important: given June's later emphasis on respect for authority and loyalty to mainstream political parties, apparent in her interview, her early union militancy might be more embarrassing then heroic. In a city where radicalism remains a fringe, not a respectable ideology, her dismissal of her early activism becomes quite comprehendible.

While June's deprecation of the strike is thus understandable, Edith's public support for the strike becomes all the more exceptional and interesting. Edith played an extraordinarily vocal and militant role in the conflict; she was often was the only visible female leader in bargaining meetings dominated by men. Edith's radical persona led to criticisms that she was ignoring her family and not acting with enough feminine decorum. This didn't seem to deter her. Her assumption of a vocal and public role in the strike indicates that dominant gender ideals, though certainly influential, have also been challenged by some women. Those challenges emerge not only from the material and social context, but also from the exceptional character, courage, and intellectual bravery of individual women. Though most clearly evidenced in Edith's response, this courage was also a small part of many women's willingness to take a public stand on the picket line.

Conclusion

My conclusions are shaped by both the moral stance of Denise Riley's assertion that, in the interests of a feminist praxis, we must lay political claim to women's experience of oppression,[63] and secondly, by a belief that poststructuralist insights must be situated in a feminist materialist context. While an emphasis on language and narrative form has enhanced our understanding of oral history, I worry about the dangers of emphasizing form over context, of stressing deconstruction of individual narratives over analysis of social patterns, of disclaiming our duty as historians to analyze and interpret women's stories. Nor do we want to totally abandon the concept of experience, moving towards a notion of a depoliticized and 'unknowable' past. We do not want to return to a history that either obscures power relationships or marginalizes women's voices. Without a firm grounding of oral narratives in their material and social context, and a probing analysis of the relation between the two, insights on narrative form and on representation will remain unconnected to any useful critique of oppression and inequality.

A glimpse of the workplace after the strike brings us back to questions of social relations, power, and its effects. There was one reality that all the women agreed on: their working conditions did not improve after the strike. The union lost; industrial unions were defeated for some time in the city; and the status quo in labour/capital relations was reasserted. Women at the Bonnerworth were still earning less than the minimum wage for a twelve-hour day; moreover, they immediately experienced a work speed-up. I cannot present such an ending without recourse to value judgments, moral outrage, and with a clear characterization of class power and fixed notions of exploitation that some poststructuralist writing has rejected along with other elements of Marxism.

Women's strike stories must be situated within social relations and structures of power that are real and "knowable."[64] We need to ask how these narratives reflect as well as shape women's social and economic lives; why certain narratives emerge and take precedence; and whom these particular scripts benefit. The experience of these women workers was not created out of many possible discourses, but out of a limited range of discourses that are the product of the power relations of class, ethnicity, and gender, as well as people's resistance to those relations. Moreover, women's narratives do reflect certain knowable experiences, always mediated by cultural codes, which may in turn, come to shape their interpretation of experience in a dialectical sense.

How we, as feminist oral historians, define experience and whether we think it is even a useful concept is central to this discussion. Locating experience, however difficult that project, however many dangers it encompasses, should remain one of our utopian goals. Otherwise, our feminist project of understanding and challenging inequality will always be one in which we gaze longingly through a distorted mirror, never able to make women whole again, but more important, never attempting to. Negating an understanding of experience as a 'lived reality' for women carries with it the danger of marginalizing and trivializing women's historical voices and their experiences (however varied) of oppression — a trivialization that practising oral historians have heard only too often. If, as Joan Scott argues, we cannot really locate women's experience because it lies within constructions of language and if women's agency "is more wish than reality,"[65] then will we not come to discount women's agency as a force in history? While Margaret's understanding of her resistance during the strike is couched in a narrative of humour and disparagement, this does not negate her momentary courage in the face of many structural constraints: her attempt to remake her own and other women's history should not be diminished in any way.

So, it is true that women's stories of the strike appear dissimilar. Women have forgotten their role in the strike. Women tried to hide their role in it. Women only remembered how it related to their wedding day. Women explained their role by saying they were young and frivolous. Women denied that there was any violence, and women remembered violence. But these narratives, rather than being simply contradictory and ambiguous, or individual representations of memory, are reflections of, and active rejoinders to, women's work and family experiences, dominant ideals of femininity, the existing power structures of capitalism and patriarchy, and sometimes even women's resistance to those structures.

Notes

1 Personal Narrative Group and Luisa Passerini, "Truths" and "Women's Personal Narratives: Myths, Experiences, and Emotions," in *Interpreting Women's Lives: Feminist Theory and Personal Narratives*, ed. Personal Narrative Group (Bloomington: Indiana University Press, 1989), 261, 197.

2 For example: Women's History Issue, *Oral History: The Journal of the Oral History Society* 5, no. 2 (1977); special issues of *Frontiers* in 1977 and 1983; Mary Chamberlain and Paul Thompson, "International Conference on Oral History and Women's History," *Oral History Review* 12, no. 1 (1984); Sherna Gluck, "Introduction," in *Rosie the Riveter Revisited: Women, the War and Social Change* (Boston: Twayne Publishers, 1987); Sara Diamond, "Women in the B.C. Labour Movement," *Canadian Oral History Association Journal* (1983), 6. On Women's Studies, see K. Anderson, K. Armitage, S. Jack, and D. Wittner, "Beginning Where We Are: Feminist Methodology in Oral History," in *Feminist Research Methods*, ed. Joyce Nielsen (Boulder, CO: Westview Press, 1990).

3 Susan Geiger, "What's So Feminist About Women's Oral History?" *Journal of Women's History* 2, no. 1 (1990): 169–70.

4 Wayne Roberts, "Using Oral History to Study Working Class History," paper presented at the Canadian Oral History Association conference, Toronto, 1991.

5 Henry Hodysh and Gordon McIntosh, "Problems of Objectivity in Oral History," *Historical Studies in Education* 1, no. 1 (1989): 137–47.

6 My argument here is indebted to Ronald Grele, *Envelopes of Sound: The Art of Oral History* (Chicago: Precedent Publishing, 1975).

7 The term 'poststructuralist' is an umbrella expression, actually referring to a number of theoretical positions. In this article I deal primarily with theories shaped by linguistic and deconstructive approaches, which explore the construction of subjectivity and cultural meaning through language. As Chris Weedon argues, these positions generally argue that "experience has no inherent essential meaning." See Chris Weedon, *Feminist Practice and Post-structuralist Theory* (Oxford: Basil Blackwell, 1987), 34.

8 Michael Frisch, "The Memory of History," *Radical History Review* 25 (1981): 16. See also Michael Frisch and Dorothy Watts, "Oral History and the Presentation of Class Consciousness: The *New York Times* Versus the Buffalo Unemployed," *International Journal of Oral History* 1, no. 2 (1980): 88–110.

9 These warnings come from Grele, *Envelopes of Sound*.

10 Michael Frisch, "Report on the International Conference on Oral History," in *Oral History Journal* (1983): 8. See also his "The Memory of History," 25. Both older and some newer articles reflect these tendencies. See, for example, Eliane Silverman,

The Last Best West: Women on the Alberta Frontier, 1880–1930 (Montreal: Eden Press, 1984), and Marilyn Mayer Culpepper, "Views from Fourscore and More: Youth and Maturation in the Oral Histories of Elderly Women," *International Journal of Oral History* 10, no. 3 (1989): 194–209.

11 Gwendolyn Etter-Lewis, "Black Women's Life Stories: Reclaiming Self in Narrative Texts," in *Women's Words: The Feminist Practice of Oral History*, ed. Sherna Berger Gluck and Daphne Patai (New York: Routledge, Chapman and Hall, 1991), 48. This does not appear to be the case in Julie Cruikshank's analysis of northern Canadian Native women's histories in *Life Lived Like a Story* (Vancouver: University of British Columbia Press, 1992). The importance of culture in shaping women's narratives is thus also crucial.

12 This is reflected overtly in language: women tended to use 'on,' men, 'je.' See Isabel Bertaux-Wiame, "The Life History Approach to Internal Migration: How Men and Women Came to Paris Between the Wars," in *Our Common History: The Transformation of Europe*, ed. Paul Thompson (New Jersey: Humanities Press, 1982).

13 Geiger, "Life Histories," 348.

14 See Claudia Salazar, "A Third World Women's Text: Between the Politics of Criticism and Cultural Politics," in *Women's Words*, ed. Gluck and Patai; Doris Sommer, "Not Just a Personal Story," in *Life/Lines: Theorizing Women's Autobiography*, ed. Bella Brodzki and Celeste Schenk (Ithaca: Cornell University Press, 1988); Julie Cruikshank, "Myth and Tradition as Narrative Framework," *International Journal of Oral History* 9, no. 3 (1988): 198–214. I have chosen to emphasize class and gender in this article because the city I am studying was overwhelmingly homogeneous in ethnic composition.

15 Interview with M.H., 18 July 1989.

16 Interview with M.A., 27 June 1989.

17 On collective scripts, see John Bodnar, "Power and Memory in Oral History: Workers and Managers at Studebaker," *Journal of American History* 75, no. 4 (1989): 4.

18 Interview with C.E., 27 June 1989. This issue is dealt with in more detail in my "The Softball Solution: Male Managers, Female Workers and the Operation of Paternalism at Westclox, 1923–1960," *Labour/Le Travail* 32 (1993): 167–99.

19 Interview with R.M., 27 Aug. 1989.

20 For discussion of silences and jokes, see Luisa Passerini, "Work, Ideology and Working-Class Attitudes to Fascism," in *Our Common History*, ed. Thompson.

21 This conclusion, which is detailed elsewhere, is supported in an article on women teachers of this period that also uses oral histories. See Cecilia Reynolds, "Hegemony and Hierarchy: Becoming a Teacher in Toronto, 1930–80," *Historical Studies in Education* 2, no. 1 (1990): 95–118.

22 Ruth Roach Pierson, *They're Still Women After All: The Second World War and Canadian Womanhood* (Toronto: McClelland and Stewart, 1986). For a popular Canadian book that stresses women's positive memories, see Jean Bruce, *Back the Attack! Canadian Women During the Second World War, at Home and Abroad* (Toronto: Macmillan. 1985). For a scholarly discussion of women's memories and how "women were changed by war work in subtle and private ways," see Gluck, *Rosie the Riveter Revisited*, 269.

23 See Grele, *Envelopes of Sound*, for a discussion of how notions of hegemony and ideology may be useful in analyzing oral histories. On the use of hegemony, see also Jackson Lears, "The Concept of Cultural Hegemony: Problems and Possibilities," *American Historical Review* 90, no. 3 (1985): 567–93.

24 My conscious reshaping of Dorothy Smith's words from *The Everyday World As Problematic* (Boston: Northeastern Press, 1987).

25 Here, I am not only referring to Smith, noted above, but also Nancy Hartsock, "The Feminist Standpoint: Developing the Ground for a Specifically Feminist Historical Materialism," in *Feminist Methodology*, ed. Sandra Harding (Bloomington: Indiana University Press, 1987). See also Alison Jaggar, *Feminist Politics and Human Nature* (Totowa: Rowman and Allanheld, 1983), 369–71, and Sandra Harding, *The Science Question in Feminism* (Ithaca: Cornell University Press, 1986), chaps. 6 and 7.

26 Ann Oakley, "Interviewing Women: A Contradiction in Terms," in *Doing Feminist Research*, ed. Helen Roberts (London: Routledge, Kegan and Paul, 1981).

27 Janet Finch, "It's Great to Have Someone to Talk To: The Ethics and Politics of Interviewing Women," in *Social Researching: Politics, Problems, Practice*, ed. Colin Bell and Helen Roberts (London: Routledge, Kegan and Paul, 1984), 78.

28 Judith Stacey, "Can There Be a Feminist Ethnography?" in *Women's Words*, ed. Gluck and Patai. See also Daphne Patai, "U.S. Academics and Third World Women: Is Ethical Research Possible?" also in *Women's Words*.

29 See Personal Narrative Group, *Interpreting Women's Lives*, 201, for the recommendation that we replace "researcher-subject" with "life historian-producer."

30 Ruth Pierson, "Experience, Difference, Dominance and Voice in the Writing of Canadian Women's History," in *Writing Women's History: International Perspectives*, ed. Karen Offen, Ruth Roach Pierson, and Jane Rendall (Bloomington: Indiana University Press, 1991).

31 Ibid.

32 For example, in Karen Olson and Linda Shopes, "Crossing Boundaries, Building Bridges: Doing Oral History with Working-Class Women and Men," in *Women's Words*, ed. Gluck and Patai, one author notes that she puts her working-class interviewees 'at ease' with a measure of self-disclosure, yet the example she

selects leaves me somewhat unsettled: "Informants are more willing to reveal their own experience when they learn that I have shared many of the family problems that plague them — a father who was chronically unemployed, a son whose adolescent acting-out included run-ins with juvenile services, a trouble marriage that ended in divorce." (194). Are there certain 'assumptions' about working-class life inherent in this statement? For a critique of proceeding from such assumptions about 'representativeness,' see Geiger, "What's So Feminist About Women's Oral History?"

33 Louise Tilly, "Gender, Women's History, Social History and Deconstruction," *Social Science History* 13, no. 4 (1989): 443.

34 Etter-Lewis, "Black Women's Life Stories," in *Women's Words*, ed. Gluck and Patai, 44.

35 Gluck and Patai, "Introduction," in *Women's Words*, 9.

36 Etter-Lewis, "Black Women's Life Stories," in *Women's Words*, ed. Gluck and Patai, 44.

37 Jerome Bruner, "Life as Narrative," *Social Research* 54, no. 1 (1987): 54.

38 Vincent Crapanzano, "Life Histories," *American Anthropologist* 86, no. 4 (1984): 955.

39 Vincent Crapanzano, "Hermes' Dilemma: The Masking of Subversion in Ethnographic Description," in *Writing Culture: The Poetics and Politics of Ethnography*, ed. James Clifford and George E. Marcus (Berkeley: University of California Press, 1986), 74. For a feminist critique of this book, see Frances Mascia-Lees, Patricia Sharpe, and Colleen Ballerino Cohen, "The Postmodernist Turn in Anthropology: Cautions from a Feminist Perspective," *Signs* 15, no. 1 (1989): 7–33.

40 For a taste of this discussion, see Joan Scott, *Gender and the Politics of History* (New York: Columbia University Press, 1988); Denise Riley, *"Am I That Name?" Feminism and the Category of "Women" in History* (Minneapolis: University of Minnesota Press); Judith Newman, "History as Usual? Feminism and the 'New Historicism'," in *The New Historicism*, ed. Harold Veeser (London: Routledge, 1989); and *Radical History Review* 43 (1989). See the replies to Scott in *International Labor and Working-Class History* 31 (1987), and critical reviews of her book in *Women's Review of Books* 6 (Jan. 1989), and *Signs* 15, no. 4 (1989). For a critique by a working-class historian, see Bryan Palmer, *Descent into Discourse* (Philadelphia: Temple University Press, 1990), or, for a Marxist critique, Ellen Wood, *The Retreat from Class* (London: Verso, 1986).

41 Indeed, some of these insights have been inspired by feminist writing. See Jane Flax, "Postmodernism and Gender Relations in Feminist Theory," *Signs* 12, no. 4 (1987): 621–43; Linda Alcoff, "Cultural Feminism Versus Post-Structuralism" *Signs* 13, no. 3 (1988): 405–36. Linda Gordon also points to ways in which some new insights of poststructuralism are not really that new in her review of Joan Scott's "Gender and the Politics of History," *Signs* 15, no. 4 (1990): 853–58. Her conclusion applies to the field of oral history.

42 Daryl McGowan Tress, "Comment on Flax's Postmodernism and Gender Relations in Feminist Theory" *Signs* 14, no. 1 (1988): 197. For other semi-critical assessments, see Mariana Valverde, "Poststructuralist Gender Historians: Are We Those Names?" *Labour/Le Travail* 25 (1990): 227–36; Michael Walzer, "The Politics of Foucault," in *Foucault: A Critical Reader*, ed. David Hoy (Oxford: Basil Blackwell, 1986); Myra Jehlen, "Patrolling the Borders," *Radical History Review* 43 (1989): 23–43; and for a more severe critique, N. Hartstock, "Foucault on Power: A Theory for Women?" in *Feminism and Postmodernism*, ed. Linda Nicholson (New York: Routledge, 1990).

43 Stephen Tyler, "Post-Modern Ethnography: From Document of the Occult to Occult Document," in *Writing Culture*, ed. Clifford and Marcus.

44 Mascia-Lees, Sharpe, and Cohen, "The Postmodernist Turn in Anthropology." These authors are understandably sceptical of some postmodern theories implying that "verbal constructs (voices) do not relate to reality, that truth and knowledge are contingent, that no one subject position is possible" (15) developed by Western, white academic men at precisely the moment these men are being challenged by women's and third world voices.

45 Pierson, "Experience," 91–94.

46 Michele Barrett, "The Concept of Difference," *Feminist Review* 20 (1987): 29–46.

47 Liz Stanley, "Recovering Women in History from Feminist Deconstruction," *Women's Studies International Forum* 13, nos. 1/2 (1990): 151–57.

48 Tilly, "Gender, Women's History, Social History and Deconstruction." See the responses in *International Journal of Oral History* 6, no. 1 (1985). This was also well characterized as a debate between hermeneutic and ethnographic methods in oral history by Daniel Bertaux and Martin Kohli, "The Life Story Approach: A Continental View," *Annual Review of Sociology* 10 (1984): 215–37. Again, analysis of linguistic structure and narrative form and explorations of how the writer 'creates' the historical document, for example, are all long-standing in the debates on oral history.

49 See Julie Cruikshank's examination of myth, narrative form, and social and economic structures in "Myth and Tradition as Narrative Framework."

50 Gluck and Patai, "Introduction," in *Women's Words*, 3.

51 P. Steven Sangren, "Rhetoric and Authority of Ethnography: Post-modernism and the Social Reproduction of Texts," *Current Anthropology* 29, no. 3 (1988): 405–24.

52 Geiger, "What's So Feminist About Women's Oral History?"

53 All quotes from Interview with Rosa, 2 Aug. 1989.

54 Ibid.

55 Interview with June, 31 July 1989.

56 Interview with Amelia, 29 Aug. 1989.

57 Interview with Edith, 26 June 1989.

58 Harding, *The Science Question in Feminism*, 194.

59 Interview with D.M., 25 Aug. 1989.

60 Veronica Strong-Boag, *The New Day Recalled: Lives of Girls and Women in English Canada, 1919–39* (Toronto: Copp Clark Pitman, 1988).

61 Interview with H.L., 29 Aug. 1989.

62 For example, see the discussion of the 1974 Fleck strike in Heather Jon Maroney, "Feminism at Work," *New Left Review* 141 (1983): 51–71.

63 Riley, *Am I That Name?*

64 Tilly, "Gender, Women's History, Social History and Deconstruction," 463.

65 Joan Scott, "Review of Heroes of Their Own Lives," *Signs* 15, no. 4 (1990): 850.

FOUCAULT, FEMINISM, AND POSTCOLONIALISM

The impact of the 'posts' — poststructuralism, postmodernism, and post-colonialism — on the writing of Anglo-American women's and gender history was considerable, though this varied according to the thematic area covered, existing national and local historiographies, and the temporal, social, and political context in which the historian was writing. Poststructuralism's emphasis on decentring grand theory, on questioning all metanarratives and attending to the power of discourse, and on challenging western narratives of the self and of human progress likely had more influence on areas such as cultural history than on labour history, the latter perhaps clinging to unstated materialist suppositions. Writing emanating from the United States appeared more deeply influenced by poststructuralism than that from Britain and Canada, though the sheer volume and variety of gender history coming out of the US makes me wary of any firm conclusions in this regard.[1] While some American-based feminists have balked at the claim by one social historian that Marxist social history maintained stronger roots in Britain,[2] there may be some element of truth to this — that is, while Marxist- and socialist-feminists existed and continue to exist in the United States, they may have become even more marginalized (especially so Marxist-feminists) than in other countries. Some American scholars have argued that US-based feminism became (to its detriment) equated with poststructuralism, or that some poststructuralist writing 'made sense' to academics precisely because it was a loose 'fit' with the juggernaut of liberal, and even neoliberal ideology that had gained popular hegemony by the late 1980s.[3] This was not so much a conscious political choice to abandon the Left for liberal ideas (indeed many academics believed they were still progressives committed to social change) as much as an ideological convergence that occurred in the wake of the decline of the Left, dismissals of Marxism, and the insidious ideological diffusion of liberal assumptions into all crooks and crannies of cultural life. Certainly, national and social contexts matter in the reception of new theoretical paradigms. There is some evidence, for instance, that writing on gender and labour in developing areas such as Latin America or Africa embraced poststructuralism less completely and enthusiastically, simply because these historians, influenced by the anti-imperialist struggles around them, continued to explore women's lives using methods drawn from social history, political economy, and historical materialism. Postcolonialism, to be sure, had an impact on these historiographies, but it was also ambiguous, complex, and critical.[4]

Where did Canadian women's history fit in? Perhaps we stood somewhere in between Britain and the United States, continuing to use theoretical approaches associated with the new (now 'old') social history, yet also sometimes challenging those with, and through 'post' theories. The specific variety of 'post' writing, and what area of history it addressed, also mattered a great deal. Arguably, the most influential thinker for Canadian feminist historians was Michel Foucault, whose explorations of regulation, discipline, and the discursive construction of sexuality greatly influenced feminist writing on criminalization, the law, sexuality, and the body. Postcolonial theory also made a strong impression, dovetailing with a significant expansion of research on First Nations women, 'internal' colonialism, and imperial history. The productive and sometimes provocative impact of both Foucault and postcolonial studies was clear by the 1990s, in writing by Mariana Valverde, Stephen Maynard, Mary Louise Adams, Mona Gleason, Sarah Carter, and Adele Perry, to name a few authors.[5]

Both Foucauldian and colonial studies are represented in this section, suggesting either (positively) that I was moving with the times or (negatively) that I was caught in the fashion of the times. The writing on criminalization and delinquency, however, was also the unintended outcome of my "Pardon Tales" research: explorations of crime and punishment led me to records dealing with juveniles and inevitably to writing on moral and sexual regulation. The contrast between women's courtroom pardon tales — sometimes inventive and brazen — and the case files of girls in court or incarcerated could not have been greater. Reading the latter, in particular, could not but evoke an emotional response (not the least because I had teenage daughters at the time). While girls entangled in the juvenile justice system cannot be seen simply as victims (and I tried not to portray them so),[6] the circumstances of abuse, violence, poverty, neglect, and racism that jumped off page after page of these records were difficult, disheartening, and angering to read. I can recall driving home to Peterborough from the archives in Toronto, with girls' unhappy, scared, and sometimes defiant voices playing repeatedly in my head. I say this knowing full well that these sources, and particularly case files, are hardly unmediated sources, offering us the 'true,' inside story: quite the contrary. The records, as I admit in "Girls in Conflict with the Law," were shaped profoundly by expert discourses and by their interpretations of the girls' behaviour, and these documents may tell us more about those expert discourses than about the girls' actual experiences. I think one can 'fall into' these records too easily, accepting the experts' priorities, and in a subsequent article I tried to correct my earlier tendency to do so. Because the experts of the time were so concerned, if not obsessed, with describing sexual misbehaviour, I inevitably focused on this issue, perhaps downplaying another crucial aspect of the disciplinary solution they were promoting: honest work and the work ethic.[7]

Still, I would argue that girls' case files — especially in conjunction with other sources — offer snatches of girls' own interpretations and important traces of their social and material existence. That social existence was crucial to my argument that a feminist appropriation of Foucault was not enough: without understanding the relations of production and social reproduction that framed these girls' lives (including patriarchal familial relations), and without understanding the legacies of colonialism, we could not completely understand how many girls became designated as delinquents by the experts, by the state, and by their own families. Foucault helped me understand the 'how' of criminalization, but not entirely the 'why.' Feminist theoretical writing that recognized how Foucault's writing had enriched and pushed feminist discussion in new directions, yet still engaged with it critically, was essential to my thinking, along with older writing informed by historical materialism. Whether they were describing Foucault's slighting of agency, the contradictions inherent in his notion of resistance, his tendency to downplay the coercive power of the state, or his failure to analyze some forms of patriarchal power, these feminist and critical legal theorists provided me with indispensible insights on criminalization and moral regulation.[8]

Postcolonial writing probably had a stronger impact in Canadian literary studies than in history, where one was less likely to find the 'foundational' writing by Homi Bhabha, Gayatri Spivak, and Edward Said used and quoted. It was not these celebrated texts as much as critical legal studies that shaped my thinking on Aboriginal women and the law, as well as the work of anthropologists like John and Jean Comaroff and Ann Stoler (herself influenced by Foucault), which elucidated the connections between sexual regulation, the imposition of 'white' domesticity, and colonial conquest, even though they were discussing quite different colonial situations.[9] In trying to understand the overincarceration of Canadian Aboriginal women in particular, I was influenced by the writing of First Nations scholars like Teressaa Nahanee and by anthropologists like Jo-Anne Fiske, who had developed a complex interpretation of customary law that incorporated both a critique of colonialism and a feminist analysis.[10]

Also, one could not talk about the criminalization of women without talking about race, not least because it stared us in the face in contemporary revelations about the overincarceration and mistreatment of women of colour and Aboriginal women in Canadian penal institutions. This was brought home when I read Yvonne Johnson's powerful and moving life history, A Stolen Life, as well as in the official, and disturbing, reports about Kingston's P4W,[11] and my involvement with Elizabeth Fry offered constant reminders of the practical, daily struggles of criminalized women, whose lives were not only 'governed from a distance.' As my colleague Gillian Balfour warned, the scholarly drift towards Foucaudian governmentality as *the* explanatory paradigm of choice risked severing feminist criminology from an activist, political scholarship and praxis that exposed both the social causes of criminalization and the "brute" force of the neoliberal state on women's lives.[12]

My own experience at Trent also pushed my writing in the direction of Aboriginal history: Indigenous Studies was not only an influential presence within the university, but also an integral part of our graduate program, so I was continually challenged by my own students and colleagues to integrate Aboriginal women more effectively into my writing. Post-colonial scholarship was so much 'in the air' in these endeavours that it undoubtedly had an impact on my thinking, stimulating new questions about the changing cultural meanings of colonialism. Those questions then came to the fore when I began to explore white women's travel books and images of Aboriginal peoples in popular culture. Ironically, it was many trips to second-hand bookstores in the United States with my book-collecting partner that led to my discovery of so many travel books on the Canadian North. Postcolonial scholarship on literature, travel writing, and visual culture then helped me 'see' literary devices and discursive strategies I might not have noticed otherwise when I began to analyze them for my article on the construction of the 'Eskimo' wife. Even still, in all these articles,[13] I often circled back to 'postcolonial' scholars like Arif Dirlik, who offered what I thought was an incisive critique of postcolonial writing that concentrated on the cultural, while ignoring the social and material context of global capitalism.[14] Neither Aboriginal women's criminalization nor the discursive expressions of colonial 'mentalities' could be understood apart from the context that framed them, including the incessant drive for capitalist accumulation as well as the social relations that accompanied colonial conquest.

Notes

1   Some critical theorists did argue that the American academy was especially receptive to postmodernism. "Much postmodernism has sprung from the United States, or at least has taken rapid root there, and reflects some of that country's most intractable political problems": Terry Eagleton, *The Illusions of Postmodernism* (Cambridge: Blackwell, 1996), 122.

2   Ava Baron and Eileen Boris, "In Response: Dichotomous Thinking and the Objects of History; or, Why Bodies Matter, Again," *Labor: Studies in Working Class History of the Americas* 4, no. 2 (Summer 2007): 62.

3   Barbara Epstein,"Why Poststructuralism Is a Dead End for Women," *Socialist Review* 5 (1995): 83–119; Rosemary Hennessy, *Profit and Pleasure: Sexual Identities in Late Capitalism* (New York: Routledge, 2000), 83. A related, though not identical, argument was put forward by Nancy Fraser, who argued that American feminism was abandoning a politics of redistribution for one of recognition of 'identity.' See Nancy Fraser, "Mapping the Feminist Imagination: From Redistribution to Recognition," *Constellations* 12 (2005): 295–307.

4 For a discussion of the posts in African history, see Paul Zeleza, "The Troubled Encounter Between Postcolonialism and African History," *Journal of the Canadian Historical Association* 17, no. 2 (2006): 89–129. A recent celebration of Joan Scott, "AHR Forum: Revisiting 'Gender: A Useful Category of Historical Analysis,'" *American Historical Review* 113 (Dec. 2008): 1344–45, includes a piece by a Latin American historian (Heidi Tinsman, "A Paradigm of Our Own: Joan Scott in Latin American History") that points to Scott's influence on that continent, but I suspect there are differences between those historians trained in the United States and those not, between those writing for an Anglo-American market and those not, and between different countries. As Barbara Weinstein argues, gender did not have the same importance and meaning in Latin America as in Anglo-American writing: "Where Do New Ideas About Class Come From?" *International Labor and Working-Class History* 57 (Spring 2000): 55.

5 Mariana Valverde, *The Age of Light, Soap and Water: Moral Reform in English Canada, 1885–1921* (Toronto: Oxford University Press, 1991); Mary Louise Adams, *The Trouble with Normal: Postwar Youth and the Making of Heterosexuality* (Toronto: University of Toronto Press, 1997); Steven Maynard, "Horrible Temptations: Sex, Men and Working-Class Youth in Urban Ontario 1890–1935," *Canadian Historical Review* 78, no. 2 (1997): 191–235; Mona Gleason, *Normalizing the Ideal: Psychology, Schooling and the Family in Postwar Canada* (Toronto: University of Toronto Press, 1999); Sarah Carter, *Capturing Women: The Manipulation of Cultural Imagery in the Canadian West* (Montreal: McGill-Queen's University Press); Adele Perry, *On the Edge of Empire: Gender, Race and the Making of British Columbia, 1849–1871* (Toronto: University of Toronto Press, 2001).

6 My thinking was influenced by my collaboration with Tamara Myers: "Retorts, Runaways and Riots: Patterns of Resistance in Canadian Reform Schools for Girls, 1930–60" *Journal of Social History* 34, no. 3 (Spring 2001): 669–97.

7 Joan Sangster, "Domesticating Girls: The Sexual Regulation of Aboriginal and Working-Class Girls in Twentieth-Century Canada," in *Contact Zones: Aboriginal and Settler Women in Canada's Colonial Past*, ed. Katie Pickles and Myra Rutherdale (Vancouver: University of British Columbia Press, 2005), 179–204.

8 These were probably more apparent in *Regulating Girls and Women: Sexuality, Family and the Law in Ontario, 1920–1960* (Toronto: Oxford University Press, 2001), 4–16. See Kate Soper, *Troubled Pleasures: Writing on Politics, Gender and Hedonism* (New York: Verso, 1990); Linda Alcoff, "Dangerous Pleasures: Foucault and the Politics of Pedophilia," in *Feminist Interpretations of Michel Foucault*, ed. Susan Hekman (University Park, PA: Pennsylvania State University Press, 1996): 99–135, and "Feminist Politics and Foucault: The Limits to Collaboration," in *Crises in Continental Philosophy*, ed. Arleen Dallery et al. (Albany: SUNY University Press, 1990), 69–86; Nancy Hartsock, "Foucault on Power: A Theory for Women?" in *Feminism/Postmodernism*, ed. Linda Nicholson (New York: Routledge, 1990), 157–75; Alan Hunt, *Explorations in Law and Society: Toward a Constitutive Theory of Law* (New York: Routledge, 1993).

9   Ann Stoler, "Making Empire Respectable: The Politics of Race and Sexual Morality in 20th Century Colonial Cultures," *American Ethnologist* 16, no. 4 (1989): 634–59; John and Jean Comaroff, *Ethnography and the Historical Imagination* (Boulder, CO: Westview Press, 1992). Of course, some critical legal studies were also influenced by postcolonialism.

10 Teressa Nahanee, "Dancing with a Gorilla: Aboriginal Women, Justice and the Charter," in Royal Commission on Aboriginal Peoples, *Aboriginal Peoples and the Justice System: Report of the National Roundtable on Aboriginal Justice* (Ottawa, 1993), 359–82; Jo-Anne Fiske, "From Customary Law to Oral Tradition," *B.C. Studies* 115/116 (1997–98): 267–88; and "The Supreme Law and the Grand Law," *B.C. Studies* 105/106 (1995): 183–99.

11 Rudy Wiebe and Yvonne Johnson, *Stolen Life: The Journey of a Cree Woman* (Toronto: Alfred Knopf, 1998); Canada, Commission of Inquiry into Certain Events at the Prison for Women in Kingston [the Arbour Commission] (Ottawa: Public Works, 1996).

12 Gillian Balfour, "Re-imagining a Feminist Criminology," *Canadian Journal of Criminology and Criminal Justice* 48, no. 5 (2006): 749.

13 Joan Sangster, "*The Beaver* as Ideology: Constructing Images of Inuit and Native Life in Post–World War II Canada," *Anthropologica* 49 (2007): 191–209.

14 Arif Dirlik, *The Postcolonial Aura: Third World Criticism in the Age of Global Capitalism* (Boulder, CO: Westview Press, 1997). See also Aijaz Ahmad, *In Theory: Classes, Nations, Literatures* (New York: Verso, 1992).

GIRLS IN CONFLICT WITH THE LAW
EXPLORING THE CONSTRUCTION OF FEMALE 'DELINQUENCY' IN ONTARIO, 1940–1960

On the eve of World War II, Gloria, a fifteen-year-old from Hamilton, was sentenced to the Ontario Training School for Girls (OTSG) after she was charged with the theft of some clothes. The Children's Aid Society (CAS) claimed in Family Court that the mother was not supporting her children and was sexually immoral. She had an illegitimate child and was involved with a married man, often "parking her children with a friend on relief" while she "is in a hotel," the social worker commented disapprovingly. Gloria also confessed to the CAS that she had allowed a forty-three- year-old man to have sexual relations with her in return for a coat and some money (though she later fearfully denied this in court) and admitted to other 'wild' behaviour: she had skipped school with her sister and was apprehended by police for "wheeling away" babies from local parks.[1]

Training school was supposed to provide Gloria with an education in useful work and proper sexual behaviour, protecting her from physical neglect and the moral contamination of her mother. Psychiatric and social work experts in the 1950s would likely have agreed with the isolation of Gloria, given their emphasis on deficient families as a major cause of delinquency. Yet in the 1970s, a historian reinterpreting her case might point to the poverty of the family, and their vulnerability to harsh policing due to the structural dynamics of class. Feminists would also critique the court's fixation with sexual misconduct, linking the control exercised over Gloria and her mother to patriarchal legal structures. By the 1990s, scholars might stress the power of experts — social workers and psychiatrists — to define Gloria's delinquency; disciplinary techniques, not class relations and patriarchal control, would become the codes used to interpret Gloria's conflict with the law.

Gloria's case highlights the ongoing theoretical, methodological, and interpretive dilemmas we encounter when exploring the history of 'female delinquency.'[2] Drawing on and comparing a range of historical sources, including reform organization and government records, popular and professional writing, court documents, and case files of convicted female juveniles sent to training school,[3] this paper will examine the criminalization of girls in the 'affluent' Ontario of the 1940s and 1950s, concurrently questioning the dominant theoretical paradigms we are utilizing to uncover the history of criminality. Asking how female delinquency was defined by the courts, and how girls and their families responded to this criminalization, inevitably invokes current debates between materialist, feminist, and poststructuralist streams of thought, and in particular, the prevailing influence of Foucauldian explications of crime and punishment.[4]

Over the past decade, studies of crime and social marginality have assumed increasing importance in Canadian history, displacing, or at least radically reinterpreting, the contours of working-class history.[5] Given contemporary politics, the shift of our scholarly scrutiny from earning to stealing is understandable, as governments at all levels have intensified economic and social marginality for many Canadians, and simultaneously promoted a 'law-and-order' approach to crime and delinquency, encouraged by neoconservative thinking that consciously divorces crime from the economic, social, and emotional traumas intertwined with capitalist social relations. This current construction of delinquency harkens back to the 1950s, when governments attributed youth problems to negligent parenting and immoral families.[6] Rhetorically, however, the solutions at that time at least stressed "child saving" rather than the more punitive, current emphasis on "child blaming."[7]

At the same time, the displacement of a "politics of redistribution,"[8] and the sidelining of political economy in academic discourse have encouraged interpretations of crime downplaying class conflict and accenting discourses and disciplinary techniques. In history, law, and criminology, these new theoretical trends followed in the wake of trenchant critiques of Marxist and social control paradigms, often constructed by materialists themselves.[9] Feminist analyses, which initially challenged the oppression of women within the criminal justice system and especially the 'sexualization' of women in that system,[10] have also edged towards the discursive, and questioned the value of 'grand' explanatory theories stressing class or patriarchal structures of oppression. Carol Smart's writing, a bellwether of such theorizing, has argued for a "decentring of the law," shying away from "general theories" and exploring instead the specificities of "how the law operates in different fields."[11]

Although some theories of patriarchy have lurched erroneously towards the ahistorical or general, and like materialist theories have grappled with difficulty with the complexities of class, gender, and race oppression, a renunciation of these theoretical traditions means the perilous abandonment of a critique of the *systems* of social and gender inequality that are so clearly entrenched in the criminal justice system. As Dawn Currie argues, "to de-centre the law in our analysis is one matter; to de-centre it in real life is another" given that the "law and its application are about the centralization of power."[12] The need to develop a materialist and feminist "emancipatory critical knowledge"[13] is essential if we are to prevent our gaze from slipping into infinite deconstructions of criminality and direct our thoughts instead to the transformation of those oppressive social relations that sustain crime, delinquency, and marginality.

This article, then, attempts to use the critical insights of materialist and feminist-Foucauldian perspectives to develop a more comprehensive analysis of young women in conflict with the law. Foucauldian thought illuminates the discursive creation of the category of delinquency by the experts, and exposes, with penetrating clarity, methods of legal and penal discipline; materialist-feminism necessarily grounds representation and discipline in social life and capitalist social relations. The first two sections of the paper, on the experts' construction of female delinquency and disciplinary practices, indicate how Foucauldian concepts have effectively challenged and enriched feminist and Marxist appraisals of criminality. The following sections, exploring power relations in the court, the social context of criminalization, and the state emphasize the continuing importance of a materialist perspective that connects the discursive and nondiscursive forces creating delinquency; class, gender, and race must be located within a feminist and materialist framework that exposes the constituents of power shaping a legal system that was skewed to punish, rather than aid, working-class girls.

Defining Juvenile Delinquency: Power/Knowledge at Work

The 1940s and 1950s are often characterized as a relatively prosperous era, marked by democratized consumerism and political stability, though the stultifying ideological, political, and sexual conformity of the Cold War period is acknowledged. Despite the prosperity generated by the war, juvenile delinquency immediately became a major social concern. "Jitters over juveniles"[14] were voiced, especially early in World War II, as rising numbers of juveniles before the courts were designated a 'new' and alarming trend. While juvenile arrests did rise in the early war years, these were concentrated in certain cities[15] and were probably related to demographic changes and policing trends as much as increased crime rates.[16]

The media, however, claimed delinquency was increasing, and attributed this to absent fathers, the appeal of materialism and urban life, and especially working or negligent mothers. One *Chatelaine* author, for example, described a working mother who left her preschoolers all day "with only a few crusts to gnaw on"; another single mother supposedly abandoned her children to carouse with her "new beau" and only the vigilance of a (male) neighbour saved the children from a fire.[17] Other magazine articles described teens enticed into early factory work, lured into 'pick up' sex and street gangs, while their fathers served overseas.[18] Though less sensational, the official reports of psychiatrists working for Family Courts often concurred that lack of a decent home life, especially the "lack of responsibility on the part of parents,"[19] was leading to escalating delinquent behaviour. In addition, media reports announcing the increased use of probation and the loss of training school places (training schools were lent to the armed forces and smaller buildings found for the inmates) then fed the flames of public panic. Without the threat of training school, citizens wrote to the Ontario government, children would develop "disrespect for the law," and school boards implored the government to "restore training school places [as] juvenile delinquency is increasing."[20]

Anxiety about delinquency in the press persisted after World War II, though it altered its tone and targets,[21] and a few writers now even dared to question the "panic" about delinquency.[22] It was feared that youth crime originated in "economic inequalities and slum conditions," though bad parenting, "inadequate leisure, and psychological trauma" were also blamed.[23] Moreover, "adverse economic conditions" easily slid into condemning the individual, as in the *Saturday Night* article that described the juvenile delinquent Margaret, who turned to crime because her "parents could not meet her *extravagant* tastes."[24]

Anti-delinquency rhetoric also overlapped with post-World War II attempts to reinforce the 'traditional' family and contain sex within heterosexual marriages — a project connected to the concurrent ideological assault on communism.[25] Although the introduction of family allowances, increased prosperity, suburbanization, and the baby boom might have signalled faith in the nuclear family, considerable anxiety actually reigned about its fate. Fears concerning the inadequate family were voiced by the Ontario Training School Advisory Board (TSAB), which repeatedly recommended compensatory initiatives to provide healthy and respectable recreation for youth, and the teaching of parenting skills. Advocates of stricter treatment of juvenile delinquents also fixed their sights on inadequate and immoral families. In 1953, a conservatively inclined Ontario Legislature Committee on Delinquency began to question the reigning emphasis on psychological treatment and child saving. These politicians wanted fewer "luxuries" and the possibility of corporal punishment in training schools, and some recommended banning common-law unions, even sterilizing 'promiscuous' women.[26]

Public anxiety aside, the actual laws defining delinquency changed very little over the 1940s and 1950s. Most children aged seven to sixteen were brought before the courts under the federal Juvenile Delinquents Act (JDA), first enacted in 1908, though the (1939) provincial Training School Act (TSA) was also used. Both laws defined delinquency extremely broadly. Aside from actually breaking a law, children could be simply "sexually immoral," "liable to be sentenced in the future," "unmanageable and incorrigible," definitions that permitted delinquency to be a very flexible status offence.[27] The JDA encouraged the use of informal options, such as foster care or probation, with correctional institutions a last resort; once under the jurisdiction of the court, however, children could be scrutinized, held, or transferred to other institutions until they were adults. Moreover, under the TSA children could be originally incarcerated on the recommendation of the CAS or through the minister, thus completely bypassing the courts. Rhetorically, 'treatment not conviction' was to be the essence of juvenile justice, but this simultaneously entailed arbitrary, wide-ranging powers over those designated delinquent.

In this context, the power of medical and social work experts to define delinquency was extremely important. Though the influence of such experts extended back long before the 1940s, it was augmented in this period as Juvenile and Family Courts expanded their personnel and strength.[28] Not only did the court professionals, or 'psyche' experts,[29] construct the dominant definitions of delinquency, they also advised judges on how to sentence girls according to those definitions. Moreover, because of the emphasis on a girl's personality and sexual practices as signs of criminality, these experts were arguably more pivotal to the fate of delinquent girls than delinquent boys.

Foucault argued that power and knowledge were deeply implicated in each other: "power produces knowledge . . . there is no power relation without the correlative constitution of a field of knowledge, nor any knowledge that does not presuppose and constitute . . . power relations."[30] Expert knowledges produced by the psyche professions, for instance, defined normality and abnormality, setting out boundaries within which "populations and bodies" were encouraged to act.[31] The experts produced "classifications and typologies" of delinquency, "constituted individuals AS cases" to be investigated, and explored their actions as overt signs of covert 'feelings'[32] that could best be discovered by (their) social work investigation or psychoanalysis.

As Foucault argued in *Discipline and Punish*, it appeared that the law was being replaced by the norm;[33] the emphasis was not on legal infractions as much as the child's psychological deviance and the need to reconstruct her conscience. "The Juvenile Court," agreed Jacques Donzelot, "does not really pronounce judgement on crimes; it examines individuals."[34] The matrix of law and the medical/social sciences that characterized judgments on delinquency was made clear in court transcripts as judges eschewed discussion of the law, and referred instead to the child's familial and emotional relationships. Sentencing one girl in the 1950s, a Toronto Family Court Judge lectured her mother first, claiming incorrigibility often "emerged from relations between mother and daughter; it is this relationship that lies at the back of it."[35] His statement symbolized the central place psychiatry had captured within discourses on delinquency.

Until a critique of psychiatry emerged in the late 1960s, this alliance of psychiatrists and judges —"to prevent suffering. . . . [and] treat the ills of mankind"[36] as one psychiatrist rather pretentiously put it — rarely met with professional or public criticism.[37] Until then, law and psychiatry represented a powerful "double force of authority" in the juvenile court.[38]

Psychologists and social workers also provided expertise for the juvenile justice system, though the latter especially were influenced by psychiatry.[39] Psychology and psychiatry were sometimes used interchangeably, though in larger courts psychologists primarily assessed ability and intelligence, while the psychiatrists' role was to penetrate deep into the shadowy corners of the delinquent's disturbed mind. Still, IQ tests were significant; these fixed, often impermanently, the authorities' plans for the child's education, vocational training, future work, and transfers to institutions for the 'mentally retarded.'[40]

Common to the all the court professionals was a strong faith in 'scientific' investigation, and this confidence was shared by emerging reform groups like Elizabeth Fry, which valued positivist criminology and trained professionals at the helm of correctional institutions. Using medical language, many criminologists in this period argued that one could detect a state of "pre-delinquency"; delinquency itself was described as a progressively disruptive illness, moving from first symptoms, "the broken home" to later, terminal illness, "serious illegalities."[41] Similarly, Sheldon and Eleanor Glueck's American study, *Five Hundred Delinquent Women*, which was cited by Canadian professionals, statistically plotted women's "promiscuity," based on categories of sexual relations, frequency, partners, and so on. Though cloaked in scientific garb, their negative view of extramarital sex was nonetheless moralistic in tone.[42]

The statistical categories established by the TSAB in their reports mirrored similar moral judgments; the causes of delinquency were listed as "immoral parents, no control in the home, parents separated" and so on.[43] The TSAB then solicited public sympathy for their work by portraying "negligent parenting" as a disease that might be 'cured': "it is true that some wards appear to be psychopaths in the bud, but by modern treatment antisocial behaviour can be discovered, as we diagnose illnesses. Most wards deserve pity . . . due to the[ir] irresponsible, cruel parents and the . . . neglect and oppression they receive instead of care and control."[44]

Interpretations of delinquency in sociological and psychiatric literature did change over this period, but one constant was the relative paucity of attention paid to girls.[45] A few influential studies, including the Gluecks,' focused especially on 'broken homes' as the common denominator for female delinquents,[46] while others suggested that girls became delinquent because they had improperly absorbed appropriate roles relating to sexuality, domesticity, and motherhood. Delinquent girls, like women, were more likely to be analyzed as psychiatric problems:[47] as a study of OTSG girls by a government consultant concluded in the 1960s: "girls are more masochistic . . . more [emotionally] disturbed than male offenders."[48] Psychiatric reports of girls in the Training School conveyed similar ideas about the cause of delinquency: "girl is seeking affection in lieu of father's support. . . . [needs to be] stabilized to accept her father's rejection"[49] are typical.

The rising star of Freud — apparent since the thirties — had much to do with the discursive construction of female delinquency.[50] Social stresses, though important, had to "find a preparedness"[51] in one's psyche to produce delinquent behaviour. Good psychological health meant progression towards heterosexual and familial maturity (i.e., sex within marriage, motherhood, passive femininity), which coincidentally approximated middle-class sexual and familial norms. Delinquency could be precipitated by lack of love (or inordinate cravings for love), a warped Electra complex, or by failure to liberate oneself from a pre-Oedipal mother. Criminologists claimed that girls' "basic feminine needs to serve . . . be loved . . . and fear of rejection" could lead to delinquency, while the increase in runaways in the fifties was due to "maternal dominance" in the home.[52]

Underlying all these discussions of female delinquency lay a final assumption: "the predominant expression of [female] delinquency in our society is promiscuous sexual activity."[53] Postwar discourses on sex and teens, argues Mary Louise Adams, literally equated delinquency with errant sexuality.[54] Although Kerry Carrington claims that explaining the creation of female delinquency with the concept of 'sexualization' "essentializes" girls, thus ignoring the "multiplicity of discourses"[55] shaping delinquency, I would argue that nonconformist sexuality was still a central component of the criminalization of working-class girls. The powerful knowledge created by medical and social work professionals

designated nonmarital sex as the most significant marker of girls' devia-
tion. Although 'deviant' sex was sometimes included in the list of problems associated with boys before the court, it never occupied the central
focus that it did with girls. Girls' misdemeanours were by extension more
serious, pathological, and deep-seated: "Even the unenlightened know,"
wrote the OTSG superintendent in the fifties, "that girls are committed
to training school for 'boy trouble' whereas boys are usually committed
for theft, a more acceptable offence [in the public mind.]"[56]

Disciplinary Practices/Docile Bodies

As these definitions of delinquency, embodying languages of the medical
and social sciences, were institutionalized in the practices of the juvenile
justice system, the knowledge/power axis 'went to work on' the bodies
of young women, making promiscuity, venereal disease, and pregnancy
into mental and social pathologies of a criminal nature.

By asking how bodies and souls are constituted by strategic knowl-
edge/power relations, and how bodies become invested with those power
relations, Foucault posed a question already long on the agenda for feminists.[57] Portraying sexuality as a social and historical construction, a
"dispersed system of morals, techniques of power, discourses and procedures designed to mould sexual practices to certain strategic ends,"
he inspired new feminist critiques of the female body as a "strategic site
of power."[58] Since sexual practices are of central political importance to
modern societies, Foucault also argued, we must understand the way
in which 'life processes' relating to the individual body and the larger
population are 'managed' by experts and institutions.

The need to oversee and manage girls' errant sexuality was vividly out-
lined in sentencing and incarceration practices. In the 1940s and 1950s, for
instance, girls were far more likely to be charged with status offenses of
incorrigibility and vagrancy in the Toronto Family Court, while boys faced
theft charges.[59] Though boys outnumbered girls in court, the latter were
more likely to be placed under court supervision, and were more likely
to face institutionalization. Girls sent to OTSG from across the province
were more likely than boys to face incarceration after no, or only one,
court appearance. Girls, it was presumed, needed immediate isolation and

treatment.[60] As one social worker told a reporter in the 1950s: The "promiscuous girl is more ostracized than the boy who commits homicide." They therefore had to be "protected from themselves."[61]

The case files of Galt inmates strengthen this conclusion: sexual activity — perceived, possible or real — was often the lightning rod precipitating incarceration. Even if sexual behaviour was not the cause of arrest, it easily became the issue of concern. Judges quickly steered their questions towards sexual practices. One fifteen-year-old faced two theft charges, but in court the discussion centred on her 'bad' sexual reputation in high school and an incident when she "stayed out all night with an older boy." Her probation rules dictated no nights out, no trips in cars with boys, and morning church going; these centred on sexual danger, not the temptations of theft.[62] Since juvenile courts permitted evidence based on suspicion and rumours collected by probation officers, even suspected intercourse constituted cause for concern. Making girls submit to gynaecological exams was a standard means of resolving the gravity of the situation. If the doctor proclaimed "she was not virginal,"[63] this encouraged further surveillance or treatment. Concerns with sex usually came in a package of accusations — incorrigibility, running away, and sexual immorality — with the first two code words for sexual immorality. Girls who ran away were courting disaster, for they might be pressured into sex by men who, as one judge warned a girl, "will use you then kick you out when they are through. . . . If you remain on the street, you are headed for a life of misery . . . kicked from pillar to post, with no home, no friends, the worst life in the world."[64] Nor were such concerns illusory, for many runaways had little sexual knowledge, and most had no money and only their sexuality with which to barter food, lodging, and transportation.

Although the various experts defining delinquency did not agree on every case, there were common themes in their prognoses. Promiscuity was usually seen as sex with many or little-known partners, with older men, or occasionally, men of 'unacceptable' racial backgrounds.[65] Second, the attitude of the girl towards sex and authority was crucial. If a girl rejected her parents' right to set curfews and bar unacceptable boyfriends, or the court's power to oversee her sexual life, she was a clear probation risk. Third, girls who were too 'forward,' or talked incessantly about or invited male attention, were deemed "boy crazy," a label that positively invited isolation in OTSG. During World War II, this had a new twist: "She is soldier crazy," complained the police to a judge during World War II, "she waves at them all, is hitchhiking to other places, going out in cars with soldiers."[66] Girls were sometimes sent to OTSG simply to be inoculated against immorality. When a thirteen-year-old Native girl was charged with incorrigibility by her grandmother, she denied sexual contact with boys she had spent the night with, but the court, undoubtedly influenced by racist stereotypes, simply presumed her current or future promiscuity and sent her to OTSG.[67]

A key means of judging girls was the measurement of sexual guilt through the confessional, that is "ritualized interviews, interrogations, consultations, autobiographical narratives" that were deeply inscribed with power relations. The girl confided to her social worker or psychiatrist, the authority who then "intervenes in order to judge, punish, forgive or console."[68] The desired end was the reconstruction of her sexual conscience within the bounds of 'normality.' Girls who recounted sexual experiences with little regret, interest, or emotion, or who boasted about countless sexual exploits, were portrayed as mentally unbalanced, needing treatment. Racially inappropriate partners also signified that the girl had not internalized appropriate sexual norms; primarily, this meant white girls having sex with Afro-Canadian boys or men.[69] A fifteen-year-old white girl who twice spent the night with a "coloured boy in a car" was warned by the CAS that "these coloured boys are like tom cats that chase alley cats." The judge agreed that she did not understand the "seriousness of the situation" and should be sent away to OTSG.[70] Parents too brought daughters to court for transgressing racial lines; one mother initiated a complaint, worried that her white daughter was "socializing with coloured in dance halls. . . . [and that] she will have a black baby."[71]

Normalizing judgments applied to families as much as to the girls. If the girl came from an 'immoral' family, she was more likely to face incarceration, no matter what the charge against her. Children, it was assumed, might "follow in the footsteps" of their relatives.[72] Pre-sentencing social work reports on the family investigated the presence of other illegitimate children and evidence of parental adultery or promiscuity; neglect, poverty, alcoholism, desertion, and prison terms were also taken into account. Parents (but especially mothers) who lived common law could potentially poison the child's moral environment; sexual immorality on the mother's part was especially troubling, as the girl then lacked a "feminine role model."[73] Recommending OTSG for a girl charged with theft and truancy, the Hamilton CAS offered this rationale: "The mother is "agency prone. . . . and [immoral] for "she had an illegitimate child after the father's death. . . . giving birth the same time as her son had a baby [a fact considered somehow in bad taste]."[74]

Definitions of delinquency might connect with girls' experiences of sexual abuse, though the experts at that time interpreted the reasons far differently than we do today. At least 12 percent of the girls in my OTSG study reported sexual abuse by relatives, especially fathers; many more recounted seeing and experiencing domestic violence in their homes.[75] By the 1950s incest was cited by some who worked with girls at OTSG as a cause of their problems.[76] Yet paradoxically, it was still portrayed by many court professionals as either the rare product of backward, ignorant, and poor families, or occasionally as the girl's "fabrication"[77] or unconscious desire. The runaway girl, one criminologist surmised in the fifties, may be simply trying to "ward off the unconscious threat of an incestuous relationship with her father";[78] his comment revealed how the influence of Freudian ideas offered professionals the "opportunity to explain away incest."[79] Many psychiatrists examining girls in OTSG also betrayed persisting suspicions that the girl bore some complicity in the abuse.[80]

One or two girls were incarcerated after incest was proven against male relatives simply because the judge presumed OTSG would teach new them sexual standards to overcome their moral 'contamination.' In most cases, criminalization worked in two other ways. First, girls ran away from homes where they experienced sexual abuse, and were subsequently brought before the courts, sometimes by the very father who had abused them. Overlapping with running was many girls' rejection of the dominant standards of femininity and sexual purity. Girls' resistance to incest often became integrated with a "more general youthful rebellion,"[81] including illicit sexual activity with other boys and men. Ironically, in rejecting their proper roles as obedient and passive daughters (which had kept many in abusive situations), they embraced aggressive, sexually active roles that then led to their classification as delinquents.

In one case, for example, one small-town judge lectured a thirteen-year-old girl, Carine, about "keeping late hours with older boys, not obeying her mother." The police matron's report concentrated on an incident when Carine went off with an eighteen- and a twenty-year-old man from a local beach, and on her one runaway attempt. "Has there been any admission of intercourse?" with boys, the judge demanded of the mother. "I supposed she does not appreciate the trouble she will get into with boys twice her age," he concluded as he sentenced her to OTSG. Yet the father's recent conviction for sexual assault of Carine stared the judge in the face; the idea that her 'rebellion' might be connected did not occur to him.[82]

Normalization within the juvenile justice system took many forms, from the intermittent surveillance of probation, under the auspices of the Family Court or Big Sisters, to the more extreme surveillance, observation, and examination offered for the intractable: the Training School. For sex delinquents, OTSG offered an education in 'clean thinking' designed to redirect sexual fantasies into dreams of marriage and motherhood. Girls were encouraged to "break their home ties,"[83] erase the past, and reinterpret their previous 'promiscuity' as dangerous, leading to pregnancy, disease, and prostitution. When trying to scare one group of troublesome girls in detention, the superintendent painted a picture of their unreformed future: "Your sexually delinquent behaviour is nothing to be proud of. Your associations with criminal men will only bring you misery and poor health — if you live to be 30, you'll be old, worn out hags."[84]

Young women were to become "their own prison wardens,"[85] internalizing discourses on proper femininity, sexuality, and the work ethic. To do this, rewards and incentives — privileges, holidays, early release, praise, and support — were parleyed with reprimands and censures. Physical coercion was not totally absent; limiting girls' freedom, placing them in (solitary) detention, even strapping them, were used as strategies of control. The rhetoric of 'treatment' was inevitably compromised by this disciplinary regime, with staff focusing on law and order and a behaviourist system of rewards and punishment to prevent rebellion and disorder. Indeed, it may be wrong to overemphasize the medicalization of delinquent girls by psychiatric discourses when some girls seldom saw a psychiatrist, and others would have welcomed the confessional instead of the carceral regime of solitary confinement that they endured.

Medical experts sometimes clashed with the penal staff, warning them that detention might only cause more resentment, and that girls needed emotional care as well as strict discipline.[86]

Once they were released from OTSG, usually into domestic or factory jobs, though occasionally to continue school, surveillance continued. Placement (like probation) officers met with the girl, interviewed her relatives, neighbours, and employers to determine if she was dating, sexually active, promiscuous, pregnant, and so on. Girls who found steady, 'respectable' boyfriends, who avoided dangerous locales such as beverage rooms or riding in cars at night, who dressed without sexual flamboyance, were given good reports. If a teen lapsed into sexual promiscuity, contacted VD, or became pregnant, she could be returned to OTSG. Not surprisingly, placement workers saw marriage, even at sixteen or seventeen, as welcome sexual containment (as long as the husband had their approval) and cause to terminate their surveillance of the girl.

While many penal workers believed that it was possible to create a new moral conscience, they saw a few girls as too pathologically promiscuous or too "vicious"[87] to change. Penal staff, as well as many judges, could not refrain from categorizing girls, even within OTSG, into polar images of 'good' and 'bad.' There are the "bewildered, confused unhappy girls who want our help"[88] and there are "those only interested in sex, smoking and jiving . . . who can't be helped by mental health professionals. . . . Not all delinquents come from broken homes . . . some are just born that way,"[89] commented an OTSG superintendent. For all the emphasis on the scientific treatment, notions of 'innate' pollution and corruption were still apparent in the juvenile justice system.

Dispersed Power/Subjugated Knowledges

Foucault's analysis of power has encouraged a conception of decentralized power and emphasis in academic discussion on *how* power operates. Not only is power "productive not repressive" in Foucauldian texts, but it is relational, not "localized here or there, never in anybody's hands."[90] It is dispersed rather than centralized, and it needs to be analyzed first at the 'microlevel.' Moreover, power is "coextensive with the social body"; there is no system of power, no "primal liberty" existing outside or between networks of power.[91] Directly challenging Marxist theories, the Foucauldian schema sees power moving "from bottom to top as well as top to bottom in socioeconomic hierarchies of society."[92] These concepts have encouraged us to extend our gaze beyond the monolithic state to the networks of interlinked power relations, the informal regulatory processes operating throughout society. In the juvenile justice system, for example, girls' delinquency was interpreted and acted on differently by the court professionals, judges, Training Schools staff, families, and girls themselves.

The power of social workers and psychiatrists emerged from their professional ability to treat the problem as they had already defined it. These experts sometimes clashed in contests for professional ascendency, but their interpretations were more likely to overlap; both focused on dysfunctional families, and they often advocated family reconstitution or counselling as a solution. Nor did they see the central irony of their approach. The family was seen the cause of delinquency, but also as potential salvation. Although inundated with positive familial ideology, most girls in conflict with the law could not approximate such ideals in their own lives — a contradiction that followed them through the courts, training school, foster homes, and their work placements.

Although judges relied heavily on advice from these court professionals, on occasion they also overruled their recommendations. Judges represented the supreme authority within the juvenile justice system; their pronouncements became defences and justifications for the truths underpinning the system itself. Their decisions might also set out new precedents that social workers had to grapple with.[93] Delivering their verdicts with paternalist and sometimes harsh authority, judges chastised, warned, lectured, and also cajoled girls and their parents. Addressing a girl who ran away from her foster home with a man to a hotel, one judge warned, "there is nothing wrong with sex, but there is proper place for it and you have not found the proper place. Don't cheapen yourself. . . . you will thank us [for sending you to training school]." Judges expressed anger with girls who were saucy, insufficiently apologetic, and whose actions had betrayed temperate, respectable parents, though parents too were subject to indignity when they failed to respond with deference and concern. "Do you want shame and humiliation on your doorstep?" demanded one judge angrily of parents who would not follow his advice.[94]

While the authority of the judge and psyche experts was considerable, families, and especially male heads of families, were not completely colonized, as Jacques Donzelot suggested, by an all-powerful "tutelary complex."[95] Parents were a major cause of complaints *against* their daughters; they used the courts to maintain lines of authority within the family and establish control over wayward daughters — more so than errant sons.[96] Fear of sexual corruption, concern that the daughter was not contributing to the family economy or getting an education, activated their complaints, which then might buttress the agenda of the court workers. Rather than stressing their own failure to approximate an ideal family, though, parents spoke of their fears for their daughters' safety and future, the disruptions she was causing to the family, and their own mental anguish. Some parents wanted other siblings protected and warned away from similar behaviour; others claimed they wished to prevent an illegitimate pregnancy by having their 'promiscuous' daughters dealt with by the court. Parents also used the courts to pry daughters away from unacceptable mates. When a fifteen-year-old from a "respectable" working-class family ran away repeatedly with an older boyfriend who was in trouble with the law, the parents saw OTSG as a way to separate her from this "obsession."[97]

Once enmeshed in the court apparatus, though, parents found they had little power. Court workers and judges could pressure, persuade, and ultimately impose their views. Often, parents who wrote to OTSG or the government trying to secure the release of their daughters maintained they never understood the original sentence to be indeterminate; they had expected to see their daughters in three months. The judge's discretionary power over parents was particularly obvious in smaller courts without extensive probation alternatives, or where other factors, such as racism, held sway. In the 1950s, more Native girls were being sent to OTSG by courts anxious to remove them from reserve environments, though the training school was reluctant to take them, feeling they were "unreachable" as their "cultural patterns were little understood."[98] Presiding over the hearing for a Native girl, the judge listened to an RCMP officer and the local Indian agent describe the drinking and sexual habits, and school and church attendance, of her and her family: their observations were privileged over those of the Native parents who came to court to "discuss the problem," but did not want incarceration.[99] Another Aboriginal father who worked as a school janitor on a reserve reacted angrily to the Indian agent's testimony, first pointing out he needed his daughter's help in his daily work as he had arthritis, then disputing her immorality: "there are so many rumours about her, that to be true, she would have to be a woman of 50."[100]

Like this father, some parents rejected the moral prerogative of the Juvenile Court: they hid daughters' pregnancies and sexual affairs from probation officers, and took open issue with the court's right to judge their own moral lives. But these parents were less likely to exert influence on the court's decisions. Indeed, power *did* operate hierarchically in the court: it was concentrated in certain networks, not in others. Court workers and judges clearly exercised more power than parents, parents more power than children. And certain interpretations of delinquency took precedence by virtue of the knowledge, interests, and authority they represented. Tying together the parental and professional desire to control delinquent daughters was an ideology that stressed the authority of parents over children, of men over women, and the importance of keeping sexuality confined within the bounds of heterosexual marriage. These meanings came to take precedence precisely because they reflected and supported existing systems of familial and gender power.

The majority of girls were cowed into silence or acquiescence in the courtroom, though a minority raged against families they hated, or declared their rejection of all authority. Undoubtedly, some knew how to craft their stories to please the authorities, like the girl who claimed that she just fell in with "bad company."[101] However, they also tendered interpretations of their delinquency that were strikingly different from those offered by the courts and the experts. Their responses might be considered "subjugated" knowledges, that is, "naive knowledges, located down on the hierarchy, beneath the required level of scientificity. . . . disqualified by the experts, but a still a form of local . . . knowledge existing in opposition to the knowledge of the experts."[102]

Running away (referred to as 'running'), for example, was portrayed by the authorities as "a childish response to problems,"[103] but girls explained their actions as an escape from unhappiness, or searching out something better. Since many girls came from homes where there was little material benefit to staying, running seemed a legitimate means of seeking their fortunes. Some used running as a means of cementing ties with boyfriends and exploring sexual activity; others saw it as a means to avoid punishment, or to escape abuse. One girl who ran away to Toronto from a small town, for instance, claimed her father sexually abused her, but was not believed after a gynaecological examination by a CAS doctor.

Tragically, children's stories of violence and cruelty were sometimes disbelieved, further accentuating their alienation. Emotional abuse was especially difficult to prove since parents' words generally commanded more authority in court, and accounts from 'troublesome' foster children were often held suspect. Social workers also had an image of a 'typical' violent parent — male, working-class, badly educated — that then shielded less 'obvious' offenders. Most girls, for instance, did encounter violence from a male relative, but mothers were not always blameless. One father finally admitted his runaway daughter's claims were true; the scar on her face was the result of repeated beatings by her mother.[104]

Running could combine escape from unhappiness and a desire for adventure. Both the police and a reluctant mother testified against a girl who ran away three times to different cities with friends, and was also spending her nights on the "main street with soldiers" stationed nearby. Her wanderings combined a quest for friends and romance with escape from a home she detested; while her mother worked, she had to care for her ill father, who constantly berated her.[105] In running, girls also became caught up in a basic search for survival, trapped by circumstances over which they commanded little power. An Oshawa teen ran away from a local gang she was involved in, was picked up by an older truck driver, and was kept by him as a sexual partner in Toronto. She claimed to dislike him, but also told the court that she did not try to leave. The judge was most horrified about her admission of "constant" sexual acts with this man. Yet her testimony indicated bewilderment and confusion, rather than pleasure and confidence in her escapade.[106]

Although children's rationalizations of their running were often disregarded, subsequent events sometimes proved their claims had validity. One fifteen-year-old who stole a car and ran away with her boyfriend was incarcerated (here, the judge rejecting the recommendations of a psychiatrist). Her claim that her mother hated her was little believed, until social workers conceded much later that her mother "often locked her out" and thoroughly disliked her. Despondent and suicidal in the institution, she finally was paroled to her boyfriend's family and married him at seventeen. Her claims that "he was the only one who cared about her" may not have been totally absurd.[107]

Girls also forwarded interpretations of other crimes, such as theft, truancy, and disobedience, thatdiffered from those of the authorities. And their resistance stretched from the courts to the training school, where verbal disagreement might be followed by physical, even violent, opposition to their circumstances — though such resistance often met with defeat.[108] In their testimonies, girls' subjugated knowledges are tucked away in offhand comments, asides, almost silenced by the more definitive power of those surveying them. Indeed, many of the historical documents used to reconstruct delinquency are problematic, implicitly reinforcing a Foucauldian view by the very nature of their aims and authorship. By looking at the discourses of experts, court judgments, and psychiatric, training school, and probation reports, we are skewing the process of historical recovery towards an emphasis *on* power/knowledge and the regulation of 'docile' bodies. OTSG reports monitoring girls' work, social, and sexual lives were the incarnation of disciplinary techniques. Psychiatric assessments examined a girl within a paradigm of sexual dysfunction, with the aim of reconstructing her conscience.[109]

Just as the incarceration of some girls should lead us to question how 'dispersed' power really was, girls' explanations of their delinquency should induce us to ask what was left out or stifled in the documents we are examining. What do we make of a teen, for instance, who complained to her social worker when she was placed out that she hated the "hard work" demanded of her and that she was not really part of the family?[110] Her first comment received *no* commentary, while the latter received extensive psychological analysis about her lack of a feminine role model. If we are to avoid reproducing the definitions of delinquency offered by the experts in the 1950s, we must therefore broaden our analysis, examining also the context of class relations that was so crucial to the criminalization of these working-class girls.

Historical Determination

To understand the construction of delinquency we need to survey the material and social circumstances of girls' lives, as well as expert discourses on sexual immorality, exploring their mutual imbrication. Explaining the complex relationship between the discursive and nondiscursive is a contentious issue, with some critics of Foucault arguing that his writings "do not and cannot explain the connection between discursive and non-discursive social practices."[111] While Foucault explored the "conditions of possibility" shaping discursive formations, this did not mean "viewing them in a material context" with the presumption of a causal, explanatory relationship between the two.[112] The concept of historical determination was anathema to Foucault; he worked outside this Marxist problematic, rejecting, in Michele Barrett's terms, the "dumb reality of the pre-discursive."[113]

A materialist framework, however, need not be the "reductionist" or "totalizing discourse"[114] that is portrayed by some Foucauldian followers. Drawing on insights about discourse, power, and subjectivity, while still allowing for a measure of determination, historical materialism makes intelligible how material life shapes the possibilities of discourse and social practice, how the materiality of discourse mediates social practices. However important the discourse of sexualization was, we must ask why it was applied, in training schools, *overwhelmingly*, to poor, working-class, and Native girls.[115] Indeed, one psychiatric expert acknowledged that middle-class girls were unlikely to come into conflict with the law even when they engaged in the very same practices as working-class girls.[116]

Anxieties about delinquency must be linked not only to the project of nuclear family containment, but also to the persistence of poverty amidst the dream of suburban plenty. Despite the increased economic stability of the working class, pockets of abject poverty on reserves, in rural and urban areas remained, sustaining fears of a persisting, unreformable 'underclass.'[117] After the war, in a time of ideological conformity and a desire for normalcy, such social 'blights' may have appeared all the more glaring. Training schools were justified in the fifties because of their ability to transform the underclass into a respectable working class. As the Galt superintendent argued: "I know there is a curve in the living standards of our released wards. They grew up in the sordid slums and they now live in respectable working class districts."[118]

Economic insecurity, if not blatant poverty, stares one so clearly in the face when examining incarcerated girls that it is hard to avoid the conclusion that class had a fundamental correlation to criminalization. Class was crucial to the apprehension of girls, their rejection of dominant social norms, and their treatment once in the juvenile justice system. Who was even brought to court, to begin with, was conditioned by policing methods that saw certain neighbourhoods and family forms (especially single parents) as 'high risk.' Families with few resources at hand also turned to the court for protection, mediation, and economic aid. Once under surveillance, the chances of a child's court apprehension increased. The close information networks between schools, welfare, social services, and the courts meant that damning intelligence was traded back and forth, and families known to any one agency were more likely to be referred to others.

By the 1950s socialized justice was steering many children into probation or a psychiatric clinic. In the Toronto Family Court, for instance, occurrences overseen by the probation department outnumbered formal court hearings by 3 to 1.[119] But the dominant psychiatric thinking of the time presumed therapy would primarily benefit "reflective" white, middle-class clients with "better cognitive skills and ego strengths."[120] A funnelling process took place, with middle-class children brought to court more likely to get probation, poor children incarceration. Middle-class and respectable working-class families could utilize various strategies, such as moving to a better neighbourhood, to protect their daughters from incarceration; they could convince probation officers that their church attendance, participation in wholesome leisure activities, work prospects, and well-furnished houses made their daughters good probation risks.

The economic instability of the poor also engendered familial and geographical transience that produced a profound insecurity in some girls. Parents unable to work and care for children left them with friends or relatives little able to care for them, occasioning feelings of rejection and resentment. Other parents who worked at low-paying jobs such as charring or farm help could not provide child care; and without supervision, these children often became involved in street life and problems with the law. Wilful neglect, moreover, did sometimes overlap with extreme poverty. One thirteen-year-old, deserted by her parents in the late 1940s, fled to her brother, but he did little to help her so she went to live on a beach near Hamilton with two transient, older men. When taken in, she had not been to school in years, was physically run-down, "absolutely filthy," and had venereal disease.[121] The real question, of course, was whether this should have occasioned her incarceration.

Confined to lower-paying jobs, cut off from Mothers' Allowance for any moral infractions, single mothers were especially vulnerable to surveillance that was then extended to their daughters. Joan, who stole some cash from a settlement house, was sent to OTSG though she begged the judge for her freedom. The mother was deemed "incapable of handling her," but her main shortcoming seemed to be her single parenthood: "she had married a man who deserted and was a bigamist . . . she has tried to support the family . . . and seems close to nervous breakdown."[122] Some courts also tended to view the background of Aboriginal girls from reserves as more likely to lead to immorality, and material deprivation was blamed more on their "lackadaisical"[123] nature than on long patterns of colonialism. Since attempts to make one Aboriginal girl "go to school or work" had failed, it was decided "there was no other option besides Training School." Her delinquency was also assumed from her position as "one of nine children in an overcrowded [reserve] home, economically marginal, mother out of the home."[124]

The insecure conditions of labour and life for many of the working poor also contributed to the criminalization of their daughters. While popular culture, along with rising wages after the war, reflected and promoted teen consumption, many children from these families had little money to spend on clothes, makeup, and restaurants, making temptations of petty theft attractive. Also, some girls were removed from school at fifteen to be used as child minders, or to find work as part-time domestics or waitresses, neither of which offered economic security. Parents with jobs that were 'unacceptable' (such as working in a bar) or that did not conform to a nine-to-five day were also disadvantaged. Working mothers with partners were chastised by judges for not "realizing how important it is to have a stable home life and a mother in the home."[125] And parental indifference was read into parents' inability to appear in court: "Why isn't the father here if you can't control [your daughter]," a Toronto judge demanded of a distraught mother who tried to explain that the father "worked in building and works away." "If your husband is not going to come, I'll have to send her away," he concluded, and did.[126] Also, some working-class parents did not want to throw away the little material security they had, for one problematic child. One father, who was fired from his labourer's job when police repeatedly came to his worksite to report on his daughter, finally said "he does not want to see her at home at all" and to send her to OTSG.[127]

Economic instability, desertion, and transience were also likely to lead to foster care, which made some children feel "ashamed" and "worthless."[128] Is it any wonder, a psychiatrist once asked, that a girl who had been in fifteen homes in seven years was "impulsive, rough, boy crazy and insolent?"[129] Once enmeshed in a cycle of rejection, girls often saw little payoff in conforming to social norms, and foster parents could simply send the girl back if she had problems. Indeed, there were few homes that would take female teens — unless they were going to scrub the floors. Though some foster children found love and care, other children's stories of physical and sexual abuse were discounted. The outward respectability of foster parents impressed social workers who later sometimes were forced to admit their mistakes. Social workers' faith in the foster parents' religiosity as a sign of their good parenting was tragically displayed when one OTSG ward became pregnant by a well-respected "church going" foster father. Even though he clearly "took the blame," the CAS and OTSG decided not to prosecute him, knowing that the girl's record included 'sex delinquency,' which might be used in court to place blame her — an interpretation even they entertained.[130]

Poverty also discouraged women from leaving violent partners, thus increasing the risk of their daughters' running away. And it accentuated illness and disabilities, leaving parents poorer, angry and frustrated, and children isolated and alienated. Nine years after a "deaf" girl was first designated a CAS "problem," OTSG finally pressured the parsimonious government into providing a hearing aid. By this time she had been incarcerated for running and immorality, though her claim of familial sexual abuse was rejected. "She is not crazy, though a little paranoid," commented the psychiatrist reasonably, "due to the fact she can't hear."[131]

Economic insecurity was often inextricably intertwined with sexual misconduct. An "immoral" fifteen-year-old was removed from her rural home after a pregnancy exposed her ongoing sexual relationship with the family's landlord. Sex with him, and also her stepfather, she claimed, had been encouraged by her mother. The court and OTSG worried primarily about taming her sexuality to prevent future pregnancies, obscuring the way in which her sexual behaviour was connected to economic survival. In return for sex, she had lived in the house rent-free, looking after five younger siblings, while her parents travelled elsewhere looking for work.[132]

For those who were very poor, despair, resignation, and anger literally became inscribed on their psyches. As one girl commented, why should I "grow up when all adults are unhappy . . . I do not know one good marriage" "Look at my mother," she added, who knew only poverty, "illness, one child after the other" and death from tuberculosis.[133] Girls' consciousness of the hardships faced by their families and concern for siblings sometimes drew them back to families they were told to forsake, even those families that had mistreated them. Well aware of the way in which the material shaped their lives, these girls were just not encouraged to speak about it by experts more concerned about their sexual activity.

Finally, girls' refusal or inability to support themselves contributed to court appearances and became a rationale for a training school sentence. Probation officers often worried about girls' failure to embrace the work ethic, but girls may have realistically assessed the insecure and poorly paid jobs of mothers and fathers and concluded they were little interested in entering the job market.[134] Parental support for an OTSG sentence was also secured by the promise of vocational training for their daughters; in practice, though, wage work was stressed over extended education. Some concerned superintendents had to *beg* for the paltry funds necessary for 'exceptional' girls to continue with their high school education. By sixteen, government bureaucrats claimed, "they should be earning their keep."[135] This meant preparing girls for jobs that fit their sex/class position, and their presumed intelligence level. While a minority of good students were encouraged to move into pink- or white-collar jobs, the overwhelming number of girls were channelled into factory and domestic work; even in the prosperous 1940s, girls deemed successful became good maids who "knew how to serve."[136] The probation officer could not have been clearer about the prescribed class position these girls were to assume. The discursive construction of delinquency, therefore, cannot be disentangled from the material context of girls' lives. In the eyes of the authorities, reform of girl delinquents necessitated interconnected moral lessons about working-class labour, femininity, and sexuality.

Whither the State?

In the World War II and postwar period, the treatment model and socialized or 'informal' justice offered by Family Courts expanded its reach across Ontario, though at the same time the numbers of children before Ontario courts increased, as did the number of youth institutionalized in training schools. In fact, Ontario's Tories positively bragged about the construction of new youth institutions in the late 1950s, offering this as a proof of the 'Progressive' side of their political label. The expansion of socialized justice did not mean less surveillance of juveniles, nor was it autonomous from the state; indeed, it was linked to the formal state apparatus at many contact points.

Yet in recent writing, the Foucault effect has led to a 'downgrading' of the state, and suggestions that we redirect our analytical gaze to decentralized, local networks of power.[137] Linked to Foucault's understanding of power was a critique of Marxist conceptions of the state, which *supposedly* portrayed the state as a dominating, overarching presence, a reflection of centralized, key interests.[138] Power, Foucault argued in contrast, is not located or held by agencies like the state, but rather expresses itself through tactics and technologies that can only be tracked at the micro level. Modern society was less characterized by state domination, more by "governmentalization of the state," that is, the many regulatory techniques and activities, including those in daily life, that govern conduct between and among individuals, organizations, and even within the self.[139]

Although Foucault argued that the law was a form of power imposing its own truths, he also saw it as "invaded" by new methods of power; the centre of gravity had shifted to discipline and normalization.[140] Thus, our critique should focus not on the 'pre-modern' form of juridical power, but more on disciplinary power. Yet even legal scholars sympathetic to Foucault have taken issue with this downgrading of juridical power and the state, arguing that he eclipses the historical evolution of the democratized modern state, artificially divides the law from the disciplines, and obscures the fact that "juridical power is still formidable."[141]

In the 1940s and 1950s, the state actually extended its command over the juvenile justice system. In the previous decade, for example, the provincial government had taken over industrial schools, previously overseen by boards of the philanthropic elite.[142] Arguing that the conditions and education provided by private charity were inadequate, the government decisively extended its own regulatory control, which culminated with legislation subsuming industrial schools under training schools in 1939. The government at first designated training schools as 'welfare'-related institutions, but increasingly, they were placed (where they belonged) within the orbit of correctional institutions.

During World War II and after, provincial bureaucrats gave directions to these institutions on everything from appropriate group outings, smoking, and church going to more basic questions of discipline for runaways. Very little escaped their view; when OTSG allowed *one* girl to drive a tractor, they were reprimanded by the government for encouraging "inappropriate work" for a young girl! Psyche experts were drawn into the service of the state bureaucracy, as consultants and researchers, shaping these policies, and using their connections to social work (or criminology) schools to further the correctional agenda. But the psyche experts were not omnipotent, and some policies emerged from the government's political agenda. For instance, one of the most contentious issues at the Galt school was solitary confinement, or "detention." OTSG used a wing of the Mercer reformatory for its "unmanageables" until 1957, when it opened its own model detention rooms. The prison-like construction of these quarters, and practices of cutting food rations, removing girls' day clothes, disallowing reading material — and more — brought sharp public criticism, especially from the Elizabeth Fry Society. The ensuing debates pitted bureaucrats, including the 'psych' experts, against the law and order superintendent, who argued for strict rules as there was "no point to staff spending their time with a bunch of psychopaths."[143] Though the psyche experts won the debate, officially relaxing the punitive rules, their influence emanated very much from the government's fear of political fallout and scandal.

The state and the judiciary did provide a crucial means of advancing the power of the disciplines, integrating them into the practice of socialized justice. It was the great latitude offered by the JDA and TSA that allowed words like 'incorrigible' to become the focus of psychiatric and social work knowledge, the mode by which delinquency was delineated. However, in ideological terms, it was the law and the courts that commanded and imposed the supreme claim to final truth. The power of the psyche court professionals was enhanced by the prestige offered to their definitions by the court, and it was ultimately the judge who decided how, when, and if their assessments would be used. The law both advanced the power of the disciplines and "retained some say in how their knowledge would be used."[144] Rather than presuming the ascendency of discipline over the law, it may be more useful to ask how and why law and the disciplines together produced a criminal justice system that institutionalized girls more than boys, pursued only girls for sexual crimes and targeted poor, racialized, and working-class girls.

As Dorothy Chunn also points out, many so-called specialized Juvenile Courts were actually extensions of adult justice, using the same judges and probation officers in a different time slot. Nor were girls from rural areas, reserves, and small towns likely to be examined by an array of social work and medical experts; even after they entered OTSG, these services were circumscribed. Indeed, OTSG superintendents often begged the government for additional psychiatric help.[145] Of an incest victim, an OTSG psychiatrist remarked, "she needs intensive psychotherapy which we cannot provide here."[146] As Ruth Alexander points out,[147] the official discourses defining delinquency sometimes stopped short at the reformatory gates; after incarceration, juvenile justice had as much to do with restraint and detention as with normalizing judgements — or more accurately, the two worked hand in hand.

As legal reformers began to argue in the 1960s, due process and legal safeguards for children were lacking in the delinquency laws; as a result, children and parents were disempowered, often exposing the blatant class biases inherent in the application of the law.[148] The arbitrary, authoritarian legal regime permitted by the JDA reinforced juridical authority, even if the courts were rhetorically denying their will to power by claiming that psychological 'treatment' of the offender was their primary aim. When a civil rights critique of the delinquency laws became a political force for legislative change in the 1960s, some bureaucrats and child welfare advocates opposed this agenda, defending their more 'arbitrary' but nonetheless welfarist/treatment model, with all the services they had built up. Yet, as Paul Havemann argues, the treatment lobby lost out in the long run. The new Young Offenders Act was a marriage of a strong 'law and order' lobby with the 'civil rights' discourse, with the latter increasingly dominated by the former. The contemporary emphasis on 'child blaming' that has so tragically assumed dominance ultimately reflected the political power of conservative governments, bent on reducing social services to the marginalized and embracing an ideology of child and family culpability for delinquency.[149]

Conclusion

In order to understand how and why girls were made into delinquents in Ontario during this period, we need to explore the origins *and* operation of power, the connections linking the discursive and the nondiscursive, asking not only how power 'circulated' through the juvenile justice system but what values and whose interests it ultimately served. Foucauldian concepts illuminate the process of constructing criminality, particularly the way in which expert knowledge became an authoritative force — equated with 'science' — that located the causes of delinquency in a bad environment, dysfunctional families, and (female) sexual deviance. Discourses concerning the sexualization of girls — so important to definitions of delinquency — were "shot through with power and became institutionalized as practices" within the juvenile justice system.[150] Within this complex system, there were many sites of normalizing conduct, from the nuclear family to the psychiatric clinic, but it was juridical power that drew these together into a powerful force determining the fate of many girls.

We must also ask why particular constructions of delinquency came to dominate. Otherwise, we may revert to the paradigms of the 1940s and 1950s, which explained delinquency with explorations of the deviant's 'inner soul' but ignored structural patterns of poverty, violence, colonialism, and marginalization shaping their lives. In a myriad of ways, material factors shaped, mediated, and legitimized the criminalization of girls; even the discourse of sexualization was inescapably intertwined with the material in its articulation.

When examining those girls sent to OTSG, the physical, spatial, and sensory experience of poverty should not be underestimated as a stimulant to disobedience and disregard for the law, and as a basic cause of their apprehension and incarceration. Once in OTSG, sexual control, training for working-class labour, and subdued femininity were seen as combined answers to delinquency; both the analysis of delinquency and its treatment reflected systems of power and established 'interests,' based on class, gender, and race.

Foucauldian concepts of power/knowledge and dispersed power thus advance feminist explorations of women's criminalization, but too rigidly applied, they may also lead to an overgeneralized, linear assumption of the medicalization of girl offenders, an eclipsing of juridical and state power, a failure to ask why power/knowledge sustains relations of ruling and oppression. Though they attempt to avoid the 'top-down' social control analyses, Foucauldian versions of regulation can also become 'top-inward' renditions of regulation, sidestepping questions of political economy, human agency, and resistance.

If we look not only for the inscription of power upon the bodies of delinquents but also at the responses of girls to their criminalization, resistance becomes more evident. Investigating girls' reactions and replies — however fragmented and muffled — in court or in training school as 'subjugated' knowledges, helps to highlight the silences and omissions in historical records that are largely disciplinary in their perspective. These silences suggest that power/knowledge was sometimes less than effective in colonizing the souls of delinquent girls. While the experts asked questions about sexuality, girls responded with tales of hard work, alienating foster care, violence and sometimes, just plain adolescent rebellion. Girls' responses and rebellions indicate, again, the need to contextualize expert knowledge in a feminist and materialist context. They may also suggest some hope that the more oppressive aspects of the juvenile justice system have been, and will continue to be, challenged by the young women who are caught in disciplinary design.

Notes

1 Archives of Ontario (AO), RG 60, Galt Training School for Girls (later Grandview) Ward Files (hereafter AO, Grandview), file 310, 1940s.

2 My use of the term 'delinquent' recognizes the historical and social construction of the term and does not denote an embrace of the negative designation of these girls as 'deviant.'

3 Along with public, published material in the popular and professional presses, I have utilized Training School Advisory Board reports, Family Court Files from the County of York, Ontario Government records from Public Welfare and the Department of Reform Institutions, Elizabeth Fry and Canadian Welfare Council Papers, and also 220 case files from the Galt (OTS or Grandview) Training School. Family Court papers offer more examples of girls on probation, Training School files girls most 'at risk.' The latter also offer a diverse picture of offenders from north and south, rural and urban areas, as well as some reserves.

4 In this article I focus on Michel Foucault's works that have been influential in academic discussions of crime and moral regulation and have also led to a 'popularization' of his concepts, including *Discipline and Punish: The Birth of the Prison* (New York: Pantheon Books, 1977); *The History of Sexuality*, vol. 1 (New York: Vintage, 1980); his essays in Colin Gordon, ed., *Power/Knowedge: Selected Interviews and Other Writings, 1972–77* (Brighton: Harvester Press, 1980); Graham Burchell, Colin Gordon, and Peter Miller, eds., *The Foucault Effect: Studies in Governmentality* (Hemel Hempstead: University of Chicago Press, 1991).

5 On the 'turn' in social history and theory from "production to perversion," see Terry Eagleton, *The Illusions of Postmodernism* (Oxford: Blackwell, 1997), 69. Some recent Canadian works embrace discourse analysis and/or draw on Foucauldian ideas: Carolyn Strange, *Toronto's Girl Problem: The Perils and Pleasures of the City* (Toronto: University of Toronto Press, 1996); Mariana Valverde, *The Age of Light, Soap and Water: Moral Reform in England Canada, 1885–25* (Toronto: McClelland and Stewart, 1991); Mariana Valverde, ed., *Studies in Moral Regulation* (Toronto: Centre for Criminology, 1994); Mary Louise Adams, *The Trouble with Normal: Postwar Youth and the Making of Heterosexuality* (Toronto: University of Toronto Press, 1998).

6 As late as 1965, the federal government task force on juvenile delinquency noted that the most common cause of delinquency cited in all submissions was 'the family': Canada, Department of Justice Committee, *Juvenile Delinquency in Canada* (Ottawa, 1965), 16.

7 Paul Havemann, "From Child Saving to Child Blaming: The Political Economy of the Young Offenders Act, 1908–84," in *The Social Basis of the Law: Critical Readings in the Sociology of Law*, ed. Stephen Brickey and Elizabeth Comack (Toronto: Garamond Press, 1986), 225.

8   Nancy Fraser, *Justice Interruptus: Critical Reflections on the "Postsocialist" Condition* (New York: Routledge, 1997), 11. On the displacement of materialist analyses of capitalism and labour with 'ludic' feminism, see Teresa Ebert, *Ludic Feminism and After: Postmodernism, Desire and Labor in Late Capitalism* (Ann Arbor: University of Michigan Press, 1996).

9   Marxism was challenged for presenting too instrumentalist or too structuralist a view of law or for "abdicating its responsibility for a theory of morality and justice": Colin Sumner, *The Sociology of Deviance: An Obituary* (New York: Continuum, 1994), 304. See also Elizabeth Comack and Stephen Brickey, "Recent Developments in the Sociology of Law," in *The Social Basis of Law*, at 19 and 20. On social control, see Shelley Gavigan and Dorothy Chunn, "Social Control: Analytical Tool or Analytical Quagmire?" *Contemporary Crises* 12 (1988): 107; Linda Gordon, "Family Violence, Feminism and Social Control," *Feminist Studies* 12 (1986): 453.

10 The literature is vast. For a few different examples, see Carol Smart, *Women, Crime and Criminology: A Feminist Critique* (London: Routledge and Kegan Paul, 1976); *Feminism and the Power of the Law* (London: Routledge, 1989); Pat Carlen, *Women, Crime and Poverty* (Philadelphia: Open University Press, 1988); Lorraine Gelsthorpe and Allison Morris, eds., *Feminist Perspectives in Criminology* (Philadelphia: Open University Press, 1990). For Canadian examples, Ellen Adelberg and Claudia Currie, eds., *Too Few to Count: Canadian Women in Conflict with the Law* (Vancouver: Press Gang, 1987); Karlene Faith, *Unruly Women: The Politics of Confinement and Resistance* (Vancouver: Press Gang, 1993). On sexualization, see Meda Chesney-Lind, "Judicial Enforcement of the Female Sex Role, the Family Court and Female Delinquency," *Issues in Criminology* 8 (1977): 51; Steven Schlossman and Stephanie Wallach, "The Crime of Precocious Sexuality: Female Juvenile Delinquency in the Progressive Era," *Harvard Educational Review* 48 (1978): 65; Gloria Geller, "Young Women in Conflict with the Law," in *Too Few to Count*, ed. Adelberg and Currie, 113; Indiana Matters, "Sinners or Sinned Against? Historical Aspects of Female Juvenile Delinquency in British Columbia," in *Not Just Pin Money: Selected Essays on the History of Women's Work in British Columbia*, ed. Barbara Latham and Roberta Pazdro (Victoria: Camosun College, 1984), 265; Mary Odem, *Delinquent Daughters: Protecting and Policing Adolescent Female Sexuality in the United States, 1885–1920* (Chapel Hill: University of North Carolina Press, 1995).

11 Smart, *Feminism and the Power of the Law*, 163–64.

12 Dawn Currie, "Feminist Encounters with Postmodernism: Exploring the Impasse of Debates on Patriarchy and Law," *Canadian Journal of Women and the Law* 5, no. 1 (1992): 76, 82.

13 Rosemary Hennessy and Chrys Ingraham, "Introduction: Reclaiming Anticapitalist Feminism," in *Materialist Feminism: A Reader in Class, Difference and Women's Lives*, ed. Rosemary Hennessy and Chrys Ingraham (New York: Routledge, 1997), 4.

14 Jeffrey Keshen, "Wartime Jitters over Juveniles: Canada's Delinquency Scare and Its Consequences, 1939–45," in *Age of Contention: Readings in Canadian Social History, 1900–45*, ed. Jeffrey Keshen (Toronto: Harcourt Brace, 1997), 364.

15 Library and Archives Canada (LAC), Canadian Council on Social Development (CCSD) [previously the Canadian Welfare Council], MG 28 I 10, vol. 56, file 474: letters from judges in 1942 showed some small towns and rural areas were not experiencing an increase in juvenile crime.

16 Keshen, "Wartime Jitters over Juveniles," 372.

17 Adele Saunders, "Is Home Life Breaking Up?" *Chatelaine* (June 1943): 8.

18 Mary Brechin, "Danger: Child Growing Up" *Maclean's*, 15 Aug. 1943, 48.

19 Dr. Anderson and Dr. Blatz, "Report from the Psychiatric Department," in Toronto, *Annual Report of the Family Court* (1945), 31.

20 AO, Department of Reform Institutions (RG 20 Series 16-2), Container J1, "Juvenile Delinquency" file.

21 There was new concern with male gangs and female teenage pregnancy. On the former, see Kenneth Rogers, *Street Gangs in Toronto: A Study of the Forgotten Boy* (Toronto: Ryerson Press, 1945).

22 Sidney Katz, "It's a Tough Time to Be a Kid," *Maclean's*, 15 Dec. 1950, 7; 15 Jan. 1951, 14. See also Roderick Haig-Brown, "Problems of Modern Life and Young Offenders," *Saturday Night*, 28 May 1955, 9.

23 Brechin, "Danger: Child Growing Up," 8; Gerald Zoffer, "Underworld Evils Breed Juvenile Delinquenncy," *Saturday Night*, 12 January 1946, 6.

24 Gerald Zoffer, "Juvenile Crime Rooted in Economic Refuse," *Saturday Night*, 26 Jan. 1946, 6. Emphasis is mine.

25 Elaine Tyler May, *Homeward Bound: American Families in the Cold War Era* (New York: Basic Books, 1988); Ruth Roach Pierson, *They're Still Women After All: The Second World War and Canadian Womanhood* (Toronto: McClelland and Stewart, 1992); Susan Prentice, "Workers, Mothers, Reds: Toronto's Postwar Daycare Fight," *Studies in Political Economy* 30 (1989): 115; Mary Louise Adams, *The Trouble with Normal*; Gary Kinsman, "Character Weaknesses and the Fruit Machines: Towards an Analysis of the Anti-Homosexual Security Campaign in the Canadian Civil Service," *Labour/Le Travail* 35 (Spring 1995): 133; John D'Emilio, "The Homosexual Menace: The Politics of Sexuality in Cold War America," in *Making Trouble: Essays on Gay History, Politics and the University*, ed. John D'Emilio (New York: Taylor and Francis, 1992).

26 AO, RG 20, 16-2, Container J 36, "Select Committee on Reform Institutions" quotes from *Globe and Mail* clipping, 10 November 1953.

27 Juvenile Delinquent Act, S.C. 1908, ch. 40; Training School Act, S.O. 1939, chap. 51. On the JDA, see Canadian Welfare Council, *The Juvenile Court in Law* (Ottawa: Canadian Welfare Council, 1941); Neil Sutherland, *Children in English Canadian Society: Framing the Twentieth Century Consensus* (Toronto: University of Toronto Press, 1978); Marge Reitsma-Street, "More Control than Care: A Critique of Historical and Contemporary Laws for Delinquency and the Neglect of Children in Ontario," *Canadian Journal of Women and the Law* 3, no. 2 (1989–90): 510; Jean Trépanier, "Origins of the Juvenile Delinquents Act of 1908," in *Dimensions of Childhood: Essays on the History of Children and Youth in Canada*, ed. Russell Smandych, Gordon Dodds, and Alvin Esau (Winnipeg: Legal Research Institute, 1991).

28 Dorothy Chunn, *From Punishment to Doing Good: Family Courts and Socialized Justice in Ontario* (Toronto: University of Toronto Press, 1992). From 1912 to 1952, the number of probation officers in the Toronto Family Court increased from four to fourteen, and they handled 900 percent more cases on an occurrence basis: John Hagan and Jeffrey Lyon, "Rediscovering Delinquency: Social History, Political Ideology and the Sociology of Law," *American Sociological Review* 42 (1977): 594.

29 By 'psyche' professions I am referring to psychiatrists, psychologists, and social workers, all used, in overlapping ways, in court assessments.

30 Michel Foucault, *Discipline and Punish: The Birth of the Prison* (New York: Pantheon, 1977), 27.

31 Foucault, *Discipline and Punish*, 177, and *History of Sexuality*, 144. For feminist re-interpretations of such Foucauldian concepts, see Sandra Lee Bartky, *Femininity and Domination* (London: Routledge, 1990); Susan Bordo, "Feminism, Foucault and the Politics of the Body," in *Up Against Foucault: Explorations of Some Tensions Between Foucault and Feminism*, ed. Caroline Ramazanoglu (London: Routledge, 1993), 179.

32 Nancy Fraser, "Michel Foucault: 'A Young Conservative?'" in *Feminist Interpretations of Michel Foucault*, ed. Susan J. Hekman (Pennsylvania: Pennsylvania State University Press, 1996), 26.

33 Foucault, *Discipline and Punish*, 222–23. As Allan Hunt notes, Foucault explores the interdependence of the law and the disciplines, but there is still a tendency for the disciplines to dominate the law. See Alan Hunt and Gary Wickam, *Foucault and Law* (London: Pluto, 1994), 47 and 49.

34 Jacques Donzelot, *The Policing of Families* (New York: Pantheon Books, 1979), 110.

35 AO, York County Family Court Records, Box 1524, unnamed file, 1950s.

36 Roy Brillinger, "The Judge and the Psychiatrist — Toward a Mutual Understanding" *Canadian Journal of Corrections* 1, no. 2 (1958). Brillinger was the director of the Hamilton Mental Health Clinic and did many assessments of incarcerated juveniles.

37 An exception is Michael Hakeem, "A Critique of the Psychiatric Approach to the Prevention of Juvenile Delinquency," in *Juvenile Delinquency: A Book of Readings,* ed. Rose Giallombardo (New York: John Wiley and Sons, 1966), 454.

38 Gloria Geller, "The Streaming of Males and Females in the Juvenile Justice System," (Ph.D. diss., University of Toronto, 1981), 121.

39 Sumner, *Sociology of Deviance,* 76.

40 I use terms like 'retarded' in their historical context. By the 1950s there are *some* OTS psychologists and psychiatrists who note that IQ tests are shaped by "socio-economic factors" (AO, RG 60, Grandview file 2353, 1950s) and are "only a starting point."

41 Paul Tappan, "The Nature of Juvenile Delinquency," in *Juvenile Delinquency,* ed. Giallombardo, 9.

42 Sheldon and Eleanor Glueck, *Five Hundred Delinquent Women* (New York: Knopf, 1934), 302. With "this swarm of defective, diseased, anti-social misfits," the Gluecks concluded, it is a "miracle" the proportion that do get rehabilitated. For one Canadian citation, see Margaret Strong, "Women and Crime in Canada," *Canadian Welfare* (July 1947): 12.

43 Ontario, *Annual Report of Ontario Training Schools,* 1933–59. These categories do change over time but focus very much on the 'home' as the cause of delinquency.

44 Ibid., 1959.

45 Doreen Elliott, *Gender, Delinquency and Society* (Aldershot: Avebury, 1988); Sumner, *Sociology of Deviance*; Ngaire Naffine, *Female Crime: The Construction of the Women in Criminology* (Sydney: Allen and Unwin, 1987); Shelley Gavigan, "Women's Crime: New Perspectives and Old Theories," in *Too Few to Count,* ed. Adelberg and Currie.

46 Sheldon and Eleanor Glueck, *Five Hundred Delinquent Women.* Many girls were arrested to begin with *for* running away from home. Also, girls' files may have stressed broken homes, given the assumption that this especially emotionally harmed girls. See Elliott, *Gender, Delinquency and Society,* 45.

47 Hilary Allen, *Justice Unbalanced: Gender, Psychiatry and Judicial Decisions* (Philadelphia: Milton Keynes, 1987).

48 AO, RG 20-148 Container 11, "Minister's Advisory Council on the Treatment of the Offender" file, Tadeusz Grygier, "Social Adjustment, Personality and Behaviour in Ontario Training Schools" (1966), 52.

49 AO, Grandview file 1560, 1950s; file 2292, 1950s.

50 Seymour Halleck, *Psychiatry and the Dilemmas of Crime* (New York: Harper and Row, 1967), 95–97; Sumner, *Sociology of Deviance.*

51 Kate Friedlander, quoted in Halleck, *Psychiatry and the Dilemmas of Crime,* 96.

52 Herbert Herskovitz, "A Psychodynamic View of Sexual Promiscuity"; Peter Blos, "Three Typical Constellations in Female Delinquency," in *Family Dynamics and Female Sexual Delinquency,* ed. Otto Pollak and A. Friedman (Palo Alto, CA: Science and Behaviour Books, 1969), 93 and 103.

53 Herskovitz, "A Psychodynamic View of Sexual Promiscuity," 89.

54 Adams, *The Trouble with Normal,*

55 Yet this statement seems to contrast with her other conclusion that the "real issue is the nexus between the welfare and criminal *systems* [my emphasis]": Kerry Carrington, *Offending Girls: Sex, Youth and Justice* (Sydney: Allen and Unwin, 1993), 107 and 27.

56 AO, RG 20 16-2, Container J21 "Galt" file, Letter of OTS Superintendent to Deputy Minister, 6 November 1952.

57 Kate Soper, "Productive Contradictions," in *Up Against Foucault,* ed. Ramazanoglu, 31.

58 Karlene Faith, "Resistance: Lessons from Foucault and Feminism," in *Power/Gender: Social Relations in Theory and Practice,* ed. H. Lorraine Radtke and Henderikus J. Stam (London: Sage, 1994), 55.

59 Trends in the Toronto Family Court are significant, as it was the largest one in the province. My conclusions are taken from a larger statistical study based on Toronto, *Annual Report of the Family Court,* 1940–1953 (after 1953, it became the Metro Family Court and similar statistics are not available), using the category "Offenses Which Brought Children to Court" for girls and boys. To give one example: in 1950, 56 percent of the boys and 26 percent of the girls were brought for theft, while 6 percent of the boys and 47 percent of the girls were brought for incorrigibility.

60 The larger statistical analysis of Toronto Family Court, ibid., supports these conclusions. See also Ontario, *Annual Report of Ontario Training Schools,* 1940–1959, under their category "Number of Times Before the Court." In 1955–56, for instance, 71 percent of the Galt girls had no court appearances and 24 percent only one. However, 39 percent of Bowmanville boys had no court appearances, 31 percent one appearance, and 16 percent two appearances. (It is true that more girls may have been processed as 'occurrences,' thus biasing these numbers.) For similar conclusions on institutionalization, see Dorothy Chunn, "Boys Will Be Men, Girls Will Be Mothers: The Legal Regulation of Childhood in Toronto and Vancouver," *Sociological Studies of Child Development* 3 (1990): 87.

61 AO, RG 20 16-2, Container J 48, "Mercer" file, quoted in clipping, *Toronto Star,* 10 Sept. 1957.

62 AO, Grandview file 2230, 1950s. The judge stressed that she must attend church in the morning, as evening services presumably posed more after-church temptations.

63 AO, Grandview File 972, 1940s.

64 AO, Grandview file 480, 1940s.

65 Venereal disease and illegitimate pregnancies might also be signs of delinquency, though by the 1950s, pregnancy might be 'treated' with other kinds of isolation. See AO, RG 20 16-2, Container J76, File "Training Schools," Statement from TSAB to Child Welfare Council, 1962: "Training School is no place for a girl in this condition. . .[although] in a sense, all unmarried mothers have been delinquent."

66 AO, Grandview file 460, 1940s.

67 AO, Grandview file 2170, 1950s.

68 Foucault, History of Sexuality, 61–62.

69 In the 1940s there is some evidence that white women were also targeted for sexual relations with Aboriginal and Asian men. However, there was not the same concern about the sexual transgressions of ethnic or religious boundaries. See Joan Sangster, "Incarcerating 'Bad Girls': The Regulation of Sexuality Through the Female Refuges Act in Ontario, 1920–1945," Journal of the History of Sexuality 7, no. 2 (1996): 239. Also, Aboriginal (and Afro-Canadian) women were not similarly punished for sex with white men. On Aboriginal women, see Joan Sangster, "Criminalizing the Colonized: Ontario Native Women Confront the Criminal Justice System, 1920–1960," Canadian Historical Review 80, no. 1 (March 1999): 32–60.

70 AO, Grandview file 843, 1940s.

71 AO, York County Family Court Records, Box 1514, unnamed file.

72 AO, Grandview file 365, 1940s.

73 AO, Grandview file 2289, 1950s.

74 AO, Grandview file 2127, 1950s.

75 The 12 percent is taken from my larger, overall study of 350 Galt inmates, from files sampled in the years from 1933 to 1960. This only includes girls who clearly reported incest. Others referred to "bad experiences," abuse, and ill treatment by male relatives but refused to give other details.

76 In the 1950s, the superintendent once remarked, "G— is one of our many victims of incest": AO, Grandview File 1565, 1950s. See also June Callwood's discussion of Galt: "The Most Heartbreaking Job in Canada," Maclean's, 1 Dec. 1953, 12.

77 AO, Grandview file 1560, 1950s.

78 Ames Robey, "The Runaway Girl," in *Family Dynamics and Female Sexual Delinquency*, ed. Pollak and Friedman, 127.

79 Linda Gordon, *Heroes of Their Own Lives: The Politics and History of Family Violence* (New York: Viking, 1988), 208.

80 The 1950s were characterized by a "denial" of incest, in part due to the influence of Kinsey and Freud: Diana Russell, *The Secret Trauma: Incest in the Lives of Girls and Women* (New York: Basic Books, 1986), 5. On different interpretations of incest, see Vikki Bell, *Interrogating Incest: Feminism, Foucault and the Law* (London: Routledge, 1993).

81 Gordon, *Heroes of Their Own Lives*, 242.

82 AO, Grandview file 2277, 1950s.

83 AO, Grandview file 290, 1940s.

84 RG 20 16-2, Container J 21, "Galt Inmates" File. Memo to Detention by Superintendent Isobel Macneil. The government was extremely upset with Macneil when the memo was leaked to them.

85 Linda Alcoff, "Feminist Politics and Foucault: The Limits to a Collaboration," in *Crises in Continental Philosophy*, ed. Arleen Dallery et al. (Albany: SUNY Press, 1990), 79.

86 On the contested relations between medical and prison officials, see Stephen Watson, "Applying Foucault: Some Problems Encountered in the Application of Foucault's Methods to the History of Medicine in Prisons," in *Reassessing Foucault: Power, Medicine and the Body*, ed. Colin Jones and Roy Porter (London: Routledge, 1994), 132.

87 AO, RG 20 16-2, Container J 21, "Galt Inmates" File, Memo of Isobel MacNeil to Deputy Minister, 6 Nov. 1952.

88 Ibid.

89 Ibid., Container 54, "Galt" File. Newspaper clipping, 20 Jan. 1959, of speech by Ruth Bentley, who resigned as superintendent.

90 Foucault, in *Power/Knowledge*, ed. Gordon, 98.

91 Ibid., 98 and 128.

92 Quoted in Alcoff, "Feminist Politics and Foucault," 75.

93 For example, Judge Orde's decision in *R. v. James Vahey* (1931), rejected a common law union as an inevitably "immoral" influence on children. Many social workers opposed this view and, aided by the Canadian Welfare Council, pressed for legislative changes to *make* common law unions a sign of immorality. See LAC, CCSD Papers MG 28 I 10, vol. 31 file 151, and vol. 32, file 151.

94   AO, Grandview file 420, 1940s.

95   Donzelot, *The Policing of Families*, chap. 4. Donzelot implies that fathers were "silenced" in court, unlike mothers (104), a situation that was not true here. Nor was the family necessarily a "sanctuary" (98) for children, offering protection from an omnipotent state.

96   For example, data collected from Toronto, *Annual Report of Family Court*, 1940–52, indicates that parents were more likely to bring complaints against daughters than sons, while the police were more likely to bring complaints against boys.

97   AO, Grandview file 850, 1950s.

98   AO, Grandview file 1647, 1950s. The *Annual Reports* listed committals by "race" and "nationality," but these statistics are problematic: for example, "Indian" may refer only to status Indians, and the province's definition of "nationality" changed over time. However, it seems that few Native girls (usually one or two a year, less than 3 percent of committals) were sent in the 1930s and early 1940s. After 1948, their numbers rose: for instance, in 1948, they were 4 percent of committals, in 1954, 8 percent, in 1955, a high of 15 percent, in 1959, 7 percent. On the causes of overincarceration of Native women in the 1950s, see Sangster, "Criminalizing the Colonized."

99   AO, Grandview file 2084, 1950s.

100 AO, Grandview file 1555, 1950s.

101 AO, Grandview file 1610, 1950s.

102 Foucault in *Power/Knowledge*, ed. Gordon, 82.

103 AO, Grandview file 90, 1930s. Although the quote comes from the 1930s, the attitude persisted in subsequent decades.

104 AO, Grandview file 2040, 1950s.

105 The mother wanted her put in a "Christian home," not OTS, but the judge disregarded her. AO, Grandview file 470, 1940s.

106 AO, Grandview file 2356, 1950s.

107 AO, Grandview file 1495, 1950s.

108 A thorough account of girls' experiences in OTS is not possible here. For a contemporary discussion of resistance, see Marge Reitsma-Street, "Girls Learn to Care; Girls Policed to Care," in *Women Caring: Feminist Perspectives on Social Welfare*, ed. Carol Baines (Toronto, McClelland and Stewart, 1991), 106. For a historical view, Tamara Myers and Joan Sangster, "Retorts, Runaways and Riots: Resistance in Girls' Reform Schools, 1930–60," paper presented at the Social Science History Association conference, Chicago, November 1998.

109 Foucault's analysis is especially apt for delinquent girls who were accused of immorality, but economic and property offences — the more common offences for all people — fit the analysis less aptly. See Hunt and Wickam, *Foucault and Law*, 58.

110 AO, Grandview file 2289, 1950s.

111 Rosemary Hennessy, *Materialist Feminism and the Politics of Discourse* (New York: Routledge, 1993), 25. See also Maureen Cain, "Foucault, Feminism and Feeling; What Foucault Can and Cannot Contribute to Feminist Epistemology," in *Up Against Foucault*, ed. Ramazanoglu, 83 and 84.

112 Terry Eagleton, "Frere Jacques: The Politics of Deconstruction," in *Against the Grain: Selected Essays* (London: Verso, 1986), 85.

113 Michele Barrett, *The Politics of Truth: From Marx to Foucault* (Stanford: Stanford University Press, 1991), 138.

114 Ibid., 139.

115 The vast majority of girls sentenced to OTS came from working-class families, and many had fallen on hard times and were seen as an 'underclass': their parents were underemployed, unemployed, on relief or welfare, or had simply deserted. In a sample of one hundred cases where the parents' background was quite clear, for example, only six families could be called 'middle-class' or were better-off farmers.

116 Halleck, *Psychiatry and the Dilemmas of Crime*, 139.

117 James Struthers, *The Limits of Affluence: Welfare in Ontario, 1920–70* (Toronto: University of Toronto Press, 1994), 142, points out that the poor were extremely marginalized in the 1950s as they "slipped even further behind the rising prosperity."

118 AO, RG 20 16-2 Container J 15, "Galt" file. OTS Superintendent to Deputy Minister, 18 Nov. 1953.

119 Chunn, "Boys Will Be Men," 99.

120 Gerald Markowitz and David Rosner, *Children, Race and Power: Kenneth and Mamie Clark's Northside Centre* (Charlottesville: University of Virginia Press, 1996), 84. See also Grygier, "Social Adjustment, Personality and Behaviour in Ontario Training Schools," 37: "psychotherapy was not favoured for subjects of low socio-economic status."

121 AO, Grandview file 905, 1940s.

122 AO, Grandview file 1440, 1950s.

123 AO, Grandview file 1521, 1950s.

124 Ibid.

125 AO, Grandview file 2080, 1950s.

126 AO, Grandview file 420, 1940s.

127 AO, Grandview file 2120, 1950s.

128 AO, Grandview File 2289, 1950s. On the connection between state care and girls' conflicts with the law, see Pat Carlen, *Women, Crime and Poverty* (Philadelphia: Open University Press, 1988), 73.

129 AO, Grandview file 320, 1940s.

130 AO, Grandview file 2295, 1950s.

131 AO, Grandview file 853, 1940s.

132 AO, Grandview file 2326, 1950s.

133 AO, Grandview file 320, 1940s.

134 As Gisela Konopka, *The Adolescent Girl in Conflict* (New Jersey: Prentice Hall, 1966), 73, points out, middle-class social workers saw work outside the home as "positive," but the girls knew theirs would more likely resemble drudgery.

135 AO, Grandview file 830, 1940s.

136 AO, Grandview File 825, 1940s.

137 Nikolas Rose, "Beyond Public/Private Division: Law, Power and the Family," in *Critical Legal Studies,* ed. Peter Fitzpatrick and Alan Hunt (London: Basil Blackwell, 1987). For a critique of his approach see Boris Frankel, "Confronting Neo-liberal Regimes: The Post-Marxist Embrace of Populism and Realpolitik," *New Left Review* 226 (1998): 57.

138 This is a simplification. Susan Boyd, "(Re)Placing the State: Family, Law and Oppression," *Canadian Journal of Women and the Law* 9, no. 1 (Spring 1994): 39.

139 Burchell et al., eds., *The Foucault Effect*, 2–3 and 102–3.

140 Foucault, *Discipline and Punish*, 170.

141 Smart, *Feminism and the Power of the Law*, 4.

142 AO, Acc 11525, Records of the Industrial Schools Association of Ontario, AOMU 1408, Series A-1, Minutes of the Executive of the Industrial Schools Assoc. of Toronto, Feb. 9 and 14, 1934, and Series B, "A History of the Industrial Schools Association," typescript.

143 AO, RG 20-16, Container 47, "Galt" file, Minutes of meeting to discuss detention, 8 Jan. 1958, quote from OTS Superintendent.

144 Hunt and Wickam, *Foucault and Law*, 49.

145 AO, RG 20 16, Container J 15, "Galt" file. Memo from OTS Superintendent to A.R. Virgin, Director of Rehabilitation, 1951.

146 AO, Grandview file 1651, 1950s.

147 Ruth Alexander, "The 'Girl Problem': Class Inequality and Psychology in the Remaking of Female Adolescence, 1900–30" (Ph.D. diss., Cornell University, 1990).

148 Bernard Green, "The Determination of Delinquency in the Juvenile Court of Metro Toronto" (SJD thesis, University of Toronto, 1968); and "Trumpets, Justice and Federalism: An Analysis of the Ontario Training Schools Act of 1965," *University of Toronto Law Journal* 16, no. 2 (1966): 407.

149 Paul Havemann, "From Child Saving to Child Blaming," 231.

150 Janet Ransom, "Feminism, Difference and Discourse," in *Up Against Foucault*, ed. Ramazanoglu, 123.

CRIMINALIZING THE COLONIZED
ONTARIO NATIVE WOMEN CONFRONT
THE CRIMINAL JUSTICE SYSTEM, 1920–1960

Over the past decade, Aboriginal women's conflicts with the law and their plight within the penal and child welfare systems have received increasing media and government attention. Framed by the political demands of Native communities for self-government, and fuelled by disillusionment with a criminal justice system that has consistently failed Native peoples — both as victims of violence and as defendants in the courts — government studies and royal commissions have documented the shocking overincarceration of Native women.[1] At once marginalized, yet simultaneously the focus of intense government interest, Native women have struggled to make their own voices heard in these inquiries. Their testimony often speaks to their profound alienation from Canadian society and its justice system, an estrangement so intense that it is couched in despair. "How can we be healed by those who symbolize the worst experiences of our past?" asked one inmate before the 1990 Task Force on federally sentenced women.[2] Her query invokes current Native exhortations for a reinvention of Aboriginal traditions of justice and healing; it also speaks directly to the injuries of colonialism experienced by Aboriginal peoples.

Although we lack statistics on Native imprisonment before the 1970s, overincarceration may well be a "tragedy of recent vintage."[3] This article explores the roots of this tragedy, asking when and why overincarceration emerged in twentieth-century Ontario; how legal and penal authorities interpreted Aboriginal women's conflicts with the law; and in what ways Native women and their communities reacted to women's incarceration. Drawing primarily on case files from the Mercer Reformatory for Women, the only such provincial institution at the time,[4] I investigate the process of legal and moral regulation that led to Native women's incarceration from 1920 to 1960. Admittedly, such sources are skewed towards the views of those in authority: inmate case files are incomplete and partisan, strongly shaped by the recorder's reactions to the woman's narrative. Arrest and incarceration statistics are also problematic: they homogenize all Native and Métis nations under the designation 'Indian,'[5] and they predominantly reflect the policing of Aboriginal peoples and the changing definitions of crime. However partial, these sources reveal patterns of, and explanations for, increasing incarceration; women's own voices, however fragmented, are also apparent in these records, offering some clues to women's reactions to incarceration.[6]

Native women's criminalization bore important similarities to that of other women, who were also arrested primarily for crimes of public order and morality, who often came from impoverished and insecure backgrounds, and whose sexual morality was a key concern for the courts. The convictions of Aboriginal women are thus part of a broader web of gendered moral regulation articulated through the law — the disciplining of women whose behaviour was considered unfeminine, unacceptable, abnormal, or threatening to society. This 'censuring' process of distinguishing the immoral from the moral woman was also sustained by the medical and social work discourses used within the penal system; these attitudes constituted and reproduced relations of power based on gender, race, and economic marginality.[7] Granted, the law was one of many forms of regulation — accomplished also through the church, the school, and the family — but it remained an important one. As the "cutting edge of colonialism,"[8] the law could enact the 'final lesson' and perhaps the most alienating one for Aboriginal women: incarceration.

The experiences of Native women were also profoundly different from those of other women: they were shaped by racist state policies of 'over-regulation' linked to the federal Indian Act, by the racialized constructions of Native women by court and prison personnel, and by the cultural chasm separating Native from non-Native in this time period. In short, the legal regulation of these women was an integral component of the material, social, and cultural dimensions of colonialism.[9]

Native women's increasing conflicts with the law thus reflect overlapping relations of power, based on gender, class, and race. Masculinist and class-biased definitions of crime, already inherent in the criminal justice system, were further complicated by the relations of colonialism and race. As Colin Sumner argues, colonialism often sparks the clash of two cultures and legal regimes, with unequal power relations operating within as well as between those cultures. The supposedly 'modern' Western legal regime often dominates, displacing older modes of regulating behaviour, and converting "attempts to preserve the old ways, resist the new order and accommodate to its hardships . . . into criminal behaviour."[10]

Arguing for a separate Aboriginal justice system, activists and scholars have recently stressed the fundamental, perhaps unbridgeable, differences between Euro-Canadian and Aboriginal value systems.[11] While I have found evidence of culturally distinct notions of wrongdoing, justice, and sanction, my conclusions also highlight some complications in this picture. Though certainly alienated from the dominant criminal justice system, some Native families, leaders, and communities also used this system to address social problems and effect social controls in desperately difficult times. As a result, they also participated in the incarceration of their own wives, daughters, and mothers.

As the only provincial reformatory for women, the Mercer, located in Toronto, took in women from across the province who received sentences varying from three months to two years.[12] Although extreme caution should be exercised in using the Mercer numbers, they do suggest patterns of emerging overincarceration.[13] The most striking fact of Native women's imprisonment at the Mercer was its increase over time. In the 1920s, few Native women appear in the prison registers; three decades later, Native women were listed on virtually every page. Of overall "intakes" (women admitted, repeaters or not) in the 1920s, only thirty-nine were Native women, or about 2 percent of the prison population. Every decade thereafter, the number of Native women taken in not only doubled but increased as a proportion of admissions — from 4 percent in the 1930s to 7 percent in the 1940s to just over 10 percent in the 1950s. Yet over these years, the Native population remained constant at about 1 percent of the general population.[14] The turning point clearly came after World War II when the number of Native women admitted increased substantially.[15] A survey of minor charges in Kenora supports this pattern; by the 1950s the number of Native women incarcerated in the local jail was increasing rapidly, with the vast majority of repeaters charged with alcohol offences.[16]

Although the patterns were amplified in certain areas, Aboriginal women's incarceration followed the trends of sentencing for all women at the Mercer. There were increasing numbers of women sentenced over time, more and more liquor offences by the 1950s, and a larger number of recidivists with shorter, definite sentences. Younger women, particularly those in their twenties, dominated at the Mercer in the interwar period; in the 1940s and 1950s, women from twenty to forty were still the majority, though slightly more women over forty were being sentenced. Most offenders were listed as housewives or domestic workers, or gave no occupation, and they were primarily sentenced for crimes of public order and morality. By the 1950s, however, Native women were overrepresented in liquor charges. Overall, alcohol offences represented about 50 percent of the admissions, but for Native women they were as high as 70 percent.[17]

For Native women, crimes of public poverty and moral transgression always dominated over crimes against private property or the person. Vagrancy, an elastic offence that included everything from prostitution to drunkenness to wandering the streets, dominated as the most significant charge for Native women in the 1920s (50%) and 1930s (31%). In both these decades, prostitution and bawdy house charges came second, and, by the 1930s, breach of the Liquor Control Act (BLCA), especially the clause prohibiting drunkenness in a public place, was assuming equal importance. In the next two decades, alcohol-related charges came to dominate as the reason for incarceration (32% in the 1940s, and 72% in the 1950s), with vagrancy and prostitution convictions ranking second. Theft, receiving stolen goods, and break and enters comprised only 6 percent of the convictions in the 1940s and 1950s, while violence against the person represented only 2 percent of the charges in these years. That issues of sexual morality and public propriety were central to Native incarceration can be seen in the increasing use of the Female Refuges Act (FRA), which sanctioned the incarceration of women aged sixteen to thirty-five, sentenced, or even "liable to be sentenced," under any Criminal Code or bylaw infractions for "idle and dissolute" behaviour. While this draconian law was used most in Ontario the 1930s and 1940s, for Native women it was increasingly applied in the 1940s and 1950s.[18]

A higher proportion of charges was levelled against women for neglecting, abandoning, or "corrupting" their children (5% and 9% in the latter two decades) than for assaults against adults.[19] Prosecutions under this charge point to a crucial theme found within the case files: even if the official charge was not alcohol-related, the crime was often attributed to alcohol consumption. One woman charged with both assault and contributing to juvenile delinquency, for instance, had struck another woman on the street while intoxicated, and in the presence of her own fourteen-year-old daughter.[20] Women often lost custody of their children when both alcohol problems and poverty indicated neglect to the authorities; sometimes the children were deserted; sometimes they were left in the hands of relatives who, poor themselves, could not cope easily. One poverty-stricken woman left her children aged three to nine in a tent, and they were later found looking for food in garbage cans. Incarcerated for intoxication, she immediately lost her children to the Children's Aid Society (CAS).

Theft charges were also linked to poverty and alcohol consumption. Two Native women found themselves severely punished when they "destroyed private property"; after drinking in a bar in a northern mining town, they asked two men for a ride home. Refused, they threw matches into the car and destroyed it. In another case, a woman "helped herself to $19.00 from the wallet of an intoxicated bushworker drinking with her." As she was five months pregnant, she reasoned that "she needed it more than him." The link between prostitution charges and women's poverty was also clear; despite the fact that a woman might be literally "malnourished and destitute," incarceration was deemed the appropriate response.[21] Even the few violent crimes were often explained in the files by alcohol problems; in one tragic case, a woman who was drunk unknowingly assaulted her sister with a beer bottle and killed her. She served less than two years for manslaughter, the judge noting her lack of murderous intent and her own mental anguish. Other women attacked family members in anger or frustration, or attempted suicide; their violence was often unsuccessful or half-hearted, desperate but not calculated.

One reason that liquor charges dominated at the Mercer by the late 1950s was overcrowding in women's cells at the local Don Jail. The crush was relieved by sending some women to the Mercer.[22] This explanation also may account for the increasing number of recidivists: by the 1950s, at least 50 percent of all the Native women admitted had already been in the Mercer before. A few women, often homeless and sometimes with alcohol problems, were being admitted twenty or thirty times.[23] One recidivist case was typical: in the late 1930s, Susan, a seventeen-year-old, was brought up before a small-town magistrate on a charge of "corrupting children." An orphaned foster child now working as a domestic, she was arrested for engaging in sex with a local man at his family home in front of children. The initial report also claimed she had no occupation, "has been mixed up in other immorality and was correspondent in a divorce case."[24] After serving her term, and giving birth to a child in prison, Susan stayed in Toronto, but she had few skills and little education. Two years later, she was incarcerated under the Venereal Diseases Act, perhaps a sign that she had turned to prostitution to support herself. Struggling with alcohol problems, she went back and forth between her home town and Toronto, trying with little success to collect enough relief to survive. When relief officials tried to force her into the local refuge, she went to live in her brother's abandoned henhouse. Eventually she was sent back to Mercer for two years, convicted under the FRA as an "idle and dissolute" woman. She remained in Toronto and, over the next fifteen years, was jailed repeatedly under BLCA charges: by 1959 she had thirty-six admissions. Often convicted on the standard thirty days or a $25 fine penalty, she — like many Native women — could not afford the fine, so spent time in the Mercer.

Many women at the Mercer came from families that had suffered significant losses; a parent or siblings had died of pneumonia, gangrene, an accident, or alcoholism. Tuberculosis claimed many lives on reserves, even after it was declining within the general population.[25] When a middle-aged woman who lost all her eight siblings to disease and her father to alcoholism told the Mercer doctor that her own drinking was "unfortunate but unchangeable," one can perhaps understand her tone of resignation. Family dissolution, domestic violence, intense poverty, low levels of education, the likelihood of foster care, or CAS intervention in the family were also evident in many women's backgrounds. Despite family dissolution, women struggled, sometimes against great odds, to sustain family ties even when illness, transience, or removal of children made it difficult. "She never knew her parents but she has five younger siblings [spread over residential schools and cas care] . . . whom she writes to try and keep the family together," noted the reformatory psychiatrist in one instance.[26]

Women's geographical origins and the location of their convictions are significant, indicating one of the major causes of overincarceration: the spiralling effects of economic deprivation and social dislocation. In the interwar period, the majority of women were convicted in southern Ontario, especially Toronto and Hamilton, or in Sarnia, Sault Ste. Marie, or Sudbury — cities close to many reserves.[27] Following World War II, more Native women originally came from more remote areas further north. By the 1950s, even though the majority of convictions were in southern Ontario, the place of origin, in over a third of these cases, was Manitoulin, North Bay, Thunder Bay, or other northern places.[28] This moving "frontier of incarceration" suggests the importance of urbanization and/ or deteriorating economic and social circumstances as the stimulus for women's conflicts with the law.[29]

In the interwar period, Natives living on many reserves were finding themselves in difficult economic straits. No efforts were made to encourage new economic development, a reform desperately needed because many reserves had a fixed resource base and a growing population. The Depression accentuated subsistence problems, reducing some Aboriginal communities to relief far below the already pitiful levels in the cities.[30] Similar dilemmas increasingly plagued more isolated reserves after the war, when corporate resource development, the decline of fur prices, and new transportation routes began to have a dramatic impact on northern communities. As the effect of colonization permeated further north, the consequences were increased social dislocation and conflict, and more intervention by Euro-Canadian police forces, especially when Aboriginal peoples were off their reserves.[31] Indeed, women who fled to cities in search of jobs and social services often found little material aid, but faced the complicating, intensifying pressure of racism.[32] One of the most dramatic examples of the colonial "penetration" of the North was that of Grassy Narrows. When this isolated community was relocated closer to Kenora, the community's sense of spatial organization, family structure, and productive relations were all undermined. Proximity to the city brought increased access to alcohol and the malignancy of racism; "the final nail in the coffin" was mercury poisoning of their water and their fish supply.[33]

The stresses experienced by Native families in this time period were never simply material. For example, official federal policies of acculturation, though increasingly viewed as unsuccessful, persisted in projects such as residential schools, which were experienced by as many as one third of Native youth in the early decades of the twentieth century. While some historians argue that girls may have acquired a few useful skills in the schools, almost all accounts agree that the isolation of children from their communities, the denigration of their culture and language, and the emotional and physical abuse left many women scarred for life.[34] It is impossible to ascertain exactly how many Mercer inmates came through residential schools, but it is clear that when residential school inmates appeared in court, magistrates and judges claimed bluntly that they should know "the difference between right [and] wrong."[35] Although the legal authorities assumed the moral superiority of the Euro-Canadian, religious instruction of residential schools, Aboriginal leaders now argue that violence, alcoholism, and alienation were actually the direct results of such schooling.[36]

Because alcohol charges were the primary cause of incarceration, it is worth examining them in greater depth: these cases demonstrate how social dislocation interacted with cultural alienation and racism to prompt overincarceration. Despite evidence that prison was no solution to "alcoholism"[37] and may have worsened the problem, penal punishment continued to be the response of the authorities. One important reason for the high numbers of alcohol arrests, especially for women, was their poverty and thus their inability to pay fines. At the same time, the public character of Native drinking made it particularly distasteful to the dominant classes and culture. It was sometimes linked to sexual 'misbehaviour,' including miscegenation, and, given the image of Native women as weak and corruptible, authorities believed that alcoholism would spread easily by example. Native drinking had for some time been feared as a precursor to alcoholism, and, although consumption of alcohol was increasingly seen as an addiction rather than as evidence of weakness of character, the latter characterization never entirely vanished from the judgments of the legal and medical authorities.

Not a crime as long as it is hidden from view, alcohol-induced behaviour by the well-heeled drinker was easier to ignore than that by the impoverished one. Moreover, the means of consuming alcohol and the way in which the effects of alcohol are exhibited are socially and culturally specific. By the late 1960s, critics of existing theories of alcoholism among Native peoples argued that there was no direct evidence that "Indians were more susceptible" to alcoholism and that the precise forms that "out-of-control" behaviour took had more to do with culture than biology.[38] Since that time, the dominant interpretations of alcoholism have stressed the social and economic context of colonialism and oppression giving rise to alcohol consumption, some even seeing it as a muted form of "protest."[39] Perceptions of alcoholism as a disease that Natives are especially vulnerable to have not totally disappeared, however, even within Aboriginal testimonies.[40]

Alcoholism may have existed as a problem for some Native women, but magistrates failed to see it as an outcome of systemic social problems. While many regretted the unfortunate background of women brought before the court, pointing to family breakups or alcoholic parents, their laments were specific rather than structural. They were insensitive to the assaults on Native culture, traditional economic production, and family and community organization that were occurring in the twentieth century. Court pronouncements also divulged a fatalistic equation of Natives and alcohol: "She is an Indian girl and probably will never stay away from the drink," noted one magistrate in 1945. A decade later the same complaint was advanced: "They spend up to 8 months in jail and are the biggest problem I have . . . I do not know any remedy for this type of person."[41]

The authorities were especially concerned with the links between visible sexual behaviour and alcohol consumption. Native women suspected of prostitution, or who engaged in sex for no money and with no obvious moral regret, were especially vulnerable to incarceration, as were non-Aboriginal women who engaged in "casual" sex and rejected the ritual of confession and moral guilt.[42] Women accused of having sex in public or with multiple partners were targeted by police, who described them in terms tinged with moral outrage: "She is known as a prostitute and often intoxicated . . . her conduct is disgraceful to say the least, one night she hung around the naval barracks, took off her clothes and jumped in the creek." Alcohol and sexual misbehaviour became so linked in the mind of the police that the mere fact of Aboriginal men and women drinking together suggested sexual immorality; when two women were found in a cabin, drinking with some men, the arresting officer noted "there was no evidence of sex but the proximity of the sexes with intoxicants can have undesirable results."[43] These descriptions were fuelled by the racist stereotype of the Indian woman easily debauched by alcohol and lacking the sexual restraint of white women. By the late nineteenth century, political and media controversies had created an image of Native women in the public mind: supposedly "bought and sold" by their own people as "commodities," they were easily "demoralized" sexually, and a threat to both public "morality and health."[44] While the Native was essentialized in the dominant cultural discourse, Aboriginal women did not assume the (male) role of the "noble savage" or the "lazy ingrate," but rather of the licentious "wild woman" symbolizing sexual excess and the need for conquest or control.[45] In one sense, there was less moral panic about Aboriginal women engaging in interracial sex than there was for white women; the latter might even be incarcerated for sexual liaisons with non-white men.[46] This lack of concern with miscegenation, however, emanated from a racist stereotype that saw Native women as less "pure to begin with."

Incarceration was also justified for paternalistic motives: magistrates claimed that, by incarcerating Native women, they were protecting them from becoming an "easy target for the avaricious" or the "victim of unprincipled Indian and white men."[47] A similar rationale of protecting the weak underlay some of the prohibitions against prostitution in the Indian Act.[48] This paternalism was evident in the trial of a young Aboriginal woman from southern Ontario who was sent to the Mercer for two years on FRA charges of being "idle and dissolute." The arresting RCMP officer insisted she was "transient, with no work and has been convicted on many alcohol charges over the past few years." She had been caught "brawling with white men," he continued, "and has been found wandering, her mind blank after drinking." Moreover, it was believed that she was a "bad influence on a fifteen year old who has also been led astray." The magistrate lectured the woman: "My girl, I hope that by removing you from unscrupulous white men and Indian soldiers and alcohol that you will start a new life. It is too bad that such a good looking Indian like you should throw your life away. Other men buy the liquor for you, then you suffer, and they escape."

This example also points to another precipitating factor in many arrests: the public nature of the woman's alcohol consumption. In large cities, Native women who were jailed were not always recidivists, but simply those targeted by police because of loud, disruptive behaviour or inability to find their way home. One such woman calmly told the psychiatrist that she was not an alcoholic and "only drinks heavily on occasion." He was forced to admit she was right.[49] It is difficult to escape the conclusion that these women were simply more heavily policed because they were poor and Native.[50]

The complaint that women who drank heavily would easily corrupt others was also common. In some cases, it was Native families who feared this prospect: "She should serve her whole term; she is better in there," wrote one father, fearing that his daughter, if released, would be influenced by her mother, who also drank. Often, it was the Indian agent or the police who advocated removing the offender so she would not lead others astray. Sentencing one woman to a term in Mercer, a magistrate noted that the woman must be kept away because she was "a bad influence on the girls on the island"; when she was released, he urged that she be sent "away from the Island." Women whose children had been removed because of their mother's drinking were seen as a special burden on the state, and, therefore, candidates for incarceration. "She has had four children with the CAS," noted one magistrate, "she has chosen the wrong path, now her children are a public charge." Such women were also portrayed as poor material for rehabilitation. As one magistrate noted of a deaf woman charged under the Indian Act: "There is no doubt that children will continue to the end of her reproductive age, or until a pathological process renders her sterile. She is also likely to drink steadily. The prospect of improvement is remote. Institutionalization, if available, is suitable."[51]

Incarceration was thus used as punishment, as banishment from public view, and as an attempt to protect women from further alcoholism or immorality. Declarations of "protection," however, were clearly inscribed with both gender and race paternalism, for they presumed an image of proper feminine behaviour, stressing sexual purity and passivity within the private nuclear family, and the need for Native women to absorb these "higher" Euro-Canadian standards. Similarly, teachers in the residential schools often claimed that Native girls were easily sexually exploited, prone to returning "to the blanket."[52] Aboriginal women were thus both infantilized as vulnerable and weak, and also feared as more overtly and actually sexual.

Unfortunately, a gulf of considerable magnitude divided Native women from those convicting them and from the penal authorities in the Mercer. Indeed, the interpretation of Native crime offered by the legal and penal "experts" contributed to the process of overincarceration by legitimizing an image of Native women as morally weak and easily corrupted. Even after incarceration, these attitudes were significant because they shaped possibilities of parole, alcohol treatment, and rehabilitation; convinced that Native women would be recidivists, authorities did little to discern their needs. Not surprisingly, many women became even more alienated within the reformatory.

Like other women, First Nations women were separated from prison personnel by class and cultural differences. Inmates encountered revulsion, antipathy, resignation, and sometimes sympathy from the experts whose "scientific" language of clinical analysis and case work often masked subjective, moral judgments. Native women, however, were also seen through the particular lens of race paternalism. For example, the very word 'reserve' had a different meaning from words like 'poor or bad neighbourhood' used between the 1930s and 1950s to describe the backgrounds of white women: reserves were associated with degeneracy, backwardness, and filth. One 'progressive' social worker, writing about Indian juveniles in the 1940s, decried racial prejudice and the poverty on reserves, but at the same time reiterated many racist images, describing Indians as "savage, childish, primitive and ignorant."[53]

A picture of Aboriginal women as weak and lacking in moral fibre followed them through the court and penal systems. Magistrates would comment, "We can't expect miracles from this home," while the presiding prison psychiatrist would often conclude, "It is doubtful if successful rehabilitation could be achieved.'[54] The image of the reserve as a place of hopelessness was especially evident in probation reports. Native families sometimes offered probationers accommodation, even when houses were crowded, yet officials equated such offers with a lack of awareness about the need for basic moral and social standards. They were especially critical of congested conditions, likely seeing proximity of the sexes as encouraging immorality. They were also suspicious of those living a transient life, "in the Indian mode,"[55] who might easily succumb to alcohol use, unemployment, and poverty. "Home conditions primitive ... the home is a disreputable filthy shack on the reserve," were typical observations. Aboriginal people who did not fit this stereotype were then portrayed as unusual: "Above average Indian home which is adequately furnished, clean and tidy," noted one probation report, while another officer claimed a father was "one of few Indians in the area who does not drink."[56]

Not all these Native women came directly from reserves, but the stigma of primitiveness was carried with them into the city, resulting in overzealous policing and victimization. One older woman was arrested, along with an intoxicated friend, for "indecent exposure"; her crime was simply swimming nude at a lake where nude boys were also swimming. Her claim that she was in prison "unjustly" seemed to be shared by the psychiatrist, but he did not advocate release. A young woman who had stolen a purse she found in a store change room became distraught at the "humiliation" her possible incarceration would cause her siblings, so tried to return some of the money. Her honesty cost her a prison term. Again, the Mercer psychiatrist's report noted she was a "bright, alert, pleasing" woman with a good employment history. She had been incarcerated, however, on the basis of reports from CAS and school officials in Sault Ste. Marie that portrayed her as a "typical" problem Native: she was an orphan, had one illegitimate child, and a "poor" attitude — in their view, she was destined for trouble.[57]

Probation reports also revealed a Catch-22 that Native women faced in terms of rehabilitation. Social workers debated whether reserve or city life would be more corrupting for released women, but they often recommended removing women from their original home or reserve. However well-intentioned the effort to isolate her from past problems, this strategy left women in foreign surroundings, alienated by language and cultural differences, and often directly faced with racism. This situation was well-captured in a parole report that claimed one woman was now "an outlaw on the Reserve" because of her promiscuity, and her parents there were heavy drinkers who lived in a "small, filthy home." It was unwise to return her there, the officer noted, but added: "We realize the extreme difficulty in placing an Indian girl in some other centre, where society is loath in accepting her." Grandmothers often tried to care for children left behind or born in jail, but families were frank about the lack of economic resources and employment available for the released women, and they agonized over the prospects of help with alcohol problems. One mother pointed out that she also drank and that if her adult daughter returned home, "she would lose her mother's allowance and so they would have no money." "The mother really does not want her home," observed the agent, "but she would not say [the daughter] could not return."[58]

If a woman came from a reserve, her incarceration might be the product of the Indian agent's powers to charge her with crimes such as drinking, prostitution, or immorality. Agents were endowed with the powers of justices of the peace under the Indian Act, thus creating an extra layer of oppressive legal regulation for Native women. The level of surveillance of the economic, social, and moral lives of Native families by the agent was astounding. When called on to assess parole, his report might comment on the family's church attendance, the marital status, education, employment, and social lives of siblings and parents, his judgment of their moral standards, and intimate details of the woman's life. The agent could initiate the proceedings sending a woman to the Mercer, or assist police efforts to incarcerate her. He had the power to make or break a case for parole, and might exile her to another area. Moreover, the evidence presented by the agent could be little more than hearsay. "There are complaints that she is hanging around the hotel, going into rooms with men . . . we hear that she is in the family way," testified the police chief in one case. The Indian agent supported him, claiming he had spoken with her doctor and discovered she was pregnant.[59]

While the agent's power was never absolute, and might be opposed by band members, the mere awareness of his ability to survey and penalize wrongdoers buttressed his authority. His surveillance was also patriarchal in character, for federal Indian policy to "assimilate and civilize" was developed with the specific image of a downtrodden, sexually loose woman in need of domestic education and moral guidance in mind.[60] Criminal charges provided one means for agents to enforce moral standards, and both alcohol consumption and sexual immorality were policed this way.[61] In 1930, for instance, a woman spent a month in a northern Ontario jail after the agent, the RCMP, and the chief charged her with "act[ing] in a profligate manner." Women were the special focus of control, but men could be targeted as well. In one case a woman charged with sexual immorality was given a suspended sentence because she was ill and had a child, while her male "accomplice" in immorality spent a month in jail.[62]

State policies encouraging regulation were buttressed by both social-work and psychiatric discourses that claimed to offer expert knowledge of the Native woman's psyche and character. Inclined to see Natives as weak, impassive, and possibly immoral, social workers and psychiatrists by the 1940s were beginning to attribute such weaknesses to environmental or social conditioning rather than racial traits.[63] Ironically, women sometimes found more sympathy from the magistrates who sentenced them than from the psychiatrists who became increasingly influential after World War II: "She has no one to look after her, is badly in need of care and treatment for alcoholism," pleaded one magistrate in his sentencing report.[64] Psychiatrists who examined women's suitability for "clinic" (alcohol) treatment were seldom so supportive. Repeatedly, a woman's silence, a means of coping with alien surroundings (and, in some cases, related to language differences), was read negatively as evidence of a passive personality. It is also revealing that a psychiatrist's assessment denoting "low intelligence" often came immediately after a statement describing the woman as Native, a psychological slip of some consequence.[65] These doctors "saw" only one Native personality type: "taciturn"; "the usual Indian reserve"; "finds it difficult to verbalize as do most of our Indians"; "incoherent and withdrawn" were opinions frequently stated.[66]

There is no evidence that these experts read any of the contemporary anthropological literature, especially on the Ojibwa women who dominated at the Mercer. Irving Hallowell, for instance, argued in the 1940s that culture shaped personality structure and that the Ojibwa were highly reserved emotionally, avoiding direct confrontation or anger with others; this restraint, he argued, was a product of their hunting and gathering way of life, their spiritual beliefs, and their social organization.[67] Contemporary participant observation has suggested similar conclusions. In both Ojibwa and Iroquois cultures, it is often considered wrong to "speak of your hurts and angers . . . to indulge your private emotions." Once past, the past should "be buried and forgotten"; moreover, faced with the unfamiliar, "conservation withdrawal" is the best survival tactic: you must "step back into yourself and conserve your physical and psychic energy."[68]

Medical and social work experts at the Mercer had a different measuring stick. What was crucial in their world view, especially by the 1950s, was an embrace of the "confessional" mode, introspection, a critical understanding of one's family background as the "cause" of addiction, and a professed desire to change one's inner self. Native women in the Mercer almost invariably refused to embrace this therapeutic model. Furthermore, their honesty about their drinking simply confounded the psychiatrist. A woman who had both her children taken away because of her drinking and "had never coped with this" spoke doubtfully about whether she could change. "She might use antabuse," he noted, but then was shocked by her final admission: "but she still laughs and says she will go on a big spree when she gets out of here." "She regards her drinking as a feature of her personality which is unfortunate but unchangeable . . . not motivated to improve, nothing to do to help her when she is discharged," he concluded, as fatalistic as he claimed the women were.[69]

This cultural gap was conversely apparent in Native women's reactions to their incarcerations. Women's silences — perhaps a form of resistance — make it difficult to judge their responses to incarceration. Displaying a level of realism, honesty, acceptance, and stoicism that the authorities interpreted as passive fatalism, Native women often openly admitted to the charge against them, making no excuses. "She freely admits neglect of [her children] and does not make any further comment," a psychiatrist mused; he was even more baffled by a woman's "extraordinary honesty about her unwillingness to work."[70] Several contemporary legal workers noted that honesty about the "crime" and guilty pleas, rather than any demand for the system to prove one guilty, distinguished the Ojibwa value system.

Not all women accepted their fate easily; the removal of children was agonizing for some, and a minority sent to the Mercer objected to their punishment. Most commonly it was younger women who tried to run away, or who argued or fought with the matrons. When one "fractious" young woman, already a fugitive from an industrial school and a training school, ended up at the Mercer, she attempted a third escape to her home near Fort William. The more rebellious Aboriginal women sometimes came to the Mercer because they had caused trouble elsewhere, as with the teen accused of trying to "start a riot" at the Galt Training School for Girls. There were women who 'denied everything" and argued with the psychiatrist that they did not belong in a reformatory. More often, they resisted by resorting to silence, by answering 'no' to every question posed by the psychiatrist, or rejecting the "help" they proffered: "on the whole seems to be able to run her own show the way she wants it," the doctor commented on a Mohawk woman in the Mercer for one month for alcohol problems. She did not want his advice or any contact with the other Native women, whom she disdainfully dismissed as "primitive Ojibwas."[71]

Families also had mixed responses to women's sentences, but there were some clear distinctions between what families and the authorities condemned as wrong. In contrast to the authorities, many Native families rejected the idea that behaviour caused by alcohol was a crime, a perception that remains strong in many Aboriginal communities today.[72] "I do not believe that my wife should be punished for drinking," wrote one distressed husband; "some soldiers bought the whisky to our reserve and I thought they were our friends." A father and daughter from southern Ontario appeared one day at the Mercer office, asking for the release of the mother. They appealed to the authorities by saying she could get employment in the tobacco fields, and added that there was no reason to keep someone just because of occasional disturbances while drunk: "She is fine unless under the influence of alcohol," they implored, to no effect. Like some white working-class families, relatives also demanded the woman's release so she could resume her familial duties: "We are old and can't look after [our daughter's] two children, as well as her sister's 15 year old," one elderly couple pleaded.[73]

Most Native families and communities failed to see drinking as a crime, and they also had difficulty understanding why incarceration was the punishment. In more isolated Ojibwa communities, the chief and council, or sometimes elders, had imposed different sanctions for wrongdoing than those imposed by the Euro-Canadian justice system. Social control was effected through elders' lectures about good behaviour, connected to spiritual instruction, or through fear of gossip or of the "bad medicine" of supernatural retribution. If a person broke communal codes, shaming and confession were crucial to rehabilitation; indeed, when the confession was public, the "transgression" was washed away.[74] Only in extreme cases was banishment of the individual considered the answer.[75] Similarly, in Iroquois societies, ostracism, ridicule, or prohibitions on becoming a future leader were all used to control behaviour, admittedly an easier prospect in smaller, tightly knit communities in which the clan system also discouraged conflicts.[76]

Many observers claimed that these traditional mechanisms of social control were breaking down in Aboriginal communities at this time owing to the social stresses on reserve life and the debilitating effects of colonialism. Moreover, there is little historical evidence of the gendered applications of sanction,[77] punishment, and social control, or on the way in which traditional values did, or did not, follow women and men into the city. While recognizing the dangers of essentializing or romanticizing "traditional" Aboriginal social control, the cultural gaps between Aboriginal and Euro-Canadian notions of wrongdoing and sanction still remain clear.

On some occasions, local attempts by the families or communities to alter women's behaviour were combined with the strategies of the Euro-Canadian justice system. Maria's case is a good example. Charged repeatedly with intoxication and with neglect of her children, Maria lost them to various institutions: three children were sent to a residential school, one was in CAS care, and one was in the sanatorium. The Indian agent complained to the crown attorney that she resumed drinking as soon as she was released. The chief on the reserve wanted to help her and tried to work out a plan for her rehabilitation, promising the return of her children and a house on the reserve if she could refrain from drinking for two months. Her failure to meet his conditions may speak not only to her addiction but to the desolation she still felt about losing her children.[78]

Seldom did the women, their families, or the communities offer a straightforward political critique of the discriminatory nature of the justice system: that is, Natives' lack of access to legal counsel; their limited cultural understanding of the courts' alien legal concepts and rituals; language and translation difficulties; and racist treatment by police or legal officials. Nonetheless, a pattern of estrangement was visible. In a rare case, one mother articulated her anger against what she justly perceived to be overly harsh treatment of her daughter: "I dearly love my daughter, I want my grandson to come home here. This is our country, especially Canada, and there is a lot more I could say. [If a] woman anywhere in this country committed murder they would get out free, but my daughter gets two years for less crime [a drunk charge]."[79]

There is also some evidence of Native support for the incarceration of women. Histories of juvenile delinquency have indicated similar patterns of working-class parents seeking state help for their unmanageable daughters.[80] But given the evidence of Native alienation from the criminal justice system, how do we explain the fact that some families and communities accepted its premises and punishments, even encouraging the removal of relatives or acquaintances by the authorities? A few women claimed they "wanted to go to the reformatory," as they were overwhelmed by addiction problems, venereal disease, or were pregnant and had nowhere to go. As one pregnant twenty-two-year-old convicted of prostitution discovered, her stepmother had informed the authorities that she "wishes her daughter to stay in for a full term as she will not listen to advice." "I believe she pleaded guilty just to have a place to go during her confinement," concluded the magistrate. The most common pattern was one of family and community pressure to incarcerate the woman. In one southern Ontario community, a woman called the Indian agent to tell where her sister had hidden stolen goods, thus incriminating her. The sister responded by "threatening to burn her house down," which did not do her case any good. In other cases, parents participated in the criminalization of daughters for immorality or incorrigibility: in one urbanized family, the father "said he wanted [his daughter] sent to Training School as he could do nothing with her."[81]

Families sometimes felt a sense of shame at a woman's conflicts with the law — this was all the more difficult on reserves where each family's history was well known — and thus encouraged her removal. One Ojibwa woman on a reserve told the CAS that "she did not want anything to do with her sister, as she [engages in prostitution] and sends men to her sister who does not want this kind of life." "She has been refused care by the people of her own community, so we had to take the children," a social worker's report concluded. Some relatives indicated to probation officers that they would not take the women back into the family after incarceration. One trapper from the North wrote a letter to the Mercer, relaying similar sentiments: he "did not want his [wife] to return," as he could not deal with her drinking and would rather "support his children on his own."[82]

Reserve communities sometimes discussed these problems together, with or without the Indian agent, then asked for legal intervention. More than one community signed letters or petitions about moral problems they perceived in their midst. One petition included signatures from the woman's grandparents, cousins, aunts, and uncles, who said, "in the interests of morality on the Reserve and of the accused, she should be sent to the Mercer Reformatory." The fact that an uncle stood with her in court "as a Friend," as well as the wording of the petition, suggests that the Indian agent had a role in the petition, and that her relatives had been persuaded that this "banishment" would help her and restore peace on the Reserve.[83]

In cases like this one, customary community controls and Euro-Canadian law are intertwined,[84] though the latter clearly assumed more power. Why, then, was Euro-Canadian legal regulation accepted, perhaps increasingly so, during this time period?[85] First, not all these women were reserve and/or treaty Indians. Many had become urban dwellers; some were of mixed-race descent. Moreover, not all women came from reserves where traditional forms of justice were fully preserved; the continuance of customary controls depended on the power of the Indian agent and local police, the geographical isolation and economic and social equilibrium of the reserve, and the political will of its occupants to vigorously defend their right to rule themselves.[86] Second, Christian schools and missions had made substantial inroads in Native communities and, along with the agents, were trying to use their power to alter social and sexual relations and impose "superior" Anglo/white values.[87] As communities were increasingly influenced by the Euro-Canadian justice system and by attempts to acculturate them, they may have acquiesced to some of the premises of this governing system.[88] However disassociating the influence of the Euro-Canadian criminal justice system was, it came to exert some ideological sway over communities, a process of hegemony that was unavoidable given the colonial imbalance of power and the ongoing assault on Native societies by those claiming cultural superiority.

Furthermore, by the twentieth century, not all the suppositions of Canadian law, such as the condemnation of certain behaviours, were unfamiliar to Native value systems. The censure of violence, the fear of disruptive alcoholic behaviour, and the "promiscuity" of women (and sometimes men) could be viewed negatively by Aboriginal communities — even if their notions of sanction were different. Domestic violence, according to some anthropologists, was absent in many Native cultures until the influence of European contact, but it was condemned after that. Even though alcohol "abuse" was not seen as criminal, it was seen as a problem; overwhelmed by the tragic toll it was taking on sisters, daughters, and mothers, families might agree to banish the person, perhaps hoping that the reformatory would actually reform. Faced with few options, families and communities used legal options to deal with problems undermining their communities, and their efforts must be seen in the context of the colonial marginality and social dislocation creating these social strains.

In many cases of internal condemnation and control, crimes of sexual immorality occasioned the most concerted opposition from the community. Historians and anthropologists agree that, at first contact, there was more sexual autonomy for Native women, more egalitarian practices of marriage and divorce, and more acceptance of illegitimate children within many Aboriginal cultures.[89] But these traditions were challenged by European values, and, by the early twentieth century, observers in both Iroquois and Ojibwa communities stressed the great importance placed on lifelong marriage, as well as disapproval of some kinds of sexual behaviour.[90] Ethnographic texts written from the 1930s to the 1950s pointed to the "mixture of conflicting beliefs,"[91] both European and Native, in Aboriginal cultures, especially in relation to marital and sexual norms, and in views of chastity and adultery. One highly controversial text claimed that northern Ojibwa women were increasingly subject to violence as their social importance and sexual autonomy were undermined within the community.[92]

Anthropological reports and oral traditions in the mid-twentieth century also indicate that chiefs acted as custodians of morality, discouraging women from leaving their husbands for new partners, and deterring the practice of serial monogamy if they felt it undermined the stability of the community. "Yes, the Indian Agent on the reserve did try to make people stick to their marriages, [but] so did the chief and council," remembers one northern Ojibwa woman.[93] Although her observation referred to the sexual regulation of men and women, other evidence suggests that sexual/ social control was likely to focus more stringently on women: the political and social effects of colonialism on gender relations had provided male leaders with access to such power and furnished ideological encouragement for the patriarchal control of women's sexuality.

All this evidence points to a complicated situation in which dominant culture, bent on "civilizing" Aboriginal peoples with the two-headed bludgeon of religion and the law, undermined older patterns of community social control. In this process, some overlapping proscribed behaviours became easier for the Canadian authorities to punish, for they could co-opt Native concerns and customary practices, drawing on the support of Native leaders. Customary law in Aboriginal communities was a dynamic 'process,' shaped by the political, economic, and cultural influences and conflicts upon and within Aboriginal life.[94] And the latter cannot be ignored: as Tina Loo has argued, "some native peoples also brokered" the extension of Euro-Canadian law, using both the Indian Act and the Criminal Code as means of asserting or reasserting power and control within their own communities, or sometimes as means of coping with the effects of colonialism.[95]

This complicated process of domination, conflict, and overlap in notions of crime and justice was bound to work itself out in both racialized and gendered ways, to the detriment of Native women. Whatever the overlap in values, the ongoing process of colonialism — encompassing the loss of economic security, increased familial instability, and the denigration of Native culture as inferior — meant that the Euro-Canadian "solution," incarceration, triumphed over more traditional Native community controls. Moreover, the Euro-Canadian standards applied by the Indian agent were decidedly patriarchal, propping up an image of the ideal family that was far from the Native reality of life, condemning women for sexual behaviour that was more acceptable for men, and marginalizing women who could lose their Indian status[96] and who had fewer economic resources outside the family and community to support themselves.

In the mid-twentieth century, particularly after 1945, contemporary patterns of overincarceration of Native women became apparent at the

Ontario Reformatory for Women. The majority of First Nations women sent to the Mercer were criminalized on the premise of moral and public order infractions linked to alcohol, or for prostitution, venereal disease, or child neglect charges. Like other women sent to the reformatory, the lives of these Aboriginal women were framed by economic marginality, family dissolution, violence, and sometimes previous institutionalization. The background of Aboriginal women, however, was also marked by high levels of ill health and intense poverty, and their experience of the criminal justice system was profoundly shaped by their own cultural alienation and by the authorities' perceptions of their cultural and racial deficiencies. Three crucial, interconnected factors shaped the emerging process of overincarceration: the material and social dislocation precipitated by colonialism, the gender and race paternalism of court and penal personnel, and the related cultural gap between Native and Euro-Canadian value systems, articulating very different notions of crime and punishment.

Unlike the women housed in local jails who were seen as hopeless repeaters, women sent to the Mercer were supposedly targeted for rehabilitation. Yet before they even entered the Mercer's towered gate, Aboriginal women were exposed to extra layers of surveillance and suspicion, and their reformation was presumed to be unlikely. Women who came from reserves were subject to the authoritarian powers of the Indian agent and the Indian Act, designed to assimilate Native peoples to the more "progressive" patriarchal, Christian, Euro-Canadian culture. If the Aboriginal woman could not be remade in a new image, she would be chastised, hidden, or punished. The process of censuring Native women demarcated colonial and racial power as well as gender hierarchies; legal and moral regulation through incarceration was in turn an integral component of colonialism.[97]

Before World War II, Native women were assessed within legal, medical, and social work discourses that assumed that the environmental, even hereditary legacy of their "primitive" origins ran deep. As psychiatry became more influential in the 1950s, Native women were no less disadvantaged: the silences that doctors faulted them for became part of the ongoing racist construction of Native women as lower in moral stature and insight than white women. In neither era did the sentencing or the "helping" authorities really see the structural crises faced by

Native women and communities; alcoholism, for example, was still interpreted as a loss of self-control, rather than as a "symptom of cultural devastation, powerlessness, marginality, [also acting] to precipitate those conditions."[98]

The experiences of these women, incarcerated for moral or public-order crimes involving alcohol, indicates the extent to which the very definition of crime is a contested question of political consequence: even the statistics showing the increasing incarceration of Native women reflected interpretations of what the dominant social groups thought was a crime, not what Aboriginal groups believed was wrong. This cultural gap underscores the extent to which the moral regulation of First Nations women through incarceration was first and foremost a "legitimated practice of moral-political control, linked to conflicts and power relations, based on class, gender and race."[99]

While women's actual voices, feelings, and responses are difficult to locate within this regulatory process, the general pattern of Aboriginal alienation from Euro-Canadian justice — particularly for more isolated communities unused to Canadian policing — is a repeated theme in women's stories. However, customary Aboriginal practices could be refashioned and used by Canadian authorities, so much so that Native communities and families might also use the legal system to discipline their own. Native acceptance of Canadian law was one consequence of ongoing attempts to assimilate Aboriginal people, but it was not a simple reflection of European dominance. It also revealed attempts to cope with the negative effects of social change that were devastating individuals and families: in the process of struggling to adjust to the dislocations of colonialism, communities sometimes abetted the incarceration of Native women.

Native women seldom found solace or aid in the reformatory and, tragically, many returned to prison repeatedly. First Nations women often responded to their estrangement from the law and the reformatory with silence and stoicism — perhaps in itself a subtle form of noncompliance — though a very few, along with their families, voiced unequivocal renunciations of this system, their voices a preview to the current sustained critique of the inadequacy of Euro-Canadian 'justice' for Aboriginal peoples.

Notes

I want to thank Peter Kulchyski, Bryan Palmer, and Jean Manore for their comments on an earlier version of this paper.

1   Native women are disproportionately represented in federal prisons — an area not dealt with in this article. There are also considerable regional variations in overincarceration. In Ontario, 1980s' statistics showed Native people to be about 2 percent of the population, while Native women comprised 16 percent of provincial admission to correctional institutions; in the North, local arrest rates were far higher. See Ontario, Ontario Advisory Council on Women's Issues, *Native Women and the Law* (Toronto, 1989); Carol LaPrairie, "Selected Criminal Justice and Socio-Economic Data on Native Women," *Canadian Journal of Criminology* 26, no. 4 (1984): 161–69; Canada, Royal Commission on Aboriginal Peoples, *Aboriginal Peoples and the Justice System: Report of the National Round Table on Aboriginal Justice* (Ottawa, 1993); Canada, Law Reform Commission, *Report on Aboriginal Peoples and Criminal Justice* (Ottawa, 1991); Manitoba, *Report of the Aboriginal Justice Inquiry of Manitoba* (Winnipeg, 1991).

2   Anonymous, quoted in Canada, Correctional Services, *Creating Choices: The Report of the Task Force on Federally Sentenced Women* (April 1990), 9.

3   Bradford Morse, "Aboriginal Peoples, the Law and Justice," in *Aboriginal Peoples and Canadian Criminal Justice,* ed. Robert Silverman and Marianne Nielsen (Toronto: Butterworths, 1992), 56. In Manitoba it is surmised that Native inmates began to predominate after the Second World War. Manitoba, *Report of the Aboriginal Justice Inquiry,* 1: 87; and John Milloy, "A Partnership of Races: Indian, White, Cross-Cultural Relations in Criminal Justice in Manitoba, 1670–1949," paper for the Public Inquiry into the Administration of Justice for Native Peoples of Manitoba.

4   The Mercer Reformatory for Women was used because it drew inmates from across the province for a variety of common 'female' crimes. Few women at this time were sent to the federal penitentiary. City and county jail registers sometimes noted race, but a statistical study of all Ontario's city and county registers has yet to be undertaken.

5   Under "complexion," the Mercer register noted if an inmate was "Indian" or "negress." The designation Indian included Indian and Métis, treaty and non-treaty women. Statistics taken from the Mercer register are also problematic because women might be charged with one crime but incarcerated for other reasons as well. Women sometimes gave different names and altered their ages. Because of the various problems with statistics, the registers are used primarily to suggest some overall trends.

6   The problems and possibilities of using such case files are explored in Linda
Gordon, *Heroes of Their Own Lives: The Politics and History of Family Violence* (Boston:
Viking, 1988), 13–17; Steven Noll, "Patient Records as Historical Stories: The Case
of the Caswell Training School," *Bulletin of the History of Medicine* 69 (1994): 411–28;
Regina Kunzel, *Fallen Women, Problem Girls: Unmarried Mothers and the Professional-
ization of Social Work, 1890–1945* (New Haven: Yale University Press, 1993), 5–6.

7   Colin Sumner, "Re-thinking Deviance: Towards a Sociology of Censure," in
Feminist Perspectives in Criminology, ed. Loraine Gelsthorpe and Allison Morris
(Philadelphia: Milton Keynes, 1990), and "Foucault, Gender and the Censure
of Deviance," in Sumner's edited collection, *Censure, Politics and Criminal Justice*
(Philadelphia: Milton Keynes, 1990).

8   Martin Chanock, *Law, Custom and Social Order: The Colonial Experience in Malawi
and Zambia* (Cambridge: Cambridge University Press, 1985), 4.

9   Many studies of colonialism have focused on the eighteenth and nineteenth
centuries, especially on kin and productive relations; fewer carry the story into
the twentieth century. Karen Anderson, *Chain Her by One Foot: The Subjugation of
Women in Seventeenth-Century New France* (New York: Routledge, 1991); Sylvia Van
Kirk, *Many Tender Ties: Women in Fur Trade Society* (Winnipeg: Watson and Dw-
yer, 1979); Jennifer Brown, *Strangers in Blood: Fur Trade Company Families in Indian
Country* (Vancouver: University of British Columbia Press, 1980); Carol Devens,
Countering Colonization: Native American Women and Great Lakes Missions, 1630–1900
(Berkeley: University of California Press, 1992); Eleanor Leacock, "Montagnais
Women and the Jesuit Program for Colonization," in her edited collection,
Myths of Male Dominance (New York: Monthly Review Press, 1981), 43–62; Carol
Cooper, "Native Women of the Northern Pacific Coast: An Historical Perspec-
tive, 1830–1900," *Journal of Canadian Studies* 27, no. 4 (1992–93): 44–75; Jo-Anne
Fiske, "Colonization and the Decline of Women's Status: The Tsimshian Case,"
Feminist Studies 17, no. 3 (1991): 509–36. On Iroquois women, see Judith Brown,
"Economic Organization and the Position of Women Among the Iroquois," *Eth-
nohistory* 17 (1970): 151–67; Sally Roesch Wagner, "The Iroquois Confederacy: A
Native American Model for Non-sexist Men," in *Iroquois Women: An Anthology,* ed.
William Spittal (Ohsweken: Irocrafts, 1990), 217–22; Elizabeth Tooker, "Women
in Iroquois Society," in *Iroquois Women,* ed. Spittal, 199–216. On Ojibwa women,
see Patricia Buffalohead, "Farmers, Warriors, Traders: A Fresh Look at Ojibwa
Women," *Minnesota History* 48 (1983): 236–44. For interrogation of the dominant emphasis on the decline of women's status, see Jo-Anne Fiske, "Fishing
Is Women's Business: Changing Economic Roles of Carrier Women and Men,"
in *Native Peoples, Native Lands: Canadian Inuit, Indians and Metis,* ed. Bruce Cox (Ottawa: Carleton University Press, 1987), 186–98; Nancy Shoemaker, "The Rise or
Fall of Iroquois Women," *Journal of Women's History* 2 (1991): 39–57.

10 Colin Sumner, "Crime, Justice and Underdevelopment: Beyond Modernization
Theory," in *Crime, Justice and Underdevelopment,* ed. Colin Sumner (London: Heine-
mann, 1982), quotation at 9.

11 The Aboriginal world view is fundamentally different in terms of "culture, tradition, spirituality": Patricia Monture-Okanee, "Reclaiming Justice: Aboriginal Women and Justice Initiatives in the 1990s," in Law Reform Commission, *Report on Aboriginal Peoples and Criminal Justice*, 112.

12 Some women came in with sentences of less than three months.

13 I examined 598 files for basic information on the charge, conviction, age, and place of birth, but many files were incomplete beyond this point, so I concentrated on a core of 300 files as the basis of my analysis.

14 The numbers for the decades are as follows: 39 in the 1920s, 80 in the 1930s, 109 in the 1940s, and 370 in the 1950s. Population statistics taken from Census of Canada, 1931, vol. 2, table 31, show Ontario Indians as 0.9 percent of the total population; Census of Canada, 1941, vol. 1, table 11, lists Indians as 0.8 percent of the total; Census of Canada, 1951, vol. 2, table 32, also shows 0.8 percent.

15 A similar trend took place at the Ontario Training School for Girls: in the 1930s, seven "Indian" admissions; in the 1940s, eight admissions, and in the 1950s, fifty-eight admissions. These statistics are drawn from Ontario, *Annual Report of the Ontario Training Schools*, 1933–59.

16 This statement is based on an analysis of the Kenora jail registers, 1920–59. In the 1920s, Indian and half-breed women were about 13 percent of all admissions; in the 1930s, 16 percent; in the 1940s, 50 percent (with the last three years of the decade the most crucial for increases); and in the 1950s, 76 percent. While most liquor charges at the Mercer came under the Liquor Control Act, the Kenora arrests showed a greater number of women arrested for breach of the Indian Act.

17 Ontario, *Annual Report of the Inspector of Prisons and Public Charities*, 1920–60.

18 Although FRA convictions for Native women remained a small proportion (about 5%) of overall incarcerations from 1920 to 1960, the act was used more in the later period. On the FRA, see Joan Sangster, "Incarcerating 'Bad Girls': Sexual Regulation Through the Female Refuges Act in Ontario, 1920–1945," *Journal of the History of Sexuality* 7, no. 2 (1996): 239–75.

19 By "corrupting," I'm referring to charges of contributing to juvenile delinquency.

20 Ontario Archives, Department of Corrections (RG 20), Mercer Reformatory Records (hereafter, OA, Mercer) case file 9869, 1940s.

21 OA, Mercer case file 10328, 1940s; case file 8966, 1940s; case file 15508, 1950s.

22 In the interwar period, recidivists were sent to local jails, and those considered "reformable" to the Mercer, but by the late 1940s this distinction was breaking down, especially for Native offenders. See Wendy Ruemper, "Formal and Informal Social Control of Incarcerated Women in Ontario, 1857–31" (Ph.D. diss., University of Toronto, 1994), 219–20.

23 Changes to the Indian Act in 1951 allowed provinces to legalize the sale and possession of intoxicants (previously illegal) to Indians off the reserve: Sharon Venne, ed., *Indian Acts and Amendments, 1865–75* (Saskatoon: University of Saskatchewan Native Law Centre, 1981), 344–45. However, this change made little difference to Native women in the Mercer, who were usually charged, throughout this whole period, under the provincial liquor laws. Local law enforcement may have used the Indian Act more. See Ontario, *Annual Report of the Inspector of Prisons and Public Charities*, 1920–60.

24 OA Mercer case file 12128, 1940s (the first charge was in the late 1930s). For the initial charge, the man was convicted of selling liquor and received a jail sentence.

25 Pamela White, "Restructuring the Domestic Sphere — Prairie Indian Women on Reserves: Image, Ideology and State Policy, 1880–1930" (Ph.D. diss., McGill University, 1987), 220. See also George Wherrett, *The Miracle of Empty Beds: A History of Tuberculosis in Canada* (Toronto: University of Toronto Press, 1977), chap. 7.

26 OA, Mercer case file 15510, 1950s; case file 16665, 1950s.

27 I recognize that these women came from different First Nations, but the records do not reveal their specific Aboriginal identity. Authorities claimed that women from Ojibwa groups dominated, though there were clearly some Iroquois and Cree women as well.

28 In other cases, the conviction takes place in a northern city — for example, Kenora or Thunder Bay — but the place of origin is a more isolated reserve or town.

29 Some scholars argue that "economic marginalization" was most noticeable in the twentieth century, especially after 1945. See Vic Satzewich and Terry Wotherspoon, *First Nations: Race, Class and Gender Relations* (Toronto: Nelson, 1993), 49–50. On the (contrasting) case of the late nineteenth century, see R.C. Macleod and Heather Rollason, "'Restrain the Lawless Savage': Native Defendants in the Criminal Courts of the North West Territories," *Journal of Historical Sociology* 10, no. 2 (1997): 157–83.

30 Robin Brownlie, "A Fatherly Eye: Two Indian Agents in Georgian Bay, 1918–39" (Ph.D. diss., University of Toronto, 1996), 52, 418.

31 R.W. Dunning, *Social and Economic Change Among the Northern Ojibwa* (Toronto: University of Toronto Press, 1959), chap. 7.

32 David Stymeist, *Ethnics and Indians: Social Relations in a Northwestern Ontario Town* (Toronto: Peter Martin, 1971).

33 Anestasia Shkilnyk, *A Poison Stronger than Love: The Destruction of an Ojibwa Community* (New Haven: Yale University Press, 1985).

34 "It seems unlikely that before 1950 more than one-third of Inuit and status Indian children were in residential school." J.R. Miller, *Shingwauk's Vision: A History of Native Residential Schools* (Toronto: University of Toronto Press, 1996), 411. On gender, see *Shingwauk's Vision*, chap. 8, and Jo-Anne Fiske, "Gender and the Paradox of Residential Education in Carrier Society," in Jane Gaskell and Arlene Tigar McLaren, eds., *Women and Education* (Calgary: Detselig, 1991), 131–46.

35 OA, Mercer case file 9332, 1930s.

36 Assembly of First Nations, *Breaking the Silence: An Interpretive Study of Residential School Impact and Healing as Illustrated by the Stories of First Nations Individuals* (Ottawa, 1994).

37 The term 'alcoholism' was used at the time in connection with these women, but we don't really know if they were alcoholics, or simply being policed for alcohol use.

38 Craig MacAndrew and Robert Edgerton, *Drunken Comportment: A Social Explanation* (Chicago: Aldine, 1969).

39 Nancy Oestreich Lurie, "The World's Oldest On-going Protest Demonstration: North American Indian Drinking Patterns," *Pacific Historical Review* 40 (1971): 311–33.

40 Some family members testified that the women charged were extremely susceptible to alcohol and became "another person" when intoxicated. OA, Mercer case file 11002. For a more recent book including this view, see Brian Maracle, *Crazywater: Native Voices on Addiction and Recovery* (Toronto: Viking, 1993).

41 OA, Mercer case file 9955, 1940s; and case file 13139, 1950s.

42 Sangster, "Incarcerating 'Bad' Girls," 251.

43 OA, Mercer case file 9955, 1940s; case file 12081, 1950s.

44 Sarah Carter, "Categories and Terrains of Exclusion: Constructing the 'Indian Woman' in the Early Settlement Era in Western Canada," in Joy Parr and Mark Rosenfeld, eds., *Gender and History in Canada* (Toronto: Copp Clark, 1996), 40–41. See also Daniel Francis, *The Imaginary Indian: The Image of the Indian in Canadian Culture* (Vancouver: Arsenal Press, 1992), 122. On an earlier period on the eastern seaboard, see David Smits, "The 'Squaw Drudge': A Prime Index of Savagism," *Ethnohistory* 29, no. 4 (1982): 281–306.

45 Sharon Tiffany and Kathleen Adams, *The Wild Woman: An Inquiry into the Anthropology of an Idea* (Cambridge: Schenkman, 1985).

46 Sangster, "Incarcerating 'Bad' Girls," 257–58.

47 OA, Mercer case file 10978, 1940s; and case file 7393, 1930s.

48 Clauses on prostitution in the Indian Act of 1880 placed more onus on the men encouraging the "use" of Native women in brothels; after 1884, the clauses were more punitive towards Aboriginal women: Constance Backhouse, "Nineteenth-Century Prostitution Law: Reflection of a Discriminatory Society," *Social History/Histoire sociale* 18, no. 36 (1985): 387–423.

49 OA, Mercer case file 9004, 1940s; case file 15489, 1950s.

50 For contemporary parallels, see John Hagan, "Towards a Structural Theory of Crime, Race and Gender: The Canadian Case," *Crime and Delinquency* 31, no. 1 (1985): 136.

51 OA, Mercer case file 7644, 1930s; case file 11419, 1950s; case file 8646, 1940s; case file 16461, 1950s.

52 That is, Native unions unsanctified by the church: Miller, *Shingwauk's Vision*, 227.

53 Mary T. Woodward, "Juvenile Delinquency Among Indian Girls" (MA thesis, University of British Columbia, 1949), 2, 21. Similar images of the reserve that stressed a "culture of poverty" can also be seen in the Hawthorn report as late as the 1960s. See H. Hawthorn, *A Survey of Indians of Canada* (Ottawa, 1966), 1: 56–57.

54 OA, Mercer case file 14413, 1950s.

55 For example, those living in a tent in the summer when the family was trapping: OA, Mercer case file 15034, 1950s.

56 OA, Mercer case file 14305, 1950s; case file 14768, 1950s; case file 12984, 1950s.

57 OA, Mercer case file 15455, 1950s; case file 16665, 1950s.

58 OA, Mercer case file 14413, 1950s; case file 14305, 1950s.

59 OA, Mercer case file 9332, 1940s. In this case the magistrate corrected police for offering hearsay evidence, but this criticism was rare.

60 White, "Restructuring the Domestic Sphere," chap. 4.

61 Policies on "immorality" on reserves varied over this period and were not uniformly applied. Agents, however, were supposed to discourage adultery, illegitimacy, and sexual "promiscuity." On the local enforcement of Indian policy in general, see Ken Coates, *Best Left as Indians: Native-White Relations in the Yukon Territory, 1840–1973* (Montreal and Kingston: McGill-Queen's University Press, 1991); Sarah Carter, *Lost Harvests: Prairie Indian Reserve Farmers and Government Policy* (Montreal and Kingston: McGill-Queen's University Press, 1990). On the reservation system, see Brian Titley, *A Narrow Vision: Duncan Campbell Scott and the Administration of Indian Affairs in Canada* (Vancouver: University of British Columbia Press, 1986), and J.R. Miller, *Skyscrapers Hide the Heavens: A History of Indian-White Relations in Canada* (Toronto: University of Toronto Press, 1989).

62 Library and Archives Canada (LAC), RG 10, Indian Affairs Department, vol. 8869, reel C 9744, file 487, 18-6, Report of agent to Ottawa, 18 Sept. 1930; 14 Aug. 1933.

63 "They are backward, but it is more background than Native intelligence to blame": Woodward, "Juvenile Delinquency among Indian Girls," 18.

64 OA, Mercer case file 14176, 1950s. One 1967 inquiry (which included Native members) claimed that some judges were "in general lenient and compassionate," at least more so than the police. See Canadian Corrections Association, *Indians and the Law* (Ottawa, 1967).

65 The comment, "Bright alert and pleasing. Looking only slightly Indian," is yet another example: OA, Mercer case file 16665, 1950s.

66 OA, Mercer case file 14154, 1950s.

67 Irving Hallowell, *Culture and Experience* (Philadelphia: University of Pennsylvania Press, 1955). This collection included earlier articles, published in major psychiatric, sociological, and anthropological journals in the 1940s, such as "Some Psychological Characteristics of the Northeastern Indians" (1946), "Aggression in Saulteaux Society" (1940), and "The Social Function of Anxiety in a Primitive Society" (1941).

68 Rupert Ross, "Leaving Our White Eyes Behind," *Canadian Native Law Reporter* 3 (1989): 3.

69 OA, Mercer case files 15214, 15510, 15505, 1950s.

70 OA, Mercer case file 16664, 1950s.

71 This attitude was partly due to a language difference, but she may also have seen her Iroquois heritage as somewhat superior: OA, Mercer case file 16669, 1950s. For other cases cited in this paragraph, see case file 6369, 1920s; case file 8082, 1930s; case files 9161 and 10396, 1940s.

72 Shkilnyk, *A Poison Stronger than Love*, 25.

73 OA, Mercer case file 8681, 1940s; case file 11096, 1940s; case file 10328, 1940s.

74 Hallowell, *Culture and Experience*, 272. Sickness could be interpreted as a form of punishment for sexual or moral transgressions; private confession could be the cure: Irving Hallowell, "Sin, Sex and Sickness in Saulteaux Belief," *British Journal of Medical Psychology* 18 (1939): 191–97. Contemporary accounts also suggest that the public confession, not incarceration, is considered the "disciplinary end" in some Aboriginal cultures. See Patricia Monture-Angus, *Thunder in My Soul: A Mohawk Woman Speaks* (Halifax: Fernwood, 1995), 238–40; Rupert Ross, *Dancing with a Ghost: Exploring Indian Reality* (Markham: Octopus Books, 1992); Kjikeptin Alex Denny, "Beyond the Marshall Inquiry: An Alternative Mi'kmaq Worldview and Justice System," in Joy Mannette, ed., *Elusive Justice: Beyond the Marshall Inquiry* (Halifax: Fernwood, 1992), 103–8.

75 Hallowell, *Culture and Experience*; Shkilnyk, *A Poison Stronger than Love*; Edward Rogers, *The Round Lake Ojibwa* (Toronto: University of Toronto Press, 1962).

76 Michael Coyle, "Traditional Indian Justice in Ontario: A Role for the Present?" *Osgoode Hall Law Journal* 24, no. 2 (1986): 605–33.

77 Some writers argue that European patriarchal ideals influenced Native cultures. See Teressa Nahanee, "Dancing with a Gorilla: Aboriginal Women, Justice and the Charter," in *Aboriginal Peoples and the Justice System*, 359–82.

78 OA, Mercer case file 11232, 1950s.

79 OA, Mercer case file 15182, 1950s.

80 For example, Mary Odem, *Delinquent Daughters: Protecting and Policing Adolescent Female Sexuality in the United States, 1885–1920* (Chapel Hill: University of North Carolina Press, 1995); Tamara Myers, "The Voluntary Delinquent: Parents, the Montreal Juvenile Delinquents Court and Internment in Early 20th Century Quebec," paper presented to the Social Science History meeting, October 1996.

81 OA, Mercer case file 7715, 1930s; case file 7989, 1930s; case file 8957, 1940s; case file 8480, 1940s.

82 OA, Mercer case file 9318, 1940s; case file 7609, 1930s.

83 It was clear they did not accept her behaviour, which was claimed to be "promiscuous": OA, Mercer case file 7057, 1930s.

84 The relationship between customary law and Euro-Canadian law with regard to sexuality is discussed in Joan Sangster, "Regulation and Resistance: Native Women, Sexuality and the Law, 1920–60," paper presented to the International Development Institute, Dalhousie University, April 1997.

85 Given the paucity of historical studies, it is difficult to ascertain if this practice was increasing, decreasing, or stable. A period characterized by intense social dislocation and/or increased federal regulation might have led to increased use of the Euro-Canadian laws.

86 Some communities, even less isolated ones in the south, had a stronger history of rejecting Euro-Canadian "rule" and maintaining their own sovereignty. A case in point is that of the Six Nations Reserve.

87 Peter Schmalz, *The Ojibwa of Southern Ontario* (Toronto: University of Toronto Press, 1995), 10; Sally Weaver, "The Iroquois: The Consolidation of the Grand River Reserve in the Mid-Nineteenth Century, 1847–1875," in *Aboriginal Ontario: Historical Perspectives on the First Nations*, ed. Edward Rogers and Donald Smith (Toronto: Dundurn, 1994), 182–257.

88 This was true of some elected chiefs who came to ally themselves politically and ideologically with the Indian agent.

89 Many studies examined Iroquois and Huron nations, and fewer looked at Ojibwa nations. Studies of plains and northern peoples indicate different gender roles and possibly asymmetry. See John Milloy, *The Plains Cree: Trade, Diplomacy and War, 1790–1870* (Winnipeg: University of Manitoba Press, 1988); Laura Peers, *The Ojibwa of Western Canada, 1780–1870* (Winnipeg: University of Manitoba Press, 1994); Joan Ryan, *Doing Things the Right Way: Dene Traditional Justice in Lac La Martre, NWT* (Calgary: University of Calgary Press, 1995).

90 Hallowell, *Culture and Experience*, chap. 13, and his "Sex and Sickness in Saulteaux Belief," in Rogers, ed., *The Round Lake Ojibwa*; Weaver, "The Iroquois"; R.W. Dunning, *Social and Economic Change Among the Northern Ojibwa* (Toronto: University of Toronto Press, 1959).

91 Rogers, ed., *The Round Lake Ojibwa*, B47.

92 Ruth Landes, *The Ojibwa Woman* (New York: AMS Press, 1938). Landes described a culture affected by colonization, rather than earlier, "traditional" Ojibwa culture: Devens, *Countering Colonization*, 124–25.

93 Informant quoted in Shkilnyk, *A Poison Stronger than Love*, 89.

94 Monture-Angus uses the concept of Aboriginal justice as a "process" in *Thunder in My Soul*.

95 Tina Loo, "Tonto's Due: Law, Culture, and Colonization in British Columbia," in *Essays in the History of Canadian Law: British Columbia and the Yukon*, ed. Hannar Foster and John McLaren (Toronto: University of Toronto Press, 1995), 129.

96 Women's loss of status because of the Indian Act contributed to their further marginalization: OA, Mercer case files 1432 and 15032, 1950s.

97 For more lengthy discussion of the relationship between sexuality and colonial power, see Ann Stoler, "Making Empire Respectable: The Politics of Race and Sexual Morality in 20th Century Colonial Cultures," *American Ethnologist* 16, no. 4 (1989): 634–60.

98 Shkilnyk, *A Poison Stronger than Love*, 232.

99 Sumner, "Crime, Justice and Underdevelopment: Beyond Modernisation Theory," 10.

CONSTRUCTING THE 'ESKIMO' WIFE
WHITE WOMEN'S TRAVEL WRITING, COLONIALISM, AND THE CANADIAN NORTH, 1940–1960

In her travel narrative describing her trip to Povungnetuk, Baffin Island, in 1946, to become the wife of a Hudson's Bay Company (HBC) trader, Wanda Tolboom recounts her anticipation of her perfect wedding, with bouquet, cake, and ceremony, in the land of ice and snow. There were few couples like us, she noted, who could boast that their wedding was "attended by every white couple within 600 miles."[1] The promotion of these white weddings as romantic 'firsts' in an uncharted, empty land — captured visually in the *Beaver's* photograph of a Pangnirtung wedding — was symbolic of changes in the Arctic in the post-World War II period, denoting an increased influx of white women sojourners in the north, the promotion of new and 'proper' domestic, marital, and consumptive roles linked to the Euro-Canadian presence, and also a cultural erasure of the existing Arctic bride — the Innu woman.

The images of Inuit life in white women's travel narratives published from the 1940s to the 1960s are the subject of this article. Women's sojourning narratives were part of a well-established, popular form of writing extending back to the nineteenth-century settler accounts of life in the 'wilds' of Upper Canada. Women's accounts of the twentieth century Arctic, published within Canada and internationally, offered powerful portrayals of cultural encounter and difference at a critical point in the history of the Canadian North. We need to ask what the "reciprocal relationship" between the "political and textual practices"[2] of colonialism was in this travel literature: what were the likely readings, and thus political and social consequences, of the 'knowledge' circulated in women's travel narratives? Even if the images of the Inuit bore little resemblance to the identity of the Inuit themselves, their potential power as an arbiter of public opinion was important, particularly because they were published as the Canadian state was extending its control over the Arctic, as Canadian society revealed a renewed, popular fascination with the 'North.'[3] These sojourners' portraits of Inuit life,[4] consumed as authentic accounts of exotic peoples, thus created the cultural landscape on which political and economic decisions could be rationalized.

Sojourners' renditions of their encounters with the Inuit of the eastern Arctic stressed themes of racial and cultural difference, often arguing for understanding and tolerance between whites and Indigenous peoples. Yet this cultural relativism could also operate as a form of "anti-conquest,"[5] articulating liberal tolerance while nonetheless reaffirming Euro-Canadian cultural and social hegemony. Writers employed a variety of techniques of colonial discourse, surveying, classifying, sometimes even idealizing their Inuit neighbours.[6] Contemplating the strange behaviour of the 'other' — the Eskimo — sojourners' accounts ultimately suggested dichotomized images of civilized and primitive, modern and premodern. As such, they became part of Canada's distinct history of internal colonialism, sustaining unequal relations of gender, race, and class, sanctioning a story of the inevitability of white settlement coupled with the transformation/displacement of more 'primitive' Aboriginal ways.

By illuminating the dominant constructions of the imaginary Inuit North, we can also uncover prevailing cultural images of the postwar 'south,' however overly simplistic that term may be, for colonial visions often imagined the metropolis as the "antithesis of the colony."[7] At the time, most Canadians presumed that peace, order, and progress moved in one direction — northward — but in fact, a dialectical relationship was created through this image: by constructing the Inuit north as primitive and untouched, the predominantly Euro-Canadian south became the very epitome of progress and development. Postwar images of Canada's economic progress, its embrace of modernity, its celebration of consumption, were also the mirror image of the Eskimo North, the land, we learned in the incredulous language of our school texts, where people still lived in igloos and rode on dogsleds.

Gender, Race, and Colonialism in Canada's North

Looking primarily at women's narratives foregrounds the question posed in recent writing on women, travel, and imperialism: what was the role, rationale, and meaning of white women's participation in colonial ventures, their "investment in the racial hierarchies of colonialism"?[8] The risk in over-valorizing a singular binary of race or colonialism within this query, however, may be the erasure of other axes of power, such as class, age, and gender, thus eclipsing the complexities of gender relations as they were lived out in colonial contexts. Women's travel accounts were to some extent shaped by their gender, and they are useful texts precisely because women were especially curious about Inuit women, their work, and their family life. At the same time, women's responses were shaped by age, race, and social position. For instance, although white women sojourning in the North were less likely to adopt the masculine persona of the "bold hero adventurer,"[9] their narratives sometimes overlapped with those of male northern travellers, revealing a colonial, superior surveillance of Inuit ways.

That superiority has much to do with 'orientalist' ways of seeing. The white person's Inuit was manufactured using discursive strategies such as disregarding, essentializing, and generalizing about their cultures; as a consequence, their subject position was erased, and they remained curious objects of colonial scrutiny, often counterpoints to whites' self-portrayal as modern, rational, progressive, and scientifically superior. Hugh Brody put it well: the "Eskimo are seen by whites *only as* Eskimo," never as individuals. Drawing on stock, repeated stories, whites construct tales depicting the true, original essence in all Eskimo people, often doing so by pointing to the bizarre in their culture. "They are *illustrations*."[10] Orientalism was also gendered. White women played an active role in constructing orientalist discourses through cultural forms such as travel writing, while Aboriginal, non-white women were often perceived as sexualized, rendered passive, the objects of masculine as well as colonial fantasy and conquest.

One inherent problem with our focus on colonial *representations* is the way in which we can lose sight of the *subjective* position and experiences of Inuit men and women, ironically making them, again, the objects of our inquiry, rather than active subjects. I offer no definitive solution to this conundrum, though we can also read these accounts against the grain, paying attention to the silences and subtle articulations of displeasure or disagreement expressed by the Inuit, an indication that sojourners' views were not shared by the Inuit themselves.

Moreover, our explorations of the cultural 'contact zone' of colonialism should not ignore the historically specific, economically and socially structured inequalities of colonialism. An analysis of travel narratives must also *historicize*, linking them to the prevailing politics, social relations, state practices, and labour regimes.[11] Most eastern Arctic Inuit communities at this time were facing a rapidly changing social and economic context, shaped not only by continuing missionization but also by the changing intentions of capital (not limited to the Hudson's Bay Company) and of the Canadian state. The accounts discussed here were published precisely as the North was being invoked by political visionaries and economic leaders as Canada's last frontier to be developed, and as the government strove to reassert Canadian sovereignty/property rights in the paranoid atmosphere of Cold War international politics.[12] In the eastern Arctic especially, the Inuit economy was in precarious shape due in part to drastic fluctuations in the traditional fur trade economy.

By the later 1950s, the state abandoned hope that 'benign neglect' would allow traditional economies to survive; its interventionist approach now attempted to integrate the Inuit into the dominant economic order and a wage economy, creating new services for the Inuit by centralizing and relocating them. This strategy, shaped by their penchant for economy as well as paternalism, inevitably undermined existing social, cultural, and economic links between individuals, families, and communities, the most infamous of which was a coerced, highly contentious relocation of some Inuit to the high Arctic.[13] The provision of new services was imagined by the state as an aid to the Inuit's assimilation into the 'equal citizenship' of the welfare state, and they were encouraged by experts like anthropologist Diamond Jenness, who portrayed the Inuit as a primitive group, unintentionally undermined by the forces of modernity, now in need of "wise" federal policies reflecting Ottawa's "moral responsibility for its Inuit."[14] In the midst of these changes, portrayals of the Inuit as stubborn adherents to an premodern culture could only reinforce existing power relations, perpetuating Canada's distinctive brand of internal colonialism, which involved not only 'geographical incursion' but also the *ideological* construction of a hierarchy of white progress, culture, and history.[15]

Impressions of an Alien Environment

White women's travel accounts varied considerably in style. Some used conventions of the autobiography and the exploration narrative; others utilized anecdote, irony and 'humour'; one author recounted immense scientific and environmental data; and some were more openly pedagogical in nature.[16] Commonalities were nonetheless evident. Most women stressed that they were anomalies in a land inhabited by few whites: "I was [a] museum curiosity, remembered Wanda Tolboom of her arrival, "fingered by old women."[17] However, this rhetorical technique of self-effacing reversal, as Mary Louise Pratt argues, can also mask, as much as undo, relations of power and hegemony.[18] Women's sense of difference was also relayed in the language of exploration and conquest as they stressed their presence in an empty, silent, unknown land, a technique that negated the Inuit human presence.

Women writers identified their travels with the histories of famous white explorers and their accounts proclaimed their place as 'firsts': the first white woman on a particular island, the first white woman to negotiate a particular journey or the "most northerly wedding."[19] Even accounting for language differences, when white women spoke initially of loneliness, they clearly longed for the company of other white women. Yet, as Mena Orford recounted in her *Journey North*, the same longing was not true for children; hers quickly made Inuit friends, with whom they chatted, played, and visited in their homes.

White women saw themselves as bonded by their common isolation, and they often claimed that divisions of class or female rivalry were not a part of their northern experience. In part, this may have been their autobiographical reluctance to reveal uncomplimentary views of themselves and others, though the northern (western) autobiography of HBC trader's wife Jean Godsell is replete with tales of hostile, nasty, competitive, and class-conscious white women.[20] Many of the Arctic sojourners discussed in this article, of course, came from similar backgrounds: most were high-school– or university-educated, Anglo-Saxon Protestants, from farm or middle-class families. Manning was a graduate nurse, trained in Halifax, working in Montreal, Marjorie Hines a British-born welfare teacher, and Katherine Scherman a scientist from the United States. Miriam McMillan, much younger than her explorer husband, came from a cultured, middle-class New England family. Orford, too, came from a comfortable prairie family who saw her marriage to a poor rural doctor husband as something of a decline in status. Elsie Gillis, who had attended university, actually joked that she was a "spoiled city girl"[21] whose farthest travels had been to New York City, while Tolboom, though she came from rural Manitoba, was also educated and middle-class in outlook.

Their cultural distance from Inuit women was accentuated by the fact that the latter were often employed by them as domestic servants, thus making the racial simultaneously a class relation. White women embraced the use of paid help in a domestic environment they found overwhelmingly difficult, if not impossible, to survive in. Manning's ability to survive entirely on her acquired skills was seen as extremely unusual and "courageous" by local HBC traders who dubbed her a veritable "white Eskimo."[22] More common was the experience of Mena Orford, who, when she arrived, was told, in the language of household effects, that her maid Nukinga "went with the house."[23] Faced with unending dishes, Gillis looked around the settlement for an Inuit woman who might "have some vague idea of white man's ways." "I would be glad to have Inooyuk as my maid," she told her husband, who then had the HBC trader strike the "bargain" for Inooyuk by paying her in HBC credit.[24] Most sojourners, publishing in the 1940s and 1950s, would not have portrayed *themselves* as imperious employers; rather they tried to employ humour and anecdote to describe their cultural estrangement from their hired help, though this too often revealed a clear sense of hierarchy.[25]

White women were also understood to be a potential liability due to their inability to weather the physical surroundings. As a result, their narratives were characterized by an ambivalence, awkwardness, and a need to justify their presence, dissimilar to the tales of many men. Of course, unlike nineteenth-century middle-class women travellers, these modern sojourners had citizenship rights, participated in the professions, and had recently been exalted during the war for their equal embrace of male labour. Even the professional women, however, commented on the difficulties they encountered. "It's a man's country," was the recurring theme Hines found when she applied for jobs in the North: "Had I been a man it would have been fairly easy to find a job in Arctic Canada at that time. . . . Nursing and teaching had been undertaken by [female] missionaries — but neither missions nor matrimony attracted me!"[26] Manning, who accompanied her husband on his geodetic surveys, had trouble persuading the government to make her an assistant on the second expedition, nor could she find an RCAF person who would fly both of them into the North. The idea was greeted with a "burst of laughter" and only a strategy of immense persistence worked. While Hines and Manning could position themselves as adventurous, path-breaking explorers, those who went as wives often cast themselves as reluctant or intrepid partners in their husband's Arctic ventures.

Women were considered potential problems in an environment associated with hostile natural forces, danger, masculine bravery, and contact with 'primitives.' Writing of her earlier travels before World War II, MacMillan described how she had to prove herself relentlessly, taking on task after task to prepare for her husband's expeditions, and when she was finally allowed on board, also taking her night watch like the men. Despite her husband's claim that the "crew would not want a woman on board,"[27] the crew eventually produced a petition calling for "Lady Mac's" participation in the trip. Women also found their distinct space by stressing their feminine roles and attributes. In North Pole Boarding House, Gillis, like some other narrators, became a social, domestic focus of the all-male community, a surrogate mother or sister to other local white, single men, helping to celebrate birthdays and provide domestic rituals and Xmas celebrations.

Moreover, in the post-World War II period, white women were increasingly welcomed in the North, in feminized professions (as nurses and teachers), and also as wives of fur traders. The earlier HBC practice of traders marrying Indigenous women was now discouraged and every effort was made to make the white HBC wife comfortable with chesterfields, canned food, even washing machines. Not surprisingly, these white HBC wives often portrayed liaisons between white men and Inuit women as undesirable or unworkable. Some depicted Inuit/white liaisons as a remnant of the whalers' (irresponsible) past, though others, drawing on nineteenth-century racial theory, implied that their 'mixed blood' progeny might produce a "superior" type of Eskimo.[28] A man from white "civilization" who married "an Eskimo woman," an RCMP constable told scientist Scherman, "would be dragged down."[29] Gillis related an incident in which a young white man at their weather station was teased about the attention he was receiving from an older Inuit woman. He then received a warning: "an Eskimo woman's skin, so I was told, looks very brown to a white man during his first year in the Arctic. In the second year, it may not look so brown. If, in the third, it looks white, then it's high time for a man to get out. He's in danger of becoming bushed."[30] While Hines was less critical of interracial marriage, she was scathing about white men's sexual use of Inuit women, and she suspected that the fascination with wife-trading tales of the Eskimo had much to do with the predatory voyeurism of white males.

Women, then, were conscious of their status as precarious outsiders even though they were favoured as partners for white men. Like white men, they were preoccupied with physical survival in an environment that was equated with danger: the North was described as physically inhospitable, frightening, literally at the end of the universe. Both men and women invested considerable detail in discussions of the making and wearing of Arctic dress, travel by komatik, the building of snow houses, hunting for food, and the preparation of skins and meat afterwards. Their detailed descriptions of daily survival became a form of anthropological and scientific "classification,"[31] a technique that carried with it an air of authorial certainty.

Women, however, were more self-deprecating about their own uselessness and vulnerability. When she first arrived, Manning imagined the Inuit women thinking — with justification — who is this useless woman who knows nothing about preparing skins and clothing?[32] On the other hand, some of the wives informed their readers that their white husbands became such skilled, masculine outdoorsmen that they were "almost Eskimo," respected for their survival skills. Some also waxed eloquent on their husbands' paternal kindness to the Eskimo. "He loved these simple people," said MacMillan of her husband, and according to her, they revered him.

Ice and snow were not the only dangers described. More than one woman recounted the tale of an RCMP wife "torn to pieces" by husky dogs."[33] Since this *one* incident took place in the 1920s, and was still being recounted in the late 1940s, it had clearly become an 'Arctic myth' symbolizing the vulnerability of white women in the North. The Inuit were also a potentially menacing presence. Despite the dominant picture of the passive, jolly Eskimo, many narratives included at least one tale of a vicious murder and/or cannibalism, suggesting the Inuit might lack an evolved sense of humane compassion. Since many women had read standard Arctic travellers' accounts, they called up incidents from these works reinforcing this point of view — sometimes citing the very same cannibalistic "event" from Peter Freuchen's book.[34] These descriptions of death in the Arctic often lacked intensive knowledge of the Inuit culture; they might also dwell on the gruesome details of death, perhaps included consciously as a means of inciting the reader's interest in the narrative.

Nor was their picture only one of male violence. Hines recounted a much-repeated story of a woman in her community who, years before, had participated in a religious-crazed, cold-blooded murder of some of her family, sending them out to the ice floes. On one of their ship's stopovers north, Gillis's husband was commandeered on to a makeshift jury trial for an Inuit woman accused of murdering her husband. Gillis characterized her as a woman without remorse, creating an image of an amoral primitive: "Her beady brown eyes looked unconcernedly at us and her face broke into happy grin. This is really serious business, I thought, shocked at her deportment . . . Then I remembered that here was a daughter out of another era, a child out of the stone age, suddenly thrust among people thousands of years distant from her. . . . Obviously she was completely unable to understand all this colour and ceremony to teach white man's ways to her and her people."[35] Even a quick glance at Gillis's account suggests a more complex situation: the woman, pressed into a marriage she did not want, claimed she was abused and threatened with a knife; a signed "confession" in syllabic was produced even though she did not write, and the trial was undertaken in English, which she did not speak. Gillis, a newcomer to the North, ventured that her sentence of banishment was *desired* as a mark of prestige, further proof of the need to impose new values on those who could so cold-bloodedly take a human life. Since the interwar period the state had slowly tried to impose its superior legal norms on the Indigenous North. Travellers' accounts could only reinforce support for this project, since they evoked a sense of fear about the occasional but unpredictable violence of the Inuit.[36]

The more preponderant image of the Inuit was that of the primitive and simple, happy, and good-natured people, a cultural motif often replayed in popular magazines like the *Beaver*, with photos of "The Cheerful Eskimo."[37] Descriptions of these "stone age" peoples in women's narratives were so numerous than one cannot begin to recount them. Katharine Scherman's first impressions will suffice: titling her opening chapter "Back to the Ice Age," she describes the Inuit as "exotic gnomes" with oriental eyes, men of the "stone age" who had the "simplicity and directness of children" and who taught her scientific party what it was like to be "uncivilized" again. Describing Idlouk, the guide who sustained their expedition to Bylot Island, Scherman's use of temporal metaphors stressed the 'cave man' image: "he was cut off from us by a barrier of many thousands years of progressive civilization, the counterpart of our Asian ancestors who drifted east and west out of an unknown, faintly remembered Garden of Eden."[38] While Scherman was there to study birds, her stature as scientist also endowed her observations of the Inuit with the impression of veracity.

In their descriptions of Inuit society, writers utilized orientalist techniques, such as generalizing and essentializing, to create an image of a Stone Age people in a collision course with modernity. Scherman's book recounted many Inuit stories, collected by the local HBC trader from elders; these myths, she explains, with their animalistic spirits, were not "abstract or symbolic," as in more developed cultures; they were merely full of "magic."[39] Other writers claimed that the Inuit had no real forms of governance, only "hunting leaders," that they embraced superstitious fantasies, especially about the spirits of the dead, and even "drilled holes in the heads" of those who appeared insane.[40] Although some women also wrote of Inuit "intelligence," even this was dependent on white assessment. MacMillan, for example, cites her expert husband: "they could be as intelligent as whites . . . and my husband had evidence to prove it."[41] This repeated language of 'primitiveness' inevitably had a cumulative ideological impact. 'Primitive' denotes 'barbaric, savage, prehistoric, crude,' designating someone less technologically and intellectually advanced, without a complex social organization, cultural world, or history. Denying non-Western indigenous peoples a history, as David Spurr argues, is one of the key rhetorical means of denying them humanity.[42]

The trope of the noble savage was also used by some writers. Manning noted that she found the interior Eskimo, "poor but gentle," their character proof that those Eskimo with "the least contact with whites were the finest."[43] The Inuit were presented as a communal people lacking in individualistic selfishness, an image that idealized, but also essentialized in its simplicity.[44] Some northern travellers saw themselves as escaping the pressures and spiritual vacuum of modernity, claiming that the simple Inuit had not yet absorbed the bad traits of a materialist society: "Eskimos" Gillis related, "never stole even when they were hungry."[45] Hines had little use for such romanticization, noting that there were "good and bad" in all peoples, and that Inuit could certainly steal, including from her: "When Eskimos know the English language well enough to read what has been written about them," she concluded sardonically on this score, "they'll get enough laughs to last a life-time."[46]

Despite immense respect for Inuit environmental skills, whites were still portrayed as those in leadership roles, with the best interests of the Native in mind, a view also reflected in some 'progressive,' social democratic attempts to improve the lives of northern Native peoples at this time.[47] Utilizing the language of British imperialism, authors described the Inuit as "children" and whites as their paternal protectors. While fur trade history does suggest relations of some reciprocity,[48] HBC sojourning wives tended to portray the company as paternalism incarnate, emphasizing instances of credit, food, and medicine humanely extended. When families faced "hunger and hardship," and men came to the post, destitute, Tolboom explained, they gave them their old clothes, and spread the biscuits "thick with lard" (the company ration) to help them out.[49]

Like the traders, the RCMP were also benevolent and fair. Retired chief of the Eastern Arctic Government Patrol, McKeand, noted Gillis, was a "great white father" to the Eskimo, while Scherman reassured her readers that the northern RCMP "are good men who want to do something for the native, not exploit them."[50] Because the Inuit did not understand what was best for their children, writers explained, payment of family allowances was overseen by the RCMP. Without this humane check, Eskimo parents might have purchased useless luxuries rather than the pablum they should have. These paternal metaphors are ironic given the way that the Inuit saw whites. Describing the early RCMP on Baffin Island, elders remember "they were just like kids . . . like children," as they had to have everything done for them — clothes made for them, posts cared for, igloos built, and even their tea mugs held in the cold![51]

Not all accounts, however, described religious missions and residential schools favourably. Reflecting a more secular age after World War II, authors like Scherman noted that judgmental, moralistic missionaries had destructively disparaged Inuit traditions. Other women praised the missionary work of whites in the North (usually referring to a few heroic individuals), but overall, women writers were less adamant about the need for conversion than nineteenth-century writers had been.

Many sojourners' accounts debated the pros and cons of whites' incursions into the North; though framed within relativist terms, these did not always reflect a true 'reciprocity'[52] of equals, as much as a subtle paternalism premised on some of the same sentiments as missionization. Furthermore, the image of a less materialistic people, living a "timeless gypsy life"[53] was used not only to idealize, but also to suggest the Inuit's lack of initiative, shiftlessness, and a premodern fatalism. Recounting the three most noteworthy things about the Inuit (who had been indispensable to their expedition), Scherman lists: "no sense of time, laziness and unending sociability."[54] In Orford's account, her doctor husband becomes exasperated if not enraged because he claims that the Inuit won't save food or plan for the future. As a result, families are starving: "They are just too bloody fatalistic and improvident to provide for tomorrow."[55] Yet most whites learned how to cache food under rocks from the Inuit, and material goods always had a different meaning for hunters who had to carry things with them. Like the poor, blamed for their own unemployment, the Inuit were viewed as architects of their own fate. Inuit "fatalism" explained why the Inuit were starving, rather than trade conditions, the depletion of resources, or social dislocation. Conservation by the Eskimo, Manning wrote, was completely inadequate due to their lack of modern understanding of firearms. Citing her husband as expert, she claimed that the Inuit fired "wantonly" on seals and needed whites to oversee the walrus hunt in order to protect this species.[56] Hines's harsh judgments about Inuit relocation are especially salient: those who were relocated "were supplied with everything necessary for the undertaking. . . . Inertia on their part was the cause of poor return. . . . now that there is a good market for Eskimo handicraft there is no need for any Eskimo to be penniless."[57]

Inuit culture was thus celebrated as a remnant of a nobler, simpler past, but impugned for its primitive, fatalistic ways. The image of the Innu woman as "post native" made this clear: she *should* become civilized, but she could never really be so. Inuit women might "act white" but never embrace whiteness.[58] Inuit labour was essential for northern whites, yet sojourners warned of the danger of "post natives" becoming "spoiled," as they wanted the same luxuries without working for them. Describing a woman working as a servant for the HBC, Scherman noted that "Makpa was one of the few examples I had seen of Eskimos ruined by coddling. They were easy to spoil, being adaptable and lazy. . . . It was obvious that this elegant, neat, lazy girl could never again live the life of her people. . . . She was no longer a true Eskimo but neither was she anywhere near being a woman of our civilization."[59] Since it was children who were normally spoiled, this language suggested the infantilization of the Inuit in the eyes of their white 'parents.'

Family, Sexuality, Consumption

One of the signs noted by many writers of the 'spoiled Eskimo' was her taste for the dress and makeup of white women. Women sojourners' narratives offered detailed descriptions of Inuit women's dress, work, family life, domesticity, and consumption, categories of particular fascination because Inuit women were portrayed as highly valued for their work, but nonetheless subordinate members of patriarchal households. Authors often equated primitive with patriarchal, referring to a recent past of Inuit men fighting violently for women, of female infanticide, or arranged marriages. There was some interest in the notion of 'wife trading' too, though this was more often discussed in men's accounts of their lives in the North.[60] Ignoring anthropological evidence of egalitarian relations between Inuit men and women, white narratives adhered to the image of their own social order as more progressive, egalitarian, and fair to women. Although white women were sometimes equated with vulnerability, they also became symbols of modernity, particularly in discussions of sexuality, family, and consumption. As in other colonial situations, the imposition of 'superior' white norms, especially relating to domesticity, was accomplished *not* by direct coercion but rather by repeated example, image, and subtle ideological persuasion.[61]

Inuit childbirth was often endowed with notions of the primitive, portrayed as easily accomplished, with less pain and disruption than for white women.[62] Writers noted how soon Inuit women were back at their work, though this may have been a necessity, as it was for some working-class women. While there is some evidence that white nurses in the North were trying to relate Inuit practices to new ideas of "natural" childbirth,[63] many sojourners' accounts still invoked images of primitive reproduction. Manning's one example was telling: "The [woman] was too lazy to do more than she had to do any time, but I did think she would make something ready. As an Eskimo baby's layette consists of a single garment, a hood, there is little sewing to be done. . . . there wasn't even a hood ready, and as soon as the baby was wiped — with her hands — she snatched the filthy rag of a hood that Lizzie had made for her doll. Neither did a sepsis have any place in the whole procedure."[64] Manning may well have been unaware of the Inuk tradition of not making clothes for a child until it was born.[65] Mena Orford was horrified to find out that her young daughters had witnessed an Inuit home birth and didn't want them to give her curious husband a description (especially at the dinner table), fearing the children might be "damaged" by witnessing this primal scene. Pressed on by the doctor who had not yet seen a Native birth, their description convinced him that midwives were ignorant, not tying the cord properly, causing women's deaths. Mena's most modern northern birth, in contrast, took place in the hospital, while she was under anaesthetic, "out like a light."[66]

Rituals such as marriage became markers of domestic difference. Bouquet, dress, bridesmaid, all had to be in place for Tolboom's wedding, and though she is gently self-mocking in her description of her vigilance with respect to custom, it is clear that this symbolized the proper standards of marriage. The fact that a white wedding denoted a virginal one was made clear with contrasts to Native weddings. When the Anglican minister made a visit to Povungnetuk, Tolboom recounts, he was perturbed to find a Native couple who had their child baptized, then announced they wanted to be married. Facing an "impatient and annoyed" minister, the "couple grinned foolishly" and in response to his lecture about the proper place of marriage, they explained, "we forgot."[67] Some women's accounts also lauded the existence of long-lasting Inuit unions — particularly to counter accounts of wife trading — but the underlying sense that marriage might be taken *less seriously* by the Inuit remained.

Nowhere was the difference between the primitive and the modern more evocatively symbolized than in descriptions of food and dress. Consumption defined white domesticity, indicated by the pantries of white women, often provisioned for a full year by the visit of the *Nascopie* (or other ships after its sinking in 1947). Describing the arduous work of unpacking, Tolboom notes that her shelves included everything from "staples" to "shredded coconut, olives and strawberries, and cases of fresh potatoes, eggs and oranges."[68] Gillis's shelves were so full after ship time that they "looked like a full grocery store." Using ready-made ingredients, she describes their desserts alone of "canned fruit, pies, cakes, puddings, jello . . . Apple pie, raisin, dried apricot, pumpkin, caramel, chocolate, butterscotch, lemon."[69] The contrast with the "biscuits covered in lard" served to the Inuit is striking. On a visit to a local tent, Tolboom realized that her garbage was being recycled as household items; her table scraps went to Inuit families. Gillis relays her charity in sending her rotten eggs and potatoes to thankful families.[70] For white women, now accustomed to consuming, not producing food, the thought of losing ship provisions was disastrous. The nine hundred pounds of meat sent north for Gillis's boarding house never made it, resulting in her images of "starvation" and incessant "public complaints"— the latter so embarrassed her husband that he became publicly enraged with her.[71] Some women, however, also came to value Inuit food, especially the meat provided by local hunters, and Hines was understandably critical of both the introduction of infant formula and the government's attempts to tell Inuit women how to preserve game![72]

Household items and dress also marked out 'the modern.' Many white women wanted to create familiar domestic space, importing everything from wallpaper to crystal, silver, and china, and a full closet of clothes. Sojourners had to have winter clothing made for them by Inuit women, as otherwise they would have frozen, yet white fashions — from nail polish to stockings — remained a symbol of social prestige, as the Eskimo baggy 'shift' was disparaged. Some writers portrayed the advent of the catalogue, the harbinger of consumption, as a ray of hope for the untidy Inuit women, dressed in "shapeless, long, ugly cotton skirts" (admittedly a Christian mission influence).[73] Immediately after Gillis accused her maid of being spoiled by proximity to whites, she explained how she had acted as a role model in terms of fashion and manners: "On Sundays, of course, I always wore one of my best silk dresses [for dinner]. On Inooyuk's first Sunday with me [as an extra maid] she came dressed as usual. She did not again make that error."[74]

Yet when Inuit women imitated white dress, they were often ridiculed. Appearing for Christmas incongruously mixing white and Native costumes, Kowtah (the maid) wore a "lady's maroon felt ribbon trimmed hat, over her black braids . . . a wine-coloured coat, draped with a huge fur collar. On her feet were ladies fur trimmed velvet overshoes. In her ears were ear-rings, and her lips and finger-tips were daubed with bright red. . . . It was all I could do to keep the smile from becoming a shout of laughter. Kowtah imagined herself a fashion plate straight out of one of the magazines she had seen at Jimmy's. Her fifth avenue costume had no doubt come out of some missionary bale."[75] Reviewers of these books clearly found such accounts amusing.[76] Could these descriptions of Native women 'dressed up as whites' be characterized as colonial mimicry? Perhaps they were for Inuit women, though those with the discursive power in this case were white women whose texts reinforced mocking colonialist images, rather than subverting them with 'hybridity.'[77]

Women offered detailed descriptions of Christmas celebrations as they tried to recreate 'home' in an alien environment. Christmas also became a means of establishing new modes of consumption and cultural practice. Women transported Christmas trees, candles, decorations, serviettes, and other paraphernalia to celebrate properly amidst the 'natives.' At their celebration for the Inuit, the Tolbooms offered up "party favours" (unsold HBC items from the trading post), games, and refreshments: "What a party we had. . . . into the office and waiting room porch crowded 87 men, women and children. Never since have I seen so many joyful, perspiring Eskimo faces." The HBC couple distributing the party favours were impeccably dressed 'parents,' imperial in image: "I felt gala in my red woollen dress, high heels and nylon stockings. Perfume, nail polish and a little corsage of evergreen and holly berries provided special touches. [Wulf] wore his good suit. Oh, but we did feel like the Lord and Lady of the Manor."[78]

The fact that Inuit women's bodies were objects of merriment in these descriptions bore some similarity — but also difference — to earlier accounts of southern First Nations women.[79] The fact that whiteness was equated with cleanliness, while Indigenous women were "dirty, greasy," and unkempt was found in both sets of racist discourses. However, Inuit women were not sexualized as degenerate or promiscuous temptresses in the same manner as Native women, perhaps because nudity was equated with sexuality, and Inuit women's layers of dress precluded this. Inuit women were rendered more childlike than voluptuous, with Inuit men cast in the 'cave man' role of sexual possessors — a stereotype, argues Brody, reflecting white sexual desires/anxieties more than anything else.[80] Nonetheless, Inuit women's sexual *availability* was implied, with references to their easy liaisons with whalers, their acceptance of past polygamy, their lack of inhibitions concerning privacy in one-room homes, and their supposedly seasonal sexual coupling. "In early summer in every Eskimo encampment," wrote Tolboom, "Sex rears its head. But here it is not an ugly one. It is looked on as . . . the changing of the seasons. It is accepted as simply as the matings of all wild things in this Land."[81]

Inuit women's domestic labour, especially their provision of food and dress, however, was vigorously extolled as readers were offered many examples of Inuit aid without which whites would have perished. Writers nonetheless absorbed the reigning anthropological and popular images of a patriarchal Inuit culture, with male hunting at the pinnacle of prestige and power. Since many sojourners saw men trapping, trading furs, and acting as guides, and women doing 'inside' labour such as sewing and child care (deemed feminine and valued less in their own culture), it was assumed that the gendered division of labour reflected the power of men. This assumption was not necessarily shared by a few writers who spent more time immersed in Inuit culture, speaking the language; one HBC fur trader stressed the co-operative partnerships of Inuit husbands and wives, as well as women's crucial role in directing decisions about extramarital liaisons.[82] Though women sojourners were sometimes critical of the *sexual* status of Inuit women, they easily accepted the gendered division of labour; some even recommended more and better domestic training for Inuit girls.

Some women's narratives also became tales of increased respect for the Inuit over time. In one small incident, Tolboom's favourite dog had to be shot, and her husband warned her that the skin *had* to be used by locals, who were in desperate straits, for warm mitts. Initially upset, she came to understand that the careful use of all resources for daily life was a positive part of Inuit life. When Gillis first saw her maid polishing the glasses by spitting on them, she recounts, "I was just sick with disgust."[83] But after a discussion with her husband, she admitted that in a culture where so much of women's work involved chewing, this was simply a logical use of a "tool."

Discussions of child rearing were used, most notably, to symbolize Mena Orford's transformation from critic to acolyte of Inuit culture. Many accounts lamented the lack of discipline for Inuit children, but then lauded the good behaviour of children and the intense love of parents for their offspring. Mena Orford's first impression of her Inuit helper, Nukinga, literally betrayed physical disgust, yet this was followed by a quick revelation of her children's different response: "A churning started in the pit of my stomach. . . . as I watched this gross woman with the dark-skinned perspiring face encircle my two in her wide arms and in turn, rub each of their noses with her own. . . . but as [the children] left, their faces shone with a contentment and happiness I hadn't seen for some time."[84] More dramatic was her realization that the Inuit aversion to the physical discipline of children was perhaps more compassionate than her own belief in spanking. When she hit one of her children in front of her two Inuit helpers, she encountered pure horror in their eyes. She began to question her superior knowledge, acknowledging that the Inuit make "a pretty good job" of child rearing.[85]

The Political Implications of Colonial Writing

Inuit women were often portrayed as docile in descriptions of the Arctic, but the reactions of Orford's helpers, and their refusal to accept her methods of child rearing, indicate that they were not. If they disagreed with the white women they worked for, they might simply stop coming or indicate, without words, their disapproval. White women often took silence for approval, yet Inuit women were likely showing "ilira," a show of deference to intimidating individuals that "reflected the subtle but pervasive result of inequality."[86] Scherman, among others, also noted instances where Inuit women and men seemed to simply disregard advice or orders; clearly, even those Inuit working for whites maintained a strong sense of their own needs, values, and judgments. Hines was more likely than some authors to endow her Inuit neighbours with complex reactions and agency, and she too noted instances in which Inuit would simply not do things that they were ordered to, if they judged them to be unsafe or unwise, no matter how insistent whites were.

In some instances, then, travel narratives might be read against the grain, indicating not the 'jolly, docile' Eskimo woman but a far more complex human being, one coping with rapid social change, and sometimes less enamoured with Euro-Canadian incursion than whites understood. However, assessing the *dominant* messages behind these sojourning narratives is still important. How would the Inuit have been imagined by readers in postwar Canada? On one level, there were messages of tolerance, respect for Inuit skills, and compassion for other human beings. One night as Mena Orford went to have tea and chat with her Inuit neighbour, she saw her neighbour's boy mauled by a dog; there is no doubt that she felt compassion for his devastated mother, a woman she did come to call a friend.

But tolerance and compassion can coexist with paternalism, also a theme in many narratives. The image of a primitive and fatalistic culture, facing the painful fact of inevitable adaption, appeared repeatedly, along with the notion that whites were well placed to oversee the difficult, uphill path to modernization. Rhetorical and discursive strategies of colonial representation — superior surveillance, scientific classification, modernist idealization, and eroticization — were all woven into sojourners' accounts. As a result, the non-Indigenous south was portrayed, in the light of modernization theories of the time, as more progressive, modern, urban, and industrial, the repository of knowledge that might allow the Inuit to develop socially and economically.[87]

These images were also deeply political, especially in an era when the North was an increasingly important economic frontier and military concern, and as government intervention in Inuit lives was increasing. The fate of northern Indigenous residents was being debated by popular writers, some of whom extolled the North for its resource potential, while others offered exposées of starving Indigenous peoples, abandoned by a callous government.[88] Whether the racism and poverty that engulfed the lives of southern Aboriginals would be replicated in the North was also a point for concerned debate.

On one hand, sojourners' respect for Inuit environmental survival skills and their hopes for positive Inuit adaption to 'modern' ways endowed the women's narratives with a tone of liberal tolerance and relativism. Writing on the Arctic Inuit did not simply replicate earlier writing on southern Aboriginal peoples; within colonialist discourse, there was some distinction between a language of northern Inuit 'primitivism' and the language of Indian 'savagism,' with the latter arguably even more pessimistic and negative in character. Nonetheless, both perspectives ultimately reflected broader patterns of colonialist thinking on history, white settlement, and 'modern' development: both were part of a long tradition of colonialism within Canada.

As cultural producers of sojourning narratives that juxtaposed 'primitive' Inuit peoples with the encroachment of more progressive, modern Canada, women authors played an active constitutive role in the creation of colonial texts. The cultural images created by white sojourners with direct experience or scientific 'knowledge' of Inuit life were undoubtedly endowed with the weight of a certain veracity, authenticity, and memorability: it was assumed that actual experience of living in the 'wild' gave them more immediate insight into their Indigenous neighbours. The tone of superior surveillance of Inuit life assumed by many women writers thus had much in common with works authored by men, although women's less confident relation to the 'wild' North — particularly if they came as helpmates — and their more detailed descriptions of women's lives, domesticity, and consumption also made their narratives distinct. Perhaps most important, sojourners' admissions that Inuit women and men retained different views and values than whites, and sometimes disagreed with them, also suggested that paternalist traditions were not unchallenged in the North. Inuit efforts to sustain their culture and organize to defend their lands indicated that the culture of colonialism was never monolithic or unassailable.

Notes

I wish to thank Shelagh Grant, Janet McGrath, and Caroline Langill for their comments and suggestions on this research.

1   Wanda N. Tolboom, *Arctic Bride* (New York: William Morrow and Co., 1956), 37.

2   Deirdre David, *Rule Britannia: Women, Empire and Victorian Writing* (Ithaca: Cornell University Press, 1995), 5. Women's travel narratives were a popular form of writing extending back to Upper Canada: for example, Anna B. Jameson, *Winter Studies and Summer Rambles* (Toronto: McClelland and Stewart, 1965); Georgina Binnie-Clark, *Wheat and Woman* (Toronto: University of Toronto Press, 1979); Agnes Deans Cameron, *The New North: An Account of a Woman's 1908 Journey Through Canada to the Arctic* (Saskatoon: Western Producer Prairie Books, 1986). For analysis, see Marian Fowler, *The Embroidered Tent: Five Gentlewomen in Early Canada* (Toronto: Anansi Press, 1982); Jennifer Henderson, *Settler Feminism and Race Making in Canada* (Toronto: University of Toronto Press, 2003); Barbara Kelcey, *Alone in Silence: European Women in the Canadian North Before 1940* (Montreal: McGill-Queen's University Press, 2001).

3   The 'North' had long exercised an important role in the imaginary construction of the Canadian nation, though renewed interest was evidenced in postwar Canada by accounts like Pierre Berton's *The Mysterious North* (Toronto: McClelland and Stewart, 1957) and numerous articles in magazines like *Maclean's* and *Saturday Night*. For some discussion of the imaginary North, see Shelagh Grant, "Arctic Wilderness and Other Mythologies," *Journal of Canadian Studies* 32, no. 2 (1998): 27–42; Janice Cavell, "The Second Frontier: The North in English-Canadian Historical Writing," *Canadian Historical Review*, 83, no. 3 (2002): 364–89; Carl Berger, *The Sense of Power* (Toronto: University of Toronto Press, 1970); David Heinimann, "Latitude Rising: Historical Continuity in Canadian Nordicity," *Journal of Canadian Studies* 28, no. 3 (1993): 134–39; Sherrill Grace, *Canada and the Idea of North* (Montreal: McGill-Queen's University Press, 2001); and "Gendering Northern Narratives," in *Echoing Silence: Essays on Arctic Narratives*, ed. John Moss (Ottawa: University of Ottawa Press, 1997), 163–82.

4 Although the 'North' is a contested concept referring to geographical, environmental, social, even cultural boundaries, I have concentrated on seven texts published after 1940 about the eastern Subarctic and Arctic, though a broader sample of northern travel writing has been consulted. Many of these seven texts were reviewed positively in Canadian magazines and journals. They are Marjorie Hines, *School House in the Arctic* (London: Geoffrey Bles, 1958); Katharine Scherman, *Spring on an Arctic Island* (Boston: Little, Brown, 1956); Mrs. Tom Manning, *A Summer on Hudson Bay* (London: Hodder and Stoughton, 1949), and *Igloo for a Night* (University of Toronto Press, 1946); Elsie Gillis, with Eugenie Myles, *North Pole Boarding House* (Toronto: Ryerson Press, 1951); Mena Orford, *Journey North* (Toronto: McClelland and Stewart, 1957); and Miriam MacMillan, *Greens Seas and White Ice* (New York: Dodd, Mead and Co., 1948). Others consulted include Eva Alvey Richards, *Arctic Mood* (Caldwell, ID: Caxton Publishers, 1949); Constance and Harmon Helmericks, *We Live in the Arctic* (New York: Little Brown and Co., 1947); Jean Godsell, *I Was No Lady: I Followed the Call of the Wild* (Toronto: Ryerson Press, 1959); Doug Wilkinson, *Land of the Long Day* (Toronto: Clarke Irwin and Co., 1955); Ritchie Calder, *Men Against the Frozen North* (London: George Allen and Unwin, 1957); Frank Illingworth, *Highway to the North* (New York: Philosophical Library, 1955); Joseph P. Moody, *Arctic Doctor* (New York: Dodd Mead and Co., 1953); Duncan Pryde, *Nunaga: Ten Years of Eskimo Life* (New York: Walker and Co., 1971); and one travel narrative of northern Ontario, Gordon Langley Hall, *Me Papoose Sitter* (New York: Thomas Crowell Co., 1955).

5 Mary Louise Pratt, *Imperial Eyes: Travel Writing and Transculturation* (London: Routledge, 1992), 7. Other works include Inderpal Grewal, *Home and Harem* (Durham: Duke University Press, 1996); Sara Mills, *Discourses of Difference* (London: Routledge, 1991); Dea Birkett, *Spinsters Abroad* (Oxford: Blackwell, 1989); Alison Blunt, *Travel, Gender and Imperialism: Mary Kingsley and West Africa* (New York: Guildford Press, 1994); Helen Callaway, *Gender, Culture and Empire* (London: Macmillan, 1987); Antoinette Burton, *Burdens of History* (Chapel Hill: University of North Carolina Press, 1994); Ellen Jacobs, "Eileen Power's Asian Journey, 1920–1: History, Narrative and Subjectivity," *Women's History Review* 7, no. 3 (1998): 295–319; Laura Donaldson, *Decolonizing Feminisms: Race, Gender and Empire Building* (Chapel Hill: University of Northern Carolina Press, 1992); Karen Dubinsky, *The Second Greatest Disappointment: Honeymooning and Tourism at Niagara Falls* (Toronto: Between the Lines, 1999), 55–85; Antoinette Burton, ed., *Gender, Sexuality and Colonial Modernities* (London: Routledge, 1999); Clare Midgley, ed., *Gender and Imperialism* (Manchester and New York: Manchester University Press, 1998; Anne McClintock, *Imperial Leather: Race, Gender and Sexuality in the Colonial Context* (London: Routledge, 1995); Ann L. Stoler, *Race and the Education of Desire: Foucault's History of Sexuality and the Colonial Order of Things* (Durham: Duke University Press, 1995).

6 David Spurr, *The Rhetoric of Empire: Colonial Discourse in Journalism, Travel Writing and Imperial Administration* (Durham: Duke University Press, 1993).

7 Antoinette Burton, "Rules of Thumb: British History and 'Imperial Culture' in Nineteenth- and Twentieth-Century Britian," *Women's History Review* 3, no. 4 (1994): 483.

8 Ann Stoler, "Making Empire Respectable: The Politics of Race and Sexual Morality in 20th Century Colonial Cultures," *American Ethnologist* 16, no. 4 (1989): 634–59; Ruth R. Pierson and N. Chaudhur, "Introduction" to their edited *Nation, Empire and Colony: Historicizing Gender and Race* (Bloomington: Indiana University Press, 1998), 4; Jane Haggis, "Gendering Colonialism or Colonizing Gender: Recent Women's Studies Approaches to White Women and the History of British Colonialism," *Women's Studies International Forum*, 13, no. 1 (1990): 105–15; Angela Woollacott, "All This Is Your Empire, I Told Myself: Australian Women's Voyages 'Home' and the Articulation of Colonial Whiteness," *American Historical Review* 102, no. 4 (1997): 1003–29.

9 Mills, *Discourses of Difference*, 22.

10 Hugh Brody, *The People's Land* (London: Penguin Books, 1975), 79. On orientalism, see Edward Said, *Orientalism* (New York: Vintage Books, 1979); Reina Lewis, *Gendering Orientalism: Race, Femininity and Representation* (London: Routledge, 1996).

11 I draw here on authors who offer more materialist critiques of postcolonial theories, including Himani Bannerji, "Politics and the Writing of History," in *Nation, Empire, Colony*, ed. Pierson and Chaudhuri; Arif Dirlik, "The Post-Colonial Aura: Third World Criticism in the Age of Global Capitalism," *Critical Inquiry* 20 (Winter 1994): 328–56; Ella Shohat, "Notes on the Post-Colonial," *Social Text* 31/32 (1992): 99–113; Ajiz Ahmad, *In Theory: Nations, Classes, Literatures* (Verso: London, 1992).

12 Shelagh Grant, *Sovereignty or Security? Government Policy in the Canadian North, 1936–50* (Vancouver: University of British Columbia Press, 1988).

13 Peter Kulchyski and Frank Tester, *Tammarjnit (Mistakes): Inuit Relocation in the Eastern Arctic 1939–63* (Vancouver: University of British Columbia Press, 1994).

14 Diamond Jenness, "Enter the European," *The Beaver* (Winter 1954): 23–38.

15 James Frideres, *Native People in Canada: Contemporary Conflicts*, 2nd ed. (Scarborough: Prentice-Hall Canada, 1993), 295.

16 Some had precise descriptions of northern flora and birds (Manning), others offer more direct opinions (Hines), while some attempt a more 'light-hearted' description of northern life (Gillis). Differences were also apparent in men's accounts, with one unusual one written by an English author, Gordon Langley Hall, *Me Papoose Sitter* (New York: Thomas Crowell, 1955). Despite the terrible title, his portraits of his northern neighbours often appear less essentialized 'racial' stereotypes than a collection of stock characters reminiscent of some eccentric British village.

17 Tolboom, *Arctic Bride*, 3.

18 Pratt, *Imperial Eyes*, 84.

19 Gillis, *North Pole Boarding House*, 10, 124.

20 Godsell, *I Was No Lady*. Manning refers briefly to such conflicts in *A Summer*, 53.

21 Gillis, *North Pole Boarding House*, 6.

22 Provincial Archives of Manitoba (PAM), Hudson's Bay Company Papers (HBC), Wolstoneholme Post Journal, B 397/a/9, Jan. 1940.

23 Orford, *Journey North*, 17.

24 Gillis, *North Pole Boarding House*, 88.

25 Again, Godsell was different, discussing attempts to teach the servants "who was master": *I Was No Lady*, 45.

26 Hines, *School House*, 15.

27 MacMillan, *Green Seas*, 75.

28 Scherman, *Spring on an Arctic Island*, 105.

29 Ibid., 188.

30 Gillis, *North Pole Boarding House*, 165.

31 Spurr, *The Rhetoric of Empire*, 61–75.

32 E. Wallace Manning, "Explorer's Wife," *The Beaver* (Sept. 1942): 12.

33 Gillis, *North Pole Boarding House*, 15. The incident is also mentioned in men's narratives. See Moody, *Arctic Doctor*, 9.

34 Peter Freuchen, *I Sailed with Rasmussen* (New York: Julian Messner, 1959). On the themes of death, mystery, and violence in popular narratives, see Grace, *Canada and the Idea of North*, 179.

35 Gillis, *North Pole Boarding House*, 48.

36 Shelagh Grant, *Arctic Justice: On Trial for Murder, Pond Inlet, 1923* (Montreal: McGill-Queen's University Press, 2002).

37 "The Cheerful Eskimo," *The Beaver* (March 1952).

38 Scherman, *Spring on an Arctic Island*.

39 Ibid., 180.

40 Ibid., 138.

41 MacMillan, *Green Seas*.

42 Spurr, *The Rhetoric of Empire*, 167.

43 Manning, *A Summer*, 26.

44 Ibid., 127.

45 Gillis, *North Pole Boarding House*, 184.

46 Hines, *School House*, 161.

47 David M. Quiring, ccf *Colonialism in Northern Saskatchewan: Battling Parish Priests, Bootleggers, and Fur Sharks* (Vancouver: University of British Columbia Press, 2004).

48 Arthur Ray, *The Canadian Fur Trade in the Industrial Age* (Toronto: University of Toronto Press, 1990).

49 Tolboom, *Arctic Bride*, 173.

50 Gillis, *North Pole Boarding House;* Scherman, *Spring on an Arctic Island*, 192.

51 Timothy Kadloo and Sam Arnakallak (Pond Inlet), quoted in Shelagh Grant, *Arctic Justice*, 232.

52 Pratt, *Imperial Eyes*, 84.

53 Scherman, *Spring on an Arctic Island*, 117.

54 Ibid., 138.

55 Orford, *Journey North*, 95.

56 Manning, *A Summer*, 140.

57 Hines, *School House*, 154–55.

58 This would echo some of Homi Bhabha's characterizations. The Native might be "anglicized but could never be 'English'": Bart Moore-Gilbert, *Postcolonial Theory: Contexts, Practices, Politics* (London: Verso, 1997), 120.

59 Scherman, *Spring on an Arctic Island*, 189.

60 Notably Duncan Pryde's description of his own participation in spouse swapping in *Nunaga*.

61 Notions of the proper domesticity were central to many other colonial projects. See Jean Comaroff and John Comaroff, *Ethnography and the Historical Imagination;* K. Hansen, ed., *African Encounters with Domesticity* (New Brunswick, NJ: Rutgers University Press, 1992).

62 Patricia Jasen, "Race, Culture and the Colonization of Childbirth in Northern Canada," in *Rethinking Canada: The Promise of Women's History*, ed. Veronica Strong-Boag, Mona Gleason, and Adele Perry (Toronto: Oxford University Press, 2002), 353–66.

63 Judith Bender Zelmanovits, "Midwife Preferred: Maternity Care in Outport Nursing Stations in Northern Canada," in *Women, Health and Nation: Canada and*

the United States Since 1945, ed. Georgina Feldberg et al. (Montreal: McGill-Queen's University Press, 2003), 161–95.

64 Manning, *Igloo*, 55.

65 My thanks to Janet McGrath for this information.

66 Orford, *Northern Journey*, 113.

67 Tolboom, *Arctic Bride*, 102. Since these women did not discuss their own sexuality, one can only infer from other vague references to their premarital 'shyness,' their belief in sex only after marriage. The fact that their sexuality was not mentioned, but that of Inuit women was, again placed the latter in the category of more sexualized 'other.'

68 Ibid., 62.

69 Gillis, *North Pole Boarding House*, 57, 75.

70 Ibid., 151.

71 This may not have been in response to their proximity to less affluent Inuit, but because, after a radio message home, he worried that everyone knew their business: "If you ever mention food again . . . I'll kill you." Was the author aware how negative a view she presented of her husband? Gillis, *North Pole Boarding House*, 62, 75.

72 Hines, *School House*, and Kulchyski and Tester, *Tammarnit*, 85.

73 Manning, *Igloo*, 21.

74 Gillis, *North Pole Boarding House*, 95.

75 Ibid., 137.

76 A review by anthropologist Douglas Leechman of Gillis's book in *Canadian Geographic Journal*, Feb. 1952, ix, notes that her description of the "oddities" of the Eskimos made it an entertaining book.

77 As Grace points out, "mimicry is unstable and uncontrollable; it can also backfire on the mimics": *Canada and the Idea of North*, 100. See also Diana Fuss for discussion of differences between feminist characterizations of mimicry as 'dissent' and the different characterization of Homi Bhabha: "Interior Colonies: Franz Fanon and the Politics of Identification," *Diacritics* 24 (1994): 20–42.

78 Tolboom, *Arctic Bride*, 93.

79 For earlier images, see Sarah Carter, *Capturing Women: The Manipulation of Cultural Imagery in Canada's Prairie West* (Montreal: McGill-Queen's University Press, 1997), and, on twentieth-century images of Indians, Daniel Francis, *The Imaginary Indian: The Image of the Indian in Canadian Culture* (Vancouver: Arsenal Pulp Press, 1992).

80 Hugh Brody, *The Other Side of Eden* (Toronto: Douglas and McIntyre, 2000), 263.

81 Tolboom, *Arctic Bride*, 225.

82 Pryde, *Nunaga*.

83 Gillis, *North Pole Boarding House*, 90.

84 Orford, *Journey North*, 20.

85 Ibid., 70–72.

86 Brody, quoted in Grant, *Arctic Murder*, 17.

87 Catherine Scott, *Gender and Development: Rethinking Modernization and Dependency Theory* (London: Routledge, 1996).

88 Farley Mowat, *The People of the Deer*, rev. ed. (Toronto: McClelland and Stewart, 1975).

EMBODIED EXPERIENCE

Whether our primary sources are textual, visual, or oral, they hold unexpected surprises, joys, disappointments, and interpretive dilemmas. Feminist historians have never approached our sources as Ms. Grandgrinds, looking for 'the facts and nothing but the facts,' although the impression that we are hopelessly mired in empiricism may linger in some quarters. We rarely trumpet the need for pure objectivity, declare that we have found *the* truth, assume a naive empiricism, or claim absolute insider knowledge; our interrogations of our sources usually fall somewhere on a "continuum between objectivity and relativism."[1] Nonetheless, there are differences of opinion among historians on how to treat sources, ranging from a primary preoccupation with their discursive construction to an emphasis on evidential truthfulness and a search for a measure of objectivity. The first paper in the section, on women's letters to the Royal Commission on the Status of Women (RCSW), grew out of an accidental discovery in the archives that in turn pushed me to consider how we interpret sources like these in light of long-standing debates about experience, working-class history, and feminist theory.

I was researching a chapter on the labour movement's interactions with the RCSW that was supposed to explore their policy proposals relating to wage-earning women and was disappointed, not because the trade union briefs were too brief — quite the contrary — but rather because they were a little repetitive and boring (a subjective view, I know). I opened a box I had not intended to use, containing personal letters to the RCSW, and was immediately captivated. I admit to feeling as if I had finally found a *better* source, a more intimate and honest source, a source that would let me understand women's changing experiences of work. I had a sense of mining the primary documents at a deeper level, yet I also knew that my preconceived notion of personal letters as a more intimate source (and perhaps the historian's well-known love of gossip), along with my generational interest in social history 'from below' and in 'recovering women's voices,' were likely shaping this very subjective assessment. I was not naïve enough to think that I had arrived at women's truest thoughts, that the letters were evidence of women's truly 'authentic' experience as opposed to the thoroughly 'ideological' trade union briefs. However, there was something very compelling about the letters: they drew me in, as they were emotive, warm, funny, angry — in other words they conveyed some *feeling.* I imagined tired women at their kitchen tables firing off their thoughts to the head of the commision, Florence Bird, in between dishes and bedtime stories, something I could relate to. And I was also surprised at how many letters were eloquent, perceptive, and critical of the sex-gender system — and what feminist is not cheered by signs of resistance, however small?

My initial impulse was to read the letters as emblematic of women's experiences, but if I was to use that highly charged term, I had to return to theoretical debates discussing our use of that concept. Just contemplating what was to follow, I became deflated: the letters were becoming a chore not a joy, more opaque, a source not to be listened to but justified, and ironically, an *object* of my 'third-person' feminist gaze, rather than the sentient source I had first encountered. The state of feminist theory, specifically our critical reflections on experience, voice, and identity — productively provoked by postmodern writing — was ruining my archival enjoyment. My response speaks to the influence of poststructuralist writing on the concept of experience in Anglo-American feminist writing; critiques by Joan Scott and others unsettled some of the assumptions embedded in an earlier feminist 'moment of discovery' in history writing, though questions about experience were not entirely new, as they had been central to earlier debates within Marxist social history. Although a younger colleague told me while I was writing this paper that the discussion of 'experience' was, well, generally *over,* I did not think so. Debates about experience may be somewhat ubiquitous, unsolvable, and always with us, but they are still important, not the least because they are often emblematic of significant differences in our political sensibilities and theoretical perspectives; they are tied, for instance, to debates about human agency and the (death of the) subject in history. Perhaps social historians in general have been tortured more by this question (many economic historians I know are not wracked with doubt about whether 'reality' is discursively constructed), or perhaps debating experience has just become part of our own historical socialization and ongoing practice.

As I read through the letters, I kept going back and forth to feminist and Marxist theoretical writing, including feminists who have expressed some concern that we are in danger of losing a sense of feeling or affectivity in our writing, something I often instinctively felt when I was reading endless descriptions of discourses *about* women. Poststructuralist writing had been eye-opening precisely because it revealed much about the power of discourses and how they operated, but if experience became completely discursive, then what happened to the subject, human agency, and resistance? I was drawn, on the one hand, to Sonia Kruks's suggestion (not unlike Susan Friedman's model that I described in the introduction) that experience could be described as either "subjectively lived or as a discursive effect" and that, interpretively, we go back and forth between these poles, "depending on the nature of our questions and goals." Experience could thus be seen from both a "first and third person"[2] perspective, but to see it only as discursive was to obscure the role of human agency in subverting or choosing discourses, returning us to "high altitude thinking" and a "disembodied subject."[3] The latter comments also reminded me of E.P. Thompson's much earlier claim — admittedly a little more sarcastic and directed towards structuralists — that experience was not only ideological, to be discovered by intellectuals. His notion of experience as a 'junction concept' between social being and social consciousness, and his argument that lived experience might exist in "friction with imposed consciousness," opening up the possibility of alternative ideas emerging,[4] still resonated for me. True, his definition suggested a 'foundational' investment in a prediscursive reality, in social relations framed by the structural relations of capitalism, but that was precisely the positive benefit of a materialist feminism.

Maintaining a materialist grip on the concept of experience was not unrelated to the second article in this section, on the working-class body. The idea emerged initially from reading white women's comments in their travel narratives about Inuit women's bodies. In order to put these in context, I tried to catch up on 'body studies,' a whole new academic category that seemed to be everywhere. Suddenly, everything was embodied or about the body, even topics that had not before been 'body identified.' The influence of both feminism and Foucault, sometimes the intermingling of the two, registered all through body studies, but little was written about work and the body: "the libidinal body," as Terry Eagleton noted, was "in, the labouring body was out."[5] This was dispiriting, since body studies did offer potential insights into labour-related topics such as sexual harassment, the gendered division of labour, and the work process. It also seemed that the body, now named, had been an unnamed presence in previous writing, such as Marx's discussion of alienation, writing that was still relevant and useful, yet often dismissed. Moreover, feminists had done such a good job of denaturalizing the body, and of arguing it was socially constructed rather than biologically limited, that it was hard to talk, without being seen as essentialist, about the actual suffering, violated, maimed body — that is, the bodies of both workers and women. Body theory seemed to circulate in such abstract, esoteric forms: were we losing sight of the labouring body, the material body? By linking research on Indigenous and working-class history, specifically the labour that went into the making of a fur coat, it seemed possible to address some of these issues.

Notes

1   Linda Gordon, "Comments on *That Noble Dream,*" *American Historical Review* 96 (June 1991): 685. As Perez Zagorin points out, historians' own critiques of objectivity are long-standing, predating postmodernism: "History, the Referent, and Narrative Reflections on Postmodernism," *History and Theory* 38, no. 1 (Feb. 1999): 2.

2   Sonia Kruks, *Retrieving Experience: Subjectivity and Recognition in Feminist Politics* (Ithaca: Cornell University Press, 2001), 141.

3   Kruks, quoting Merleau-Ponty, ibid., 143.

4   E.P. Thompson, "The Politics of Theory," in *People's History and Socialist Theory,* ed. Raphael Samuel (London: Routledge and Kegan Paul, 1981), 406.

5   Terry Eagleton, *The Illusions of Postmodernism* (Oxford: Blackwell, 1996), 71.

WORDS OF EXPERIENCE/EXPERIENCING WORDS
READING WORKING WOMEN'S LETTERS
TO CANADA'S ROYAL COMMISSION ON THE
STATUS OF WOMEN

> The work that historians do in order to find texts, which they make into
> evidence, inclines some to a sense that the sources speak to us. I have exper-
> ienced research as requiring me to be very quiet when reading documents
> so that I can "hear" them speak to me.[1]

Historians may experience some texts as more revealing or moving than
others, but their predilections are often quite different from those who
originally created and classified these documents. When the Liberal government set up the Royal Commission on the Status of Women (RCSW)
in 1967 to investigate women's status and make recommendations to
enhance female equality, women's organizations and trade unions welcomed the opportunity to contribute written briefs, many of which were
presented in public.[2] Indeed, the commission had been established after
vigorous lobbying by the Committee for Women's Equality, a coalition of
women's organizations, led by white, professional, educated women, as
well as at least one prominent trade unionist. While scholars have somewhat different views of the RCSW's politics and impact — some stressing its liberal feminist orientation and others seeing it as a moment of
possibility for women's public, 'civic resistance'[3] — most would concede
that this royal commission, more than others, encouraged input from
'ordinary' women, solicited through newspaper ads, surveys, TV and radio coverage, and letters to community and women's organizations.[4]

The seven appointed commissioners,[5] and especially their staff, had
clear ideas about which briefs were most useful, and should be published
for posterity, favouring ones that provided 'hard' evidence, social-science
style, that had statistics (presumed not to lie), and concrete, pragmatic,

realistic policy suggestions. They did not like submissions that were "belligerently" feminist or appeared to describe individual "grievances"; nor, of course, did they have any use for 'wild' socialists trying to criticize the capitalist system.[6] Given the RCSW's preconceived notion of usefulness, it is not hard to see why the roughly one thousand private letters submitted often assumed a lower priority: they were perceived to be more subjective, particularistic, and opinionated. The analysts, in fact, sometimes scribbled "no value" or "little value" at the top of these letters. Historians might disagree.

One could argue that both sources offered insights into women's experience, one through empirical, social-scientific ways of knowing, and the other through a more flexible, variable, and personal means of communication. While the trade union briefs were characterized by a fixed style of presentation, and were formal, distanced in tone, and, despite some differences between unions, structured around similar categories, the letters were more personal, emotive, and passionate, even if they appeared contradictory, disorganized, or hurriedly written. Since this 'private' mode of communication gave women more leeway to say the unspoken, the letters offer a unique standpoint from which to view women's interpretations of the changing economic and social landscape of the postwar period, including the way in which women invoked their *own* personal experiences as meaningful and authoritative evidence for the commission to consider. To read the letters through this particular lens, however, necessitates critical engagement with the very concept of experience, which has been the lightning rod for intense debates within Marxist, feminist, and poststructuralist writing since the 1970s. Using the letters as evidence, I want to revisit these debates, reaffirming the value of a feminist historical materialist analytic in women's history, as well as the importance of a political sensibility that, as Catherine Hall so presciently put it, conveys a sense of "feeling"[7] for the past.

Debating Experience

Our preconceived notion of personal correspondence as a privileged source of information, my own feminist perspective, and perhaps a lingering impulse (in the vein of the new social history) to 'rescue women's voices' and to see the subject as wilful and intentional, undoubtedly shaped my assessment of the letters, though I also recognized that the letters represented only a "trace"[8] of the larger story of women's work. Some poststructuralist critics would go further, arguing, as Joan Scott has, that experience is better seen as a "linguistic event" that "doesn't happen outside established meanings."[9] Scott's contention that experience is an epistemologically flawed foundational concept, too often used to privilege certain historical sources as "unassailable"[10] and 'authentic' has undoubtedly altered the way we think about our subjects. If feminist historians once gave epistemic "privilege to experience,"[11] we later came to express far more epistemic doubt about experience. Following Scott's lead, other social theorists also contend that experience is not merely a "problematic building block" for social history, but also a dangerously 'essentializing' and universalizing concept that potentially leads to "tribalized" identities.[12]

Poststructuralist reappraisals of the concept of experience have undeniably had an influence on historical writing and feminist theory. In the Canadian context, a much-praised historiographical article penned by Joy Parr in 1995 also argued that "experiences were claims, not irrefutable foundations," for "meaning precedes experience,"[13] while two European social historians have argued recently that Joan Scott's critique effectively "disposed" of E.P. Thompson's use of the concept.[14] Debates about experience, however, will likely continue: after all, they have been dogging historians over the entire twentieth century, and in one sense, most historians have long recognized that without mediation of some kind there is no experience. Early twentieth-century historians like Oakeshott "challenged the *authority* of experience, doubted all attempts to re-experience history," and emphasized instead the active role of historians in constructing the past.[15]

Experience later became the focus of vigorous debate within social history and British Marxism, stimulated by Raymond Williams' and especially Edward Thompson's efforts to move away from sterile structuralism and reductive economism by stressing the lived experience of working-class people as a means of "re-insert[ing] the subject" into history.[16] Thompson was taken to task by structuralist Marxists for his neglect of objective conditions, as well as the way in which he endowed experience with far too much "authenticity" and "epistemological privilege"— the latter criticism ironically similar to that of later postmodernists.[17] Experience, he maintained in response, was a humanist concept worth defending, rather than a thoroughly ideological construct needing "scientific discovery by intellectuals."[18] He defined experience as both "lived events" and humans' processing and consciousness of them, but the relationship between the two was not automatic and predictable, and they also informed each other: experience was implied in consciousness and realms of the cultural were also part of experience.[19] Experience thus operated as a mediating or "junction concept," creating a dialectical "dialogue between social being and social consciousness that goes in both directions."[20]

Thompsonian notions of experience left an imprint on an earlier generation of socialist-feminist labour historians who expanded on New Left efforts to reconceptualize labour history beyond the limited category of "the economic,"[21] while also altering its masculinist orientation by integrating women and gender into the narrative.[22] While socialist-feminist historians wrote in a materialist mindset, it was hardly an economistic one: the pressures of material conditions shaping daily life, the consideration of culture and ideology as part of class formation, and an emphasis on the reflective human subject making history all shaped their writing, along with questions concerning male domination and patriarchal cultures. Certain Thompsonian *sensibilities* about experience, humanism, and politics, in other words, were germane to their thinking: they were interested in creating a narrative through the eyes of historical actresses; they questioned the existence of a politically neutral objectivity; and they were unafraid to employ a language of moral approbation about oppression and exploitation. As Linda Gordon put it, socialist-feminist historians saw the importance of "listening to" and understanding their historical subjects, creating a "subjective, imaginative and emulative communication" with the past.[23]

Even historians sympathetic to Thompson point to inconsistencies in his definitions of experience,[24] but the most thoroughgoing feminist critiques came from postmodernists like Scott, who faulted Thompson for his 'foundational' investment in experience and in "class as an identity rooted in structural relations that pre-exist politics"[25] — though this latter position is hardly surprising given Thompson's debt to historical materialism. Scott's characterization of experience broke not only with

Thompson's writing, but also with earlier, 'modernist' feminist scholarship that assumed recuperating women's words, even reading men's words about women against the grain, offered us realistic glimpses of lives lived. These scholars were not trying to prove an "empirical" point,[26] as much as a feminist point about the need to counter male-defined history with women's stories. There was undoubtedly an initial tendency, especially for those using oral history and personal narratives, to assume women's words were a taken-for-granted point of origin for consciousness, including feminist 'oppositional consciousness,' though feminist historians soon began to interrogate the construction of memory, and ask how personal narratives were shaped by cultural norms and conventions.[27]

Although poststructuralist writing has productively unsettled an inclination to read experience as a direct 'point of origin' for consciousness, and sharpened our scrutiny of narrative conventions, texts, and historical contingency, earlier 'modernist' or humanist notions of experience have never been totally abandoned, and indeed they have been defended by many feminist writers. Some feminist standpoint theorists, who originally borrowed from historical materialism, have registered their objection to poststructuralist writing on experience, sensing that it severs social consciousness from the social location and daily activities — productive and reproductive — of the oppressed, and fails to address how an alternative perspective about the world might be achieved through human agency and political reflection. Nancy Hartsock implicitly assumes, as did Thompson, the existence of different levels of experience, and the potential for disjunctures between material being-in-the-world and our consciousness of it. "What sort of oppositional subjectivities," she asks, "grow out of the experience of being native, women, poor?" One's "location in the social order" and the "liminality" of the oppressed *matter*, she adds, but there is no direct, determinate line from experience to political consciousness, for the views 'from below' are multiple and contradictory, sometimes critical of, but also "vulnerable to the dominant culture."[28] Dorothy Smith's explication of the 'relations of ruling' also assumes that an alternative standpoint located in women's "every day, every night" experience[29] can emerge as a political possibility, not the least because a feminist analysis must start with a 'knowable' world "brought into being by human activity."[30]

Marxist-feminists who have not completely abandoned the concept of social determination, or who remain committed to Marx's methodology of exploring the 'conditions of possibility' that underlie class conflict, also invoke women's experience in their writing, not as an unproblematic, transparent, and readily readable reality, but as a reality embedded in social relations, and encompassing language, ideology, and culture.[31] A materialist-feminist like Rosemary Hennessy, while directly engaged in debates with queer and 'post' writing, nonetheless positions her analysis of sexuality within the material conjuncture of late capitalism, and she refers to Thompson's writing in her discussion of the "dis-identification" that can transpire between feelings considered legitimate under capitalism and those 'outlawed,' between the "identities promoted by the dominant culture and the lived experience of social relations not summoned up by these terms."[32]

In a somewhat different vein, Sonia Kruks's critique of poststructuralist writing on experience starts by challenging the false 'transition narrative' that has emerged about the rupture between outdated modernism and superior postmodernism. This manufactured narrative, she suggests, has blinded feminists to the insights of Simon de Beauvoir's existential writings, particularly her emphasis on lived experience and the "sentient, emotional subject."[33] In de Beauvoir's view, she argues, gender was socially produced, but women were not without agency: they experienced a "constrained, situated freedom."[34] Moreover, by denying experience, and reducing human subjects to a set of "discursive effects," postmodern feminists preclude an understanding of both interiority, and the domain of "affectivity"— the latter crucial to feminist projects of understanding and solidarity.[35]

Scholars outside of Marxist traditions, who are nonetheless concerned about the textual erasure of social relations in some poststructuralist writing, are also "reclaiming" experience as a viable historical, and necessary, political concept. The notion that experience is still "epistemologically indispensable" to the recovery of history[36] is forwarded by a group of postpositivist realist scholars who challenge postmodern attempts to "de-legitimize a theoretical project that explores linkages between social location and identity."[37] While granting that experience is mediated through culture and ideology, postpositivists assert that it is still shaped by "cognitive processes," making humans capable of rendering relatively 'true' and objective knowledge about the world — recognizing that objectivity does not mean neutrality.[38] In the postmodernist critique of experience, these scholars warn, the salience of political-ethical judgements is negated, an epistemological relativism prevails, questions about how historical transformations in consciousness occur are left unanswered, and "ideology becomes total and inescapable," with humans "confined to a fixed order of meanings."[39]

Postpositivist writing has been justifiably criticized as liberal pluralist in tone, lacking an anticapitalist critique or discussion of class as a category of exploitation.[40] Indeed, these defences of experience are not theoretically homogeneous, or cut from the same ideological cloth. For cultural studies scholar Michael Pickering, Thompson's notion of experience needs to be defended less because of its absolute theoretical soundness and more because of its theoretical *sensibility.* Reflecting the theoretical shift from materialism to intersectional feminist analyses, Pickering's emphasis is primarily on the "mutually constituting"[41] intersections of social structure, representation, and subjectivities that create lived experience; productive relations do not take centre stage in his definition. Yet, dismayed by the portrayal of historical subjects as no more than "vectors" for ideology/discourse,[42] he is sympathetic to earlier Marxist efforts of historical retrieval that rejected mechanical and elitist theories (including Marxist ones) delineating society from above, in favour of efforts to listen to the collective voices of historical actors, attempting to get "inside their minds and hearts"[43]— while recognizing full well that their words are not simply transparent reflections of reality.

These somewhat disparate defences suggest that experience, as both socialist humanists and feminists have conceived it, has not been entirely 'disposed of.' Apprehensions about the slighting of attention to human agency and social causality[44] in recent historical writing have encouraged a group of "middle grounders" to seek a compromise "between discourse and experience."[45] Jay Smith, to note only one example, urges historians to resist the "lure of experience" if that concept still means exploring the social, political, and cultural contexts shaping how individuals 'read' their worlds. His alternative is to explore the "interpretive dispositions that determine how people engage, process, and learn from all that occurs," with these dispositions defined as "ever changing beliefs, ideas and values that are fragmented, disconnected, composite and contradictory." While the phrasing is different, this definition does not really break entirely from idealist and postmodern assumptions.[46] Other efforts at theoretical rapprochement have been criticized as new forms of liberal pluralism;[47] moreover, rather than sitting on the political fence, middle grounders often ultimately come down on one side or the other, most often the discursive, criticizing, for example, the "myopia of materialism."[48] Few scholars are brave enough to declare that "accommodation is an illusion" and that this "middle ground" still slights "human agency and causal explanations."[49] Our reassessment of experience may have to heed this warning, rather than following the more heavily trod path of desperately seeking a liberal compromise that is anything *but* a Marxist or materialist solution. This, at least, was my conclusion after reading hundreds of letters from working women who were determined to claim their *own* experience as the solid evidence that the Royal Commission was looking for.

Letters to Florence Bird

Read as a whole, women's letters to Florence Bird, the Head of the RCSW, suggested to me that working women's consciousness had undergone important shifts the postwar period. If the letters had only been personal laments for unhappy lives, they might have resembled women's devotional letters to St. Jude, the patron saint of lost causes; however, these women did not seek aid in becoming 'better' individuals in order to cope with their problems.[50] On the contrary, many women identified ideological barriers and structural inequalities in Canadian society, and they articulated a sense of collective grievance and desire for change. Certainly, these women spoke from a limited constituency.[51] The letters were predominantly from literate (and semi-literate) English and French-speaking women who had the confidence and skills to put their ideas to paper. In terms of race, they may have reflected the predominantly white population of the time, but racial minorities, the very poor, as well as recent European immigrants, were still underrepresented.[52] There were many white-collar working women writing, Bird suggested, because they wanted to avoid the public exposure of commission hearings, fearing reprisals on the job. One sixteen-year veteran clerical worker at Bell Telephone, who laid out multiple examples of rampant discrimination in the company, insisted that her name be "kept under cover" as she feared losing her "only means of support."[53] It was precisely this group of white-collar women, along with those in service work and the feminized professions, whose commitment to wage labour was rapidly increasing.

The letters were just one of a number of examples of the commission's information-filtering practices; many had "private" written on them, but in some cases the commission staff categorized them as private letters based solely on their method of presentation and content. Since the very satisfied would have been less likely to write, the letters were generally letters of complaint or calls for change. The anonymity of private submissions also meant that, statistically, they were skewed in political outlook: women and men who celebrated homemaking and opposed married women's work were more likely to write privately than appear in public, fearing that the "tide of [public] opinion is in favour of married women working."[54] Like the official briefs, women's letters were strategic attempts to persuade the RCSW that their concerns were important, but they did address issues other submissions did not: there are more references in these letters to sexual harassment and violence, issues the commission was later criticized for completely ignoring. "My husband beat me and tried to kill me several times," wrote one woman, "family welfare [just] told me to go home and not antagonize him."[55] The term 'sexual harassment' had yet to be coined, but women's allusions to it are quite clear. "I did not come to this country to be the boss's girlfriend" said an immigrant about her decision to leave a workplace, while another noted she had to quit a job because of the "pressure" caused when she "refused to have anything to do with a married man."[56] Although Bird claimed the commission did not address violence, as it was perceived to be a social, not a women's issue, these letters clearly said otherwise.

If we are to understand how women explained their labour in these letters, we have to consider the social relations in which they were embedded. Changes in material life shape the formation of social groups "*as well as* how they describe themselves."[57] This is not to say the relations of production and reproduction of the period were a bare economic imperative determining women's lives, but rather that the organization, thought, and practice of women's labour were imbricated in these changing economic relations. The Royal Commission itself was in part a response to the increased numbers of women working for pay. In pushing for such a commission, feminists drew not only on the political climate of the time — debates about civil rights, poverty, and equality — but pointed to women's increased role in the labour force. The postwar transformation in the labour force may have been interpreted differently, but it was not simply discursively constructed. More and more women were working for pay, and returning to wage work after child bearing. The extent and nature of these shifts was differentiated by class, immigration status, and ethnicity; indeed, one could argue that poor and racialized women had a long-standing involvement in paid labour, but that far more working- and middle-class women were now joining the workforce. Still, for all groups of women, wage-earning motherhood was becoming more and more the norm.

Women's changing productive and reproductive work roles meant they had different timetables, hours of work, job definitions, relationships with other women, and schedules with their children; in other words, the physical and mental mapping of their daily lives was altering. This is made clear in women's descriptions of their rushed double days and fast-paced multi-tasking. One woman who had previously combined wage and mother work, then dropped paid work, described her typical day with a physical analogy: "I found myself saying, 'Run, run, run as fast as you can, you can't catch me.' . . . What makes [us] run? Stop the world I want to get off!"[58] As Kathleen Canning argues, women's embodied experiences of significant physical alterations in daily life sometimes "opened the way for the transformation of consciousness."[59] Similarly, Regina Gagnier's study of British working-class women's letters about motherhood indicates how their experience of pain, uncertainty, and anxiety generated new ways of describing themselves, which in turn were utilized politically as justifications for better conditions of life for themselves and their children.[60]

Even some of the apparent tensions in women's letters to the RCSW can be interpreted in light of their struggles to come to terms with a new economic and social landscape. One repeated theme was what one writer called the "civil war"[61] between married working women and homemakers. Homemakers often claimed their work was not "esteemed or rewarded" and that they were chastised for not using their brains and talent by going out to work,[62] while working women with families believed they were stigmatized for 'abandoning' their children at home.[63] "Married women with children," wrote one homemaker, are in the unenviable position of "being 'damned if they, and damned if they don't.' On the one hand, we hear about the damaging effects on the family unit if the mother goes out to work, and on the other hand, we are being constantly urged to make more use of our potential."[64] Her claim that women were at a difficult "historical crossroads"[65] was apt, but not all writers were as even-handed. Women in the home who felt their work was "downgraded" might concede that mothers had a right to work, but there was no mistaking the judgmental tone of one such correspondent who intoned that working mothers should make "proper arrangements" for their children, who often "run wild and are a terror to the neighbourhood."[66]

The idealization of a male breadwinner and home-centred motherhood, especially for white, middle-class women, was still quite powerful, but these ideals were increasingly challenged by the needs of working families, and the growing number of married women in the labour force. This 'civil war,' then, was a reflection of women's uncertain attempts to process where they fit in the changing world around them, how to interpret and legitimate the work they performed every day. In a similar vein, single self-supporting women, single working mothers, and divorced women often made references to their 'outsider' status as workers, although they had differing explanations for this marginalization. Analyzing their different rationales is important, but so too is seeing the common denominator in their discomfort: they were responding, both consciously and unconsciously, to their exclusion from the dominant, idealized heteronormative familial ideal.

Letters that bridled with resentment or anger about this outsider status might simultaneously be articulations of entitlement. Single women and self-supporting mothers especially suggested that every citizen had a right to be independent economically, not forced into dependence on others. Some of the most painful letters to read are those from single working mothers, often deserted, who knew first-hand the injustice of divorce laws, the uselessness of trying to secure spousal support, and the daily worry of supporting their children on a woman's salary. Their budgets were so tight that a few bus tickets or an extra lunch could make the difference between ending the month in the red or the black.[67] To add insult to injury, they felt looked down upon, their children treated as "third class oddities." "Each day I go to work wondering why I'm doing it and each day I hurry home to cook or snack quickly to appease my ulcer I've been starving all day . . . you see, I can't afford lunches for the children and me as well," wrote one single mother who also knew that she would be "called down for even having a man in the house."[68] Although a few women asked why they became mothers at all, most directed their palpable anger towards laws and salaries that did not allow them the dignity they believed they and their children deserved.

Not all women articulated a clear-cut sense of collective injustice. Some women's presentations of themselves were individualist in tone, reflecting also the prevailing ideology about the deserving and undeserving poor. A single working mother, supporting three children, one an "invalid," with scarcely a penny to spare every week, insisted she still had her "dignity" and was better than others she saw lingering at the welfare office, alcohol bottle in hand.[69] Women decried the fact that women were their own worst enemies (because they denied the need for equality, were nasty to other women, or were hoodwinked into subservient femininity), or sometimes advocated their own prescription for individual 'bootstrapping.' An older woman insisted that younger women just had to assume some "backbone" in order to secure their economic independence and a share of any property in the marriage: "Girls must see from the start that they must stand up for themselves . . . . Get all the knowledge you can and use it to be a full person and not lean on men as dependents. . . . Of course no husband is going to say you are worth your salt. I'd say find out what salt you are worth, and see you are worth it." This self-help advocate, however, also incorporated a more subversive critique of the patriarchal attitudes that accounted for women's oppression. Men would "never do anything to help women as long as they can exploit them," she concluded, ending with the essentialist, but nonetheless amusing quip: "Men are a race of cads."[70]

One can often read between the lines of these letters to guess at the particular personal situation shaping women's views, but their life histories reflect more than particularistic stories, as the commission staff assumed. Many self-supporting white-collar women workers, for example, wrote to the RCSW expressing their unhappiness, resentments, and desire for something better: it was not only wages, but their sense of respectability that was on the line. The self-supporting single woman had long had some social purchase as a deserving, if pitied, wage earner, but many women writing to Florence Bird took a more assertive stance, equating their needs and rights with those of self-supporting men. White-collar women bemoaned the fine line they faced between poverty and respectability, and with good reason. Women's clerical salaries were, on average, two-thirds of men's, not even enough for an apartment, leaving them in rented rooms, or dependent on family. "I want to speak for the unmarried female workers," wrote one correspondent, "how about some tax concessions so we can rent something better than housekeeping rooms, euphemistically called bachelor suites. After all, we are past the stage when dorm living is fun."[71] Complaints about working women's lack of access to the private 'home space' they deserved came from many letter writers, though a few used this complaint to relay resentments against married working women, since the pooling of more than one salary appeared to offer couples more housing options.

The issue of housing touched a nerve because it symbolized economic independence and dignity. One immigrant woman working as a waitress protested that she could not secure a mortgage because she was single, though her anger was simultaneously fuelled by the way in which her service labour was denigrated: there is "no respect for waitresses, even less than waiters . . . [we are] too lowly to merit status" yet we are providing an "essential service." She went on to condemn the more affluent customers — including women — whom she thought looked down on her, indicating the class tensions between women also relayed in a few letters to the RCSW.[72] Single women who had looked after aged parents also found themselves, later in life, without a house or pension, uncompensated for their years of caring work, and few assets other than their high-school typing skills. "Why should a woman who has spent half of her life looking after her aged parents . . . be doomed to a life of poverty after they have died?"[73] In an inchoate way, these women understood that their unpaid contributions to social reproduction had left them vulnerable to poverty and marginalization.

Women's sense of unfairness or dissatisfaction often emerged from the fissures, contradictions, and stress points they sensed between constructions of women's economic needs and their actual material predicament, between idealized domesticity and the reality that more women were going out to work, between the expectations placed on 'good' mothers and the constraints of the double day. Women's personal narratives, suggest Patricia Ewick and Susan Silbey, are always positioned within a social context, and thus bear the marks of existing ideologies and unequal power relations. Yet these may be unsettled by countervailing 'subversive stories' that emerge in the disjuncture between the recounting of subjective experience and dominant discourses, between "biography and history."[74]

Metaphors of friction have often been used to suggest how hegemonic ideologies can be unsettled by the pressures of material relations, cultural traditions, political beliefs, and human feeling. Our social consciousness of lived traditions, institutions, and formations, Raymond Williams suggested, is never fixed or complete; we may have experiences that do not seem attuned to, or recognizable within, this consciousness, though we may feel only an "unease, displacement or reservation" about this dissonance, and any new forms of thought and feeling may remain "embryonic," tentative, before — and if — they are fully articulated.[75] Analyzing these fissures is politically crucial if we are to understand *how* resistance might emerge to taken-for-granted understandings of class and gender relations. This emphasis on tension and contradiction has been intrinsic to much writing on feminism since the 1970s, but similar notions of "double consciousness" have been at the heart of many discussions of other oppressed groups.[76] Our reflections on the "distorted" ideological constructions of our own daily experiences, gay historian William Wilkerson suggests in a critique of Joan Scott, may well lead to "transformations in [our] collective and political consciousness.[77]

Both the male breadwinner ideal and a sexual division of labour increasingly rubbed up against women's day-to-day needs and aspirations, sparking their questions, resentments, and protests. Women could see how unfair, if not irrational, the male breadwinner ideal was when a young single man in their office was paid more than a single mother supporting children, and they were not afraid to point out the contradiction. "Women office workers in this small town," wrote one woman, "are so badly paid they cannot support their families, and their qualifications are not recognized. Take the young men out of university who are installed in higher positions and imperiously tell us where to put a comma when they can't write a sentence and are paid twice as much. . . . So yes, women are discriminated against."[78] Women are "treated as if it is not quite ladylike or nice to be the sole support of the family," one woman advised, "this fallacy needs uprooting if we are to have a just society."[79]

These women understood that discrimination was systemic rather than haphazard and individual; even if they made their point using personal anecdotes, they simultaneously conveyed a sense of collective displeasure about shared social conditions. Both public submissions and private letters complained that older women were shut out of the job market, either because employers cavalierly replaced them with younger women, or because employment agencies like Drake Personnel discriminated against them. "Sorry, we have had no requests for women over 50,"[80] they told one woman, who then wrote to Florence asking that something be done about this discrimination. Since it's a well-known fact that we are "governed by older men," asked one woman pointedly, why is that older women are not allowed to work?[81]

A sense of collective injustice was also registered through women's criticisms of practices that were more often accepted as unchangeable in the interwar period: the lack of advancement for women in the professions like teaching, pregnancy bars for women workers, and the prevailing sexual division of labour. Women offered different interpretations of the sexual division of labour, but there was nonetheless unhappiness expressed with the limitations it placed on their earning and sense of fulfilment. Some protested that employment agencies streamed women only into clerical jobs, while one bank clerk pointed out that banks slyly put a different title on a woman's job, then paid a man more to do it, while "expecting us to live on a salary no single man would."[82] The "general male attitude," explained one woman looking for work, was that "anything in a skirt should be able to type."[83] A European immigrant who was an experienced photographer protested her relegation to a photofinishing factory, after being denied jobs because of her sex: when I go to work, "I have to shut off my brain, [if not] I would go out of my mind," she lamented.[84]

Women writers were not convinced the prevailing division of labour was based on inherent sex differences, though some still clung to male breadwinner images. A single office worker with thwarted technical ambitions told the RCSW she had been confined to female-typed jobs, barred from more technical, highly skilled, or highly paid ones in her company. Even though she was "fascinated with motor mechanics" and had asked to work in the warehouse doing machinery orders, she was denied this job. She believed that married women's place was primarily "in the home" but that, as a single woman, she was in a different category: "There are women like me who must make a living, not an existence, but a living, because we chose not to marry right out of high school." She abandoned the company that prevented her from "moving up" or making equal pay, and was still searching for a job where she felt she could secure the "same benefits" as men, without "sacrificing [her] femininity."[85]

Other women had a more politicized sense of 'who benefits' from women's work in female job ghettos. "Employers take advantage of working mothers," wrote one correspondent. "They know [we have to work and] . . . they discount our wages and job opportunities," using the excuse that women are "short term" workers, even though this was not the reality. "Why are [our] girls only trained for nursing and teaching" she asked; after all, "women have brains too, yet they must outwork and outperform males." As if to apologize for her radical views, she concluded more lightheartedly: "I guess I was born thirty years too early."[86]

While poststructuralist writing has been concerned with the emergence of counter-discourses, explications of the origins of such resistance are less clearly enunciated.[87] In contrast, feminist historical materialist writing has situated the possibilities of resistance within the interconnected dynamic of changing social relations, concrete human activities, and the reflective human process of meaning making. If these letters to the RCSW had been shaped only within a 'closed circuit' of discursive possibilities that constituted women's reality, it would have been difficult for women to imagine and demand something different — yet clearly many did. Women did not begin to interpret their world with new eyes simply as a result of ambiguities *within* discourses, but rather because their experience of capitalist and gendered work relations, along with an emerging vocabulary of equality, stimulated their questions. Women writers seldom employed words like 'liberation,' or cited Betty Freidan, and some even shied away from feminism, noting fearfully they did not want to "discard their femininity in the rush for equal rights."[88] Yet they were clearly articulating a changing consciousness of the centrality of paid labour in their lives, as well as a sense of grievance about workplace inequality. Their opposition was voiced by appropriating some of the very ideals sacred to the dominant social order — entitlement, rights, human dignity — not unlike generations of workers before them. "We have to make things better for our daughters," concluded one mother, while another writer put it more forcefully: "We need profound changes . . . this is a generation of angry females who will be satisfied with nothing less."[89]

Women's articulations of unfairness were not necessarily expressed in a clear and uncompromising manner. Working mothers, for instance, recognized that a male-breadwinner family was a persisting ideal, and their letters were couched in a defensive tone. They felt they were the most stigmatized, misunderstood workers, and they wanted the RCSW to hear their side of the story. They responded, defensively, to the prevailing myths about working moms. One mother countered the idea that women worked for unnecessary 'extras' by reminding the RCSW that part-time workers like her had "few benefits and lower pay," and that her money was not "spent on luxuries and riotous living. . . . it goes to the dentist bill, buys shoes to replace a pair outgrown, new curtains, paint for the kitchen ceiling . . . and countless other items that deteriorate or disappear to the embarrassment of an already strained budget."[90] The charge that working mothers neglected their children and created juvenile delinquents was the cruellest myth of all; a bookkeeper wrote to Bird denouncing a radio show caller who had referred to working mothers as mere nighttime babysitters, insinuating that they barely knew their children. Many working mothers invoked the notion of *their own experience* to counter these myths, and some suggested that they were especially misunderstood by men who had never been in their shoes: "Our legislators, predominantly male, fail to realize how hard the majority of women work to raise children, educate them, provide extras that are in no way luxuries, and ease the burden on the husband. Working mothers are helping to provide the citizens of the future."[91]

While the letters reveal perceived differences between women workers based on age or marital status, they are less revealing about the very significant divisions of class, ethnicity, and race, while sexual orientation was simply ignored. A few letters do indict the commission's "professional" bias, claiming it was paying too little attention to the "working conditions of [blue-collar] hourly wage" jobs.[92] Few of the white- and blue-collar working mothers who wrote adopted the line of some service clubs, with solidly middle-class leadership, that suggested working moms were *forced* to work largely due to poverty, but might prefer to be homemakers. Understandably, the letter writers wanted to legitimize their labour, not suggest that bringing home a pay check was a second-best option. The regional and racial complexion of Canadian poverty also revealed itself in submissions that simply asked *for* paid work of any kind for women. "There is little opportunity for women's labour in Newfoundland because of high unemployment," lamented one brief.[93] Another woman from Nova Scotia pointed out that many women workers in her town feared even raising the issue of equal pay, since decent jobs were "scarce," and their husband's seasonal work in the fisheries meant wives had little choice but to work.[94] Lacking letters from Aboriginal women, we must look to public presentations that discussed the lack of work available in their communities. An Alberta Métis woman who testified before the RCSW lamented the fate of the next generation on her reserve should they not secure work: "we need training and work . . . men could work in sawmills, girls train as supervisors in local mission schools, or as waitresses, cooks, and in beauty culture. It is sad to see so many young people walking around when so much could be done."[95] The fairly narrow work options she cited for women suggest that critiques of the sexual division of labour were less salient for those who had long been denied any paid work. The notion that Aboriginal women especially should be trained for domestic work, articulated in a long brief submitted by a white woman in the NWT, was, however, quite different, reflecting a racist understanding of character and ability.

While I have quoted predominantly from letters defending women's waged work, there was certainly a minority group of men and women who expressed hostility to married women in the workforce, and unqualified support for a naturally ordained sexual division of labour. The few responses that were steeped in misogyny, however, came predominantly from men. Feminists, wrote one man, are publicity-seeking, "mentally

sick, unfeminine, frustrated, unhappy, dictatorial, overbearing and emotionally disturbed" people who need "a good psychiatrist and tranquilliz-
ers."[96] Another man offered a long diatribe on the uselessness of women
over forty, bragging about the enjoyment of playing "slap and tickle" with
his "cute typist."[97] These letters suggest how accepted the sexualization
and ridicule of women was, though many of their authors appeared to
be on the defensive, fearful that the established familial order they idealized was disintegrating. Where will all this talk of working women end,
fretted another antifeminist: with "thousands of unemployed men" and
"demands for golf courses for women not caring for their children."[98] The
most adamant opponents of women's equality were not taken seriously
by the RCSW staff, though polite thank-you letters were required. Occasionally the staff had a little fun. When a rambling letter blamed cartoon
characters Dagwood and Jiggs for patriarchy in crisis, the RCSW reply
read: "Thank you for your letter explaining how Dagwood and Jiggs have
demoted the father as the head of the household. Yours sincerely. . ."[99]

Nor were men the only antifeminists. Some women's determination to
cling to certain aspects of the existing gender order, perhaps those they
found most ideologically reassuring, makes clear the fractured and contradictory nature of ideology. These letter writers might call for a better
deal for women workers, but then caricature their fellow female workers,
pointing to their emotive nature, their interest only in husband hunting, and their unsuitability for skilled jobs. Others opposed rights such as
maternity leave, insisting that this 'special status' contradicted notions
of equality: "Pregnancy is not an accident," noted one writer acerbically,
"if women want children, they can't have their cake and eat it too."[100]

Although they did not represent the majority, some writers laid out a
hierarchy of who the most virtuous and deserving female workers were,
assuming their right to work should be equated with need. Their views
suggest that the Depression-era equation of job rights with providing
roles, highlighted by Alice Kessler-Harris, had some residual appeal.[101]
By and large, however, all men were assumed to need a job, while some
women were more entitled than others: those who were single, in poor
families, or supporting children stood at the top of the list, though some
correspondents also conceded this right to women with special professional skills. A letter writer who deplored the bad working conditions

in department stores, noting in particular Simpson's refusal to pay one woman's sick day, then added, "this woman depends on her wages. . . . there are other women who have husbands and what they earn is extra money, but when a woman depends on her salary to live, it is not right" she should lose her sick pay.[102] Still, descriptions of the un/deserving worker were not always predictable. One woman in the Northwest Territories criticized well-off, white married women workers because so many Native youth were underemployed; do these women not know, she asked that "this still is a Depression for the native peoples?"[103]

As some of these examples illustrate, the letters are sometimes difficult to categorize, since they contained multiple themes, points of view, even seemingly contradictory ideas: a homemaker who soundly denounced working mothers might then call for day nurseries for them. This undoubtedly frustrated the commission, probably making it even less inclined to see the letters as solid evidence. Yet the topics women covered, the perspectives offered, and particularly the feeling they conveyed, did reveal something lost in the formal trade union briefs that divided women's lives up into charts and statistics, and separate boxes of work and family. Some women protested a whole series of problems, undoubtedly seeing these as connected, not confined to separate spheres. A sixty-eight-year-old widow with two sons wrote about tax relief, abortion, violence, job benefits, and equal pay. Her views, presented with both humour and indignation, are worth quoting at length. Calling, first, for "no laws at all" concerning abortion and birth control, she asked:

Why should some 80 yr old cardinals decide [about abortion] for women. It's ridiculous . . . might as well ask a eunuch to give his personal experience on sex. . . . women have to work harder, usually have longer hours and perform monotonous jobs for less than their male counterparts in most industry and particularly in offices. . . . they are subject to dismissal after years of hard work by arbitrary bosses who would rather have a younger if less efficient worker, and [the one fired] has no protection. I hope you have many responses and something will be done for women who are pushed around, worked to death, beaten up (and too scared to say anything about it) and work at two jobs a day.[104]

The last example opens up the question of how contemporary read-ers experience these letters, perhaps endorsing or enjoying sentiments like hers that the RCSW was more prone to see as outspoken and subjec-tive. Because letter writing in our culture permits us to be introspective, to express views or emotion inappropriate in the public sphere, women articulated a sense of injustice, rage, unhappiness, and hope that might have been consciously or unconsciously suppressed in public. Indeed, one could argue that the interface between the expression of emotion and changing social relations was precisely the opportunity opened up for "oppositional meaning making." In Raymond Williams's terms, the letters convey a "provisional, elusive, embryonic structure of feeling . . . a social experience which is still in process."[105]

Feelings are, admittedly, not to be naturalized. There is a social and historical dimension to emotion and affect; they are not innate, universal, or unchanging phenomena. Nor are readers' responses entirely predict-able. My feminist point of view, to be sure, plays a role in how I experi-ence and interpret the letters — and convey them to you. Feminist and Marxist writing, however, has not been unreflective about the political expenditure we invest in our efforts to retrieve women's and workers' experience and consciousness, or the way in which the past only answers the questions we pose to it.[106] The distance of objectivity, as both postmod-ernists and materialists might agree, is neither possible, nor necessarily a laudable goal. Subjecting our own interests to critical scrutiny, making our "partisanship" clear and "striving for dispassionate judgement," sug-gests Terry Eagleton, speaking for the materialist side, are preferable to the "liberal myth" of "even handed" neutrality.[107]

One could argue that these letters were strategically emotional or confessional in mode, and on one level that is absolutely true. But to see them *only* as rhetorical devices or discursive constructs misses the fact that women had something very real to complain about: if we assign no 'truth claims' to their words, concepts of exploitation, injustice, and op-pression will have little meaning. Moreover, if we accede to "the [post-modern] death of the subject," as Catherine Hall wrote perceptively in 1990, "it can lead to a . . . loss of *feeling* in [our] historical writing"[108]: that sense of affect or 'feeling' has been, and should continue to be, an inte-gral part of feminist history.

Conclusion

Women's private letters to this Royal Commission offered an array of observations, opinions, and life histories that often invoked women's own experiences as evidence, which they contrasted in turn with the experience and views of male employers and lawmakers, and, occasionally, with those of more privileged women. While class tensions between women were evident in a few of the letters, they were likely flattened out in this particular source because so many of the letters came from literate English- and French-speaking white women, in professional, white-collar, and service work. Similarly, differences of race, ethnicity, and sexual orientation are less evident, save in the overwhelming assumption by writers and the commission alike that women workers *were* predominantly heterosexual, white Canadians.

The commission staff tended to see women's personal evidence as more subjective, and of less value than the hard empirical data of social science research, yet these letters can tell us much about how women managed, negotiated, and interpreted the changing patterns and practices of paid labour during the twenty-five years following World War II, and why these women believed their experiences counted as solid evidence that would enlighten the commissioners. They were clearly articulating a changing consciousness of the centrality of paid labour in their lives, as well as an embryonic sense of grievance about workplace inequality. Their 'subversive stories' represented a challenge to the dominant norms, a sense of collective grievance, and a plea for better lives for themselves and their daughters. How and why women came to object to the status quo had much to do with frictions, fissures, and seeming incongruencies that were part and parcel of women's daily experiences of both paid and unpaid work, and their reflections on them. This is not to suggest a one-way determinate line between work and consciousness. Women's lives were bounded and pressured by the material, to be sure, but their understanding of social change was not then automatically 'translated' directly into political consciousness; rather, their experiences gave way to a range of possibilities that shaped how they handled those events — hence, the contradictory and partial character of their responses and observations. As in Gramscian writing, there existed the possibility, not inevitability, of a disjuncture between dominant and alternative ideologies.

Poststructuralist critiques of the concept of experience have sharpened our understanding of the way in which women's words are mediated through culture, made us wary of drawing a direct line between being and consciousness, and warned us of the dangers of essentialism. However useful these cautions are, the theoretical assumptions separating poststructuralist critics and 'modernist' defenders of experience are not easily resolvable in a middle-ground compromise. It is not only that class is often slighted in the postmodern academic gaze, but that key epistemological differences cannot be wished away in a liberal search for compromise. Rather than seeking an elusive 'third way,' there is value in developing a reinvigorated feminist historical materialism as a method of unravelling the intertwined making of class and gender relations. On-the-ground, empirical "excavations"[109] of women's lives are crucial to this project, offering insight into a history created by women, but not within conditions of their own choosing. Our explorations of women's experience need not entail a naive reification of experience, a denial of differences between women, or the assumption that it is unmediated by culture. Rather, our analyses can take into account the power of structuring relations, the two-way dialectic between being and consciousness, and the importance of human agency in meaning making. Although not all materialist feminists concur on how to define and use the concept of experience, a recurring metaphor of interconnected layers, encompassing contradiction and tension, is often invoked in their work. Experience is thus both lived and construed, a "point of origin for an explanation," yet also as the "object of explanation";[110] it is dialectic between "first and third person" perspectives, the former foregrounding lived experience and the latter scrutinizing our processing of that experience.[111]

These definitions, however, cannot suffice as timeless or lifeless abstract frameworks; they require the ongoing excavations of women's lives, and the challenge of intellectual critique, if we are to comprehend how gender and race are embedded in the process of class formation, how oppression and exploitation are sustained, remade, and sometimes challenged over time. Both feminist and Marxist historians have been faulted for failing to interrogate our own subjective, political ends in claiming to 'know' women's authentic experience and interiority. It is true that explicating our own investment in this history is not only essential, but will produce more honest, critical, and animated history. However, "committed history"[112] is not an unreflective history. The gap between women's experience in the past and our attempts to reconstruct it cannot be denied, but this is not a convincing reason to abandon attempts to understand the minds and feelings of historical actors. Listening to our sources, as Linda Gordon suggests, and contemplating affective links with women in the past has many dangers for historians: we may romanticize past actors, think in presentist terms, assume a false sisterhood between women, skirt over differences based on class or race, or misinterpret their interpretation of their experience. Yet, however fraught or utopian this form of time travelling is, the effort may be both politically and historically worthwhile.

Notes

1 Linda Gordon, "Comments on *That Noble Dream*," *American Historical Review* 96 (June 1991): 684.

2 Literature on the Royal Commission includes Caroline Andrew and Sandra Rodgers, eds., *Women and the Canadian State* (Montreal: McGill-Queen's University Press, 1997); Cerise Morris, "No More than Simple Justice: The Royal Commission on the Status of Women in Canada" (Ph.D. diss., McGill University, 1982), 319; Kimberly Speers, "The Royal Commission on the Status of Women: A Study of the Contradictions and Limitations of Liberal Feminism" (MA thesis, Queen's University, 1994); Kathryn McLeod, "Laying the Foundation: The Women's Bureau, the Royal Commission on the Status of Women and Canadian Feminism" (MA thesis, Laurentian University, 2006); Annis Timpson, "Royal Commissions as Sites of Resistance: Women's Challenges on Child Care in the Royal Commission on the Status of Women," *International Journal of Canadian Studies* 20 (Fall 1999): 124; Jane Arscott, "Twenty-Five Years and Sixty-Five Minutes After the Royal Commission on the Status of Women," *International Review of Canadian Studies* 11 (Spring 1995): 33–58; Barbara Freeman, *The Satellite Sex: The Media and Women's Issues in English Canada, 1966–71* (Waterloo: Wilfrid Laurier University Press, 2001). It is also discussed in Jill Vickers, Pauline Rankin, and Christine Appelle, *Politics As If Women Mattered: A Political Analysis of the National Action Committee on the Status of Women* (Toronto: University of Toronto Press, 1993); Nancy Adamson, Linda Briskin, and Margaret McPhail, *Feminists Organizing for Change: The Contemporary Women's Movement in Canada* (Toronto: Oxford University Press, 1988).

3　Timpson, "Royal Commissions as Sites of Resistance," 124.

4　See Arscott, "Twenty-Five Years and Sixty-Five Minutes."

5　The appointed commissioners, two men and five women, were white, educated volunteer or professional leaders in their fields, selected with an eye to regional and linguistic diversity. They were Florence Bird, journalist and head of the commission; Miss Elsie Gregory MacGill, aeronautical engineer; Mrs. Lola Lange, volunteer for women's farming organizations; Miss Jeanne Lapointe; Doris Ogilvie, judge; Jacques Henripin, sociologist; and John Humphrey, law professor.

6　Analyst assessment from vol. 15, brief 295 and vol. 12, brief 115, Royal Commission on the Status of Women Papers, RG 33-89 (hereafter RCSW), Library and Archives Canada (LAC).

7　Catherine Hall, "Politics, Post-structuralism and Feminist History," *Gender and History* 3 (1991): 210.

8　Carolyn Steedman, "Something She Called Fever: Michelet, Derrida and Dust," *American Historical Review* 106 (2001): 1165.

9　Joan Scott, "The Evidence of Experience," *Critical Inquiry* 17 (Summer 1991): 797. Scott does note that it is a term almost impossible to do without, and she too uses it: Joan Scott, *Only Paradoxes to Offer: French Feminists and the Rights of Man* (Cambridge, MA: Harvard University Press, 1996), 14. Her call for attention to subjectivity and language and her insights on gender as a way of signifying power have arguably had substantially more impact than her article on experience. See Joan Scott, "Gender: A Useful Category of Analysis," *American Historical Review* 91, no. 5 (Dec. 1986): 1053–75, and a recent celebration of her work as "canonical": AHR editors, "AHR Forum," *American Historical Review* 113, no. 5 (Dec. 2008): 1344.

10　Joan Scott, "The Evidence of Experience," *Critical Inquiry* 17 (Summer 1991): 793.

11　Ruth Roach Pierson, "Experience, Difference, Dominance, and Voice in the Writing of Canadian Women's History," in Karen Offen, Ruth Roach Pierson, and Jane Rendall, eds., *Writing Women's History: International Perspectives* (Bloomington: Indiana University Press, 1991), 85.

12　Craig Ireland, "The Appeal to Experience and Its Constituencies: Variations on a Persistent Thompsonian Theme," *Cultural Critique* 52 (Autumn 2002): 95. It is important to note, however, that the postmodern critiques of identity politics differ from materialist-feminists critiques that stress the 'fit' between neoliberalism and identity politics and the politicization of identity "at the expense of the politicization of capitalism." See Rosemary Hennessy, *Profit and Pleasure: Sexual Identities in Late Capitalism* (New York: Routledge, 2000), 229.

13　Joy Parr, "Gender History and Historical Practice," *Canadian Historical Review* 76, no. 3 (Sept. 1995): 364. One indication of changing interpretations of experience is Parr's most recent book, in which experience is described differently. Commenting positively on another author, she notes :"This is a stark departure from the conceptual frame of recent studies of the social construction studies of gender, sex, and race. Rather than postulating, as social constructionists have done, that meaning precedes experience and that humans know the world through the meanings they share symbolically in language . . ." Parr attributes the expression "meaning precedes experience" to Joan Scott in her endnotes: Joy Parr, *Sensing Changes: Technologies, Environments, and the Everyday, 1953–2000* (Vancouver: University of British Columbia Press, 2010), 12.

14   Geoff Eley and Keith Nield, *The Future of Class in History: What's Left of the Social?* (Ann Arbour: University of Michigan Press, 2007), 106. To be fair, they do have some other criticisms of Scott's writing.

15   Martin Jay, *Songs of Experience: Modern American and European Variations on a Universal Theme* (Berkeley: University of California Press, 2006), 424.

16   E.P. Thompson, *The Poverty of Theory and Other Essays* (New York: Monthly Review Press, 1978), 170, and, for critics at the time, Perry Anderson, *Arguments Within British Marxism* (London: New Left Books, 1980); Stuart Hall, "Cultural Studies: Two Paradigms," *Media, Culture and Society* 2 (1980): 57–72. For two (of many) later reflections on Thompson, the first more critical: William Sewell, "How Classes Are Made: Critical Reflections on E.P. Thompson's Theory of Working-Class Formation," in *E.P. Thompson: Critical Perspectives,* ed. Harvey Kaye and Keith McClelland (Philadelphia: Temple University Press, 1990), 50–77, and Kate Soper, *Troubled Pleasures: Writings on Politics, Gender and Hedonism* (New York: Verso, 1990), chap 4. Raymond Williams had perhaps a more vague definition of experience when he wrote about working-class culture — views for which he was criticized by structuralist Marxists. I do not discuss his work since it was Thompson's writing that had the most impact on historical debates.

17   Jay, *Songs of Experience*, 202, 209.

18   E.P. Thompson, quoted in ibid., 206.

19   E.P. Thompson, "The Politics of Theory," in *People's History and Socialist Theory*, ed. Raphael Samuel (London: Routledge and Kegan Paul, 1981), 406, and *The Poverty of Theory*, 8.

20   Thompson, *The Poverty of Theory*, 9.

21   Sheila Rowbotham, "New Entry Points from USA Women's Labour History," in *Working Out Gender: Perspectives from Labour History,* ed. Margaret Walsh (Brookfield, VT: Ashgate, 1999), 12. Some of the overlap in political perspectives can be seen in the interviews in Henry Abelove, ed., *Visions of History* (New York: Pantheon, 1983). See also Ellen Kay Trimberger, "E.P. Thompson: The Process of History," in *Vision and Method in Historical Sociology,* ed. Theda Skocpol (Cambridge: Harvard University Press, 1984), 211–42, and Alice Kessler-Harris's comments on her own

history in "Introduction: Conflicts in a Gendered Labor History," in *Gendering Labor History* (Urbana: University of Illinois Press, 2007), 8.

22 Carolyn Steedman, "The Price of Experience: Women and the Making of the English Working Class," *Radical History Review* 59 (1994): 108–19.

23 Linda Gordon, interview in *Visions of History* (New York: Pantheon, 1983), 77.

24 Sewell, "How Classes Are Made."

25 Eley and Nield, *The Future of Class*, 105.

26 Contra Scott, who argues that "experience was reintroduced into historical writing in the wake of critiques of empiricism": Joan Scott, "The Evidence of Experience," in *Questions of Evidence: Proof, Practice, and Persuasion Across the Disciplines*, ed. James Chandler, Arnold Davidson, and Harry Harootunian (Chicago: University of Chicago Press, 1991), 370.

27 For example, Natalie Zemon Davis, *Fiction in the Archives: Pardon Tales and Their Tellers in Sixteenth-Century France* (Stanford: Stanford University Press, 1987).

28 Nancy Hartsock, "Postmodernism and Political Change: Issues for Feminist Theory," *Cultural Critique* 14 (1989/90): 24, 27. Another important comment on Scott and experience is Laura Lee Downs, "If 'Woman' Is Just an Empty Category, Why Am I Afraid to Walk Alone at Night? Identity Politics Meets the Poststructuralist Subject," *Comparative Studies in Society and History* 35 (1993): 414–47, and for some very gentle criticisms, combined with praise: Kathleen Canning, *Gender History in Historical Practice: Historical Perspectives on Bodies, Class and Citizenship* (Ithaca: Cornell University Press, 2006), chap. 3.

29 Dorothy Smith, *Texts, Facts and Femininity: Exploring the Relations of Ruling* (London: Routledge, 1990), 6.

30 Ibid., 90.

31 Joanna Brenner, *Women and the Politics of Class* (New York: Monthly Review Press, 2000), 86, describes experience as inextricable from women's "survival projects within capitalism." It is difficult to categorize Marxist and materialist-feminist writers precisely. I use a very broad term, 'materialist feminism,' to describe those who fuse feminist and historical materialist or Marxist traditions in their writing, although when I describe historians of the 1970s and early 1980s who fit this category, I also use 'socialist feminist,' as this was how they often described themselves. There are some distinctions between (a) those locating themselves firmly in a Marxist tradition, for example, Martha Giminez, "Capitalism and the Oppression of Women: Marx Revisited," *Science and Society* 69 (January 2005): 11–32, and Teresa Ebert, "Rematerializing Feminism," *Science and Society* 69 (January 2005): 33–55; (b) those who, very similarly, refer to themselves as Marxist-feminists (Lise Vogel, *Woman Questions: Essays for a Materialist Feminism* [New York: Routledge, 1995]), though drawing more concertedly on some

feminist concepts; and (c) those who attempt to combine historical materialism and feminism in different theoretical configurations, including Anna Pollert, "Gender and Class Revisited: The Poverty of Patriarchy," *Sociology* 30 (1996): 639–50; Joan Acker, *Class Questions, Feminist Answers* (Lanham, MD: Rowman and Littlefield, 2006); Heidi Gottfried, "Beyond Patriarchy? Theorizing Gender and Class," *Sociology* 32, no. 3 (1998): 451–68; and Stevi Jackson, "Why a Materialist Feminism Is Still Possible — and Necessary," *Women's Studies International Forum* 24 (2001): 283–93. Moreover, some materialist and Marxist feminist theorists include insights from other positions, such as queer theory, though always within the context of historical materialism: e.g., Rosemary Hennessy, *Profit and Pleasure: Sexual Identities in Late Capitalism* (New York: Routledge, 2000). For an overview of the history of this theory, see Rosemary Hennessy and Chrys Ingraham, "Introduction," in their edited *Materialist Feminism: A Reader in Class, Difference and Women's Lives* (New York: Routledge, 1997). Theory may be international, but these trends differed across nations. For an earlier interpretation of the evolution of socialist feminism in the United States, see Karen V. Hansen and Ilene Philipson, "Introduction," in their edited *Women, Class and the Socialist Feminist Imagination: A Reader* (Philadelphia: Temple University Press, 1995), and for a Canadian/British view, Michele Barrett and Roberta Hamilton, "Introduction," in their edited *The Politics of Diversity* (London: Verso, 1986), 1–31.

32 Hennessy, *Profit and Pleasure*, 230.

33 Sonia Kruks, *Retrieving Experience: Subjectivity and Recognition in Feminist Politics* (Ithaca: Cornell University Press, 2001), 146.

34 Ibid., 19.

35 Ibid., 140.

36 Paula Moya, "Postmodernism, 'Realism,' and the Politics of Identity," in *Reclaiming Identity: Realist Theory and the Predicament of Postmodernism*, ed. Paula Moya and Michael Hames-Garcia (Berkeley: University of California Press, 2000), 68.

37 Ibid., 69.

38 Thomas Haskell, *Objectivity Is Not Neutrality: Explanatory Schemes in History* (Baltimore: Johns Hopkins University Press, 1998), chap. 6.

39 William Wilkerson, "Is There Something You Need to Tell Me? Coming Out and the Ambiguity of Experience," 273; John Zammito, "Reading 'Experience': The Debate in Intellectual History Between Scott, Toews and Lacapra," 298, both in *Reclaiming Identity*, ed. Moya and Hames-Garcia.

40 Barbara Foley, review of *Reclaiming Experience*, in *Cultural Logic: An Electronic Journal of Marxist Theory and Practice* 4, no. 2 (Spring 2001), http://clogic.eserver.org/. Other critics suggest that realist writing skirts close to 'relativism' in that all invocations of experience are potentially valid in its schema: see Robert Young, review in *Cultural Logic*, http://clogic.eserver.org/.

41 Michael Pickering, *History, Experience and Cultural Studies* (New York: St. Martin's Press, 1997), 176.

42 Ibid., 224.

43 Ibid., 16.

44 On the sense of crisis relating to notions of human agency, see the special issue of *History and Theory* 40 (December 2001). For example, David Gary Shaw's introduction, "Happy in Our Chains? Agency and Language in the Post-structuralist Age," notes: "It is time for historians to show how these attempts to understand the self as constituted in social history were not misguided but were essential to historical work," 3. For a discussion of whether social structure has been slighted, see Eley and Nield's *The Future of Class*, or their "Farewell to the Working Class?" *International Labor and Working-Class History* 57 (2000): 1–30, as well as the critical responses.

45 Jay Smith, "Between Discourse and Experience: Agency and Ideas in the French Pre-Revolution," *History and Theory* 40 (2001): 127.

46 Ibid.

47 See replies to Geoff Eley and Keith Nield's "'Farewell to the Working Class,'" *International Labor and Working-Class History* 57 (April 2000): 1–87.

48 Eley and Nield, *The Future of Class*, 77.

49 They are the only authors in this special issue on agency with a forthright call to "reject the linguistic turn": Michael L. Fitzhugh and William H. Leckie, Jr., "Agency, Postmodernism, and the Causes of Change," *History and Theory* 40, no. 4 (Dec. 2001): 60. While I agree with some of their critique, I have doubts about their solution: cognitive science.

50 Robert Orsi, *Thank You, St. Jude: Women's Devotion to the Patron Saint of Hopeless Causes* (New Haven: Yale University Press, 1996).

51 A note on how I selected the letters is important. I went through all the files of letters, then concentrated note taking on about two hundred. I included letters from women in all occupations (professional, blue-, and white-collar). Overall, factory workers and unorganized service workers (e.g., waitresses) were the smaller group. Women in professional jobs were a minority and those who did write were generally teachers or nurses. The largest group of writers appears to be women in various pink- and white-collar jobs or who had been in those jobs. I read letters of part- and full-time workers, and also of women who had quit work but commented on it. I also looked at some letters from men and homemakers who commented on working women. Regionally, the number of letters reflected the population: the files from Quebec and Ontario were far larger, and because more Alberta and Saskatchewan letters talked about farm women, I do not quote as often from them. I have listed the volume and file the letters are in, but not women's names, to protect their anonymity.

52 In 1967, when the commission began its demographic work, women of colour were still a small minority of the overall Canadian population, although the RCSW also tended to overlook their stories. The RCSW did not even differentiate by race and ethnicity in some of their studies of immigrant women. See RCSW, vol. 28, immigration studies: Marica Rioux, "Female Immigrants in the Labour Force"; Freda Hawkins, "Women Immigrants in Canada"; Edith Ferguson, "Immigrant Women in Canada." For a discussion of the issue of race and the RCSW, see Jane Arscott, "Twenty-Five Years and Sixty-Five Minutes," and for a differing view from a First Nations woman, Mary Ellen Turpel-Lafond, "Patriarchy and Paternalism: The Legacy of the Canadian State for First Nations Women," in *Women and the Canadian State*, ed. Andrew and Rodgers.

53 Vol. 9, Ontario file, RCSW, LAC (hereafter volume and province given).

54 Vol. 8, Northwest Territories.

55 Vol. 9, Ontario.

56 Vol. 8, Ontario, and vol. 9, Quebec.

57 William Holt, "Experience and the Politics of Intellectual Inquiry," in *Questions of Evidence: Proof, Practice, and Persuasion Across the Disciplines*, ed. James Chandler, Arnold Davidson, and Harry Harootunian (Chicago: University of Chicago Press, 1991), 393–94.

58 Vol. 8, Manitoba.

59 Kathleen Canning, *Gender History in Historical Practice: Historical Perspectives on Bodies, Class and Citizenship* (Ithaca: Cornell University Press, 2006), 97. Of course, the physical changes she is referring to were far more drastic.

60 Regenia Gagnier, *Subjectivities* (New York: Oxford University Press, 1992), 57, 62.

61 Vol. 9, Ontario.

62 Vol. 9, Quebec. Some homemakers stressed the importance of their work in comparison to wage work, but others lamented being an "unpaid servant," feeling dependent on their husbands for every purchase, and their isolation in the home. Some testimonies echoed the sentiments of *The Feminine Mystique*: "I'm in a rut . . . feeling wasted, watching soap operas and gaining weight. Also drawing into a shell" (vol. 8, Quebec).

63 Valerie Korinek identifies this theme in letters to *Chatelaine* in *Roughing It in the Suburbs: Reading Chatelaine Magazine in the Fifties and Sixties* (Toronto: University of Toronto Press, 2000), 100.

64 Vol. 8, Ontario.

65 Vol. 8, Ontario.

66 Ibid.

67 Vol. 9, Ontario.

68 Ibid.

69 Vol. 9, Ontario.

70 Vol. 8, Ontario.

71 Vol. 8, Ontario.

72 Vol. 11, brief 14, RCSW.

73 Vol. 9, Ontario.

74 Patricia Ewick and Susan E. Silbey, quoting C.W. Mills, in "Subversive Stories and Hegemonic Tales: Toward a Sociology of Narrative," *Law and Society Review* 29 (1995): 101.

75 Raymond Williams, *Marxism and Literature* (London: Oxford University Press, 1977), 130–31.

76 Nancy Hartsock, paraphrasing E.B. DuBois, in "Postmodernism and Political Change," 26.

77 Wilkerson, "Is There Something You Need to Tell Me? Coming Out and the Ambiguity of Experience," 251–79.

78 Vol. 9, Ontario.

79 Ibid.

80 Vol. 8, Ontario.

81 Ibid.

82 Vol. 8, Nova Scotia.

83 Vol. 8, Manitoba.

84 Vol. 9, Ontario.

85 Vol. 8, Alberta.

86 Vol. 8, Ontario.

87 There is a wide range of writing influenced by postmodernism, including works in which discourse is not totalizing, but many feminist critiques do focus on problems within Foucauldian writing concerning resistance. See Linda Alcoff, "Feminist Politics and Foucault: The Limits to Collaboration," in *Crises in Continental Philosophy*, ed. Arleen Dallery and Charles Scott, with P. Holley Roberts (Albany: SUNY Press, 1990), 69–86; Kate Soper, "Productive Contradictions," in *Up Against Foucault: Explorations of Some Tensions Between Foucault and Feminism*, ed. Caroline Ramazanoglu (New York: Routledge, 1993), 21–50.

88 Vol. 9, Ontario.

89 Vol. 8, Ontario, and vol. 8, Saskatchewan.

90 Vol. 8, New Brunswick.

91 Vol. 9, Nova Scotia.

92 Vol. 9, Ontario.

93 Vol. 11, brief 77, and vol. 18, brief 424.

94 Vol. 9, Nova Scotia.

95 Vol. 14, brief 252.

96 Vol. 8, Saskatchewan.

97 Vol. 9, Quebec.

98 Vol. 8, Saskatchewan.

99 Vol. 8, Ontario.

100 Vol. 8, Ontario.

101 Alice Kessler-Harris, "Gender Ideology in Historical Reconstruction: A Case Study from the 1930s," *Gender and History* 1 (Spring 1989): 31–49.

102 Vol. 8, Ontario.

103 Vol. 9, Northwest Territories.

104 Vol. 8, Ontario.

105 Williams, *Marxism and Literature*, 132.

106 Those in the past can only "speak" when "asked" questions by historians: Thompson, *The Poverty of Theory*, 222.

107 Terry Eagleton, *After Theory* (New York: Basic Books, 2003), 136.

108 Hall, "Politics, Post-structuralism and Feminist History," 210.

109 Gottfried, "Beyond Patriarchy?," 451.

110 Kruks, quoting Elizabeth Grosz, in *Retrieving Experience*, 138.

111 Ibid., 141.

112 Renate Rosaldo, "Celebrating Thompson's Heroes: Social Analysis in History and Anthropology," in *E.P. Thompson*, ed. Kaye and McClelland, 103–25.

"To most women . . . whether they are queens or chambermaids," declared Canada's largest mass magazine in 1945, "fur coats are an emotion."
Amidst wartime affluence, even factory war workers, it was claimed, were
rushing to fur salons to purchase this timeless and classless symbol of
feminine desire.[1] Although its evidence of working-class buying was rather
thin, the article did indicate how the fur coat operated as a gendered
symbol of luxury in popular culture. Feminist authors have recently explored such textual and visual meanings of fur, including fur as feminine
fashion and as fetishism, often linking the cultural representation of fur
to writing on the body. This discussion of the "symbolic value"[2] of fur is
especially important in Canadian scholarship, for fur has a central place
in the early political economy of the nation, Aboriginal-settler relations,
historical mythmaking, and cultural production.[3]

Feminist writing on fur as a gendered symbol for the nation, or as the
feminine "skin of the body"[4] reflects the continuing influence of postmodern preoccupations with the discursive, representation, and sexual
identities. While useful in their discussions of commodity fetishism,
these works tend to neglect a topic critical for working-class history: fur
as work. We also need to historicize the fur coat by examining the forms
of labour, the productive and social relationships that made it possible.
The "magic of [consumer] display," as Gary Cross warns, should not lead
us to assume that "commodities transcend political and economic relations."[5] By tracing the making of a fur coat in mid-twentieth-century
Canada, with a focus on women's labour, I want to explore some paths
not taken in feminist scholarship, examining bush production, manufacturing work, and retail labour: skinning, sewing, and selling. Although

women's bodily labour differed in each process, one connecting link was the incessant appetite of consumer capitalism for profit at the expense of Aboriginal and working-class bodies.

Since recent writing on fur is directly linked to feminist theorizing about the body, it is also useful to query if, and how, current trends in 'body studies' might aid our understanding of labouring bodies. Previous conversations between feminist theory and labour studies have been intellectually invigorating, as debates concerning capitalism and patriarchy, class and gender, materialism and feminism stimulated productive dialogue, if also intense disagreement and dissension. After the 1980s, these debates waned, as Anglo-American feminist scholars shifted their attention to postmodern theories indebted to Foucault, psychoanalysis, and literary theory, approaches stressing contingency, fluidity, and fragmentation rather than the supposedly "old fashioned"[6] metanarratives of Marxism. Connecting feminist debates with labour scholarship, however, remains critical, not only through discussions of abstract theory, but especially by theorizing through empirically based, specific studies of women's everyday labouring lives.[7] Moreover, 'old' materialist approaches, integrated with a feminist critique of gendered power relations, may still have much to offer us.

My emphasis on *historicizing*, of course, tips my own theoretical hand: embedded in my investigation of women's bodily labour are theoretical proclivities, favouring feminist historical materialism,[8] an emphasis on class and gender formation as lived processes, and on the dynamic interplay of social structures, social practices, and human agency. The body and social life, as Simone de Beauvoir wrote many decades ago, are invariably implicated and intertwined.[9] Her dialectical adage remains a useful starting point as we analyze the labouring bodies that made the fur coat possible.

The Body in Feminist Theory and Labour Studies

The body as 'project' is a sign of our scholarly times. Body studies have proliferated in recent decades, partly as a consequence of feminist scholars' efforts to 'gender' the female body, challenging its equation with biology and nature, reinserting "it within the realm of the social," though they are also aware of the more intensive embodiment of women than men in academic writing.[10] Differences in body studies abound, with sociologists in contention over whether to emphasize the Foucauldian or the phenomenological body, the "ordered, inscribed, structured or lived" body.[11] Similar questions inform historical research, particularly relating to the body and sexuality as a site of power, regulation, and resistance.[12] A voluminous feminist literature probing the relation of the body to identity, sexuality, subjectivity, and society is also far from homogenous. Though feminist debates are too extensive to detail here, at a general level, some authors are more inclined towards materialist and social constructionist views, while others, influenced by poststructuralism, are wary of the notion of a 'given' physical body, and, anxious to dispel all traces of essentialism, challenge the distinctions made between the body and culture, sex and gender.[13] Michel Foucault's discussions of the body as a site of bio-power, and its constitution within discursive fields, have been extremely influential across the disciplines, stimulating innovative and radical social constructionist thinking, though his critics have also challenged what they see as his "transhistorical discursive essentialism" in which the biological body all too easily "evaporates."[14]

Social forces are also credited with bringing the body to scholarly light, including the new demographics and anxieties of aging bodies, and the shift in advanced capitalism from the "hard work in the sphere of production" to consumption and leisure.[15] The hard work of tourism and shopping, of course, is primarily the provenance of affluent groups, not the world's poor and working classes. Perhaps this is one reason why, as one sociological expert concedes, academic "body studies have tended to neglect the subject of the wage labour in favour of consumption and culture."[16] As Terry Eagleton has wryly quipped: "if the libidinal body is in, the labouring body is out."[17] While feminist writing often pays homage to the diversity of bodies, edited collections completely neglect wage labour, leaving one wondering if bodies actually go to work any more to scrub floors, operate machinery, serve hamburgers, or care for other bodies.[18] This absence is not a mere thematic oversight. It also reflects the postmodernist shift in interest from lived experiences to textual renderings of them: there is a preoccupation with "individuation," identity, and subjectivity, though largely detached from historical context and structured social relations.[19] The results, in Toril Moi's critical words, are "fantastic levels of abstraction without delivering a concrete, situated and materialist understanding of the body."[20]

Given the long-standing influence of feminist theory on the writing of social history, how have these debates affected working-class histories of the body? Body studies have helped to stimulate important new research on themes that have stretched the field from an institutional, workplace-based *labour* history to a more inclusive *working-class* history; in the process, they have also aided the integration of gender and race, as key categories of analysis, into working-class history. Historians, for example, have productively explored the symbolic meaning of the body through clothing, makeup, gendered manners, and behaviour.[21] New attention has also centred on themes such as sexual harassment, disability, the legal regulation of the working-class body, working-class sexuality, and women's sexualized work.[22] Certainly, not all of this literature has engaged directly with body studies or with poststructuralist ideas; earlier works especially drew on social constructionist and materialist paradigms, though recently, there is more interest in poststructuralist ideas, such as Butleresque notions of 'performance.'[23] More concerning is writing that concentrates on the body as cultural object or endows discourse and language with inordinate causal weight — thus mirroring tendencies in some postmodern theory.[24] In our productive dialogue with feminist theory, we need to be wary of the persistent "dilution of the material" within much postmodern theory;[25] nor should we lose sight of the actual wage labour of bodies, a topic less 'au courant' for feminism, but still central to working-class history

Current academic writing, as David Harvey convincingly argues, reveals the danger of "body reductionism": while considered "foundational" to all politics, body studies are not grounded in an understanding of the "real temporal-spatial relations between material practices, representations, institutions, social relations and the prevailing structures of political-economic power."[26] Similarly, the danger of embracing feminist-Foucauldian proposals to thoroughly deconstruct the natural body is that the lived, suffering, and alienated body may fade from view. If bodies are recognized only within an abstract circle of discourse, will we not lose our connection to a politics of social transformation that understands that the oppression, maiming, and utilization of bodies is facilitated by particular set of social relations, economic structures, and forms of injustice?

How, then, might we historicize women's labouring bodies, paying attention to their cultural construction, without becoming trapped in the mode of the discursive? Fusing a feminist intent to critically interrogate gender and 'race' power relations in all aspects of society with a rich tradition of materialist writing in labour studies may provide a starting point. As Chris Shilling has argued, the body has been an "absent presence" in Marxist explorations of the 'embodiment' of economic relationships, including Marx's own powerful description of alienation, whereby workers within capitalism are "estranged" from their bodies, from external nature, and from humanity itself.[27] It is also present in E.P. Thompson's recounting of work time and the disciplining of industrial bodies, and in Harry Braverman's insights into the subtle transformation of the human body into a 'willing' machine for employers.[28] This materialist tradition assumes that the body is a means and instrument of labour, though it is also constituted and reconstituted by, and through, human labour and social and cultural practices. Though workers' bodies are moulded by society and political economy, and inscribed with the effects of social and economic relationships, they are not 'determined' objects; they still possess the subjective potential for critical reflection, agency, and rebellion. Materialist theories of social reproduction also suggest the mutual determination of the body and society. Bodies, in Pierre Bourdieu's terms, are located within a 'habitus' that includes our acquired cultural histories, dispositions, and values; class and gender become embodied in the most mundane, minute, unrecognized social practices of daily life.[29] Moreover, materialist critiques of colonialism offer another necessary layer of questions, asking how racialized bodies, as well as class relations, mattered to the political, economic, and cultural vitality of imperialism.[30]

Marxist, materialist, and social reproduction theories are, admittedly, quite divergent.[31] What they do share in common is a (modernist) acceptance of the 'real' experienced body, "out there to be explored";[32] the body is not simply a set of 'material effects' in the realm of the cultural. While embracing a feminist skepticism about the existence of a preordained, 'natural' body, we need to avoid the dematerialized body of much postmodern theory — admittedly a hard balancing act. There may be "irresolvable tensions" in this endeavour, but as Kathy Davis argues, feminist writing stressing the body as metaphor runs the risk of obscuring the "systemic domination enacted through the female body" and the materialist insight that bodies are "embedded in the immediacies of everyday life and lived experience."[33] The social construction of women's bodily labour as less skilled or unimportant, as racialized, feminized, or sexualized, must be viewed in relation to "the objective, sensuous and suffering body,"[34] shaped by material conditions and patterns of social and political power, as well as dominant and subterranean cultural values. A feminist and materialist approach also keeps the analytical door open to the possibility of the unfinished body, to intentionality, agency, and a notion of bodily resistance to the 'maps' of cultural and social life. However worn down, regulated, or constrained, the labouring body might also become an instrument to create new dispositions, cultural maps, or political dreams.

Skinning

Feminist historical materialism, according to one scholar influenced by E.P. Thompson, is not a set, abstract 'Theory,' but is rather a critical excavation of social experience as it unfolds. "By its very nature" it involves the empirical interrogation of gender and class formation *as historical processes,* often fraught with contradiction and conflict.[35] Let us now turn to an empirical investigation of the social experience of extractive fur labour, performed in the Subarctic and Arctic North largely by Indigenous peoples.[36] Though fur was considered fairly marginal to Canada's industrial economy by the mid-twentieth century, trapping was still the principal activity for 45 percent of its land mass in 1950, occupying at least fifty-seven thousand Aboriginal persons.[37] In the North, "bush production" of fur pelts, according to many economic studies, occupied the majority of male earners; these "breadwinners" were responsible for all the trapping "income" while women were responsible for domestic "affairs," a rather vague term that carried less significance than "income."[38]

Women's work varied across Indigenous cultures in the Subarctic and

Arctic North, but there is no doubt that such characterizations obscured women's labouring bodies from view. Fur trade studies, as feminist anthropologists argue, have sustained colonial and masculinist perspectives by ignoring women's trapping labour.[39] Historical sources, to be sure, make the search for women difficult. In many Arctic Hudson's Bay Company (HBC) Post Journals, for example, women exist on the margins of the main story. The journals were written by white traders, anxious to justify *their* output of daily work for their employers, and they recorded information according to a masculinist mindset: marriage records listed only men's names and occupations, while account books recorded trading by women "under their husband's names."[40] Constrained by Western notions of the dichotomized private and public spheres, even later anthropologists looking *for* women's labour often used a grammar of belittlement: "women *aid* men in their work . . . [they] maintain the household. . . . there seems to be no roles available for women *other than* those of wife and mother."[41] As Hugh Brody concedes, his study of the "Indian economy" in the North was premised on his observations and those of male informants; women's labour was harder to quantify, underestimated, and thus "concealed."[42]

Yet a closer examination of Hudson's Bay Post Journals, Indigenous oral histories, ethnographic studies, sojourners' accounts of the North, and visual archival evidence all reveal women's labouring bodies participating in fur extraction. After listing all the furs deposited by an Inuit trapper, the HBC trader might add that local women were "put to work"[43] washing and cleaning the furs and sewing them into bales. This labour was crucial to the production of a high-quality pelt for the market. In the 1950s, HBC posts routinely paid women 2 to 5 cents for each muskrat they skinned, a small sum considering that these rats might fetch $1.25 or more at a fur auction.[44] When the traders at the HBC Wolstonholme post were forced to wash the skins themselves, they quickly complained that it absorbed their whole day; they could now see why the Inuit did not want to do the "washing and scraping" for the paltry sum offered, as it was "strenuous work."[45]

Inuit women were also engaged by Arctic posts as part of a 'family package' of labour, supplying wood and water, drying fur, and travelling for mail.[46] Girls and women also commonly performed domestic labour for wages or credit, scrubbing floors, cleaning post houses, preparing food, making clothes, or sewing parkas for the post men.[47] Their wages were then assimilated into the family fur economy. Inuit women were not completely channelled into Euro-Canadian notions of an appropriate gendered division of labour: when 'ship time' came at the Arctic Payne Bay post, for instance, women were paid the same wages as men for unloading heavy cargo.[48] Inuit women's bodies were described by white sojourners as more robust, closer to nature, and able to endure a measure of pain and physical labour that white women could not,[49] a cultural construction that obscured the material and social basis of women's work. Inuit women's bodies had long been constituted by arduous labour shared with men, and geared towards community survival; however, this work assumed a very different ideological cast within their own culture.

Oral histories of Aboriginal women also provide examples of female trapping labour that was not seen as unusual physical work, but rather as labour integral to individual and familial subsistence. Ellen Smallboy, a northern Labrador Cree woman, learned from an early age to trap small animals in order to keep her family from starving; later, she also trapped with her husband for furs to sell. Similarly, a Saskatchewan woman's autobiographical story, "Encounters with Bears," reveals a single woman trapper who engaged in traditional bush production as an "everyday occupation."[50] For Cree women interviewed in the north of Saskatchewan, women's work was shaped by a division of labour in which women primarily skinned animals, preparing furs for the market, processing hides, and manufacturing clothing.[51] Ironically, their technical 'know-how' was similar to that of male manufacturing workers, who also had to assess skins, cut them, wet, and block them. Likewise, the intricate "freeze drying" method of preparing beaver skins used by James Bay Cree women to create unblemished[52] and thus more marketable skins was so complex that in any industrial setting, the work would have been described as artisanal and skilled.

Women's labour in fur extraction was thus expended in three overlapping areas: women worked on the trap lines, they were primarily responsible for familial and social reproduction, and they were primarily responsible for preparing skins. In both Arctic and Subarctic areas, women travelled with trapping husbands, often leaving after freeze-up for a season of intensive trapping, though this altered as the state pressured families into permanent settlements. At trading time, as one northern post manager recorded, the Inuit arrived "with furs and families," both being linked together in the extractive process.[53] Although men made the initial spending decisions, women were often by their side offering advice. Lamenting the decline of male authority in an area where women were few in number, one HBC employee employed the language of clothing and the body to underscore his dismay with this practice: "The wife wears the pants, and the poor husband has always to refer to his better half before he can buy anything."[54]

The domestic affairs of women, referred to by the earlier observer, also amounted to social reproduction of key economic significance. Historicizing women's part in bush production necessitates taking into account many forms of unpaid reproductive work, and in the case of Indigenous peoples, a recognition that these labours were also "deeply interwoven with one's culture and cosmology."[55] Women often combined familial labour with work for wages or trapping labour; sojourner narratives and visual archives repeatedly document women minding children while working on furs.[56] Indigenous peoples extracting furs also relied heavily on hunting for 'country food' for survival. Northern Cree women's contribution to hunting involved collecting wood (thirty cubic feet per household per day); netting snow shoes; manufacturing tents, clothes, and ammunition pouches; repairing traps; preparing food; and of course, caring for children, husbands and parents.[57]

This work did not simply save families funds; they could *not have existed without this unwaged labour* given how low their fur incomes were. Widespread reliance on country food thus had a direct impact on families' involvement in the capitalist production of fur; arguably, it meant that Aboriginal workers were not paid the full cost of their social reproduction through wages (or skins traded), in effect aiding the creation of surplus value.[58] Moreover, the reciprocal obligations of gendered labour characteristic of Indigenous societies were transformed, indeed undermined, by the capitalist fur economy, as relations of trade and authority were cemented with Indigenous men, while women were sidelined as 'helpmates,' or even possessions.[59] Euro-Canadian observers had long dichotomized 'traditional' hunting for subsistence and 'modern' work for wages; they did not see these interconnected patterns of women's labour in fur extraction, nor appreciate its significance for the bodily survival of their families.[60]

Indigenous women's bodies have recently been the focus of considerable scholarly attention as feminist historians have critiqued the sexualization and racialization of Aboriginal and Inuit women so intrinsic to Canada's patterns of internal colonialism.[61] Our analyses of the 'embodiment' of colonial relations, often through representation, have generally been distinct from writing on labour, but the two themes are intimately intertwined.[62] Indeed, their mutual explication makes clear the need to situate our critiques of the culturally constructed body within the material and social relations that made this construction possible — if not probable.

Historically, there were some distinctions between colonialist images of Native 'savagism' and Inuit 'primitivism,' but there was still a common exoticization of all Indigenous women's bodies. Popular images sometimes romanticized a premodern Aboriginal 'Madonna,' or a suitably acquiescent Pocahontas; however, racist ideologies also reflected the association of Indigenous women with promiscuous, primitive, sexual mores.[63] Inuit women, it was presumed, were the product of premodern, patriarchal cultures accustomed to licentious wife trading, while racist images of degenerate Aboriginal women, conditioned by alcohol, were still deeply embedded in Canadian society, justifying violence against them. While we must acknowledge the importance of these destructive discourses of the exotic or promiscuous female Indigenous body, another key aspect of colonialism was the appropriation of women's labour *as well as* their sexual dignity. Perhaps most important, we must also consider how these processes were co-implicated, how the symbolic and material interacted in this specific historical context. Accounts of women's work were shaped by a process of signification that drew on discourses of race and gender, but the significance of the material body to the creation of profit and surplus value should not be slighted in the process of meaning making. In fact, the gendered racialization of Aboriginal women's bodies *allowed them* to become 'invisible' labouring bodies in an economic and political context of both capitalist and colonial relations.

Sewing

The image of the bourgeois, fur-clad woman, a symbol of wealth and decadence, literally becoming the commodity she models, has long been utilized as a trope of class privilege, including in the labour press.[64] The role of *working-class* women in the making of the fur coat, however, has been hidden from historical view.[65] A reclamation of women's sewing labour reveals the way in which women's bodies, as factors of production, were seen as an expendable investment, even though the physical risks of fur work were similar for men and women. Their role in fur workers' unions, in contrast, underscores the need to theorize the relationship between subjectivity, agency, and the body, rather than concentrating predominantly on bodily "constraint" and containment, the latter more "predominant" in current feminist theory.[66]

In Canada, fur production was characterized by many small, competitive manufacturing and manufacturing-retailing firms doing seasonal work, dependent almost entirely on the women's coat market. In 1949, a peak year of fur production, there were 642 manufacturers across the country, some with fewer than 10 employees, though most larger factories were concentrated in three cities, Winnipeg, Toronto, and Montreal. Fur work, as well as factory ownership, was dominated by Eastern European Jewish immigrants; until the 1940s, some local union meetings were conducted in Yiddish, and membership lists in cities like Winnipeg indicated both geographical and social clustering of predominantly Jewish members,[67] though French-Canadians also laboured in fur in Montreal, and in Toronto, the 'gentiles' were actually segregated in a separate union local in the 1930s.

The most important skills needed in the translation of raw furs into coats were the preserve almost entirely of men, apprenticed to learn the techniques of sorting, wetting and stretching, blocking, then cutting the skins. Both the 'skin on skin' and newer 'drop' technique of fur preparation (used more after World War II) involved the cutter knowing how to select, cut, and recut skins countless times, so that they could be sewn together to form an elongated, almost seamless coat. From the early twentieth century, women did work as operators on sewing machines that had blowing devices to keep the fur from being caught in the seams; they also sewed linings and did the finishing of the coat. In larger factories combining pelt preparation and garment construction, women might help with preparation of the raw skin, for example, as 'greasers,' 'unhairers,' and 'fleshers,' jobs that still needed a degree of training, especially for fleshing machines, with razor sharp blades designed to remove excess flesh from the fur skin. This 'skin on skin' work was a far cry from the "sensual" experience of women wearing fur; it would be difficult to characterize it as the "many tender ties of skin, flesh and fur," referred to by contemporary feminist scholars.[68]

Not only were women's jobs considered less skilled, but after World War II their share of sewing machine operators' jobs declined, and of course, their wage rates were always consistently lower than men's, reflecting the assumption that they were temporary sojourners in the workforce. Union contracts before and after unionization in the late 1930s incorporated differential wages; even when women shared operating jobs with men, they made 25 to 33 percent less.[69] Lacking the privilege and protection of skill, women's bodies were particularly vulnerable. Like the radium girls in the United States, they were seen as expendable factors of production, surely a vivid illustration of Marx's concept of labour power as a bodily commodity, purchased by employers, sold by workers with few choices in the marketplace of work.[70] They had little manoeuvring room to deal with the stresses of work and could be more easily fired, for there was little time invested in their bodies. With small amounts of capital needed for startup, a fringe of small, struggling firms always existed; these firms tried to keep labour costs low, but did not want to risk losing skilled male cutters. This undervaluation of women's labour was clearly apparent in the records of the Ontario Department of Labour, as Toronto firms were chastised regularly by the Minimum Wage Board for paying far below the minimum, or using loopholes in the law, which were not hard to find. "Yours is one of the worst wage sheets we have ever seen," commented the board to one fur firm, and seldom moved to such moral indignation.[71]

Women's bodies were also susceptible to the physical stresses of fur work. In the 1930s women laboured in factories up to sixty hours a week, with peak production times requiring overtime that workers could not refuse and still keep their jobs. This pace was tempered substantially in the 1940s by unionization and some state-legislated industrial standards,[72] but workers had no sooner won the forty-four-hour week than the industry went into the doldrums in the later 1950s, leading to forced overtime and wage reductions. Nor could a forty-four-hour week address some of the physiological hazards in the industry. Workplaces were notoriously damp, and the high levels of fur in the air, particularly cheap, loose furs like rabbit, created breathing problems for workers. Indeed, fur workers were known to have high levels of tuberculosis. During the organizing drives of the thirties, communist organizers claimed that "unsanitary conditions" faced all fur workers, from the fumes in the drying cellars to lingering "terrible odours" of the skins after chemical treatment. Women's work was not exempt from bodily danger. They routinely laboured where "the brushing and combing from hair flies from the skin all over the place," and some "girls were forced to climb up on ladders" to hang the skins in drying departments "with all windows shut."[73]

Fur-laden air, recounts one furrier, had to be accepted as part of the job, though he did admit "he often had a cold" in these conditions.[74] Occupational hazards were thus naturalized as a bodily inevitability, and they were integrated into patterns of humour and initiation, as older (male) fur workers teased younger ones with made-up stories of workers having 'fur balls' removed from their throats. Bravado and humour were understandable coping mechanisms for those with limited choices about occupational hazards; fur work was not the "rough and tough"[75] labour often associated with the masculine body, but mechanisms for coping with the physical risks of work might still take on gendered forms. These hazards also illustrate that class was not simply displayed on the body; rather, it is embodied on a daily basis, a destructive process described in other studies of women's occupational health, poverty, and disease. Robert Connell's claims for the gendered body apply equally to class: it is not simply that bodies are defined or constructed differently, but that *different experiences* and practices literally transform the body, altering it physically.[76]

In the fur industry journal, businesses were photographed as scientific workplaces, where white-coated men in clean factories exercised their craftsmen-like expertise and skill. The industry also stressed workers' responsibility in preventing accident and health problems by caring for their own bodies.[77] Yet the same journal carried information warning about health hazards emanating from "squalor, poor ventilation, dust, poisonous fumes, poor lighting" that plagued the fur industry. The results were common respiratory ailments, such as bronchitis, asthma, and coughing, as well as skin eruptions caused either by metallic dyes or chemicals like Ursol D. There were also rare but lethal risks cited, including blood poisoning from lead, arsenic, or mercury used in fur glossing, and a disease from rabbit skins that caused fingernails to fall off.[78] Male fur workers in dressing and dyeing had more direct contact with chemicals, but similar problems emerged in factories where many women laboured making small leather goods. When one Toronto woman, disabled with "substantial injuries" from benzol poisoning in a leather factory, tried to sue her employer for damages her case was dismissed by the court, with the company hiding behind the claim that there were no warning labels on the benzol containers.[79] The health protections offered to women's bodies by the state, in other words, were small indeed. Unionization offered more protection, but by the 1950s, women's position within the industry was contracting, in part because of the 'glutting' of the labour market with furriers admitted from war-torn Europe, with single male immigrants targeted first and foremost as potential fur workers.[80]

Fur work in major urban centres tied women to machines in damp and dusty surroundings; fur organizing placed them in the precarious midst of a polarized, contentious, and sometimes violent union milieu. The battles within Canadian fur unions could fill a book. Torn apart internally by social democratic versus communist politics in the 1920s and early 1930s (with dual unions emerging in the thirties), the International Fur and Leather Workers Union (IFLWU) was occasionally unified through struggles for recognition against small employers ready to use any tactic, from injunctions to yellow dog contracts, to avoid unions. In these struggles, women workers' bodies came under direct assault. Union and Communist Party activist Pearl Wedro was taken to hospital with gash in her head needing stitches after being assaulted by a scab during a 1931 Winnipeg strike, while another communist fur worker, Freda Coodin, led fellow picketers on a march to the comfortable home of the factory owner, an affront to middle class domestic privacy that led to her being jailed. Not even five feet, she was later convicted of assaulting a scab during a strike at the adamantly anti-union Hurtig Furs. She spent a year in prison, where the fur worker's disease, tuberculosis, claimed her life. A martyr for the Communist Left, her gravestone carried the words "a victim of the Hurtig strike" until they were scratched out by angry opponents.[81]

Despite Coodin's designation as a political martyr, it is important to recognize that women might also engage in violence, attacking scabs and opponents to defend their jobs or their political loyalties. During one Toronto strike, female strikers were arrested for blocking scabs physically with their bodies and for throwing rocks at a car carrying strikebreakers, shattering a windshield. A chorus of three women were accused of intimidating another female worker and her father with threats of bodily harm, as well as teaching neighbourhood children how to throw stones at cars carrying scabs, an interesting twist on women's traditional child-rearing role. These radical women were not 'fainting away'[82] from bodily contact and violence in the heat of struggle — quite the contrary. Their willingness to put their bodies on the line probably had much to do with their youth and political commitment, though it was also likely shaped by their socialization in the rough culture of working-class immigrant streets. Class experiences thus marked the body invisibly, shaping women's willingness to use their bodies in physically confrontational ways.

At their most intense in the late 1930s and early 1940s, union battles also took on a decidedly macho tone, as men chased each other up and down Toronto's Spadina Avenue with baseball bats, trashed cars, and even hired local gangsters to beat up rivals. The conflict finally ended during the Cold War when the left-wing IFLWU, under attack by the state and anticommunist unions, amalgamated with the AFL-chartered Fur Workers Union and the Amalgamated Meat Cutters and Butcher Workmen union in 1955. All of the Communist fur leadership, whether appointed or elected, and including Pearl Wedro, were removed from office by the victorious social democrats (who had been earlier found cooking the books), ready to use any political methods to purge the union of supposed Communist influence.[83] Wedro had been denounced publicly by her rival social democrats as a "Stalinist fish wife,"[84] an anticommunist designation also meant to elicit a physical image of an overbearing, ugly, nagging old woman — like other women on the Left, she was stereotyped by sexuality and body more than men. Wedro remained completely loyal to her Communist politics, though privately she bemoaned the fact that she had been looked down on in the union, denied the same opportunities and respect as male organizers.[85]

In an industry built on the bonds of masculine skill, fur unions had difficulty effectively addressing questions of gender equality on a sustained basis, though the IFLWU made some valiant efforts in the United States before it was destroyed by the Cold War.[86] The American union attempted to mobilize women workers and workers' wives in combined women's committees, but the smaller Canadian union was only able to create homemakers' auxiliaries, dedicated primarily to "helping our men fight for better working conditions and better lives for our families."[87] Once the merger with the Butcher Workmen was achieved in 1955, women's issues all but disappeared into the resolutely masculinist title of the union. In fur production, woman's body as labouring body seemed to increasingly fade from public, political, and even trade union view.

Selling Fur

After the union merger in 1955, the former IFLWU president wrote a column on women in the Amalgamated Meat Cutter's paper, the *Butcher Workman*, without ever mentioning women *workers*. Breaking from a long tradition of fur worker militancy, he urged "cooperation" with employers in order to stabilize a faltering industry, and revival of a nineteenth-century labour strategy to boost consumption, the union label. A fund created by business and labour might then seek out a new market: the suburban housewife. She had to be convinced that fur was both practical and stylish, though he added as an afterthought that return to cheaper furs (such as rabbit) might also reach the wives and daughters of workers too.[88]

If women workers' bodies were the locus of exploitation in the production process, they became the focus of an imagined consumer in the selling process. However, if we focus only on the consumer, more visible in historical sources, we would miss another form of bodily labour: workers in the retail sector. Both women and men worked as fur sellers, though a hierarchy typical of retail work existed; it was usually men (who might be master furriers) who took on managerial positions in both large and small stores. Whatever the gender of the retail worker, the work of selling reveals much about the required posture of class distinction, deference, and service that was literally embodied within the work process. These insights on the nature of service work have been made by feminist labour historians for some time, even if the body was more of an "absent presence" in earlier writing.[89] Feminist sociologists interested in class relations, though not necessarily in Marxism, have recently turned to Bourdieu as a means of understanding the embodiment of class and gender in the micro processes of daily life, and his writing on social reproduction does help in understanding the encounter between consumer and worker in the fur salon.[90]

In the popular media, fur extraction was associated with skill, bravery, and the outdoors (the male body), and fur consumption with frivolity, fashion, and emotion (the female body). In an article on the genealogy of fur, a reporter for Canada's largest magazine began with a trapper, "Big Louis . . . a Sturdy individual" with "Leathery Coppertone" skin and "halting English" (probably meant to signify Métis) whose solitary winter work denoted a determined, muscular, and courageous male body. The story of fur ended with the woman consumer seeking the emotion and romance of fur: "When you show them an ermine wrap," reported a store manager, "they all go slightly crazy."[91]

Fur industry journals in the 1940s and 1950s generally imagined two types of female consumer. Some designs suggested practical wear, comfort, and respectability: these popular, lower-priced coats were marketed for the suburban housewife, the middle-class consumer. A contrasting image became more visible by the late 1940s: the sensual, sexy, sultry movie star model, wearing makeup, high heels, and jewellery, adorned in fox or mink. Montreal fur photographer June Sauer used images of Venus and Botticelli, naked women with seductive and inviting pouts on their faces,[92] to suggest the connection between fur, sexuality, and luxury. These latter images did reveal a trend in postwar fur consumption: more luxury furs such as mink were being purchased, at the expense of cheaper furs, previously disguised with fabricated names.[93] By 1961, the overall production of fur was declining in Canada, as the industry was hurt by the introduction of fake fur, high excise taxes, and consumers spending on other durables. Faced with hard times, fur workers begged the government to reduce its tax on luxury consumer goods, an ironic plea for working-class Canadians.[94]

Media discussions of selling also assumed that women demanded fur, though men bought it, evidenced in countless articles advising men that the most successful gift to secure (or buy back) affection was a mink for 'the wife.'[95] Women supposedly desired fur as a form of cultural capital to be displayed for others. Fur was thus a marker of class distinction in Bourdieu's terms, and as a gift, it was laden with notions of gendered power.[96] Because image and style, not warmth and comfort, were seen to be key to selling, advice to salespersons included tips on how to have the woman buyer reimagine her body. "Wear Furs and Look Younger," and "Show off that Schoolgirl Complexion with a dainty Fur," were suggested as selling pitches.[97] The workers expected to offer these lines — emotional acting being part of the work process — had to walk a fine line between deference and authority. The customer generally had "no idea what she wants and . . . because of this she is more readily influenced by the salesperson who manifests a greater knowledge than her," advised the *Canadian Furrier*.[98] "Adopting an authoritative manner," was important, but so was "sensing the woman's mood" and psychology. As a less-than-knowledgeable luxury seeker, the female consumer could be won over if the retail seller could make her feel physically distinctive and stylish — at worst, women consumers were presented as simply vain and susceptible to flattery.

Clerks had to be well dressed and coifed, knowledgeable, but also assume a posture of class courtesy to the customer. Of course, fur selling varied according to the venue. Holt Renfrew's elite carriage trade provided a different challenge than the array of customers and price tags in the Eaton's (department store) fur salon (the very name meant to denote bourgeois style), which differed again from small establishments where manufacturing and retailing were combined. Whatever the venue, many sellers felt they should offer enhanced personal service to fur buyers: they might memorize regular customer names or take on extra work, mediating with the accounts or delivery offices to speed up the transaction.

The retail fur seller, therefore, had to offer a certain bodily performance.

This emphasis on the worker's presentation of self underlines the way in which the body is both a source of labour and also something that retail workers had to *labour upon* to make it presentable and appealing. The overlap between this "official" and "cultural" body work, as Shilling points out, is often characteristic of service labour.[99] Class distinctions are subtly ingrained through the repeated gestures, inflections, and self-presentation necessary for the seller's job: the body thus becomes a "constant reminder of socio-sexual power relations"[100] in the workplace. Performance may thus help to constitute the labouring body, but there are important differences between Bourdieu's concept of performance as part of habitus, with his emphasis on the conditioning power of social norms and institutions, and postmodernist conceptions of performance as wilful, permeable, flexible — with far less consideration of the social circumstances circumscribing women's choices.[101]

In large department stores, more female clerks were involved as they moved into the fur salon from other areas of selling. A quota of sales was sometimes required, then commission paid as further incentive. In one large Montreal department store, the fur manager described his ideal fur saleswoman as someone who was extremely polite and careful with customers. He complained bitterly about one of his female workers whose posture was less than deferential; she is "impossible . . . how many clients have we lost to her bad behaviour. I had to intercede in one case and save a client" whom the seller was arguing with over whether she should buy "black or brown" fur.[102] Customers from this store also complained with great umbrage if they sensed bad treatment in the fur salon; clearly, they expected *superlative* attention from the retail workers.

There were limited avenues for resistance for the retail worker; giving a fussy customer a frank opinion on black or brown fur might have been one means of talking back, though there were undoubtedly other behind-the-scenes complaints as well.[103] As well as demanding customers, workers in this fur salon had to cope with the regular physical stresses of department store work: long hours in certain seasons, layoffs in others, standing on the job, surveillance by critical managers, and sometimes moderating contentious relations with competing salespeople or those working on renovating and mending coats. One former seller noted that the only negative aspect of work was "boredom," since crowds did not swarm the fur salon.[104] But the necessity and stress of making a sale once a customer came in was surely all the more critical.

Customer service was thus the essence of the labour process for fur sellers, and as Lan argues in a contemporary context, retail labour selling the promise of female beauty often requires a mirroring body (the stylish salesperson), a disciplined body (deferential gestures), and a communicating body (offering knowledge).[105] The last two were key for fur sellers who had to convince the customer that she would be transformed by fur. Not surprisingly, interviews with sellers suggest that they saw their work in terms of the skills needed. One seller pointed to the expertise needed to quickly assess a woman's body type and match this to the right style.[106] Another stressed the importance of selling one's specialized knowledge as well as courtesy and attentiveness —"treat every customer as you would want to be treated." Good service did not mean being overly personal; "never talk about religion or politics" to a customer was a mantra in their store.[107] Sellers recall that helping a woman visualize her future with the coat —"how long it would be a benefit, how heads would turn" — could be the key to a sale. Moreover, they had to quickly assess who was actually paying the bill; for example, parents sometimes bought their daughters fur coats as part of a trousseau, so selling to more than one person required a delicate verbal approach.[108]

The female fur-wearing body took centre stage in popular discourse, and these images were undeniably important in conveying an image of sexualized and economically dependent femininity. Feminist scholarship has effectively highlighted the sexualization of women's bodies, particularly in relation to consumption, but this should not divert our attention from the related labour of selling femininity to women. If the fur coat denoted a certain cultural capital to the buyer, it was also, quite literally, a means of making a living for the seller. These very different relations of women's bodies to fur remind us all too well that class conditions our experience of the body in a fundamentally crucial manner. In the work of retail selling, women's bodies served both as instruments of labour power and as the conduit for symbols of sensual and dependent femininity. Although the socially constructed feminine desire for fur may have crossed class lines, the ability to fulfil that desire did not.

Conclusion

There are deep ironies behind the production of the fur coat in mid-twentieth century Canada. Postwar affluence was presumed to offer women access to the consumer item that adorned icons like Marilyn Monroe. Yet this industry was contracting by the 1960s, with negative consequences for Indigenous and working-class women labouring to produce the skins and the coat. Moreover, the idealized female body may have been a sensuous one adorned with fur, but this cultural image stood in contrast to the real, living, and exploited bodies of working-class and Indigenous women. By historicizing the fur coat, we can uncover the labour and social relations that made the coat possible, and in the process, ask what these social relations reveal about women's labouring bodies.

Aboriginal women's skinning labour and their role in bush production were obscured for some time by masculinist ideologies and by the patterns of accumulation tied to capitalist enterprises and colonial institutions. Colonizers often categorized Indigenous women's bodies as primitive, unusually strong, and close to nature. Although arduous work did shape their physical, bodily existence, this labour was not seen by Indigenous women as unusual but as a necessary part of kin and community subsistence, interwoven too with cultural endurance. Prevailing colonialist images, whether the sexualized "squaw," or the idealized "Eskimo" mother with papoose, must therefore be seen as two-sided, as a racialized distortion of women's bodies *and* as an erasure of their labouring bodies. These derisive representations of the Indigenous woman cannot be analyzed only within the realms of culture and discourse, nor considered their materialized effects, for the colonialist marking of the body was closely intertwined with processes of exploitation and the extraction of surplus value. To comprehend women's embodiment, in other words, we need to connect the discursive construction of sexual and racial difference with actual social practices and experiences of women's lives in specific historical contexts.

The labour of women sewing fur coats has also been obscured, in part because of their marginalization as temporary and unskilled workers in workplaces shaped profoundly by gendered power relations. Women's secondary status in the industry meant that they were seen as a fleeting, expendable investment for capital, even though they faced many of the same bodily hazards of fur work as the more skilled artisans. After unionization in the late 1930s and early 1940s, fur workers secured improved conditions, often through another form of bodily exertion: protest, sometimes vigorously and physically asserted by politicized women workers. But it was difficult to sustain this activity or to address gender inequities in the workplace when an influx of immigrants, political repression, the Cold War, and industrial contraction characterized the industry. Retail workers selling fur have also been sidelined by the inordinate attention focussed on the imagined female body consuming the fur coat. The work of selling fur, nonetheless, reveals the embodiment of class in the requisite gestures and practices of service work, as well as very different experiences shaping the body of the woman worker and the consumer of luxury products.

Ironically, contemporary feminist writing has tended to reproduce the erasure of the labouring body in fur, with its lack of interest in women's wage labour and its fascination with the body as discursive construct or performance. Challenging this "idealist turn"[109] in feminist scholarship, and reasserting the importance of the 'material' for our studies of the working-class body have been two intertwined intentions of this article. Certainly, body studies have encouraged research that has stretched our focus beyond the workplace and pressed us to consider how the gendered and raced working-class body and social life intersected; moreover, some recent feminist writing has declared an interest in "recuperating the material" in body studies, a promising salvo.[110]

However, scholars both inside and outside of working-class history see 'old-fashioned' approaches emanating from historical materialism as too deterministic or economistic for this recuperation project. I would suggest the contrary. First, there is a "kernel" of materialist insight worth preserving, as Rosemary Hennessy argues, in the concept of surplus value: in the last resort, this inevitable expropriation of labour from workers' bodies is a driving force of capitalism.[111] Women's bodies, of course, were not only a means to surplus value; they also assumed a symbolic value related to their sexualized and racialized representation. Understanding the gendered dimensions of bodily labour thus necessitates close attention to the dialectical relationship of a sexed body to social life so crucial to Simone de Beauvoir's writing, and elaborated on later by materialist-feminist theorists.

Second, feminist historical materialism has much to recommend as a method of unravelling class and gender formation as lived historical processes. This excavation does not simply rest upon an analysis of the macro contours of capitalist accumulation (though that should not be discounted) but involves a recognition that the material permeates all aspects of class, gender, and race power relations. It also requires continual (re)theorizing 'from the bottom up,' as we examine the productive and reproductive labour and the everyday practices, interactions, and understandings of women's lives. These goals of historical recovery have been challenged by poststructuralist writing, particularly those authors stressing the irretrievable cultural and linguistic construction of experience. However, if we connect feminist historical materialism to a persistent, critical reflexivity towards our sources and assumptions, I do not believe we will rush inexorably down the slippery slope to a naive essentialism and a biological reductionism about the body.

Third, a feminist political economy of embodiment recognizes the need to critically examine the social and historical contexts in which bodies live, work, and create personal and social lives, with acute attention to questions of power, inequality, and resistance. The labouring body, as "real, living, sensuous, objective being" always exists in social relation to other bodies and the "exercise of the powers that constitute social life."[112] Those powers encompass the fault lines of gender and race as well as class; women's experience of fur work was shaped by patterns of masculine and colonial power as well as capitalism, and by women's everyday negotiation of these interconnected relationships. The structural and systemic conditions of colonialism and capitalism were important to workers' experience of their bodies, but so too were their subjective understanding of them. Fur-laden air, for instance, was considered an inevitable factor of production; it infiltrated, indeed violated the fur worker's body, irretrievably altering one's physical being. At the same time, we need to understand workers' subjective negotiation of these hazards — their bravado and jokes, as well as their rebellion and resistance — though these too were shaped by workers' constrained choices in a gender-segregated capitalist market place.

However constrained by the necessity and conditions of their labour, women's bodies cannot be reduced in our analysis to the disciplined and docile. Capturing the related processes of accumulation and reproduction on one hand, and intentionality and agency on the other hand, requires a delicate balance of the objective and subjective in our search for historical bodies, one that embraces neither "body reductionism" or "liberal illusions" of individualist, heroic self.[113] If bodies were shaped by alienation, they sometimes also became a conduit for resistance, a means of expressing alternative ideologies or cultural practices: workers maintained the ability to reflect on, and alter their working lives. In the fur business, women's bodies were implicated within and constituted by three social processes, of capital accumulation, consumption, and colonialism, yet they could also become sites of contestation for the very forces that created and shaped them.

Notes

1 *Maclean's*, 15 March 1945, 11.

2 Julia Emberley, *The Cultural Politics of Fur* (Montreal: McGill-Queen's University Press, 1997), 4; see also Chantal Nadeau, *Fur Nation: From the Beaver to Brigitte Bardot* (London: Routledge, 2001).

3 To cite one example, the staples theory of Canadian economic development starts with fur: Harold Adams Innis, *The Fur Trade in Canada: An Introduction to Canadian Economic History*, rev. ed. (Toronto: University of Toronto Press, 1999).

4 Chantel Nadeau, "'My Fur Ladies': The Fabric of a Nation," in *Thinking Through the Skin*, ed. Sara Ahmed and Jackie Stacey (London: Routledge, 2001), 194–208.

5 Gary Cross, "Time, Money, and Labor History's Encounter with Consumer Culture," *International Labor and Working-Class History* 43 (Spring 1993): 4.

6 Peter Winn, "Introduction," *International Labor and Working-Class History* 63 (2003): 3. The term is used to describe Latin American labour historians, contrasted to more 'progressive' American and American-educated ones who are more likely to integrate gender into their work. On earlier feminist-materialist debates, see Rosemary Hennessy and Chrys Ingraham, eds., *Materialist Feminism: A Reader in Class, Difference, and Women's Lives* (New York: Routledge, 1997).

7 Stevi Jackson, "Why a Materialist Feminism Is (Still) Possible — and Necessary," *Women's Studies International Forum* 24, no. 3–4 (2001): 286; see also Dorothy

Smith, *The Everyday World as Problematic: A Feminist Sociology* (Boston: Northeastern University Press, 1987).

8 Materialist theories are not synonymous with Marxist theories, and there are significant distinctions between feminist materialism, materialist feminism, and feminist historical materialism that I cannot delineate here. The first (feminist materialism) sometimes refers to the radical 'French' materialism of Christine Delphy, who sees the domestic sphere as a patriarchal mode of production; in the United States, the second (materialist feminism) might include some authors who try to integrate poststructuralist insights into a form of materialism, while a feminist historical materialism may be more indebted to Marxist writing. My understanding of the terms 'historicizing' and 'feminist historical materialism' is indebted to Rosemary Hennessy's writing, especially *Profit and Pleasure: Sexual Identities in Late Capitalism* (New York: Routledge, 2000), as well as Anna Pollert, "Gender and Class Revisited; Or, The Poverty of Patriarchy," *Sociology* 30, no. 4 (1996): 639–59, and Kate Soper, *Troubled Pleasures: Writing on Politics, Gender and Hedonism* (London: Verso, 1990).

9 Toril Moi, *What Is a Woman? And Other Essays* (Oxford: Oxford University Press, 1999), 67–68, and Elaine Stavro, "Re-reading the Second Sex," *Feminist Theory* 1, no. 2 (2000): 131–50.

10 This also meant some feminists were wary of body studies, as they did not wish to be inserted into the social *only* through their bodies: Anne Witz, "Whose Body Matters? Feminist Sociology and the Corporeal Turn in Sociology and Feminism," *Body and Society* 6, no. 2 (2000): 1–24, 2.

11 Chris Shilling, *The Body in Culture, Technology and Society* (London: Sage Publications, 2005), 9. For other sociological views, see Sue Scott and David Morgan, eds., *Body Matters: Essays on the Sociology of the Body* (London: Falmer Press, 1993); Mike Featherstone, Mike Hepworth, and Bryan Turner, eds., *The Body: Social Process and Cultural Theory* (London: Sage Publications, 1991).

12 For discussions of the body in history, see Londa Schiebinger, ed., *Feminism and the Body* (Oxford: Oxford University Press, 2000); Kathleen Canning, "The Body as Method?: Reflections on the Place of the Body in Gender History," *Gender and History* 11, no. 3 (Nov. 1999): 499–513; Caroline Bynum, "Why All the Fuss About the Body? A Medievalist's Perspective," *Critical Inquiry* 22 (Autumn 1995): 1–33. Historians approach the body in different ways: as a category of analysis, as a site of power relations, as a strategy for recovering gender in history, as a theme for exploration. This article tends to concentrate on the latter two.

13 Influential works include Elizabeth Grosz, *Volatile Bodies: Towards a Corporeal Feminism* (Bloomington: Indiana University Press, 1994); Judith Butler, *Gender Trouble: Feminism and the Subversion of Identity* (London: Routledge, 1990), and *Body Matters: On the Discursive Limits of 'Sex'* (London: Routledge, 1993).

14 Chris Shilling, *The Body and Social Theory* (London: Sage Publications, 1993), 80.

15 Ibid., 35.

16 Shilling, *The Body in Culture*, 73. Perhaps this is also a comment on the changing political proclivities of the intellectual Left, as articulated by Alex Callinicos in *Against Postmodernism: A Marxist Critique* (Cambridge: Polity Press, 1989).

17 Terry Eagleton, *The Illusions of Postmodernism* (Oxford: Blackwell, 1996), 71.

18 A few examples: Mariam Fraser and Monica Greco, eds., *The Body: A Reader* (London: Routledge, 2005); Kate Conboy, Nadia Medina, and Sarah Stanbury, eds., *Writing on the Body: Female Embodiment and Feminist Theory* (New York: Columbia University Press, 1997); *Women's Studies,* special issue, 34, no. 7 (2005).

19 On 'individuation,' see Lisa Adkins, *Revisions: Gender and Sexuality in Late Modernity* (Buckingham, UK: Open University Press, 2002), 22.

20 Moi, *What Is a Woman?* 31.

21 A few examples include Kathy Peiss, *Hope in a Jar: The Making of American Beauty Culture* (New York: Metropolitan Books, 1998); Nan Enstad, *Ladies of Labor, Girls of Adventure: Working Women, Popular Culture and Labor Politics at the Turn of the Century* (New York: Columbia University Press, 1999); Eileen Boris, "You Wouldn't Want One of Them Dancing with Your Wife: Racialized Bodies on the Job in World War II," *American Quarterly* 50 (March 1998): 77–108.

22 Some examples are Mary Odem, *Delinquent Daughters: Protecting and Policing Adolescent Female Sexuality in the United States, 1885–1920* (Chapel Hill: University of North Carolina Press, 1995); Jennifer Terry and Jacqueline Urla, eds., *Deviant Bodies: Critical Perspectives on Difference in Science and Popular Culture* (Bloomington: Indiana University Press, 1995); Joan Sangster, *Regulating Girls and Women: Sexuality, Family and the Law in Ontario* (Toronto: Oxford University Press, 2001); Stephen Meyer, "Workplace Predators: Sex and Sexuality on the U.S. Automotive Shop Floor, 1930–1960," *Labour: Studies in Working-Class History of the Americas* (hereafter *Labour*) 1, no. 1 (Spring 2004): 77–93; Elizabeth Kennedy and Madeleine Davis, *Boots of Leather, Slippers of Gold: The History of a Lesbian Community* (New York: Routledge, 1993); Daniel Bender, *Sweated Work, Weak Bodies: Anti-Sweatshop Campaigns and Languages of Labor* (New Brunswick, NJ: Rutgers University Press, 2004); Lisa Adkins, *Gendered Work: Sexuality, Family and the Labour Market* (Buckingham, UK: Open University Press, 1995); Sarah Rose, "Crippled Hands: Disability in Labor and Working-Class History," *Labor* 2, no. 1 (Spring 2005): 27–54; Claudia Clark, *Radium Girls: Women and Industrial Health Reform, 1910–35* (Chapel Hill: University of North Carolina Press, 1993). This literature does not necessarily emerge from body studies; some pieces represent efforts to offer a broader, more inclusive picture of working-class life.

23 Eileen Boris notes that "if gender is performative as Judith Butler argued, the body becomes constructed through its labor," although the concept is not fully developed in her "From Gender to Racialized Gender: Laboring Bodies That

Matter," in *International Labor and Working-Class History* 63 (Spring 2003): 9–20, 11. Given extensive feminist critiques (and not even materialist feminists') of Butler's "evasion of the historical and social" (see, for example, Lois McNay, *Gender and Agency: Reconfiguring the Subject in Feminist and Social Theory* [Cambridge: Polity Press, 2000], 19), I would be wary of embracing her notions of performance.

24 For example, Jane Marcellus, "Moderns or Moms? Body Typing of Employed Women Between the Wars," *Women's Studies* 34, no. 7 (2005): 551–74; Gregory Kaster, "Labour's True Man: Organised Workingmen and the Language of Manliness in the USA, 1827–77," *Gender and History* 13, no. 1 (April 2001): 24–64; Rosemary Pringle, *Secretaries Talk: Sexuality, Power and Work* (London: Verso, 1989); Daniel Bender's *Sweated Work*, which draws very usefully on literature on the body, sometimes allows language and performance to become overbearing concepts, as in chapter 7.

25 Alexandra Howson, *Embodying Gender* (London: Sage Publications, 2005), 72; Kathy Davis, "Embodying Theory: Beyond Modernist and Postmodernist Readings of the Body," in *Embodied Practices: Feminist Perspectives on the Body,* ed. Kathy Davis (London: Sage Publications, 1997), 1–23, 15. For recent Marxist-feminist attempts to 'rematerialize' studies of women's oppression, see *Science and Society*, special issue, 69, no. 1 (2005).

26 David Harvey, *Spaces of Hope* (Berkeley: University of California Press, 2000), 130.

27 The expenditure of bodily human labour is central to two of Marxism's key precepts: alienation and exploitation: Karl Marx, *The Economic and Philosophical Manuscripts of 1844* (New York: International Publishers, 1964), 114.

28 Harry Braverman, *Labor and Monopoly Capital* (New York: Monthly Review Press, 1974). His insights have been integrated into excellent feminist writing on the body: Pei-Chia Lan, "Working in a Neon Cage: Bodily Labour of Cosmetics Saleswomen in Taiwan," *Feminist Studies* 29, no. 1 (Spring 2003): 21–45. Michel Foucault's *Discipline and Punish* (New York: Vintage Books, 1979), 141–49, also explores the disciplining of working bodies through space and time.

29 Pierre Bourdieu defined habitus as "embodied history" in *The Logic of Practice,* trans. Richard Nice (Stanford: Stanford University Press, 1990), 57. For some feminist appreciations of Bourdieu, see Terry Lowell, "Thinking Feminism with and Against Bourdieu," *Feminist Theory* 1, no. 1 (2000): 11–32, and Moi, *What Is a Woman?* 204–99.

30 Katie Pickles and Myra Rutherdale, *Contact Zones: Aboriginal and Settler Women in Canada's Past* (Vancouver: University of British Columbia Press, 2005); Tony Ballantyne and Antoinette Burton, eds., *Bodies in Contact: Rethinking Encounters in World History* (Durham, NC: Duke University Press, 2005).

31 Bourdieu, for example, was not a Marxist. He was less interested in capitalism and structural transformation than in forms of 'capital' as power. See Alex

Callinicos, "Social Theory Put to the Test of Politics: Pierre Bourdieu and An-thony Giddens," *New Left Review* 236 (1999): 95; Craig Calhoun, "Habitus, Field, and Capital," in *Bourdieu: Critical Perspectives,* ed. Craig Calhoun, Edward LiPuma, and Moishe Postone (Chicago: University of Chicago Press, 1993), 61–88.

32 Pollert, "Gender and Class," 647, is referring to the notion of experience, but the same could be applied to the body.

33 Kathy Davis, "Embody-ing Theory: Beyond Modernist and Postmodernist Read-ings of the Body," in *Embodied Practices,* ed. Davis, 1–23, 15.

34 Marx, *The Economic and Philosophical Manuscripts of 1844,* 182.

35 Pollert, "Gender and Class," 640.

36 I use both the terms 'Indigenous' and 'Aboriginal' to refer to both Native and Inuit (First Nations) peoples. The Indigenous groups described here were di-verse in language, culture, and social organization, though I have drawn some general conclusions across these differences.

37 *Canadian Business,* 23 Feb. 1950, 66–67.

38 J.M. Kew, *Cumberland House in 1960,* Report #2, Economic and Social Survey of Northern Saskatchewan (Saskatoon, 1962), 31, 90.

39 Jo-Anne Fiske and Susan Sleeper-Smith, "Introduction," 1–12, and Jo-Anne Fiske and Caroline Mufford, "Hard Times and Everything Like That: Carrier Women's Tales of Life on the Traplines," 13–29, in *New Faces of the Fur Trade: Selected Papers of the North American Fur Trade Conference,* ed. Fiske and Sleeper-Smith (Lansing: Michigan State University Press, 1998). Writing on women's role in the eigh-teenth- and nineteenth-century fur trade included discussion of women's la-bour: Ron Bourgeault, "Race, Class, Gender: Colonial Domination of Indian Women," in *Race, Class, Gender: Bonds and Barriers,* ed. Jesse Vorst et al. (Winnipeg: Between the Lines, 1989), 87–116; Sylvia Van Kirk, *Many Tender Ties: Women in Fur Trade Society, 1670–1870* (Winnipeg: Watson and Dwyer, 1980).

40 Toby Morantz, *The White Man's Gonna Getcha: The Colonial Challenge to the Crees in Québec* (Montreal: McGill-Queen's University Press, 2002), 35.

41 My emphasis. See Patricia Ann Rogers, "Aspirations and Acculturation of Cree Women at Great Whale River," (MA thesis, University of North Carolina, 1965), 5.

42 Hugh Brody, *Maps and Dreams: Indians and the British Columbia Frontier* (Vancouver: Douglas and McIntyre, 1981), 196.

43 Provincial Archives of Manitoba (PAM), Hudson's Bay Company Records (HBC), Arctic Bay Post Journal, B 381/1/1, March 1937.

44 Leonard Mason, *The Swampy Cree: A Study in Acculturation* (Ottawa: National Museum of Canada, 1967), 49, and Kew, *Cumberland House in 1960*, 32.

45 PAM, HBC, Wolstonehome Post Journal, B 368/a/16, 23 May 1939.

46 PAM, HBC, RG 3/75A/-2, Annual Report, Padley Post, 29 June 1957.

47 PAM, HBC, RG 3/74A/2, Manager, Frobisher Bay to Manager, Ungava Section, 2 Feb. 1950.

48 PAM, HBC, RG 3/74B, Payne Bay Post Report, 11 July 1943.

49 It was also believed that Inuit women endured childbirth more easily: Patricia Jasen, "Race, Culture and the Colonization of Childbirth in Northern Canada," in *Rethinking Canada: The Promise of Women's History*, ed. Veronica Strong-Boag, Mona Gleason, and Adele Perry (Toronto: Oxford University Press, 2002), 353–66.

50 H.C. Wolfart, "Introduction," in *Our Grandmothers' Lives: As Told in Their Own Words* (Regina: Canadian Plains Research Center, 1998), 7–38, 20.

51 Miriam McNab, "From the Bush to the Village to the City: Pinehouse Lake Aboriginal Women Adapt to Change," in *Other Voices: Historical Essays on Saskatchewan Women*, ed. David De Brou and Aileen Moffatt (Regina: Canadian Plains Research Center, 1995), 131–43.

52 Hugh Conn, "Careful Fur Preparation Brings Bigger Cash Returns," *Indian News*, January 1956.

53 PAM, HBC, Cape Dorset Post Journal, B 387/a/8, 31 May 1939.

54 PAM, HBC, RG3/74B/1, Arctic Bay Post Annual Report, May 1943.

55 Fiske and Mufford, "Hard Times and Everything Like That," 16–17.

56 Even accounting for the fact that these pictures were taken by whites, perhaps fascinated by Inuit women's combination of skinning work with children on their backs, the hundreds of visuals and many sojourner accounts detailing women's work indicate that this was common practice, not simply the image that fascinated whites. For a sojourner account, see Elsie Gillis, *North Pole Boarding House* (Toronto: Ryerson Press, 1951), chap. 15.

57 Adrian Tanner, *Bringing Home Animals* (New York: St. Martin's Press, 1979), 52, 60.

58 For this argument for cannery workers, see Alicja Muszynski, "Race and Gender: Structural Determinants in the Formation of B.C.'s Salmon Cannery Labour Force," in *Class, Gender and Region: Essays in Canadian Historical Sociology*, ed. Gregory S. Kealey (St. John's: Committee on Canadian Labour History, 1988), 103–20. Native peoples were certainly critical of this relationship: John Honigman, "Incentives to Work in a Canadian Indian Community," *Human Organization* 8, no. 3 (Summer 1949): 23–28, 26.

59 Bourgeault, "Race, Class, Gender," 98–99.

60 In the contemporary politics of Aboriginal women's resistance, women have often drawn, ideologically, on the historical memory of their earlier, crucial integration into bush, and thus fur, production.

61 For a definition of internal colonialism, see Frideres. The term was out of favour in the United States, but it might be undergoing a renaissance. See Linda Gordon, "Internal Colonialism and Gender," in *Haunted by Empire: Geographies of Intimacy in North American History*, ed. Ann Laura Stoler (Durham, NC: Duke University Press, 2006), 427–51.

62 For a review of writing on Canadian Aboriginal labour, see Steven High, "Native Wage Labour and Independent Commodity Production During the 'Era of Irrelevance,'" *Labour/Le Travail* 37 (1996): 243–64. Two non-Canadian examples are Kay Saunders and Jackie Huggins, eds., *Labour History*, special issue, 65 (1994); Colleen O'Neill, *Working the Navajo Way: Labor and Culture in the Twentieth Century* (Lawrence: University Press of Kansas, 2005). The intersection of labour and the cultural contours of colonialism is dealt with in Jo-Anne Fiske's work: "Fishing Is a Woman's Business: Changing Economic Roles of Carrier Women and Men," in *Native Peoples/Native Lands: Canadian Indians, Inuit and Metis*, ed. Bruce Cox (Ottawa: Macmillan, 1988), 186–97. See also Paige Raibmon, *Authentic Indians: Episodes of Encounter from the Late-Nineteenth-Century Northwest Coast* (Durham, NC: Duke University Press, 2005), chap. 4; Joan Sangster, "Domesticating Girls: The Sexual Regulation of Aboriginal and Working-Class Girls in Twentieth Century Canada," in *Contact Zones*, ed. Pickles and Rutherdale, 179–204.

63 There is a vast literature on images of Indigenous women. A few Canadian examples include: Gail Guthrie Valaskakis, *Indian Country: Essays on Contemporary Native Culture* (Waterloo: Wilfrid Laurier University Press, 2005), chap. 5; Kim Anderson, *A Recognition of Being: Reconstructing Native Womanhood* (Toronto: Second Story Press, 2000); Sarah Carter, *Capturing Women: The Manipulation of Cultural Imagery in Canada's Prairie West* (Montreal: McGill-Queen's University Press, 1997); Sarah Carter, "Categories and Terrains of Exclusion: Constructing the 'Indian' Woman in the Early Settlement Era of Western Canada," *Great Plains Quarterly* 13 (1997): 147–61; Pickles and Rutherdale, eds.,*Contact Zones*. Some comparative international discussion includes Anne Fausto-Sterling, "Gender, Race and Nation: The Comparative Anatomy of 'Hottentot' Women in Europe, 1815–17," and Tsianina Lomawaima, "Domesticity in the Federal Indian Schools: The Power of Authority of Mind Over Body," in *Deviant Bodies: Critical Perspectives on Difference in Science and Popular Culture*, ed. Jennifer Terry and Jacqueline Urla (Bloomington: Indiana University Press, 1995), 19–48 and 197–218; Antoinette Burton, ed., *Gender, Sexuality and Colonial Modernities* (London: Routledge, 1999); Sharon Tiffany and Kathleen Adams, *The Wild Woman: An Inquiry into the Anthropology of an Idea* (Cambridge: Schenkman, 1985). Ann Stoler, "Making Empire Respectable: The

Politics of Race and Sexual Morality in Twentieth-Century Colonial Cultures," *American Ethnologist* 16, no. 4 (1989): 634–59.

64 *UE News*, 1 Feb. 1952, cartoon with bourgeois woman in fur speaking to a friend: "Why should people worry about unemployment? I've never worked a day in my life."

65 Philip Foner's classic, *The Fur and Leather Workers Union: A Story of Dramatic Struggles and Achievements* (Newark, NJ: Nordan Press, 1950), deals little with women and barely mentions Canadian workers.

66 McNay, *Gender and Agency*, refers to this dominant approach as "negative subjectification," 2.

67 Cornell University (CA), Kheel Centre for Labor-Management Documentation and Archives (Kheel), International Fur and Leather Workers Union Papers (IFLWU), Box 25, folder 29, Winnipeg Fur Workers Local 91 Membership List.

68 Nadeau, "My Fur Ladies," 195. Ironically, the term 'many tender ties' is appropriated from Sylvia Van Kirk's book on fur trade marriages, which *does* discuss women's labour in the eighteenth and nineteenth centuries.

69 Differentials varied by city and year. This average was secured by taking a snapshot of four years and comparing male and female operators' rates. Ernst Strauss, "The Canadian Fur Manufacturing Industry" (MA thesis, McGill University, 1967), 287.

70 Karl Marx, *Capital: A Critique of Political Economy*, vol. 1 (New York: International Publishers, 1971), 271: "Labour power is that which the worker is compelled to offer for sale . . . and only exists in his living body."

71 Library and Archives Canada (LAC), Joseph Cohen Papers, vol. 2, File 1145, Letter from Minimum Wage Board, 19 May 1932, to Hallman and Sable Fur Company. Cohen (known for his communist sympathies) was acting for the company in this case.

72 In tripartite negotiations over industry regulation, employers wanted recognition of the higher "stress" and "wear and tear on the nerves" in larger, more specialized fur firms. See Archives of Ontario (AO), Factory Inspection Branch, RG 7-71-0-59. No records of individual factory inspections remain.

73 *The Worker*, 9 Sept. 1933.

74 Interview with B.C., 1 Dec. 2005.

75 Ava Baron, "Masculinity, the Embodied Male Worker, and the Historian's Gaze," *International Labor and Working-Class History* 69 (Spring 2006): 143–60, 146.

76 Robert Connell, *Gender and Power* (Stanford: Stanford University Press, 1987), 87.

77 Jesse Mercer Gehman, "Your Health," *Canadian Furrier* (Fall 1942): 14.

78 "Your Health: A Practical Programme for the Furrier," *Canadian Furrier* (Fall 1942): 18. There was no distinction made between the risks to male and female health in this literature, as noted by Daniel Bender in *Sweated Work*. This may well have been a theme, but without factory reports, it is difficult to judge.

79 *Siebel v. Vereshack*, [1946] 1 DLR 225–41.

80 LAC, RG 27, Dept. of Labour, vol. 279, file 1-26-5-2, "Fur Workers"; AO, MU 9011, interview with Al Hershkovitz.

81 Roz Usiskin, "Winnipeg's Jewish Women on the Left," in *Jewish Radicalism in Winnipeg, 1905–60*, ed. Daniel Stone (Winnipeg: Jewish Heritage Centre of Western Canada, 1980), 106–22, 119; Joan Sangster, *Dreams of Equality: Women on the Canadian Left, 1920–1950* (Toronto: McClelland and Stewart, 1989), 78. "Freda Coodin" as a pseudonym has recently been resurrected by radicals writing from within the labour movement.

82 Bender, *Sweated Work*, 177–78. Bender describes women fainting in meetings, offering a "gendered performance" that "signalled the removal — the fainting away — of women from factionalism," the latter associated with the men in the union. The women may simply have been acting ideologically, using their bodies as a conscious political tactic of disruption.

83 On these illegal actions, see AO, Multicultural History Society of Ontario (MHSO), MU 9021, Muni Taub papers, file 8428, and MU 9001, Federman papers; LAC, Cohen papers, vol. 13, file 2701.

84 AO, MHSO, MU 9001, Federman papers.

85 AO, Abella Oral History Collection, interview with Pearl Wedro, n.d.

86 In part, gender issues were trumped by race concerns in the United States, though dealing with Cold War attacks by the state and other unions also took up immense union energies. My reading of gender politics is taken from the IFLWU papers, convention reports, and *The Fur and Leather Worker*, though these contained little Canadian news.

87 LAC, RCMP Papers, RG 18, vol. 3526, Pamphlets, *The Toronto Furriers Newsletter*, June 1954; CA Kheel, IFLWU Papers, vol. 25, folder 20.

88 *Butcher Workman*, Aug. 1955, 8–10.

89 Susan Porter Benson, *Counter Cultures: Saleswomen, Managers and Customers in American Department Stores, 1890–1940* (Urbana: University of Illinois Press, 1988). For recent writing on service labour, including its sexualization, see Dorothy Sue Cobble, "A Spontaneous Loss of Enthusiasm: The Workplace, Feminism and the Transformation of Service Jobs in the 1970s," *International Labor and Working-Class History* 56 (Oct. 1999): 23–44; Gail Reekie, *Temptations: Sex, Selling and the Department Store* (Sydney: Allen and Unwin, 1993); Adkins, *Gendered Work*, chap. 4.

90 Beverley Skeggs and Lisa Adkins, eds., *Feminism After Bourdieu* (Oxford: Blackwell, 2004). Feminist debates concerning Bourdieu's usefulness are now extensive. For one discussion of the weight he gives to social reproduction, see Deborah Reed-Danahay, *Locating Bourdieu* (Bloomington: Indiana University Press, 2005), 64.

91 *Maclean's*, 15 March 1945, 11. Scholarship on gender and consumption points to the association of women consumers with emotion and desire, even irrational acts.

92 Nadeau, *Fur Nation*, chap. 3.

93 After dyeing, manufacturers had previously added exotic labels — e.g., the transformation of skunk into Alaskan sable: Leonard Knott, "Furs, a Bigger Business than Ever," *Canadian Business*, Feb. 1950, 26.

94 "Mock Mink Man-made," *Life*, 5 Dec. 1955, 72–76, and LAC, Co-operative Commonwealth Papers, MG 28 IV I, vol. 491, Fur Industry 1952 file, brief for the Minister of Finance by the IFLWU. Aboriginal trappers also protested royalty taxes: see LAC, RG 10, Dept. of Mines and Resources [Indian Affairs], C 8093 v. 6732, f. 420-1-5-3, 'Royalties on furs,' 1945.

95 *Financial Post*, 13 Dec. 1958; *Canadian Business*, Feb. 1950, 24–27.

96 Pierre Bourdieu, *Distinction: A Social Critique of the Judgement of Task*, trans. Richard Nice (Cambridge: Harvard University Press, 1984), 201–2.

97 M.D. Gellman, "Get Ready for Christmas," *Canadian Furrier* (Fall 1942): 10.

98 E.C. Tarler, "How a Sales Person Should Sell Furs," *Canadian Furrier* (Fall 1941): 11.

99 Shilling, *The Body in Culture*, 72.

100 Moi, *What Is a Woman?* 283.

101 Lovell, "Thinking Feminism with and Against Bourdieu," 11–32, 15. For a materialist-feminist critique of performance, see Rosemary Hennessy, *Profit and Pleasure: Sexual Identities in Late Capitalism* (New York: Routledge, 2000), 115–20.

102 Université de Montréal, Écoles des Hautes Commerciales Archives (HEC), Dupuis Frères Papers, Box 21656, Employee file 2221.

103 Benson, *Counter Cultures*.

104 Interview with B.C., 1 Dec. 2005.

105 Lan, "Working in a Neon Cage."

106 Ibid.

107 Interview with G.L., 13 Jan. 2006.

108 Interview with B.C., 1 Dec. 2005.

109 Harvey, *Spaces of Hope*, 130.

110 Momin Rahman and Anne Witz, "What Really Matters? The Elusive Quality of the Material in Feminist Thought," *Feminist Theory* 4, no. 3 (2003): 243–61, 245.

111 Hennessy, *Profit and Pleasure*, 15.

112 Harvey, quoting from Marx, *Spaces of Hope*, 120.

113 Ibid., 119.

Books

Dreams of Equality: Women on the Canadian Left, 1920–1950. Toronto: McClelland and Stewart, 1989.

Earning Respect: The Lives of Working Women in Small-Town Ontario, 1920–1960. Toronto: University of Toronto Press, 1995.

Regulating Girls and Women: Sexuality, Family and the Law in Ontario, 1920–1960. Toronto: Oxford University Press, 2001.

Girl Trouble: Female Delinquency in English Canada. Toronto: Between the Lines Press, 2002.

Transforming Labour: Women and Work in Postwar Canada. Toronto: University of Toronto Press, 2010.

Edited Volumes

Beyond the Vote: Canadian Women and Politics, co-edited and co-introduced with Linda Kealey. Toronto: University of Toronto Press, 1989.

Teaching Women's History: Challenges and Solutions, co-edited with Bettina Bradbury et al. Edmonton: Athabasca University, 1995.

The Woman Worker, 1926–1929, co-edited and co-introduced with Margaret Hobbs. St. John's: Canadian Committee on Labour History, 1999.

Crossing Boundaries: Women's Organizing in Europe and the Americas, 1880s–1940s, co-edited with Pernilla Jonsson and Silke Neunsinger. Uppsala: University of Uppsala Press, 2007.

Labouring Canada: Class, Gender, and Race in Canadian Working-Class History, co-edited with Bryan D. Palmer. Toronto: Oxford University Press, 2008.

Articles and Chapters

"The 1907 Bell Telephone Strike: Organizing Women Workers," *Labour/Le Travailleur* 3 (1978): 109–30.

"Women and Unions in Canada: A Review of Historical Research," *Resources for Feminist Research* 10, no. 2 (July 1981): 2–6.

"Finnish Women in Ontario, 1890–1930," *Polyphony: The Bulletin of the Multicultural History Society of Ontario* 3, no. 2 (Fall 1981): 46–54.

"'A Link Between Labour and Learning': The Workers Educational Association in Ontario, 1917–1951" (co-authored with Ian Radforth), *Labour/Le Travailleur* 8 (1982): 41–78.

"Women of the 'New Era': Women in the Early CCF," in *Building the Co-operative Commonwealth: Essays on the Democratic Socialist Tradition in Canada,* ed. William Brennan (Regina: University of Regina, 1985), 69–97.

"The Communist Party and the Woman Question, 1922–1929," *Labour/Le Travail* 15 (1985): 25–56.

"Canadian Working Women," in *Lectures in Canadian Labour and Working-Class History,* ed. W.J.C. Cherwinski and Gregory S. Kealey (St. Johns: Committee on Canadian Labour History and New Hogtown Press, 1986), 59–78.

"The Making of a Socialist-Feminist: The Early Career of Beatrice Brigden," *Atlantis* (Fall 1987): 13–28.

"Introduction," in *Moving Forward: Creating a Feminist Agenda for the 1990s* (co-authored with Heather Avery), conference proceedings, Trent University, 15–17 June 1990, 7–14.

"'Pardon Tales' from Magistrate's Court: Women, Crime and the Courts in Peterborough County, 1920–1950," *Canadian Historical Review* 74 (June 1993): 160–97.

"The Softball Solution: Female Workers, Male Managers, and the Operation of Paternalism at Westclox, 1923–1960," *Labour/Le Travail* 32 (1993): 167–99.

"Telling Our Stories: Feminist Debates and the Use of Oral History," *Women's History Review* 3, no. 1 (1994): 5–27.

"Doing Two Jobs: The Wage-Earning Mother, 1945–70," in *A Diversity of Women: Ontario, 1945–1980,* ed. Joy Parr (Toronto: University of Toronto Press, 1995), 99–133.

"Women Workers, Employment Policy and the State: The Establishment of the Ontario Women's Bureau, 1963–1970," *Labour/Le Travail,* 36 (1995): 119–45.

"Facing Differences, Forging Solutions: Introduction," in *Teaching Women's History* (Edmonton: Athabasca University, 1995), 18–25.

"Beyond Dichotomies: Re-assessing Gender History and Women's History in Canada," *Left History* 3, no. 1 (Spring/Summer 1995): 109–21.

"Reconsidering Dichotomies," *Left History* 3, no. 2, and 4, no. 1 (Fall 1996): 239–48.

"Women and Wage Labour in Australia and Canada, 1880–1980" (co-authored with Raelene Frances and Linda Kealey), *Labour/Le Travail* 38 (1996): 54–89.

"Incarcerating 'Bad Girls': The Regulation of Sexuality Through the Female Refuges Act in Ontario, 1920–1945," *Journal of the History of Sexuality* 7, no. 2 (Fall 1996): 239–75.

"Criminalizing the Colonized: Ontario Native Women Confront the Criminal Justice System, 1920–1960," *Canadian Historical Review* 80, no. 1 (March 1999): 32–60.

"Girls in Conflict with the Law: Exploring the Construction of Female 'Delin-quency' in Ontario, 1940–1960," *Canadian Journal of Women and the Law* 12, no. 1 (2000): 1–35.

"Masking and Unmasking the Sexual Abuse of Children: Perceptions of Violence Against Children in 'the Badlands' of Ontario, 1916–1930," *Journal of Family History* 25, no. 4 (2000): 504–27.

"Women and Work: Assessing Women's Labour History in Canada," *Atlantis* 25, no. 1 (Fall 2000): 51–62.

"Feminism and the Making of Canadian Working-Class History: Exploring the Past, Present and Future," *Labour/Le Travail* 46 (2000): 127–66.

"Retorts, Runaways and Riots: Patterns of Resistance in Canadian Reform Schools for Girls, 1930–60" (co-authored with Tamara Myers), *Journal of Social History* (Spring 2001): 669–97.

Introduction to Part Four, "Women's Activism and the State," in *Framing Our Past: Canadian Women's History in the Twentieth Century*, ed. Sharon Cook, Lorna McLean, and Kate O'Rourke (Montreal: McGill-Queen's University Press, 2001), 201–11.

"Consuming Issues: Women on the Left, Political Protest and the Organization of Homemakers, 1920–1960," in *Framing Our Past*, 240–47.

Women's Work: Re-Examining American and Canadian Labour History," in *Amerikanische Arbeitergeschichte Heute*, ed. Irmgard Steinisch, Mitteilungsblatt des Instituts für soziale Bewegungen 25 (Bochum: Ruhr Universität, 2001), 67–88.

"Defining Sexual Promiscuity: 'Race', Gender, and Class in the Operation of Ontario's Female Refuges Act, 1930–60," in *Crimes of Colour: Racialization and the Criminal Justice System in Canada*, ed. Wendy Chan and Kiran Mirchandani (Toronto: University of Toronto Press, 2001), 45–63.

"'She Is Hostile to Our Ways': First Nations Girls Sentenced to the Ontario Training School for Girls, 1930–1960," *Law and History Review* 20, no. 1 (Spring 2002): 59–96.

"Constructing Social and Moral Citizens: Male and Female Delinquency in English Canada," in *Contesting Canadian Citizenship: Historical Readings*, ed. Robert Adamoski, Dorothy Chunn, and Robert Menzies (Peterborough, ON: Broadview Press, 2002), 337–58.

"'We No Longer Respect the Law': The Tilco Strike, Labour Injunctions, and the State," *Labour/Le Travail* 53 (2004): 47–88.

"Reforming Women's Reformatories: Elizabeth Fry, Penal Reform, and the State, 1950–1970," *Canadian Historical Review* 85, no. 2 (June 2004): 227–52.

"Mobilizing Canadian Women for World War I," in *Canada and the Great War: Essays in Honour of Robert Craig Brown*, ed. David MacKenzie (Toronto: University of Toronto Press, 2005), 157–93.

"*Robitnystia*, Ukrainian Communists, and the 'Porcupinism' Debate: Reassessing Ethnicity, Gender and Class in Early Canadian Communism, 1922–1930," *Labour/Le Travail* 56 (Fall 2005): 51–89.

"Domesticating Girls: The Sexual Regulation of Aboriginal and Working-Class Girls in Twentieth-Century Canada," in *Contact Zones: Aboriginal and Settler Women in Canada's Colonial Past*, ed. Katie Pickles and Myra Rutherdale (Vancouver: University of British Columbia Press, 2005), 179–204.

"Archiving Feminist Histories: Women, The 'Nation' and Metanarratives in Canadian Historical Writing," *Women's Studies International Forum*, 29, no. 3 (May–June 2006): 255–64.

"Remembering Texpack: Nationalism, Internationalism and Militancy in Canadian Unions in the 1970s," *Studies in Political Economy* 78 (Fall 2006): 41–66.

"Making a Fur Coat: Women, the Labouring Body, and Working-Class History," *International Review of Social History* 52 (2007): 241–70.

"*The Beaver* as Ideology: Constructing Images of Inuit and Native Life in Post–World War II Canada," *Anthropologica* 49 (2007): 191–209.

"Introduction," in *Crossing Boundaries Women's Organizing in Europe and the Americas, 1880s–1940s*, ed. Jonsson, Neunsinger, and Sangster, 9–20.

"Political Tourism, Writing and Communication: Transnational Connections of Women on the Left, 1920s–1940s," in *Crossing Boundaries: Women's Organizing in Europe and the Americas, 1880s–1940s*, ed. Jonsson, Neunsinger, and Sangster, 95–116.

"The Polish 'Dionnes': Gender, Ethnicity, and Immigrant Workers in Post–World War II Canada," *Canadian Historical Review* 88, no. 3 (Fall 2007): 469–500.

"Constructing the 'Eskimo' Wife: White Women's Travel Writing, Colonialism, and the Canadian North, 1940–1960," in *Creating Postwar Canada: Community, Diversity, and Dissent, 1945–75*, ed. Magda Fahrni and Robert Rutherdale (Vancouver: University of British Columbia Press, 2008): 23–44.

"Historia Social," *Historia Social* 60 (2008): 213–24.

"Queen of the Picket Line: Beauty Contests in the Post–World War II Labour Movement," *Labor: Studies in Working Class History of the Americas* 5, no. 4 (2008): 83–106.

"Canada's Cold War in Fur," *Left History* 13, no. 2 (Spring 2009): 10–36.

"Feminists in Academe: From Outsiders to Insiders?" in *Academic Callings: The University We Have Had, Now Have, and Could Have*, ed. Janice Newson and Claire Polster (Toronto: Canadian Scholars' Press, 2010), 178–86.

"Radical Ruptures: Feminism, Labor, and the Left in the Long Sixties in Canada," *American Review of Canadian Studies* 40, no. 1 (2010): 1–21.

"Gendering Labour History Across Borders," *Labour History Review* 75, no. 2 (August 2010): 143–61.

"Debating Maternity Rights: Pacific Western Airlines and Flight Attendants' Struggles to 'Fly Pregnant' in the 1970s," in *Work on Trial: Canadian Labour Law Struggles*, ed. Judy Fudge and Eric Tucker (Toronto: Irwin Law and the Osgoode Society for Canadian Legal History, 2010), 283–314.

"Invoking Experience as Evidence," *Canadian Historical Review* 92, no. 1 (March 2011): 135–61.

"Words of Experience/Experiencing Words: Reading Working Women's Letters to Canada's Royal Commission on the Status of Women" is a longer version of an essay that appeared in the *Canadian Historical Review* 92, no. 1 (March 2011): 135–61, under the title "Invoking Experience as Evidence" (copyright © University of Toronto Press). The author is grateful to the University of Toronto Press Incorporated (www.utpjournals.com) for permission to reprint significant portions of that essay.

¶ This book was typeset in Cartier Book Pro, Rod McDonald's revival of Carl Dair's original 1967 design.

Scrapbook
1 - movie tickets - the monster - Tiger pic
   - tims coffee - Bear

2 - victoria skate, artist pic/kiss
   - cameron

3. Boys house   4 valtinesday 5 my B-day 6 easter weekend

7 summer fun   8 trip up north 9 homecoming halloween
new cars   new apartment fish carlton Thanksgiving
Christmas